International Human Rights and Mental Disability Law

American Psychology-Law Society Series

Books in the Series

Trial Consulting
Amy J. Posey and Lawrence S. Wrightsman

Death by Design
Craig Haney

Psychological Injuries
William J. Koch, Kevin S. Douglas, Tonia L. Nicholls, and Melanie L. O'Neill

Emergency Department Treatment of the Psychiatric Patient
Susan Stefan

The Psychology of the Supreme Court
Lawrence S. Wrightsman

Proving the Unprovable
Christopher Slobogin

Adolescents, Media, and the Law
Roger J. R. Levesque

Oral Arguments before the Supreme Court
Lawrence S. Wrightsman

God in the Courtroom
Brian H. Bornstein and Monica K. Miller

Expert Testimony on the Psychology of Eyewitness Identification
Edited by Brian L. Cutler

The Psychology of Judicial Decision-Making
Edited by David Klein and Gregory Mitchell

The Miranda Ruling: Its Past, Present, and Future
Lawrence S. Wrightsman and Mary L. Pitman

Juveniles at Risk: A Plea for Preventive Justice
Christopher Slobogin and Mark R. Fondacaro

The Ethics of Total Confinement
Bruce A. Arrigo, Heather Y. Bersot, and Brian G. Sellers

International Human Rights and Mental Disability Law: When the Silenced Are Heard
Michael L. Perlin

International Human Rights and Mental Disability Law

When the Silenced Are Heard

Michael L. Perlin

OXFORD
UNIVERSITY PRESS

OXFORD
UNIVERSITY PRESS

Oxford University Press, Inc., publishes works that further
Oxford University's objective of excellence
in research, scholarship, and education.

Oxford New York
Auckland Cape Town Dar es Salaam Hong Kong Karachi
Kuala Lumpur Madrid Melbourne Mexico City Nairobi
New Delhi Shanghai Taipei Toronto

With offices in
Argentina Austria Brazil Chile Czech Republic France Greece
Guatemala Hungary Italy Japan Poland Portugal Singapore
South Korea Switzerland Thailand Turkey Ukraine Vietnam

Published by Oxford University Press, Inc.
198 Madison Avenue, New York, New York 10016
www.oup.com

Library of Congress Cataloging-in-Publication Data

Perlin, Michael L., 1946–
International human rights and mental disability law : when the silenced are heard / Michael L. Perlin.
p. cm. — (American psychology-law society series)
Includes bibliographical references and index.
ISBN 978-0-19-539323-1 1. Mental health laws. 2. People with mental disabilities—Civil rights. 3. Insanity (Law) I. Title.
K640.P47 2011
344.04'4—dc22
2011003686

9 8 7 6 5 4 3 2 1
Printed in the United State
on acid-free paper

Series Foreword

This book series is sponsored by the American Psychology-Law Society (APLS). APLS is an interdisciplinary organization devoted to scholarship, practice, and public service in psychology and law. Its goals include advancing the contributions of psychology to the understanding of law and legal institutions through basic and applied research; promoting the education of psychologists in matters of law and the education of legal personnel in matters of psychology; and informing the psychological and legal communities and the general public of current research, educational, and service activities in the field of psychology and law. APLS membership includes psychologists from the academic research and clinical practice communities as well as members of the legal community. Research and practice is represented in both the civil and criminal legal arenas. APLS has chosen Oxford University Press as a strategic partner because of its commitment to scholarship, quality, and the international dissemination of ideas. These strengths will help APLS reach its goal of educating the psychology and legal professions and the general public about important developments in psychology and law. The focus of the book series reflects the diversity of the field of psychology and law, as we continue to publish books on a broad range of topics.

I am pleased that Professor Michael Perlin is publishing his latest book, *International Human Rights and Mental Disability Law: When the Silenced Are Heard*, in the APLS series. Professor Perlin has long been a champion of the rights of individuals with mental disabilities. In 1989, he wrote a groundbreaking multivolume treatise on mental disability law and policy in the United States. Some ten years later, he published a classic book,

The Hidden Prejudice: Mental Disability on Trial, in which he made a compelling case that fear of persons with mental illness has created a bias against them that supports the violation of their rights. He coined the term *sanism* to describe this form of discrimination, which he defines as "the irrational prejudice that causes, and is reflected in, prevailing social attitudes toward persons with mental disabilities." With his current book, Professor Perlin demonstrates that the violations of human rights that he so forcefully identified in the United States are also prevalent in many countries throughout the world. Based on his analysis of law and practice, he highlights the pervasive problems that allow human rights violations to perpetuate. These include lack of comprehensive legislation, lack of independent counsel, inadequate care, lack of community programming, and inhumane forensic systems. He is not content to merely identify these human rights violations. He is an advocate and views his analysis of abuses as a foundation for his proposals for changes in law, policy, and practice that would improve the treatment of persons with mental disabilities. Indeed, creating change is at the heart of this book. As he cogently argues, it is essential that countries worldwide "devote themselves to significant and ameliorative reform of their mental health systems." I believe that this book will serve as a catalyst for the far-reaching changes that will ultimately establish Professor Perlin's call for a constitutionally based mental disability law jurisprudence.

Ronald Roesch
Series Editor

Preface

I began practicing law in 1971, and I became a full-time law professor in 1984. My primary focus—academic, advocacy, litigation—has always been on the rights of persons with mental disabilities, especially those institutionalized against their will. Until 2000—putting aside the occasional paper presented at conferences in Canada and in Western Europe—however, my work focused exclusively on U.S.-based mental disability law.

That state of affairs changed dramatically in 2000, and the years immediately following. And that change led to a substantial recalibration of all my work, and led, eventually, to this book.

As I discuss in chapter 1, during that latter time period, I embarked on a series of site visits on behalf of Mental Disability Rights International (now Disability Rights International), the most important U.S. nongovernmental organization (NGO) dealing with the application of international human rights law and principles to persons with mental disabilities. At the same time, as part of New York Law School's online, distance learning, mental disability law program, I taught courses in mental disability law in Japan and Nicaragua to cohorts of lawyers, mental health professionals, academics, legislators, and judges. I also began to lecture regularly and do advocacy trainings on mental disability law topics in Japan and throughout Central and Eastern Europe and Central and South America. In 2002 I convened a conference at New York Law School to consider the application of international human rights law to persons in institutions in Hungary and Bulgaria (see Perlin, 2002). I believe that that was the first such program ever presented at a U.S.-based law school.

This work clarified for me that the violations of fundamental freedom, dignity, decency, and humanity, the pervasive stigma that befalls persons with mental disabilities (attitudes that I call "sanism"), and the continued failure of courts and fact finders to acknowledge the depths of the problems presented by shameful institutional neglect (attitudes that I call "pretextuality") often were found to be even more pervasive in other nations than in the United States.

Soon after this, I began to turn my academic attention to these issues. With my friend and colleague Professor Eva Szeli (with whom I had done advocacy work in Estonia, Latvia, Hungary, and Bulgaria), I created a course at New York Law School: *International Human Rights and Mental Disability Law*. With Eva and three other colleagues, I published the first casebook on that topic. This all coincided with a sabbatical in 2005, during which I was fortunate enough to spend time, to research, to teach, and to lecture at the European Union Institute (in Florence, Italy), Abo Akademi University (in Turku, Finland), and Hebrew University (in Jerusalem, Israel). At each of these locales, I began to "dig deeper" into the questions that grew into this book.

When I returned to the United States, I continued that research, and began to speak frequently at other law schools and at law-and-psychology and law-and-psychiatry conferences about these topics (and I was always struck by how little otherwise-well-educated Americans knew about them, in contrast to my experiences abroad). I published frequently in this area, and expanded my geographical horizons by presenting papers and conducting workshops in Argentina, Lithuania, Uganda, Australia, and Taiwan. When I was named as a Fulbright Senior Specialist, I went to Haifa University Law School in Israel to teach the International Human Rights and Mental Disability Law course as part of that university's global law program.

During all this time, I continued to work with my friend and colleague Yoshi Ikehara, head of the Tokyo Advocacy Law Office. I had met Yoshi in 2000 at an international conference in Italy, and started to work with him in Japan, the United States, and Taiwan soon thereafter. For the last few years, he has headed a project to create a Disability Rights Tribunal for Asia and the Pacific, and I have been working with him to make his dream a reality. Chapter 9 of this book is devoted to a discussion of this tribunal. My work with Yoshi on this project has taught me more about the international human rights/mental disability law intersection than any other pro bono work I have ever done.

I have written this book for several overlapping reasons. I seek to paint a picture of the shameful state of public psychiatric institutions worldwide, a shame that is abetted by the social attitude of sanism (that I discuss extensively, see infra chapter 2), and one in which governments are complicit, either passively or, in some cases (see infra chapter 4), actively. I seek to remediate this bleaker-than-bleak picture by pointing to several beacons of hope, especially the recent ratification of the United Nations Convention on the Rights of Persons with Disabilities (see infra chapter 7). That Convention offers the potential for redemption, for demarginalization, and finally, for a universal acknowledgment of the shameful ways that we have treated persons with mental disabilities—especially those *institutionalized* because of disabilities—for hundreds of years. I have visited facilities in over half the American states, in Central and Eastern Europe, and in Central and South America. It is my hope that publication of this book leads to authentic social change that gives those still languishing in such institutions a measure of hope for the future.

Much of this book is completely new, but some chapters draw on previously published (and "in press") articles. Chapter 1 builds on *Mental Health Law and Human Rights: Evolution and Contemporary Challenges*, in MENTAL HEALTH AND HUMAN RIGHTS (Michael Dudley ed. 2011) (Oxford University Press) (with Prof. Eva Szeli) (in press). Chapter 4 is an expansion of *International Human Rights and Comparative Mental Disability Law: The Role of Institutional Psychiatry in the Suppression of Political Dissent*, 39 ISRAEL L. REV. 69 (2006). Chapter 5 relies in part on *International Human Rights Law and Comparative Mental Disability Law: The Universal Factors*, 34 SYRACUSE J. INT'L L. & COMMERCE 333 (2007). In chapter 6 the section "Law School Pedagogy" continues the ideas first developed in *"Ain't No Goin' Back": Teaching Mental Disability Law Courses on Line*, 51 N.Y.L. SCH. L. REV. 991 (2006), and *An Internet-based Mental Disability Law Program: Implications for Social Change in Nations with Developing Economies*, 40 FORDHAM INT'L L.J. 435 (2007). The chapter 6 section "Expert Evidence Law" flows from *"The Witness Who Saw, /He Left Little Doubt": A Comparative Consideration of Expert Testimony in Mental Disability Law Cases*, 6 J. INVESTIGATIVE PSYCHOL. & OFFENDER PROF. 59 (2009) (with Profs. Astrid Birgden & Kris Gledhill), and also borrows from *"With Faces Hidden While the Walls Were Tightening": Applying International Human Rights Standards to Forensic Psychology*, 7 US-CHINA L. REV. 1 (2010). The chapter 6 section "Psychotherapist-Patient Law" adds to *"You Got No Secrets to Conceal": Considering the Application of the Tarasoff Doctrine Abroad*, 75 U. CIN. L. REV. 611 (2006). Some of the ideas expressed in the chapter 6 section "Corrections Law" were first developed in *"It's Doom Alone That Counts": Can International Human Rights Law Be an Effective Source of Rights in Correctional Conditions Litigation?* 27 BEHAV. SCI. & L. 675 (2009) (with Prof. Henry Dlugacz).

Chapter 7, in part, relies on *"A Change Is Gonna Come": The Implications of the United Nations Convention on the Rights of Persons with Disabilities for the Domestic Practice of Constitutional Mental Disability Law*, 29 NO. ILL. U. L. REV. 483 (2009). Chapter 8 approaches the issues from the perspective of *"I Might Need a Good Lawyer, Could Be Your Funeral, My Trial": A Global Perspective on the Right to Counsel in Civil Commitment Cases, and Its Implications for Clinical Legal Education*, 28 WASH. U. J. L. & SOC'L POL'Y 241 (2008). And portions of chapter 10 come from *"Where The Home in the Valley Meets the Damp Dirty Prison": A Human Rights Perspective on Therapeutic Jurisprudence and the Role of Forensic Psychologists in Correctional Settings*, 14 AGGRESSION & VIOLENT BEHAVIOR 256 (2009) (with Prof. Birgden), and

"Tolling for the Luckless, the Abandoned and Forsaked": Community Safety, Therapeutic Jurisprudence and International Human Rights Law as Applied to Prisoners and Detainees, 13 Leg. & Criminol. Psychology 231 (2008) (with Prof. Birgden).

I have also presented unpublished papers at conferences over the years that have helped clarify many of the underlying issues for me. These include, but are not limited to, *The Need for a Regional Disability Rights Tribunal in Asia: What Can We Learn from the Inter-American Experience?*; *Why a Regional Tribunal Is Needed to Implement the CRPD*; *Creation of a Disability Rights Tribunal for Asia and the Pacific: Its Impact on China?*; ***Pr**omoting Social Change in East Asia: The Movement to Create a Disability Rights Tribunal and the Promise of International Online, Distance Learning*; and *"Your Old Road Is/ Rapidly Agin": International Human Rights Standards and Their New Impact on Forensic Psychologists and Psychiatrists.* I want to also thank my friend and colleague Yoshi Ikehara, with whom I collaborated on several of these papers, for his support and his being the inspiration for the project that led to chapter 9.[1]

It would have been impossible for me to have completed this book without the work of an extraordinary team of research assistants over the past years. In the past, I was helped so much by Carra Greenberg, Jackie Halpern Weinstein, Devra Nemrow, An Truong, Sabrina Antebi, Ryan Hild, Danny Gershburg, Cambridge Peters, and Rachel Hisler. But I must single out two of my assistants for work far beyond the call of duty. Simply put, I never could have completed chapter 9—the most intellectually difficult and challenging chapter in the book, I think—without the superb and prodigious work of Naomi Weinstein, whose contributions to this book are unparalleled. Finally, my never-ending thanks to Jessica Cohn, who, in the past five months, has done an astonishing job of editing, cite checking, cite "translating" (from Bluebook to APA style), and of offering me excellent suggestions that I hope have improved the final product. To all these students and former students, and to my colleagues at New York Law School to whom I presented a version of chapter 9 of this book at a faculty development workshop, my profound thanks. I also benefited from comments and suggestions at faculty development workshops and conferences at the University of Tokyo; Haifa University; European University Institute; the Philadelphia College of Physicians; Georgia State University Law School; Tulane University Law School Disability Rights Society; The Human Rights Program and the Institute for Law, Psychiatry, and Public Policy at the University of Virginia Law School; Florida International University Law School; McGeorge Law School; Stanford University Law School; Fordham University Law School; the East Asian Chapter of the Law and Society Association; Northern Illinois University Law School; the

[1] I also want to thank Tara Brach for leading me to the works on Buddhism and human rights on which I relied heavily in Chapter 9.

Asia-Pacific Development Center on Disability; the National Human Rights Commission of Korea; Renmin University Law School; Waseda University Law School; University of Washington Law School; University of Cincinnati Law School and Medical College; Washington University in St. Louis Law School; the European Association of Law and Psychology; the National Association for Rights, Protection and Advocacy; the Society of American Law Teachers; the International Academy of Law and Mental Health; the Canadian Psychological Association; the Western Psychological Association; the European Chinese Studies Association; the American Academy of Psychiatry and Law; the American Psychology-Law Society; the Asia-Pacific Center on Disability; the University of Hong Kong, and the Australian and New Zealand Association of Psychiatry, Psychology and Law.

I also want to thank Dean Richard A. Matasar , former Associate Dean Jethro Lieberman and Associate Deans Stephen J. Ellmann and Carol Buckler for their support and for their awarding me grants from the New York Law School Summer Research Grant Fund to aid me in my work on this volume. My faculty assistants, Stan Schwartz and Steven Cunningham, provided me flawless assistance (and realized that when I would say, "This is the last draft; honest!" that that might not be exactly true . . .). Special thanks also go to Liane Bass, Esq., and Professor Heather Cucolo (administrators of New York Law School's online mental disability law distance learning program) for all the work they have done and continue to do to make the programs described in "Law School Pedagogy," in chapter 6, a reality, and also special thanks to Anna Blaine, my wonderful library assistant. My coauthors of some of the articles that led to chapters in this book—Eva Szeli (who gets an extra special thanks for her help with the final naming of the book), Henry Dlugacz, Astrid Birgden, and Kris Gledhill—get a special thanks, as do Yoshi Ikehara (who conceived of the idea of the Disability Rights Tribunal for Asia and the Pacific, see Chapter 9), and Professor David Wexler and the late Professor Bruce Winick, whose monumental contribution to the world of law and society (by their creation of the school of therapeutic jurisprudence, see chapter 10), can never be overstated. I am so sad that Bruce did not live to read this dedication. I miss him so much.

My inspiration for this book also came from one of Bob Dylan's greatest and most anthemic songs, "Chimes of Freedom." Those who have read my articles know that I frequently draw on Bob's song titles and lyrics as inspiration. Rarely has the fit been better than in this work, writing about, again from "Chimes of Freedom," "the luckless, the abandoned an' forsaked." My other regret is that my friend Michael Feuerstein, who brought me back to the world of Dylan 16 years ago, did not live to see the publication of this volume. As I prepare for my next two Dylan shows, I am reminded of how much Michael brought—and still brings—to my life.

Finally, I dedicate this book to my wife Linda, and my children Julie and Alex. When I first dedicated a book to them, Julie was 8 and Alex 5. Julie is now approaching her 30th birthday and Alex his 27th. They are accomplished professionals, and every day I give thanks for their presence, and Linda's presence, in my life. Their love and support and encouragement have allowed me to "keep on keepin' on" every day.

New York City
October 19, 2010

Contents

1

Introduction and Overview

I. Introduction

"Traditionally, disability has not been regarded as a human rights issue" (Lawson, 2006, p. 462; see also, Lord, 2004). As recently as 17 years ago, it was not so broadly acknowledged (Rosenthal & Rubenstein, 1993). Although there had been prior cases decided in the United States and in Europe that, retrospectively, had been litigated from a human rights perspective,[1] the characterization of "disability rights" (especially the rights of persons with *mental* disabilities) as a social issue was not discussed in a global public, political, or legal debate until the early 1990s. Instead, disability was seen only as a medical problem of the individual requiring a treatment or cure. By contrast, viewing disability as a human rights issue requires us to recognize the inherent equality of all people, regardless of abilities, disabilities, or differences, and obligates society to remove the attitudinal and physical barriers to equality and

---

[1] E.g., *O'Connor v. Donaldson*, 1975 (unconstitutional to confine a nondangerous person capable of surviving safely in freedom to a mental hospital); *Wyatt v. Stickney*, 1971; *Wyatt v. Aderholt*, 1974 (persons with mental illness have constitutional right to adequate treatment in mental hospital); *Lessard v. Schmidt*, 1972 (a statute that fails to provide a person alleged to be mentally ill with adequate procedural safeguards is unconstitutional); *Winterwerp v. the Netherlands*, 1979 (detention on grounds of unsoundness of mind must be based on objective medical evidence of a true mental disorder, be a proportionate response, and be carried out in accordance with a procedure prescribed by law); see generally, 1 Perlin, 1998; 2 Perlin, 1999b.

inclusion of people with disabilities (see Perlin et al., 2006; see also, Jones & Marks, 1999; Hendricks & Degener, 1994; Lawson, 2006).

For the past decade, I have turned my attention to the intersection between mental disability law and international human rights law in multiple ways. First, under the aegis of Mental Disability Rights International (MDRI), a Washington, DC–based human rights advocacy NGO (now known as Disability Rights International), I have done site visits and conducted mental disability law training workshops in Hungary, Estonia, Latvia, Uruguay, and Bulgaria (see infra chapter 5). Second, through New York Law School's (NYLS) online distance learning mental disability law program (which I direct), I have taught mental disability law courses in Japan and Nicaragua, and have worked extensively in Nicaragua with local advocates and activists in an effort to build a mental disability advocacy network in that nation (one that could optimally be expanded to other nations in Central and South America), and am currently involved in expanding this program to create a new partnership in Japan, and other partnerships in China and elsewhere (see infra chapter 6). In this role, I have also collaborated with the American Bar Association's Rule of Law Asia office, the All China Lawyers' Association, and Northwest University of Politics and Law in Xi'an, to teach experienced criminal defense lawyers how to train inexperienced lawyers, using the online, distance learning methodologies developed in this program. Third, through the International Mental Disability Law Reform Project of the NYLS Justice Action Center (which I also direct), I have worked in Taiwan and in Japan, as the first step in the creation of a Pan-Asian Rim Mental Health Advocacy Network and in the creation of a Disability Rights Tribunal for Asia and the Pacific, see infra chapter 9, and in Uganda in the creation of an Institute on Criminal Justice (at Nkumba University Law School, in Entebbe).

This work—and other work that I have done in Europe, Asia, and South America—has clarified to me the extent of our societal blindness to the ongoing violations of international human rights law in the context of the institutional commitment and treatment of persons with mental disabilities.[2] Notwithstanding a robust set of international law principles, standards and doctrines—many substantially based on American constitutional law decisions and statutory reforms of the past four decades—people with mental disabilities live in some of the harshest conditions that exist in any society (see, e.g., MDRI, 1995, 1997, 1999, 2000, 2007a, 2007b). The recent ratification of the United Nations Convention on the Rights of Persons with Disabilities (CRPD) forces all nations—for the first time—to take seriously these issues, and the conditions that are faced on a daily basis by persons

---

[2] Most of the examples and cases referred to and relied on in the work involve persons with psychosocial disabilities. International human rights law must apply equally robustly to persons with intellectual disabilities. See Dimopoulos, 2010.

worldwide who are institutionalized (or who have been institutionalized) because of mental disability.

These conditions are the product of neglect, lack of legal protection against improper and abusive treatment, and, primarily, the social attitudes of *sanism* and *pretextuality* (see infra chapter 2). *Sanism* is an irrational prejudice of the same quality and character of other irrational prejudices that cause (and are reflected in) prevailing social attitudes of racism, sexism, homophobia, and ethnic bigotry; that infect jurisprudence and lawyering practices; that are largely invisible and largely socially acceptable; that are based predominantly on stereotype, myth, superstition, and deindividualization; and are sustained and perpetuated by our use of a false "ordinary common sense" and heuristic reasoning[3] in an unconscious response to events both in everyday life and in the legal process (Perlin, 2000b, pp. 21–58).[4] *Pretextuality* refers to the ways in which courts accept—either implicitly or explicitly—testimonial dishonesty and engage similarly in dishonest and frequently meretricious decision-making, specifically where witnesses, especially expert witnesses, show a high propensity to purposely distort their testimony in order to achieve desired ends (Perlin, 2000b, pp. 59–76).

In the past, I have written regularly about these attitudes in *domestic* contexts so as to "seek to expose their pernicious power, the ways in which [they] infect judicial decisions, legislative enactments, administrative directives, jury behavior, and public attitudes, the ways that these factors undercut any efforts at creating a unified body of mental disability law jurisprudence, and the ways that these factors contaminate scholarly discourse and lawyering practices alike" (Perlin, 1999a, p. 26). In this volume, I will expand this inquiry to an *international* setting.

In the last several years, I have turned my scholarly attention to the intersection between international human rights law and mental disability law. I have coauthored the only casebook available on this topic (Perlin et al., 2006), and have published (and am in the process of publishing) a series of book chapters and law review articles that both deal globally with this topic (see e.g., Perlin, 2002a, 2007b, 2008c, 2009; Perlin & Szeli, 2010a, 2010b) and that focus on such specific subissues as political dissent (Perlin, 2006a), availability of counsel (Perlin, 2008b), sexual autonomy rights (Perlin, 2008a), prison and correctional law (Birgden & Perlin, 2008; Perlin & Dlugacz, 2009), judicial construction of mental status testimony (Perlin, Birgden & Gledhill, 2009), the psychiatrist-patient privilege (Perlin, 2006b), and online education as a tool of social change in this area of the law (Perlin, 2007a). In this book, I hope to link all these ideas together.

I have thus chosen to write this book to draw attention to these issues, to shed light on a shame that governments continue to ignore, and to invigorate

---

[3] See infra note 36, this chapter; see also infra chapter 6.

[4] On the invisibility of persons with disability, see also Quinn, 2009.

the debate on a social policy issue that remains "beneath the radar" for most of the world's nations. A decade ago, I titled a book *The Hidden Prejudice: Mental Disability on Trial* (2000b) because I wanted to focus on "the invisibility of the prejudice against persons with mental disability" (Perlin, 2003a, p. 317). That book dealt with the mistreatment of persons with mental disabilities in the United States (in both institutional and community settings). Again, I am writing this book to emphasize that this is not a provincial, domestic issue, but a global one. I believe that what I am writing about in this book "matters" not simply to institutionalized persons and their families but to all concerned citizens of the world. Governmental inaction (in some cases, through benign neglect; in others, because of malignant motives) demeans human dignity, denies personal autonomy, and disregards "the most authoritative and comprehensive prescription of human rights obligations" (Weissbrodt et al., 2009, p. 9; see also, Henkin, 1981, 1989).

This is not to say that no attention is being paid on a global basis to the issues that form the core of this book. As I have already indicated, the United Nations Convention on Human Rights of People with Disabilities has been ratified and is in force in 90 nations (http://www.un.org/disabilities).[5] But the topics that are at the heart of this book—how there is a cluster of what I call "universal factors" (Perlin, 2007b) that infect the nature, substance, and procedures of public psychiatric institutionalization around the world, how the lack of systemic provision of counsel to persons with mental disabilities perpetuates the existence of those factors (Perlin, 2008a), and how sanism and pretextuality infect the legal treatment of persons with mental disabilities worldwide (Perlin, 2009)—have never previously been considered in a systematic and unified way. In arguing why the United States should ratify the UN Convention, Tara Melish focused on the "deeply entrenched attitudes and stereotypes about disability that have rendered many of the most flagrant abuses of the rights of persons with disabilities 'invisible' from the mainstream human rights lens" (2007, p. 44). I am writing this book, in significant part, to make these abuses *visible.*

The book will proceed in this manner: First, I present brief overviews of international human rights law, and will then explain both *sanism* and *pretextuality* (see e.g., 4 Perlin, 2000b, 2 Perlin, 1999b), and the significance of *dignity* to this entire inquiry (see e.g., Perlin, 1996) (chapter 2). I then consider mental disability law in a comparative law context (see e.g., Rosenthal & Sundram, 2002; Rosenthal & Rubenstein, 1993; Perlin, 2002a; Degener, 2000), and then examine comparative law examples from, e.g., the United States (see e.g., 1 Perlin, 1998 [civil commitment law]; 2 Perlin, 1999b [institutional rights law], 3 Perlin, 2000a [antidiscrimination law], 4 Perlin, 2002b [forensic issues]; see generally, Perlin, 2000b), South America (Moncada, 1994), Western Europe

[5] As of September 6, 2010, there were 146 signatories to the Convention, and 89 signatories to the Optional Protocol. In addition, there have been 54 ratifications of the Optional Protocol. Quinn, 2009.

(Gostin, 2000; Harding, 1989), and central and eastern Europe (Lewis, 2002), as well as case law examples from Europe, Latin America, and Africa (Perlin et al., 2006) (chapter 3). Following this, I will consider the specific case of the ways that institutional psychiatry has been used as a means of stifling political dissent, looking at this issue from a broader mental disability law perspective (Perlin, 2006a), stressing how we have regularly ignored the ways that nonpolitical psychiatric patients are treated in nations that use institutional psychiatry to suppress dissent (chapter 4).

I will then move on to the heart of the book: discussing and analyzing the universal factors that I have identified that must be dealt with if the human rights violations are to be corrected: as indicated above, lack of comprehensive legislation, lack of independent counsel, inadequate care, lack of community programming, and inhumane forensic systems (Perlin, 2007a), and will consider specifically how the corrosive impact of sanism and pretextuality have contributed to these problems which I am discussing (chapter 5). I argue that to maintain the status quo is to perpetuate institutionalized human rights abuses, and that it is essential that all nations devote themselves to significant and ameliorative reform of their mental health systems. Following this, I will consider the international human rights/mental disability law intersection as it applies to other specific questions: matters involving law school pedagogy, corrections law, private law, and evidence law that relates to the judicial construction of mental state testimony (e.g., Perlin, 2006b, 2008a; Perlin, Birgden & Gledhill, 2009; Perlin & Dlugacz, 2009) (chapter 6). In the context of the discussion of law school pedagogy, I discuss how the use of online distance learning can bridge the gap between nations in which there are robust programs teaching mental disability law and those where there are not (see Perlin, 2007a; chapter 6).

The book will then look carefully at the UN Convention, and will highlight Articles in that Convention that are of the most significance to the population under consideration in this volume (Perlin, 2009a; chapter 7). Then, I will look forward to the likely post–UN Convention landscape, and will conclude that the legislative and judicial creation of rights—both positive and negative—is illusory unless there is a parallel mandate of counsel that is (1) free and (2) regularized and organized (Perlin, 2008a) (chapter 8). Without the presence of such counsel, any rights articulated by a court or human rights commission or legislature become merely "paper victories" (Perlin, 2002c, p. 246). Further, to be authentically effective, counsel needs to be available both for individual cases (in which commitment—initial or extended—of the patient is being sought) and in "affirmative" cases (that is, cases consciously thought of as "public interest" or "law reform" cases (see Perlin, 2007a).

Following this, I will discuss an important gap in international human rights protection that I note in chapter 3: that there is no human rights court or commission for Asia or the Pacific. In an effort to remediate this, I propose the creation of a Disability Rights Tribunal for that region, and discuss the steps that have already been taken in this regard, looking most closely at the debate on "Asian values," and the implications of the resolution of that debate, returning again to the need for regularized, dedicated counsel (chapter 9).[6] Then, in the final substantive chapter, I consider the school of therapeutic jurisprudence (see e.g., Wexler & Winick, 1996; Winick, 2002) as it relates to all of the developments discussed in this book, and I urge scholars and policy-makers to look at this school of interpretation and policy more closely as they grapple with the difficult questions before us (chapter 10). I then offer some final thoughts and recommendations in a concluding chapter (chapter 11).

Writing in 1993, Eric Rosenthal and Leonard Rubenstein first illuminated how the Principles for the Protection of Persons with Mental Illness and for the Improvement of Mental Health Care "come from an individualistic, libertarian perspective that emphasizes restrictions on what the state can do to a person with mental illness" (p. 260).[7] A presenter at a conference held at New York Law School on the treatment of persons with mental disabilities referred to this article, and then told the audience, "[W]ithout advocates willing to get in the trenches and fight for these ideals, so that they might become a reality for persons with mental disabilities, these treaties and standards remain mere words without action" (Bliss, 2002, p. 381).

I hope that, by writing this book, I am able to place these issues into a social, legal, and political context, to encourage decision makers to take these questions seriously, and to bear witness to the reality that the voices of the persons about whom this book has been written are finally being heard.[8]

II. Disability Rights and Human Rights: An Overview[9]

A. Disability Rights Have at Last Been Recognized as Human Rights

Remarkably, the issue of the human rights of people with disabilities, particularly people with mental disabilities,[10] had been ignored for decades by the international agencies vested with the protection of human rights on a

---

[6] In this context, I will also explain why online, distance learning in mental disability law is an essential piece of rights-expansion in this area.

[7] I return to this issue in chapter 4.

[8] When I first wrote about this topic, I chose Bob Dylan's masterpiece, "Chimes of Freedom" as part of my title (see Perlin, 2002a). "Chimes" was characterized by music critic Robert Shelton as his "most political song" and an expression of "affinity" for a "legion of the abused." Shelton, 1997, p. 220. See http://www.bobdylan.com/#/songs/chimes-of-freedom (last accessed August 18, 2010). It also serves as one of the main sources of inspiration for this book.

[9] See generally, Perlin & Szeli, 2010a, 2010b.

[10] There is no single, universally accepted definition of "mental disabilities." The terminology varies from country to country, jurisdiction to jurisdiction, and even document to document. In this book, I use "mental disabilities" to encompass both psychiatric disorders and intellectual disabilities. On the political maneuvering at the

global scale.[11] Early developments in global international human rights law following World War II—and the various forms of human rights advocacy that emerged in the decades that followed—failed to focus on mental disability rights. As Dr. Theresia Degener, a noted disability scholar and activist, has observed:

> Drafters of the International Bill of Human Rights did not include disabled persons as a distinct group vulnerable to human rights violations. None of the equality clauses of any of the three instruments of this Bill, the Universal Declaration of Human Rights (1948) (hereinafter UDHR), the International Covenant on Civil and Political Rights (1966) (hereinafter ICCPR), and the International Covenant on Economic, Social and Cultural Rights (1966) (hereinafter ICESCR), mention disability as a protected category. (Degener, 2000, p. 187)

It was not until the United Nations' declaration of 1981 as the International Year of Disabled Persons (GA Resolution, 1976) that there was significant activity on an international level. The United Nations General Assembly subsequently established the World Programme of Action Concerning Disabled Persons (GA Resolution, 1982a), and declared 1983 to 1992 to be the Decade of Disabled Persons (GA Resolution, 1982b). As part of these efforts, the United Nations Human Rights Commission appointed two special rapporteurs to investigate and report on the human rights of persons with mental disabilities (Despouy Report, 1991; Daes Report, 1983), and in 1991 the General Assembly adopted the *Principles for the Protection of Persons with Mental Illness and for the Improvement of Mental Health Care* (widely referred to as the "MI Principles"; GA Resolution, 1991; see Rosenthal & Rubenstein, 1993).[12] The MI Principles established what at that time[13] were the most comprehensive

---

UN on the question of how and whether mental disabilities were to be defined in the CRPD, see Cantor, 2009.

[11] On how persons with disabilities may be "the most fragile within any society," see Gunn, 2009, p. 359. See also, Diniz, Barbosa & dos Santos, 2010, p. 65, on the oppression of persons with disability by the "culture of normality."

[12] But see Gendreau, 1997, p. 278, arguing that the MI Principles, in some ways, placed "more restrictions" on human rights; Harding, 2000, p. 24, concluding that, in some ways, the Principles "remove patients' rights rather than reinforce them." The World Network of Users and Survivors of Psychiatry has gone so far as to urge the United Nations to revoke the MI Principles. See Kaiser, 2009, p. 161 n. 90.

For a detailed discussion of the development of mental disability rights protections within the United Nations human rights system; see also, Arboleda-Florez & Weisstub, 2008.

[13] For a review of all pre-MI Principles UN documents in this area of the law, see Kampf, 2008. On how the evolution of human rights law in this area vindicates a social model of disability rights, see Dimopoulos, 2010.

international human rights standards for persons with mental disabilities, and their adoption was a critical global step in recognizing mental disability rights issues within the human rights arena.[14]

Degener's writings reflect the change that has taken place in disability rights jurisprudence. In 2000, she stated further that "disability has been reclassified as a human rights issue," and that "law reforms in this area are intended to provide equal opportunities for disabled people and to combat their segregation, institutionalization and exclusion as typical forms of disability-based discrimination" (p. 181). Yet, historically, mainstream human rights protection systems and advocacy organizations had difficulty acknowledging mental disability rights as part of their mandates (Dhir, 2008). The human rights issues encountered by persons with mental disabilities may have been perceived as too complex or esoteric. This challenge was sometimes articulated in rather unfortunate ways, such as "We work in human rights, not mental disability rights."[15] While the oblique suggestion that people with mental disabilities were not "human" was generally unintended, it may well have reflected deep-seated beliefs that they were somehow less valuable than the broader population, whose human rights merited unquestioned protection (Perlin, 2008d).[16] But while human rights are—by definition—universally

---

The MI Principles retain significance today in those nations that have neither signed nor ratified the CRPD.

[14] On mental health as a human right, see Gable, 2009; Gable & Gostin, 2009; "PAHO Position Paper," 2010. On the globalization of human rights, see Marsh & Payne, 2007; Stacy, 2009. On the relationship between human rights and global *health* governance, see Gable, 2007; Arboleda-Florez & Weisstub, 2008. On how globalization can lead nations with developing economies to "embed disability rights in their emerging institutions as part of their development efforts," see Thornburgh, 2008, p. 447. On the significance of the Article in the CRPD (Art. 32) that mandates "international cooperation" in this context, see Skogly, 2009.

On the potential impact of the globalization of law, see Halliday & Osinsky, 2006; on human rights in general, see Cheah, 1997; and on health rights as a human right, see Meier, 2007; Gable, 2007; Gable & Gostin, 2008; Ruger, 2008. Professor Rhoda Howard-Hassmann concludes that in the short term we cannot determine whether globalization "improves or undermines" human rights (2005, p. 1). On ways that the debate about public health informs the debate about human rights, see Nixon & Forman, 2008; Taylor, 1999. On globalization and constitutional rights, see Law, 2008. On the protection of human rights in a globalized world, see Shelton, 2002. On judicial globalization, see Slaughter, 2000.

[15] On the relationship between disability rights enforcement and the enforcement of rights of women and children, see, e.g., de Alwis, 2009.

[16] See Perlin, 2008d, manuscript, p. 9:

> When I have shared with others our vision of [doing mental disability law advocacy work and teaching online mental disability law courses] in sub-Saharan East Africa, those others have often scoffed, suggesting that the problems faced in that part of the world are so profound that it is almost

possessed by *all* humans, the formal recognition of the applicability of these rights in contexts specific to vulnerable populations is critical for their enforcement.[17]

To some extent, this new interest in human rights protections for people with disabilities echoes a larger international movement to protect human rights (Ramcharan, 1991),[18] and appears to more precisely follow track C. Raj Kumar's observation that "the judicial protection of human rights and constitutionalization of human rights may be two important objectives by which the rule of law can be preserved and which may govern future human rights work" (2003, p. 282). To be sure, some of the results to date have been modest. See infra chapter 3 (case law); chapter 7 (likely impact of the CRPD).[19] Few will quarrel with Douglass Cassel's observation that "[t]he direct impact of international human rights law on practice in most of the world remains weak and inconsistent." But, as Cassel perceptively noted further:

> Both this incipient body of law, and to a lesser degree its direct and even more its indirect influence on conduct, have grown rapidly in historical terms, and appear to be spreading in ways that cannot be explained by a worldview based solely on state power and rational calculations of self-interest. To appreciate its effectiveness and potential, international human rights law must be understood as part of a broader set of interrelated, mutually reinforcing processes and institutions—interwoven strands in a rope—that together pull human rights forward, and to which international law makes distinctive contributions.

Thus understood, Cassel concluded, international law "can be seen as a useful tool for the protection of human rights, and one which promises to be more useful in the future" (2001, p. 135).

Within the legal literature, the first time disability rights was directly conceptualized as a human rights issue may have been as recently as 1993. In their groundbreaking article, Eric Rosenthal and Leonard Rubenstein (1993) applied international human rights principles to the institutionalization of people with mental disabilities.[20] In the political context, disability as a human

---

frivolous to create the programs we are seeking to launch. As you might expect, I disagree, profoundly.

[17] At least one commentator has taken the position that human rights are "relatively irrelevant" for persons with mental illness (see Butcher, 2000), but it does not appear that this position has many adherents. A recent WESTLAW search revealed *no* citations to this piece in either the JLR or WORLD-JLR databases. (last searched September 12, 2010).

[18] Ramcharan is former deputy UN high commissioner for human rights.

[19] Professor Laurence Helfer has speculated that some governments may have "overlegalized" their human rights commitments (2002).

[20] This article was relied on almost immediately by scholars and activists studying the human rights implications of mental disability laws in nations as diverse as Japan

rights issue first appears to have been raised in remarks made the next year by former United States senator Bob Dole: "As a nation that has been a pioneer in promoting the dignity of its own citizens with disabilities, we have a special obligation to assume leadership in establishing the international human rights of people with disabilities" (1994, p. 931).

Meanwhile, regional human rights courts across the globe had begun to exhibit an increasing willingness to address mental disability rights issues, although, as will be discussed extensively below, see infra chapter 9, there is, as of this date, no such tribunal in Asia. In 1979, over a decade earlier than the publication of the Rosenthal/Rubenstein article, the European Court of Human Rights had already heard its first mental disability rights case, *Winterwerp v. Netherlands*, under the European Convention of Human Rights.[21] Over the following decades, the European Court heard dozens of mental disability rights cases, defining and refining the contours of human rights as applied in mental health contexts under the European Convention (Gostin, 2000; Lewis, 2002). In the Americas, the Inter-American Commission on Human Rights heard its first mental disability rights case, *Victor Rosario Congo v. Ecuador*, under the American Convention on Human Rights[22] in 1999, breaking new ground in formalizing the use of the MI Principles as a guide for interpreting and applying binding human rights standards. And subsequently, in 2003, the African Commission decided its first mental disability rights case, *Purohit and Moore v. The Gambia*, under the African Charter on Human and Peoples' Rights.[23] All of this case law has served to validate the connection between mental health and human rights, providing regional fora for recognizing and enforcing the human rights of individuals labeled with mental disabilities.[24]

However, during the late twentieth century, much of mental disability rights advocacy occurred outside of formal legal settings. Local, regional, and international nongovernmental organizations conducted investigations,

---

(Cohen, 1995, p. 35 n. 48), and Uruguay (Moncada, 1994, p. 591 n. 6).

[21] Convention for the Protection of Human Rights and Fundamental Freedoms, E.T.S. No. 5, 213 U.N.T.S. 222, opened for signature November 4, 1950, entered into force September 3, 1953. *Winterwerp* is discussed infra chapter 3. On the democratic legitimacy of the European court, see Follesdal, 2009.

[22] O.A.S. Treaty Series No. 36, 1144 U.N.T.S. 123, entered into force July 18, 1978. *Congo* is discussed infra chapter 3.

[23] O.A.U. doc. CAB/LEG/67/3 rev. 5, 21 I.L.M. 58 (1982), adopted June 27, 1981, entered into force October 21, 1986. *Purohit* is discussed infra chapter 3.

[24] We cannot fall into the trap of assuming that, simply because a court issued a decision, conditions in institutions immediately changed or that procedural safeguards were immediately instituted in response to such decisions. The history of mental disability law is all too often the history of "paper victories," and even the most rights-protective court decisions may be slow to produce significant real-life changes. See infra chapters 2 & 7.

wrote reports, and brought media attention to egregious human rights abuses suffered by people labeled with mental disabilities (see e.g., MDRI reports, cited supra, this chapter). Most significantly, the emergence of a "consumer movement" supported the natural advocacy capacities of stakeholders. By definition, the focal point of the mental disability rights movement is, or certainly should be, individuals who are identified as having mental disabilities. Yet, historically, their voices were often ignored, while others deemed to speak for those who purportedly could not speak for themselves. Referring to themselves as *consumers*, *users*, *ex-users*, *ex-patients*, or *survivors* of mental health services, individuals who had been labeled with mental disabilities began to organize not only locally but also regionally and globally (see infra, this chapter).[25] Such self-advocacy groups have since become instrumental in identifying violations of their human rights, and in advocating reform in the policies and systems that directly affect their lives (e.g., Stefan, 2003; "WUSNP position paper," 2010).[26]

B. The Disability Rights Convention[27]

Disability rights as a human rights issue subsequently took center stage at the United Nations, and the involvement of stakeholders has been critical in the most significant historical development in the recognition of the human rights of persons with mental disabilities: the drafting and adoption of a binding international disability rights convention (on the singular role of this Convention, see Megret, 2008a, 2008b). In late 2001, the United Nations General Assembly established an ad hoc committee "to consider proposals for a comprehensive and integral international convention to promote and protect the rights and dignity of persons with disabilities" (GA Resolution, 2001). The ad hoc committee drafted a document over the course of five years and eight sessions, and the new *Convention on the Rights of Persons with Disabilities* (sometimes "Convention" or "Disability Convention"; GA Resolution, 2006a) was adopted in December 2006 and opened for signature in March 2007 (GA Resolution, 2006b). It entered into force—thus becoming legally binding on States parties—on May 3, 2008, 30 days after the

---

[25] On how such interest groups are a "new form of democratic participation," see Lee, 2009.

[26] See, e.g., Gombos et al., 2002, describing the results of an extensive nationwide human rights investigation into conditions at long-term residential facilities for persons with mental disabilities, conducted by the Hungarian Mental Health Interest Forum, an organization of users/survivors of psychiatric services. For an earlier consideration in Japan, see Iwata, 1993.

[27] See generally infra chapter 7.

20th ratification (http://www.un.org/News/Press/docs/2008/hr4941.doc.htm; see generally, Melish, 2007; Stein & Stein, 2007).[28]

One of the hallmarks of the process that led to the publication of the UN Convention was the participation of persons with disabilities and the clarion cry, "Nothing about us, without us" (Kayess & French, 2008, p. 4, n. 15).[29] This has led commentators to conclude that the Convention "is regarded as having finally empowered the 'world's largest minority' to claim their rights, and to participate in international and national affairs on an equal basis with others who have achieved specific treaty recognition and protection" (Kayess & French, 2008, p. 4, n. 17;[30] see Cooper & Whittle, 1998, p. 36 [for any Convention to have positive influence on rights of persons with disabilities, it must be binding, accessible, and self-executing]), to "fundamentally enrich... the context of existing rights" (Megret, 2008a, p. 498), and to enable all persons with disabilities to "fully enjoy economic, social, cultural, civil and political rights" (Lee, 2009, p. 285).[31] Professor Gerard Quinn says simply that the CRPD "is a beacon for an international consensus on justice and disability" (2009, p. 52).[32]

---

[28] On the relationship between treaty ratification campaigns and international law theory in general, see Oberdörster, 2008.

[29] See, for example, Statement by Hon Ruth Dyson, Minister for Disability Issues, New Zealand Mission to the UN, for Formal Ceremony at the Signing of the Convention on the Rights of Persons with Disability, March 30, 2007: "Just as the Convention itself is the product of a remarkable partnership between governments and civil society, effective implementation will require a continuation of that partnership." The negotiating slogan "Nothing about us without us" was adopted by the International Disability Caucus, available at: http://www.un.org/esa/socdev/enable/documents/Stat_Conv/nzam.doc [last accessed November 13, 2007]. See Kayess & French, 2008, p. 4 n. 15.

Previously, persons with disabilities were frequently excluded entirely from the legislative drafting process. See e.g., MacKay, 2007.

[30] See, for example, statements made by the High Commissioner for Human Rights, Louise Arbour, and the Permanent Representative of New Zealand and Chair of the Ad-Hoc Committee on a Comprehensive and Integral International Convention on the Protection and Promotion of the Rights and Dignity of Persons with Disabilities, Ambassador Don Mackay, at a Special Event on the Convention on Rights of Persons with Disabilities, convened by the UN Human Rights Council, March 26, 2007, available at: http://www.unog.ch/80256EDD006B9C2E/(httpNewsByYear_en)/7444B2E219117CE8C12572AA004C5701?OpenDocument [last accessed November 13, 2007].

On the role, in general, of UN treaties and conventions in the protection of minority rights, see Alfredsson, 2009.

[31] On the way that the CRPD reconceptualized mental health rights as disability rights, see Fennell, 2008.

[32] See also, Fennell, 2008, p. 34 (CRPD provides a "moral compass for change"). On the role of NGOs in general in the development of the Convention, see Lord, 2004; on

III. Sanism and Pretextuality

There has always been great ambivalence on the part of the human rights community in its perception of the rights of persons with mental disabilities, and the *value* of those rights. I believe that the explanation for the roots of this ambivalence can be found in what we call "sanism" and what we call "pretextuality," and in the ways that we use cognitive-simplifying devices (heuristics) to distort our thinking processes (see infra chapters 2& 6). It is critical for those seriously interested in this topic to understand these concepts and how their malignancy has distorted all aspects of mental disability law, domestic and international.[33]

There is now some nascent literature on the relationship between sanism, pretextuality, and international human rights law (Perlin, 2006a, 2007b, 2008c, 2009a; Perlin et al., 2006, pp. 281–319; see also, Fischer, 2005; Katner, 2006), especially focusing on circumstances in nations with developing economies (Perlin, 2008b),[34] and it is critical that this investigation be expanded by scholars and policymakers in the justice system.[35] And this expanded consideration is especially time-urgent in light of the ratification of the new UN Convention.[36]

---

the role of NGOs in a potential Disability Rights Tribunal for Asia and the Pacific, see infra chapter 9.

[33] Professor Debora Diniz and her colleagues refer, instead, to "disablism," to reflect how persons with disabilities are "the target of oppression and discrimination" (Diniz, Barbosa & dos Santos, 2010, p. 61).

[34] By way of example, residents of nations with developing economies in Central and South America are no strangers to pretextuality in many other areas of the law and of society. See, e.g., DeSoto, 1989; Popkin, 2000; Eckstein, 2001; Galeano, 1997. On the relationship between this history and the importance of a vigorous mental health advocacy movement, see Perlin, 2007a.

[35] E.g., an analysis of the European Commission on Human Rights concluded that it has interpreted the European Convention on Human Rights "very restrictively in psychiatric cases" (Hewitt, 2001, p. 1278). The cases included in this analysis, which characterize the handcuffing of patients as "therapeutically necessary" (id., discussing *Herczegfalvy v. Austria*, 1993, or sanction the use of seclusion for "disciplinary" purposes (id., discussing *Dhoest v. Belgium*, 1987) certainly bespeak pretextuality. It is essential that such pretextuality be identified and answered (see Perlin, 2008c, discussing the UN Convention in this precise context).

[36] The Convention's focus on questions of empowerment (Kayess & French, 2008, p. 17) forces us to consider whether the legal system will continue to perpetuate the sort of sanism and pretextuality that has had such a negative impact on the lives of persons with mental disabilities, and will continue to condone teleological judicial behavior through overreliance on cognitive-simplifying heuristics. See Perlin, 2009b, p. 892, discussing the dominance and the power of the *vividness heuristic*, a cognitive-simplifying device through which a "single vivid, memorable case overwhelms mountains of abstract, colorless data upon which rational choices should be made," see also Perlin, 1997b, p. 1417; by *teleological*, I refer to outcome-determinative reasoning;

While there is a robust "psychiatric survivor" movement both in the United States and elsewhere, this voice is typically ignored (see supra; Margulies, 1992, p. 57, n. 132; Honig & Fendell, 2000, p. 185; "Taking Issue," 1997).[37] For more than 25 years, formerly hospitalized individuals and their supporters have formed an important role in the reform of the mental health system and in test case litigation. "Yet, there is little evidence that these groups are taken seriously either by lawyers or academics" (Perlin, 2003c, pp. 699–700).[38]

Finally, it is critical that we consider how any sanism-inspired blunders by lawyers can easily be fatal to the client's chance of success. By way of example, in the civil commitment context,[39] if a lawyer rejects the notion that his client may be competent (indeed, if s/he engages in the not-atypical "presumption of incompetency" that is all too often de rigueur in these cases),[40]

---

social science data that enable judges to satisfy predetermined positions are privileged, while data that would require judges to question such ends are rejected or subordinated. See e.g., Perlin, 1993; see also Asplund, 2000.

[37] See e.g., Andersen-Watts, 2008, p. 160: "If the law were to use the social model, it would hear the discontent, reasoning and knowledge from sources such as Judi Chamberlin and the Icarus Project, and it could use these perspectives in order to improve these interactions to ensure that they are not borne of ignorance nor prejudice." On an Australian perspective on why this voice should be heard, see Pearson, 2004.

[38] See also, Perlin, 2007a, p. 444 n. 39:

> [S]urvivor groups generally have opposed the constitutionality or application of involuntary civil commitment statutes, see, e.g., Project Release v. Prevost, 722 F.2d 960 (2d Cir. 1983), or supported the right of patients to refuse the involuntary administration of psychotropic drugs, see Rennie v. Klein, 653 F.2d 836, 838 (3d Cir. 1981) (Alliance for the Liberation of Mental Patients, amicus curiae), but also have involved themselves in a far broader range of litigation. See, e.g., Colorado v. Connelly, 479 U.S. 157 (1986) (impact of severe mental disability on Miranda waiver; Coalition for the Fundamental Rights and Equality of Ex-patients, amicus). The involvement of such groups in test case litigation—exercising the right of self-determination in an effort to control, to the greatest extent possible, their own destinies, see, e.g., Judi Chamberlin, On Our Own: Patient-Controlled Alternatives to the Mental Health System (197[8])—is a major development that cannot be overlooked by participants in subsequent mental disability litigation.

[39] It must be stressed that the majority of those subjected to involuntary civil commitment are poor, elderly, uneducated, or female. See Perlin, Gould & Dorfman, 1995. The relationship between this set of circumstances and human rights law is explored in de Alwis, 2009.

[40] See Perlin, 2003b, p. 193:

> In short, the presumption in which courts have regularly engaged—that there is both a de facto and de jure presumption of incompetency to be applied to medication decision making—appears to be based on an empirical fallacy: psychiatric patients are not necessarily more incompetent than nonmentally ill persons to engage in independent medication decision making) [footnote omitted].

the chances are far slimmer that s/he will advocate for such a client in the way that lawyers have been taught—or, at the least, *should* be taught—to advocate for their clients. In nations with no traditions of an "expanded due process model" (Perlin, 2007a, p. 971) in cases involving persons subject to commitment to psychiatric institutions or those already institutionalized, sanism in lawyers can be fatal to an individual's chance for release or for a judicial order mandating amelioration of conditions of confinement and/or access to treatment and/or to be free from unwanted treatment interventions.

IV. International Attention to Disability Rights

At least 42 countries have adopted disability antidiscrimination laws (Kanter, 2003, p. 249, n. 33; Chaffin, 2005, p. 138; see generally, http://www.un.org/disabilities/default.asp?id=235). Although some countries rely on the medical model of disability, others have chosen instead to incorporate a human rights perspective in their domestic legislation, thereby guaranteeing the right of people with disabilities to equality and full participation in society (see Waddington, 2001; compare Besner, 1995 [discussing possible applicability of an Americans with Disabilities Act–type law to France]; Heyer, 2000 [same, to Japan]; Cantor, 2009; Waddington, 2008 [both same, to EU nations]; Lord & Brown, 2010 [on how the CRPD requires the application of the reasonable accommodation principle]).[41] Arguably, at no previous time in history has the confluence of international and domestic efforts with and for people with disabilities challenged policymakers, scholars, and activists to reframe the meaning of equality and inclusion for people with disabilities.[42]

For people with mental disabilities, in particular, the development of human rights protections may be even more significant than for people with other disabilities. Like people with other disabilities, people with mental disabilities face degradation, stigmatization, and discrimination throughout the world today.[43] But disproportionately and more frequently, many people with mental disabilities are routinely confined, against their will, in institutions, and deprived of their freedom, dignity, and basic human rights. People with

---

41 For a rejection of a welfare-based model of disability policy, see Mor, 2006 (studying Israeli policy).

42 On the shift toward a social model reflected in international human rights standards, see Waterstone, 2004. On how the model of disability "plays the decisive role in the ultimate success or failure of legislative programs governing disability rights," see Cantor, 2009, p. 434. On how the social model has enabled "a shift of disability from private to public places," see Diniz, Barbosa & dos Santos, 2010, p. 65.

43 See *City of Cleburne v. Cleburne Living Center,* 1985, p. 462 (Marshall, J., dissenting in part), arguing that "[T]he mentally retarded have been subject to a 'lengthy and tragic history' of segregation and discrimination that can only be called grotesque," and describing a "regime of state-mandated segregation and degradation . . . that in its virulence and bigotry rivaled, and indeed paralleled, the worst excesses of Jim Crow."

mental disabilities who are fortunate enough to live outside of institutions often remain imprisoned by the social isolation they experience, often from their own families. They are not included in educational programs, and they face attitudinal barriers to employment because they have not received the education and training needed to obtain employment or because of discrimination based on unsubstantiated fears and prejudice (Stefan, 2001).

Discrimination against people with mental disabilities does not always take the form of hatred or hostility, however. More often, discrimination against people with mental disabilities takes the form of fear, pity, or patronization (see generally, Perlin, 2000b; Boyadjiev & Onchev, 2007). Yet only relatively recently have disability discrimination laws and policies in the United States and elsewhere focused on changing such attitudes and promoting the integration of people with disabilities into our schools, neighborhoods, and workplaces (see Perlin, 1993-1994, discussing "sanist attitudes" in this context).

Therapeutic jurisprudence (see infra Chapter 10) teaches us that, if the legal system is to fulfill its commitment to provide dignity to litigants, it must honor the "three Vs"—voice, validation and voluntariness (Ronner, 2008). Persons with mental disabilities who are institutionalized in barren, crowded, inhumane facilities (see infra Chapter 5) are truly the silenced. Their dehumanization invalidates them. They rarely have the opportunity to act voluntarily. My hope is that recent developments in this area of law and social policy will finally, begin to break this cycle, give them a voice, and in the words of the title of this book, allow the silenced to be heard.

It is clear that, within the past decade, there has been nothing short of an explosion of interest in the area of human rights and mental disability law by academics, practitioners, advocates, and self-advocates (Perlin, 2002–2003, p. 539). As Professor Arlene Kanter has put it: "The principle of non-discrimination and equality for people with disabilities has entered center stage in the international arena" (2003, p. 268). Again, groups such as Disability Rights International and the Mental Disability Advocacy Center have investigated conditions of institutions for people with mental disabilities and issued scathing reports about the quality of services made available in psychiatric institutions and social care homes in Eastern Europe and Latin America. Organizations such as Amnesty International and the Helsinki Committees have finally, albeit tardily, recognized that violations of persons' mental health rights are violations of human rights (see Dhir, 2008, p. 105: "For decades, the rights of mentally disabled persons were virtually ignored by the human rights movement").[44]

---

[44] Symposium 2002, p. 391 (Comments of Eric Rosenthal):

> I began my research . . . by examining the human rights studies of non-governmental organizations such as Human Rights Watch and Amnesty International. I also looked at the U.S. Department of State's Country Reports on Human Rights Practices. What I found is shocking: those human rights organizations and human rights reports criticized governments when political

And the CRPD offers the "beacon" of hope (see Quinn, 2009, p. 52) to which I have already referred. Yet, it would be unduly optimistic to suggest that the atrocities—there is no other word to be used—of the past (see infra chapter 5) are no more.

V. Conclusion

It would have been impossible to have written this book 20 years ago. Developments in recent years—culminating in the ratification of the UN Convention—have been nothing less than meteoric. But, these developments should not lull us into thinking that the historic wrongs have all been righted, and the persons with mental disabilities are treated with respect and dignity, and as full citizens. All too often, they are still–drawing on Bob Dylan's brilliant song, *Chimes of Freedom*—"the luckless, the abandoned an' forsaked/ . . . the outcast, burnin' constantly at stake" (Dylan, 1964). Throughout the world, such individuals continue to be subjected to harsh, barbaric—in some cases, almost unimaginable—conditions (see, e.g., http://www.disabilityrightsintl.org/media-gallery/our-reports-publications [MDRI website]), and most of society remains unaware of how shocking these conditions often are (see infra chapter 5).

I have written this book in an effort to call attention to that history, to share recent developments, and to help set an agenda for the future. In subsequent chapters, I will return to each of the issues I have raised here, with the hopes that I can illuminate them for the readers, and that I can inspire others to take these questions seriously.

---

dissidents were put in psychiatric facilities, but they did not speak out about the abuses against other people who may or may not have mental disabilities.

See also, Kanev, 2002, p. 435 (Amnesty International first involved itself in this issue in Bulgaria in 2001).

2

International Human Rights Law in Perspective: Legal Issues and Social Constructs

Introduction

In this chapter, I will offer a short overview of international human rights law that relates *generally* to mental disability law. I will begin with a short background of early UN documents and conventions, will then discuss more specialized civil rights documents, and then will explore some of the conceptual dichotomies that must be considered if international human rights law is to be understood in this context. I will then continue by discussing the phenomena of "sanism" and "pretextuality," why they must be understood, and how they contaminate this entire area of law and social policy, and then, the significance of dignity in any inquiry as to the relationship between international human rights and mental disability law.

Chapter 2A. International Human Rights in Legal Perspective

I. Legal Background

The idea that individuals have certain human rights independent of the rights granted to them by governments of the nations of which they are citizens can be traced to the writings of Locke and Rousseau, who argued that certain rights were beyond the scope of state control.[1] By the early twentieth century, a growing recognition of the right of individuals to self-determination led to the creation of the League of Nations. But the true "birth" of human rights law came in the 1940s in the aftermath of World War II and the revelations of the extent of death and destruction in the Holocaust. The brutality of the war "demonstrated that previous attempts to protect the individual from the ravages of war were inadequate" (Weissbrodt, 1989, p. 6, quoting Luard, 1967, pp. 20–21).[2]

Soon after the United Nations was created, members of the Human Rights Commission were charged with drafting a Universal Declaration of Human Rights (UDHR) "in a common language from a host of cultural, religious, and political traditions" (Ishay, 2004, pp. 16–17). The drafting of this Declaration "challenged the premise that universal human rights were purely a Western invention, [and instead, chose to] look at all the world's great religions and culture for the universal notions of the common good that had inspired the Enlightenment's human rights visionaries" (Perlin et al., 2006, p. 234). Between the UN Charter, the UDHR, and the subsequent international covenants (see infra this chapter), the blueprint was set in place for later documents that focused exclusively on questions of disability rights.

A. The UDHR[3]

The United Nations underscored its commitment to human rights by adopting the Universal Declaration of Human Rights (UDHR) in 1948.[4] As stated in the preamble, the UDHR sets forth a common standard of achievement for all peoples and nations. Its primary authors drew on established religious and secular philosophical traditions worldwide in crafting provisions that recognize the inherent, universal, and transcendent nature of human rights. (See generally, Pillay, 2008.) Professor David Kinley has thus concluded that human rights "are not only compatible with democracy, *they are essential to its functioning and survival*" (2007, p. 559, emphasis added. But compare Baxi, 1999, p. 198: "the paradigm of the Universal Declaration of Human Rights is being steadily supplanted by a trade-related, market-friendly human rights paradigm").

The 30 articles of the UDHR place emphasis on principles of liberty, dignity, equality, and brotherhood. The UDHR refrains from creating distinctions among categories of rights, recognizing basic civil and political rights along

[1] Compare Butler, 2009 (human rights doctrine predates the Enlightenment and can be found in earlier religious thought and doctrine).

[2] Compare Scharf, 2009, p. 46 (discussing how events following 9/11 led scholars and policymakers to conclude that international law was "just 'politics'").

[3] See generally, Perlin & Dlugacz, 2008, pp. 977–1041.

[4] On how human rights, in the context of the UDHR, serve as a body of international constitutional rights, see Gardbaum, 2008; see also, Mutua, 1996, p. 595 (human rights corpus "based on the idea of constitutionalism").

with economic, social, and cultural rights. Collective guarantees are also included, such as the right of everyone to a social and international order that will allow human rights to be realized (Art. 28). Notably, the UDHR makes specific reference to medical care and social security but stops short of announcing a right to health (Art. 25). In 1993, the Vienna World Conference on Human Rights echoed the UDHR proclamations by stating that human rights are universal, indivisible, interdependent, and interrelated (Vienna Declaration, World Conference on Human Rights, Vienna, Austria June 14–25, 1993, U.N. Doc A/CONF 157/24, at para. 5 (1993)).

The designation of the UDHR as a "declaration" rather than a treaty or convention was necessary to secure the broad support of the UN membership. Realizing the power of moral persuasion, Eleanor Roosevelt, who chaired the commission responsible for drafting the document, "believed wholeheartedly that a declaration, though not legally binding, would be much more than a vague proclamation" (Glendon, 2001, p. 86).[5] Indeed, shortly after the UDHR was approved, its principles and provisions began appearing in newly drafted national constitutions in Latin America and the Middle East.

Due to the changing nature of human rights law, a differentiation between "hard" convention and treaty-based law and so-called soft law such as the UDHR sometimes proves to be artificial (see infra this chapter). For example, the legal significance of UDHR is due in part to the fact that it took nearly three decades to implement the two "hard law" covenants, the International Covenant on Civil and Political Rights (ICCPR) and the International Covenant on Economic, Social and Cultural Rights (ICESCR). In the interim, the UDHR provided the primary reference for international human rights standards during an era when a number of new nations emerged, particularly in Africa. The UDHR also serves an authoritative interpretative function with regard to the UN Charter's protection of human rights.[6] As a result of the pervasiveness of state practice, many of the UDHR's provisions are now viewed as part of customary international law that is enforceable against the world community. Irrespective of its precise characterization, the UDHR remains the leading pronouncement on the critical importance of international human rights.[7]

---

5 On the balance between persuasion and coercion in international human rights law, see Goodman & Jinks, 2004a.

6 On how the principles articulated in the UDHR affects state behavior, see Risse & Skinnik, 1999.

7 See Anderson, 2009, characterizing it as "a place of refuge"; but see Cheng, 2008, p. 254, asserting that the UDHR "fails to achieve its goal of setting a common standard of human rights achievement for all nations because the foreign policies of various states and special interest groups politicized its formation, and because it does not instruct decisionmakers on how to determine the content and legality of its provisions"; Anghie & Chimni, 2003 p. 84, arguing that international law historically "justified and legitimatized suppression of Third World people"; Kinley, 2007, discussing how human rights have been "demonized").

B. The International Covenants

1. INTRODUCTION An International Bill of Rights was originally designed in three parts: a declaration setting forth general human rights principles and concepts, a covenant with more specific provisions, and a section with mechanisms for implementation. Beginning in 1948, the efforts of the Commission on Human Rights were directed toward drafting the covenant portion to ensure the standards of the UDHR in a binding treaty form. When it became apparent that agreement would not be easily achieved, a decision was made to create two separate documents, one to include civil and political rights and the other to address economic, social, and cultural rights.[8]

The political realities of the cold war era and the subsequent collapse of colonial regimes worldwide resulted in a global landscape markedly different from that of 1948. States were increasingly resistant to surrender their sovereignty and to make commitments to take positive steps for the protection of human rights. The United States in particular became a reluctant participant in UN-initiated endeavors. In 1953, President Eisenhower refused to reappoint Eleanor Roosevelt to the Human Rights Commission. Finally, in 1966, the two covenants were presented to the General Assembly for adoption and then sent out for approval and ratification. By the mid-1970s, the Covenants had garnered the support of the 35 states needed for implementation.

The Covenants impose binding obligations on states parties subject to any reservations that might be invoked. Both Covenants expand on the principles of UDHR. There is some overlap between the Covenants such as the right to self-determination (ICCPR Art. 1(1); ICESCR Art. 1(1)) and a prohibition against discrimination based on "race, color, sex, language, religion, political or other opinion, national or social origin, property, birth, or other status" (ICCPR Art. 2(1); ICESCR Art. 2(2)).[9] "Other status" has been interpreted to include discrimination based on disability. Protection against discrimination has been interpreted broadly to include de jure and de facto discrimination and to sanction the use of affirmative action remedies to ensure compliance (Rosenthal & Sundram, 2002, p. 506).

There is an important difference in the enforcement mechanisms of the ICCPR and the ICESCR. The ICCPR mandates that each State Party "undertakes to respect and to ensure to all individuals within its territory and subject to its jurisdiction the rights recognized in the present Covenant" (Art. 2(1)). Furthermore, the ICCPR requires each State Party to make effective remedies

---

[8] See Simmons, 2009a, pp. 437–438, arguing that the International Bill of Rights "has the power to influence the direction of rights practices in fluid political situations, but . . . cannot magically transform autocracies into liberal guarantees of civil liberties."

[9] On nondiscrimination as a universal human right, see Fellmeth, 2009. On the application of this nondiscrimination principle to sexual orientation, see Fellmeth, 2008.

available for reporting violations and subsequent enforcement (Art. 2(3)(a)(b)(c)). This is sometimes referred to as imposing an "obligation of outcome" or "obligation of result" because states make a greater commitment to effectuate the rights protected in the ICCPR. The First Optional Protocol to the ICCPR establishes procedures for individuals to file complaints about rights violations with the Human Rights Committee.

By contrast, the ICESCR provides that each State Party "undertakes to take steps, individually and through international assistance and co-operation, especially economic and technical, to the maximum of its available resources, with a view to achieving progressively the full realization of the rights recognized in the present Covenant by all appropriate means, including particularly the adoption of legislative measures" (ICESCR Art. 2(1)). The "progressive realization" language implies an "obligation of conduct" rather than an "obligation of result" and allows greater latitude to States with respect to implementation.

2. THE INTERNATIONAL COVENANT ON CIVIL AND POLITICAL RIGHTS (ICCPR) The ICCPR safeguards individual rights against government interference beginning with a right to life that is protected from arbitrary deprivation (Art. 6). There are specific prohibitions against "torture" and "cruel, inhuman or degrading" treatment or punishment and nonconsensual "medical or scientific experimentation" (Art. 7). Right to liberty and security of the person are emphasized by a ban on slavery (Art. 8) and arbitrary detention (Art. 9). Procedural due process guarantees, particularly the rights of the accused upon arrest, are prescribed in depth (Art. 9; Art. 14; Art. 15).

Freedoms of thought, conscience, and religion (Art. 18) are ensured along with freedom of expression, broadly construed to encompass the right to information (Art. 19), freedom of assembly (Art. 21), and freedom of association (Art. 22), including the right to intimate association through marriage and the family (Art. 23). The right to universal and equal suffrage is specifically guaranteed (Art. 25). Finally, individuals are afforded equal protection of the law and protection from discrimination (Art. 26).

All of these provisions have particular import for people with mental disabilities whether or not they are confined in institutional settings. Derogation[10] of all but the most fundamental freedoms is permitted "in time of public emergency which threatens the life of the nation and the existence of which is officially proclaimed" (Art. 4(1)(2)). The ICCPR also establishes a Human Rights Committee to monitor compliance (Art. 28) through a mandatory reporting system involving member states. (Art. 40). The Human Rights Committee also issues General Comments that interpret ICCPR provisions to aid States in the reporting process (Compilation of General Comments and

[10] See infra this chapter, on the significance of derogation in this context.

General Recommendations adopted by Human Rights Treaty Bodies, UN Doc. HRI/GEN/1/rev. 5 (2001)).

3. FIRST OPTIONAL PROTOCOL TO THE ICCPR This separate document permits aggrieved private parties who have exhausted all available domestic remedies to file complaints with the Human Rights Committee that allege violations by States Parties to the Protocol. The Committee is charged with the responsibility of investigating and communicating with individual complainants and the involved States Parties.

4. INTERNATIONAL COVENANT ON ECONOMIC, SOCIAL, AND CULTURAL RIGHTS (ICESCR) The ICESCR sets forth a panoply of rights in detail beginning with the right to self-determination (Art. 1). Economic rights encompass the right to work (Art. 6), which includes appropriate working conditions (Art. 7); the right to form trade unions along with the right to labor stoppages (Art. 8); and the right to social security and social insurance (Art. 9). Social rights protect the family (Art. 10) and provide the right to an adequate standard of living (food, clothing, shelter) (Art. 11), the right to the highest attainable standard of physical and mental health (Art. 12), and the right to education (Art. 13 and Art. 14). Cultural rights acknowledge the right to participate in cultural life and to benefit from scientific progress (Art. 15). Although Article 12's so-called right to health may have the most direct connection, each of these guarantees has significance for people with mental disabilities.

In order to interpret ICESCR rights, the ECOSOC periodically issues General Comments. In 1996, the ECOSOC adopted General Comment 5 on the ICESCR to provide reference points for interpreting the rights of persons with disabilities (General Comment No. 5, U.N. Doc. E/1993/22, 11th Sess., para. 3 (1994) [hereinafter, General Comment 5]). A few years later, General Comment 14 was issued to provide further edification:

> The right to health contains both freedoms and entitlements. The freedoms include the rights to control one's own health and body, including sexual and reproductive freedom, and the right to be free from interference such as the right to be free from torture, non-consensual treatment and experimentation. By contrast, the entitlements include the right to a system of health protection, which provides equality of opportunity for people to enjoy the highest attainable level of health. (The Right to the Highest Attainable Standard of Health, CESCR General Comment 14, U.N. Committee on Economic, Social and Cultural Rights, 22nd Sess. Agenda Item 3, U.N. Doc. E/C 12/2000/4 (2000))

Although the ICESCR does not contain an Optional Protocol with complaint mechanisms analogous to the ICCPR, the Committee on Economic, Social and Cultural Rights under the auspices of ECOSOC has established mechanisms including the use of General Comments (such as the aforementioned General Comments 5 and 14) to provide interpretative guidelines that can be used to encourage State compliance. (See generally, Melish, 2009; Simmons, 2009b; see also, de Albuquerque, 2010, characterizing this optional protocol as "the missing piece of the International Bill of Rights".)

5. OTHER SPECIALIZED CONVENTIONS The ICCPR and the ICESCR were the starting points for creating legally binding human rights guarantees. Recognizing that certain traditionally disempowered groups might be more vulnerable to human rights abuses, treaties (referred to as "conventions") were initiated that focus on specific populations.[11] Examples include the 1965 International Convention on the Elimination of All Forms of Racial Discrimination (CERD), the 1979 Convention on the Elimination of All Forms of Discrimination Against Women (CEDAW), and the 1989 Convention on the Rights of the Child (CRC), sometimes referred to as the "Children's Convention."[12]

As will be discussed extensively below, see infra chapter 7, more recently, the publication of the United Nations Convention on the Rights of Persons with Disabilities (CRPD) marks the first time that such persons have been recognized by the UN as worthy of specific legislative protection. (Lawson, 2007).[13] There is no question that the ratification of this Convention—obligating all state parties to "adopt all appropriate legislative, administrative and other measures for the implementation of the rights recognised in the present Convention"—will, for the indefinite future, be the most important of all UN documents dealing with the issues discussed in this book.

II. Conceptual Dichotomies

A. Introduction

In this section, I will address a grouping of questions that must be considered for a full understanding of the role of international human rights law in this context. I will briefly look at (1) why states comply with international law; (2) the issue of universalism vs. cultural relativism;[14] (3) the differences between "hard law" and "soft law"; (4) the meaning of "peremptory norms" and the difference between derogable and nonderogable rights; (5) the differences between "negative" and "positive" rights; and (6) the differences

---

[11] On the intersectionality of international human rights treaties, see Satterthwaite, 2005.

[12] On the ways that the CRC has the capacity to alter traditional family relationships, see Dillard, 2009. On the ways that CEDAW "unequivocally bars" the perpetuation of gender stereotypes, see Stark, 2009, p. 345.

[13] Globally, on the way that international human rights treaties require states to recognize a diversity of identity groups, see Koenig, 2008.

[14] I consider this at far greater length infra chapter 9.

between the way we conceptualize civil and political rights on one hand, and economic, social, and cultural rights on the other.

1. WHY COMPLIANCE? One question that needs to be addressed is why most states generally comply with the international human rights law obligations most of the time (see Henkin, 1979, p. 235, for a clear articulation of this position).[15] According to Sonia Cardenas, the motivation may be utilitarian at base: "States may also be identifying with international norms to a greater degree than in the past because they have an interest in avoiding blame (and punishment) for illegitimate acts not because they are becoming privately committed to these norms" (2007, p. 133). Alternatively, Emilie Hafner-Burton and Kiyoteru Tsutsui conclude that the emergent global legitimacy of human rights "exerts independent global civil society effects that improve states' actual human rights practices" (2005, p. 1373).[16]

There is also a strong hortatory argument. Louis Henkin argues that international human rights law "seeks to *induce* the state to improve [national law and institutions] and make them more effective" (Henkin, 1984, p. 26; emphasis added). The acceptance of international human rights documents creates "a national responsibility to protect that rests with every government in the world" (Ramcharan, 2009, p. 362). Perhaps the roots of this acceptance are behavioral (see Woods, 2010), perhaps religious (see Butler, 2009), perhaps anthropological (see Merry, 2006). Perhaps this acceptance follows the activism of advocacy networks (see Risse & Ropp, 1999). No matter: the dominant theme is that international human rights law has the real capacity to influence domestic behavior, and that reality is one that must be kept in mind at all times.[17]

2. UNIVERSALISM VS. CULTURAL RELATIVISM The universality of human rights is the subject of ongoing debate. Despite global input into the process of applicable instruments, critics point out that the dominant discourse in human rights continues to reflect a Western, liberal, developed nation perspective. Others contend that respect for human dignity is a borderless and unbounded concept.

---

[15] According to Professors Goodman and Jinks, there are three motivators for compliance: coercion, persuasion, and acculturation (2004a). See also, Goodman & Jinks, 2003 (measuring the effects of human rights treaties). On the issue of acculturation, see Goodman & Jinks, 2004b.

[16] For subsequent research by the same authors, concluding that the expansion of the human rights movement's focus on normative aims has come with the expense of underfocusing on the mechanics of enforcement, see Hafner-Burton, Tsutsui & Meyer, 2008).

[17] On the relationship between international human rights law and international law in general, see Kamminga, 2009.

Much of the criticism of the idea that human rights are universal values, shared by all, has come from what is called the "Asian values" position.[18]

As I discuss extensively below (see infra chapter 9), I conclude that the universality of human rights must predominate. "Individuals everywhere want the same essential things: to have sufficient food and shelter; to be able to speak freely; to practice their own religion or to abstain from religious belief; to feel that their person is not threatened by the state; to know that they will not be tortured; or detained without charge, and that if charged, they will have a fair trial" (Higgins, 1994, p. 96). To deny persons with mental disabilities these basic human rights on the basis of "Asian values" is an attempt to hide behind the mask of cultural relativism. "Cultural relativism is not sufficient justification for the denial of the universal application of human rights standards." (Hui, 2002, p. 199; see also, Paul, 2000, p. 13 n. 51, citing Davis, 1998, criticizing cultural relativism as deterministic and tautological; and Tay, 1996, examining the problematic character of the cultural argument in the context of Asian human rights). As Arati Rao (1995, p. 174)[19] has stated, "the notion of culture favoured by international actors must be unmasked for what it is: a falsely rigid, ahistorical, selectively chosen set of self-justificatory texts and practices whose patent partiality raises the question of exactly whose interests are being served and who comes out on top."

The resolution of this debate has grown rapidly in the context of mental disability law reform, especially in the years following the ratification of the CRPD. Virtually all of the topics to be considered in the remainder of this work need to be considered through this filter.

3. HARD VS. SOFT LAW The UN Charter and the Covenants are multilateral treaties that impose certain obligations on the part of member states.[20] By contrast, at the time of its conception, the UDHR was a resolution intended only to establish "a common standard of achievement for all peoples and all nations . . . without binding legal effect" (Perlin et al., 2006, p. 237). The UN Charter and the Covenants are sometimes considered *hard law*, while the UDHR was initially characterized as *soft law* (see generally, Fennell, 2008).

Christine Chinkin includes as soft law those norms that: (1) have been articulated in nonbinding form; (2) contain vague and imprecise terms; (3) emanate from bodies lacking international lawmaking authority; (4) are directed at nonstate actors whose practice cannot constitute customary

---

[18] On the special case of Russia (a nation partially in Europe and partially in Asia), see Wilson, 2008 (concluding that Russia is culturally averse to the rule of law).

On the schism between universalists and "cultural relativists," see Robbins, 2005.

[19] See also, from an anthropological perspective, Preis, 1995, rejecting cultural relativism; on deploying cross-cultural perspectives in this inquiry, see Lee, 2008.

[20] See generally, Kalb, 2010.

international law; (5) lack any corresponding theory of responsibility; or (6) are based solely on voluntary adherence (Chinkin, 2000, p. 230; see also Di Robilant, 2006; on the role of soft law in the international legal system in general, see Barelli, 2009).

According to Jose Alvarez (2003), "[Soft law] may guide the interpretation, elaboration, or application of hard law; constitute norms that aspire to harden; serve as evidence of hard law; exist in parallel with hard law obligations and act as a fall-back; or serve as a source of relatively hard obligations through acquiescence or estoppel" (p. 420; on the "hardening" of soft law, see also, e.g., Janis, 2008, p. 55).

Under the *Restatement (Third) of the Foreign Relations Law of the United States* (sec. 701), a State is obligated to respect the human rights of persons subject to its jurisdiction that are established "as a matter of customary international law" (sec. 702). Thus, soft law, as it hardens into "hard law," becomes part of the customary law that states are obliged to follow and enforce (see Tay, 1999, p. 263).[21]

The "hardening" of soft law in a mental disability law context is illustrated by the case of *Victor Rosario Congo v. Ecuador* (1999) in the context of the UN's Mental Illness Principles. As will be discussed extensively below, in 1991, the United Nations General Assembly adopted the United Nations Principles for the Protection of Persons with Mental Illness and for the Improvement of Mental Health Care, a detailed international statement of the rights of persons with mental illness (G.A. Res. 119, U.N. GAOR, 46th Sess., 3d Comm., 75th plen. mtg., reprinted in [1991] 45 U.N.Y.B. 620, U.N. Sales No. E.92.I.1 [MI Principles]).[22] Several years later, in the *Congo* case, the Inter-American Court on Human Rights, in its first decision regarding mental disability rights, held that these Principles functioned as an authoritative guide to the interpretation of the American Convention in the absence of a specialized convention on the rights of people with mental disabilities (Benko & Benowitz, 2001; Perlin, 2007). This decision effectively "hardened" the soft law of the MI Principles (see generally, Bederman, 2001; Kelly, 2004).[23]

---

[21] On the ways that soft law can "increase the value of legal rules over time," see Meyer, 2009, p. 916. On how the soft law of international tribunals has become an international common law, see Guzman & Meyer, 2009; compare Kelly, 2000 (characterizing customary international law as being in its "twilight").

[22] On mental health as a human right in general, see Gable & Gostin, 2009.

[23] On the significance of soft law in the development of international human rights, see Courtis, 2002–2003, pp. 113–114. On "hardening" of soft law by judicial decisionmaking in general, see Collins, 2003. See also, Johnstone, 2008, p. 88:

> This evolution proceeds as follows: operational activities occur against the backdrop of widely acknowledged but not well-specified norms; in carrying out those activities, international organizations do not seek to enforce the norms per se but typically act in a manner that conforms to them; these activities

4. PEREMPTORY NORMS, AND DEROGABLE VS. NONDEROGABLE RIGHTS Rights that cannot be altered are nonderogable; those subject to change under certain circumstances are considered derogable rights. Peremptory norms are those accepted and recognized by the international community from which no derogation is allowed. These norms are also referred to as *jus cogens* and include, for example, the prohibitions against slavery, piracy, genocide, torture, and racial discrimination. Under the provisions of some major treaties, derogation involving other rights may be permissible if certain specific conditions are met, such as in an emergency situation where good faith departure from compliance with human right standards is strictly necessary and otherwise lawful (Perlin et al., 2006, p. 239).[24] According to Sara Stapleton:

> The permissibility of derogation from provisions in human rights treaties in general is debatable; one view is that no derogation, reservation or limitation is appropriate since human rights treaties have the character of jus cogens. Jus cogens norms are those that are not subject to limitation, denial, or suspension under any circumstances, including those of public emergency. The view that all human rights norms are jus cogens is weakened by the acceptance of derogation clauses in major human rights treaties. The more prevalent view is that derogations are only acceptable if they are necessary, proportional, and subject to international scrutiny and review, as well as in accordance with the derogation clause of the treaty under consideration. Because human rights treaties attempt to create a balance between the rights of the individual and the rights of a state, it is necessary "for improved human rights to be matched by accommodations in favour of the reasonable needs of the State to perform its public duties for the common good." (Stapleton, 1999, pp. 581–582, citing Higgins, 1976–1977, pp. 281–283; Fitzpatrick, 1994, pp. 38–41)[25]

---

generate friction, triggering bouts of legal argumentation; the reaction of affected governments—and the discourse that surrounds the action and reaction—can cause the law to harden.

[24] Relevant here is the "margin of appreciation" doctrine, holding that states should be allowed some latitude in the application and interpretation of their human rights obligations. See Allo, 2009; Shany, 2006; Yourow, 1987; see also, Ghai, 2009, p. 149 ("there must be an acceptance of qualifications on rights"). The doctrine is criticized as conceptually inadequate in Singh, 1999. See also, Neumayer, 2010 (derogation more likely in authoritarian states).

[25] Note that the African Charter on Human and Peoples' Rights is the only general international human rights treaty that contains no derogation provisions. See Neumayer, 2010.

5. NEGATIVE VS. POSITIVE RIGHTS In some instances, observance of human rights law demands that governments refrain from engaging in certain types of conduct such as the arbitrary confinement of individuals. In other cases, the government may be required to take steps to affirmatively protect individual rights such as the right to be treated humanely during confinement (Perlin et al., 2006, p. 240). Explains Stephen Marks:

> Negative rights are somewhat akin to negative liberty in the sense that their enjoyment requires inaction on the part of others, whereas positive rights require action on the part of the duty holder. Thus civil and political rights, such as freedom of speech, the right to vote, or the right to physical integrity, require abstention on the part of the state from banning speech, restricting voting rights, or abusing the person of a citizen. Poverty, ignorance, illness, inability to bargain for the price of one's labor under conditions of exploitation, social inequalities, stigma, discrimination and similar factors are as constraining on an individual's liberty to be or act as he or she wishes as banning a publication or speech or assaulting or arbitrarily detaining a person. The realization of human rights requires positive action to lift such constraints, such as providing education, protecting from discrimination, or regulating the labor market. In this sense, economic, social and cultural rights are instrumental to negative freedom. (2009, p. 222)[26]

In the context of mental disability law, this divide is best seen in the distinction between the positive right of the right to treatment (and other mental health services while an individual is institutionalized) and the negative right of the right to refuse treatment (Perlin, 2008, p. 263). The general theory is that the right to refuse is a "corollary" to the right to treatment (see e.g., Cantor, 2005, p. 127 ["necessary corollary']; Wilansky, 2006, p. 832 ["logical corollary"]). Certainly, over the years, there has been a significant conflict between patients' rights lawyers (seeking to equally enforce both), the psychiatric survivor movement (that focuses its attention primarily on the right to refuse antipsychotic medications), and the psychiatric establishment (which has frequently vocally opposed the existence of the latter right; see Kahn, 1984; Stefan, 2003, p. 1351).

6. CIVIL AND POLITICAL RIGHTS VS. ECONOMIC, SOCIAL, AND CULTURAL RIGHTS The discussion whether there is or should be a hierarchy of rights is a source of tension between Western developed states with their strong commitment to individual civil rights and civil liberties and developing nations in other areas of the

---

[26] On how this distinction "tends to oversimplify the process of realizing rights in practice," see Marks, 2009, p. 221.

world that emphasize group rights. The UDHR includes provisions that acknowledge the full panoply of rights: political and civil, and economic, social, and cultural, including rights that affect larger numbers of people such as the right to self-determination (Perlin et al., 2006, p. 241).

It is common for human rights to be divided into three generations of rights. The first generation are civil and political rights, second-generation rights refer to social and economic rights, and third-generation rights are commonly understood to connote miscellaneous collective rights, such as minority rights, environmental rights, or other group rights (Beck, 2008). Javier Rehman notes that first-generation rights have often been given priority over second-generation rights on the theory that they could be implemented immediately, whereas economic, social, and cultural rights can be introduced only "progressively," and that the application of civil and political rights is less costly (as the State is required to abstain from certain activities, e.g., not to engage in torture) (2003, pp. 6–7; on "progressive realization" generally, see Gathii, 2009). As will be discussed below, Article 4.2 of the Convention on the Rights of Persons with Disabilities sets out the principle of progressive realization for the economic, social, and cultural rights dealt with in the instrument, "without prejudice to the need to implement the civil and political rights immediately" (Lawson, 2007, p. 592).[27]

III. Conclusion

This overview should set the stage for the consideration of the mental disability law–specific questions that follow. The CRPD must be seen in the context of prior UN Conventions, Covenants, and Declarations, and the application of rights to persons with disabilities must be seen in the context of the application of rights to other often-disenfranchised minorities. In the coming years, as more and more nations ratify the CRPD, it is realistic to expect that the apparent dichotomies of negative vs. positive rights and civil/political rights vs. economic/social/cultural rights will continue to grow in importance in this specific context.

Chapter 2B. Sanism and Pretextuality

I. Introduction

There has always been great ambivalence on the part of the human rights community in its perception of the rights of persons with mental disabilities,

[27] On ways that a national Disability Rights Commission can better be seen as a movement toward the realization of social rights (rather than simply civil rights), see Fletcher & O'Brien, 2006 (UK).

and the *value* of those rights. I believe that the explanation for the roots of this ambivalence can be found in what I call "sanism" and what I call "pretextuality." It is critical, I believe, for those seriously interested in this topic to understand these concepts and how their malignancy has distorted all aspects of mental disability law, domestic and international.

"Sanism" is an irrational prejudice of the same quality and character of other irrational prejudices that cause (and are reflected in) prevailing social attitudes of racism, sexism, homophobia, and ethnic bigotry. It permeates all aspects of mental disability law and affects all participants in the mental disability law system: litigants, fact finders, counsel, and expert and lay witnesses. Its corrosive effects have warped mental disability law jurisprudence in involuntary civil commitment law, institutional law, tort law, and all aspects of the criminal process (Perlin, 2000, pp. 21–58; Perlin, 2003b, p. 684; 1992; 1999).[28] It reflects what civil rights lawyer Florynce Kennedy has characterized as the "pathology of oppression" (Perlin, 2008a, p. 601, quoting Birnbaum, 1974, p. 197 (quoting Kennedy).[29] It is the reason for most of the difficulties faced by formerly institutionalized persons when they seek reintegration into society (Arboleda-Florez & Weisstub, 2008).

These attitudes are by no means limited to the United States (see, e.g., Boyadjiev & Onchev, 2007 [Bulgaria]; Heyer, 2000; Reilly, 1995; Gostin, 1987 [Japan]; Lawson, 2008 [Australia]; see also, Lindblom, 2006, p. 13, quoting Dan A. Taylor, secretary of MindFreedom, Ghana ["Most Ghanians tend to believe that anyone who has a mental illness has offended the deities or is suffering punishment for some wrongful act committed by their ancestors"]; see generally, Neaman, 1975 [discussing stereotype of persons with mental illness as being evil]; Tsang et al., 2007, p. 725 [in rural areas of China, mental illness is usually regarded as "punishment from the supernatural or spiritual world."].

"Pretextuality" defines the ways in which courts accept (either implicitly or explicitly) testimonial dishonesty and engage similarly in dishonest (and

---

28 On the related concept of "disablism," see Diniz, Barbosa & dos Santos, 2010.

29 There is a robust literature on stigma and mental illness, both in the West, see Hayward & Bright, 1997; Crisp et al., 2000; Verhaeghe, Bracke & Bruynooghe, 2008; WHO Report, 2005; and elsewhere, see Fung et al., 2007 (China); Tsang et al., 2007; Yip, 2005 (Hong Kong); Ay, Save & Fidanoglu, 2006 (Turkey); Chanpattana, 2010 (Asia); Lindblom, 2006 (Ghana). On public attitudes toward mental health facilities, see Pearson & Yiu, 1993 (Hong Kong). On stigma in the family context, see Pearson & Tsang, 2004 (Hong Kong); Phillips & Xiong, 1995 (China); Phillips et al., 2002 (China); Takizawa, 1993 (Japan). In the caregiver context, see Kung, 2003 (Chinese Americans). On the views of patients on their right to participate in decision making, see Tuohimaki et al., 2001 (Finland); Gibbs et al., 2005 (New Zealand); Canvin, Bartlett & Pinfold, 2002 (UK). On how "biological ideology" may increase stigma, see Read, 2007 (Australia). On the relationship between socioeconomic diagnosis and incidence of serious mental illness, see de Girolamo, 1996.

frequently meretricious) decision making. It is especially poisonous where witnesses, especially expert witnesses, show a "high propensity to purposely distort their testimony in order to achieve desired ends" (Perlin, 1991, p. 135). This pretextuality infects all participants in the judicial system, breeds cynicism and disrespect for the law, demeans participants, and reinforces shoddy lawyering, blasé judging, and, at times, perjurious and/or corrupt testifying (Perlin, 1999a, p. 5).

In previous works, I have explored the relationships between sanism and pretextuality in matters involving, inter alia, competency to stand trial (Perlin, 1993; Perlin, 2004), sexual autonomy (Perlin, 1993–1994a), the right to refuse treatment (Perlin & Dorfman, 1996; Perlin, 2005), "autonomous decisionmaking" (Perlin, 1997a), the Americans with Disabilities Act (Perlin, 1993–1994b), competency to plead guilty or waive counsel (Perlin, 1996), jury decision making in death penalty cases (Perlin, 1994), and the bar's attitude toward counsel with mental disabilities (Perlin, 2008a). But, these factors can be even *more* pernicious as they relate to the job that lawyers do when they represent persons with mental disabilities in court proceedings. Elsewhere, I have alleged:

> Sanism permeates the legal representation process both in cases in which mental capacity is a central issue, and those in which such capacity is a collateral question. Sanist lawyers (1) distrust their mentally disabled clients, (2) trivialize their complaints, (3) fail to forge authentic attorney-client relationships with such clients and reject their clients' potential contributions to case-strategizing, and (4) take less seriously case outcomes that are adverse to their clients. (Perlin, 2003b, p. 695)

II. Sanism, Pretextuality, and International Human Rights[30]

There is now some nascent literature on the relationship between sanism, pretextuality, and international human rights law (see Perlin, 2002, 2006, 2007, 2008b, 2009a; Perlin et al., 2006; Fischer, 2005; Katner, 2006), especially focusing on circumstances in nations with developing economies (see Perlin, 2008b). For example, an analysis of the European Commission on Human Rights concluded that it has interpreted the European Convention on Human Rights "very restrictively in psychiatric cases" (Hewitt, 2001, p. 1278).[31] The cases included in this analysis, which characterize the handcuffing of patients as "therapeutically necessary" (id., discussing *Herczegfalvy v. Austria*, 1993), or sanction the use of seclusion for "disciplinary" purposes (id., discussing

[30] See generally, Perlin & Szeli, 2010.

[31] On the ways that the European Commission is, for these purposes, similar to the Inter-American Commission on Human Rights, see, e.g., Powers, 2002; Mugwanya, 1999.

Dhoest v. Belgium, 1987), certainly bespeak pretextuality.[32] It is essential that such pretextuality be identified and answered.

This is especially timely in light of the ratification of the new UN Convention (see Perlin, 2008c, discussing the UN Convention in this precise context). The Convention's focus on questions of empowerment (see Kayess & French, 2008, p. 17) forces us to consider whether the legal system will continue to perpetuate the sort of sanism and pretextuality that has had such a negative impact on the lives of persons with mental disabilities, and will continue to condone teleological judicial behavior through overreliance on cognitive-simplifying heuristics (see, e.g., Perlin, 1997b, p. 1417, discussing the dominance and the power of the *vividness heuristic*, a cognitive-simplifying device through which a "single vivid, memorable case overwhelms mountains of abstract, colorless data upon which rational choices should be made"; see also, Perlin, 1993, pp. 684–685, defining *teleological* in this context as outcome-determinative reasoning; social science data that enable judges to satisfy predetermined positions are privileged, while data that would require judges to question such ends are rejected or subordinated).[33]

Although there is a robust "psychiatric survivor" movement both in the United States and elsewhere (see, e.g., Margulies, 1992; Honig & Fendell, 2000; "Taking Issue," 1997; see supra chapter 1), this voice is typically ignored. For at least 25 years, formerly hospitalized individuals and their supporters have formed an important role in the reform of the mental health system and in test case litigation. "Yet, there is little evidence that these groups are taken seriously either by lawyers or academics" (Perlin, 2003b, pp. 699–700).

Also, as discussed earlier (see supra chapter 1), in the civil commitment context, any sanism-inspired blunders by lawyers can easily be fatal to the client's chance of success.[34] If a lawyer rejects the notion that his client may be competent (indeed, if s/he engages in the not-atypical "presumption of incompetency" that is all too often de rigueur in these cases, see Perlin, 2003a,

---

[32] It should be underscored. There have been *many* decisions about *many* aspects of substantive and procedural civil commitment law in the ECHR and other bodies. These decisions, however, by themselves, have *not* created a robust corpus of international human rights law.

[33] See, e.g., Asplund, 2009, p. 30 ("I [have] heard stunned legal consultants telling of judges that seemed to be making decisions based on their intuitive reading of a case. . . after which their clerks might fill in references to (more or less) relevant laws").

[34] As will be discussed extensively infra chapter 5 and chapter 8, one of the core factors of comparative mental disability law is the abject lack of counsel made available to persons facing involuntary civil commitment:

> Neither counsel nor judicial review is present in most of the world's mental disability law systems. It is rare for even minimal access to counsel to be statutorily (or judicially) mandated, and, even where counsel is legislatively ordered, it is rarely provided. Moreover, the lack of meaningful judicial review makes the commitment hearing system little more than a meretricious pretext.

Perlin, 2007, p. 342. See also generally, Perlin, 2008b; infra chapter 8.

p. 193,[35] the chances are far slimmer that s/he will advocate for such a client in the way that lawyers have been taught—or, at the least, *should* be taught—to advocate for their clients. In nations with no traditions of an "expanded due process model" (see Perlin, 1997a, p. 971), in cases involving persons subject to commitment to psychiatric institutions or those already institutionalized, sanism in lawyers can be fatal to an individual's chance for release or for a judicial order mandating amelioration of conditions of confinement and/or access to treatment and/or to be free from unwanted treatment interventions. These issues are even *more* accentuated in nations where the cultural tradition attaches "shame or dishonor" to mental illness (Gostin, 1987, p. 366).

In later chapters, I discuss the use of state-sanctioned psychiatry as a tool of suppressing political dissent (see infra chapter 4), the universal factors that permeate the practice of all mental disability law (but especially *institutional* mental disability law) in all regions of the world (see infra chapter 5), and the inadequate counsel often made available to persons with mental disabilities (see infra chapter 8) In each of these chapters, I conclude that each of these factors "is tainted by the pervasive corruption of sanism that permeates all of mental disability law, and each reflects a blinding pretextuality that contaminates legal practice in this area" (Perlin, 2009a, p. 487). Subsequently, in my discussion of therapeutic jurisprudence, I argue that that method of interpretation "has the far-reaching potential to allow us to—finally—come to grips with the pernicious power of sanism and pretextuality and to offer us an opportunity to make coherent what has been incoherent—and to expose what has been hidden—for far too long" (Perlin, 2008a, p. 607 n. 103; see infra chapter 10). As I have previously noted, in her analysis of why the United States should ratify the new UN Convention, Tara Melish focused on the "deeply entrenched attitudes and stereotypes about disability that have rendered many of the most flagrant abuses of the rights of persons with disabilities 'invisible' from the mainstream human rights lens" (Melish, 2007, p. 44; see supra chapter 1, at p. 6). I will argue below, these stereotypes are the essence of sanism; vigorous, advocacy-focused counsel is needed to answer and rebut them (see also, Perlin, 2008c).

Chapter 2C. Dignity

I. Introduction[36]

Human rights are necessary for all individuals—human rights violations occur when persons are treated as objects or as a means to others' ends (Ward

---

[35] See id.: "In short, the presumption in which courts have regularly engaged—that there is both a de facto and de jure presumption of incompetency to be applied to medication decision making—appears to be based on an empirical fallacy: psychiatric patients are not necessarily more incompetent than nonmentally ill persons to engage in independent medication decision making." (footnote omitted).

[36] See generally, Perlin & McClain, 2009.

& Birgden, 2007). All citizens—including those who are institutionalized—have enforceable human rights (Birgden & Perlin, 2008; Birgden & Perlin, 2009; Perlin & Dlugacz, 2009). As noted above, the Vienna Declaration and Programme of Action (1993) and the Universal Declaration of Human Rights (1948) recognized that inherent dignity and inalienable rights of all individuals are the foundation of freedom, justice, and peace.[37] Through global covenants, individual rights of offenders are safeguarded against cruel, inhuman, or degrading treatment or punishment (International Covenant on Civil and Political Rights [ICCPR], Art. 7, 1966a); prisoners should be treated with humanity and dignity, and provided with reformation and social rehabilitation (ICCPR, Art. 10, 1966a); individuals are guaranteed the right to the highest attainable standard of physical and mental health (International Covenant on Economic, Social and Cultural Rights, Art. 12, 1966b); individuals are guaranteed respect for human rights and fundamental freedoms in forensic and correctional systems (Vienna Declaration on Crime and Justice, 2001); and prisoners should be treated in a humane manner and with dignity (United Nations Body of Principles for the Protection of All Persons under Any Form of Detention or Imprisonment, 1988; See generally, Birgden & Perlin, 2009; Perlin & Dlugacz, 2009; Ward & Birgden, 2009; see infra chapters 6 and 10).[38]

When the United Nations embarked on the drafting process of the Convention on the Rights of Persons with Disabilities, it established an ad hoc committee "to consider proposals for a comprehensive and integral international convention to promote and protect the rights and dignity of persons with disabilities" (GA Resolution, 2001). This was consonant with the perspectives of observers such as Professor Aaron Dhir: "Degrading living conditions, coerced 'treatment,' scientific experimentation, seclusion, restraints—the list of violations to the dignity and autonomy of those diagnosed with mental disabilities is both long and egregious" (2005, p. 182; for a comparative consideration of the use of seclusion and restrain, see Sailas & Wahlbeck, 2005).

As ratified, the Convention calls for "respect for inherent dignity" (Art. 3(a)).[39] The Preamble characterizes "discrimination against any person on the basis of disability [as] a violation of the inherent dignity and worth of the human person" (para. h.). And these provisions are consistent with the

---

37 See, for helpful historical background, Dicke, 2002.

38 See McCrudden, 2008, p. 670 (international human rights documents "adopted dignity as foundational. . . to human rights in general"). On the content of human dignity as a legal concept, see Mahlmann, 2010. On human dignity as a constitutional value, see Chakalson, 2002. On the role of dignity in the trial process in general, see Perlin, 1996, and see id., p. 74, n. 112, discussing US caselaw (see e.g., *Marquez v. Collins* (1984)) and scholarship (see e.g., Tyler, 1992; Nicholson, 1995) on its significance and constitutional underpinnings.

39 On the role of Art. 3 of the European Convention on Human Rights in the protection of dignity, see Lawson, 2006.

entire Convention's "rights-based approach focusing on individual dignity" (Dhir, 2005, p. 195), placing the responsibility on the State "to tackle socially created obstacles in order to ensure full respect for the dignity and equal rights of all persons" (Quinn & Degener, 2002, p. 14). Professor Michael Stein puts it well: A "dignitary perspective compels societies to acknowledge that persons with disabilities are valuable because of their inherent human worth" (Stein, 2007, p. 106). In Professor Cees Maris's summary: "The Convention's object is to ensure disabled persons enjoy all human rights with dignity" (2010, p. 1156).[40]

In his testimony in support of the UN Convention, Eric Rosenthal, the director of Mental Disability Rights International, shared with Congress his observations of the treatment of institutionalized persons with mental disabilities in central and eastern European nations: "[w]hen governments deny their citizens basic human dignity and autonomy, when they subject them to extremes of suffering, when they segregate them from society—we call these violations of fundamental human rights" (Chaffin, 2005, p. 140, quoting Rosenthal).

One way of best assuring such dignity is the provision of dedicated and effective counsel[41] (see infra chapter 8). A U.S. state case from Montana made this point most effectively nearly a decade ago: "'Quality counsel provides the most likely way—perhaps the only likely way' to ensure the due process protection of dignity and privacy interests in cases such as the one at bar [an involuntary civil commitment]" (*In re Mental Health of K.G.F.*, 2001, pp. 493–494; see Perlin, 2008, pp. 246–249, discussing *K.G.F.* in this context, and see generally, Perlin, 1992; Schwartz et al., 1983). Professor Tom Tyler's research in procedural justice has demonstrated, beyond doubt, that individuals subject to involuntary civil commitment hearings, like all other citizens, are affected by such process values as participation, dignity, and trust, and that experiencing arbitrariness in procedure leads to "social malaise and decreases people's willingness to be integrated into the polity, accepting its authorities and following its rules" (1992, p. 443).[42]

---

[40] Compare Donnelly, 2008 (arguing that the right to autonomy must be contextualized with the right to dignity). On the relationship between dignity and international human rights in a mental disability law context, see Gostin, 2004.

[41] On how a lack of lawyers available to litigants in social justice cases can lead to a lack of dignity in the judicial process, see Viljoen, 2004, p. 20, discussing (in the context of the African Court on Human Rights) how a lack of lawyers can make reliance on the law "fanciful."

[42] On the need for advocacy *beyond* legal advocacy, see Banks, 1999; Funk et al., 2005; Beaupert, 2009. On the relationship between this insight and therapeutic jurisprudence values, see infra chapter 10. On how judicial decisions in international human rights cases have the unique capacity to promote dignity, see Monsalve & Roman, 2010.

Dignity issues self-evidently affect institutionalization issues as well.[43] An intermediate appellate court U.S. case—in holding that a state welfare department regulation requiring certain patients to receive services in the segregated setting of a nursing home, rather than in their own homes, violated the Americans with Disabilities Act (ADA)—has read the ADA to intend to ensure that "qualified individuals receive services in a manner consistent with basic human dignity rather than a manner which shunts them aside, hides, and ignores them" (*Helen L. v. DiDario*, 1995, p. 334).[44] Courts in Canada have similarly stressed the role of dignitarian values in cases involving the autonomy of persons with mental disabilities: "Mentally ill persons are not to be stigmatized because of the nature of their illness or disability; nor should they be treated as persons of lesser status or dignity. Their right to personal autonomy and self-determination is no less significant, and is entitled to no less protection" (*Fleming v. Reid*, 1991, pp. 86–87, as discussed in Dhir, 2008, p. 109).[45]

In his exhaustive evaluation of dignity in the specific context of international human rights law, Professor Christopher McCrudden reviews cases from the International Court of Justice, the European Court of Human Rights, the European Court of Justice, and the constitutional courts of many nations, and finds multiple categories of cases in which "dignity" is relied on as a basis for a court's judgment:

- Cases involving prohibition of inhuman treatment, humiliation, or degradation by one person over another;[46]
- Cases involving individual choice and the conditions for self-fulfillment, autonomy, and self-realization;
- Cases involving protection of group identity and culture; and
- Cases involving the creation of necessary conditions for individuals to have essential needs satisfied. (McCrudden, 2008, pp. 686–694).

Having said this, McCrudden's reading of the case law has led him to the conclusion that "the use of the concept of human dignity has not given rise to a detailed universal interpretation" (id., p. 724). Notwithstanding this insight, however, he finds that the concept of dignity can provide "a language in which judges can appear to justify how they deal with issues such as the weight of

[43] For a recent discussion of the role of dignity in the criminal trial process in cases involving criminal defendants with mental disabilities, see *Indiana v. Edwards*, 2008.
[44] On how hearings in right to refuse treatment cases can enhance dignity values, see Perlin & Dorfman, 1996. On the ADA and dignity in general, see Perlin, 2001–2002, pp. 243–244; Law, 1991.
[45] On the relationship between dignity, human rights, and issues of accessibility for persons with physical disabilities, see Connelly, 2009.
[46] On the connection between dignity and humiliation, see Statman, 2002. The relationship between dignity and humiliation has developed into an important field of study. See http://humiliationstudies.org/index.php.

rights, the domestication and contextualization of rights, and the generation of new or more extensive rights" (id.).[47]

Conclusion

The test of whether the CRPD will have authentic meaning or will be little more than a "paper victory" (see Perlin, 2009, p. 490) will be whether, as a result of the ratification of the Convention, persons with mental disabilities—especially *institutionalized* persons with mental disabilities—are, in fact, treated with that level of dignity that they are owed as a key component of international human rights law. As of the writing of this volume, it is far too early to come to any conclusions on this point, but the question is the one that will be before us for the indefinite future.

[47] On how expanded work opportunities that may flow from enforcement of Art. 27 of the CRPD—recognizing "the right of persons with disabilities to work, on an equal opportunity with others"—can provide individuals with disabilities "a meaningful life of independence and human dignity," see Zhang, 2007, p. 518.

3

Mental Disability Law in a Comparative Law Context

I. Introduction

Professors Larry Gostin and Lance Gable have stressed the point that human rights law was important in the context of mental disability law for two fundamental reasons: first, because human rights was the only source of law "that legitimatizes international scrutiny of mental health policies and practices within a sovereign country" (2004, p. 21) and, second, that human rights "do not rely on government beneficence. . . . Human rights law provides fundamental protections without qualification or exception" (id., p. 22; see also, Sharma, 2003). Mental health policies can violate human rights and can adversely affect mental health (Gostin & Gable, 2004, p. 28). International human rights and mental health are "inextricably linked"; human rights are "indispensable" for mental health "because they provide security from harm and restraint" (id., p. 29).

This analysis leads to a logical follow-up question: to what extent *does* the body of what we categorize as "international human rights" actually offer protection to persons with mental disabilities?[1] Do the UN Conventions, treaties,

[1] An open question is whether such rights are better protected in common law than in civil law nations. Although common wisdom suggests that common law nations—with a more expansive tradition of judicial review and a more vigorous adversary system (see Perlin, Birgden & Gledhill, 2009)—would create a milieu of better human rights protection than is available in civil law nations, recent research by political scientists calls this into question. See Keith & Ogundele, 2007, p. 1065 ("We find no solid

and other documents sufficiently articulate both the positive and negative rights needed to empower such persons?[2] Will states enforce judgments entered by regional courts?[3] Do the regional courts and commissions take seriously the issues that arise in litigated and contested cases?[4] Do sovereign states take seriously their obligations to enforce the human rights of this all-too-frequently marginalized and hidden population?[5]

In this chapter, I will approach this issue from these perspectives. First, I will briefly consider the state of the law in the United States, the single nation with the most developed structure of constitutionally based mental disability law (see 1-4 Perlin, 1998–2002). Then, I will discuss the state of the law in Europe, the continent that has the most comprehensively developed international human rights scheme. Then, I will look at the case law from the regional courts and commissions in other areas of the world that have such bodies in an effort to determine the extent to which judicial tribunals take seriously the claims of persons with disabilities in individual cases.[6]

---

evidence . . . that common law system countries have better human rights behavior than civil code system countries."). On a comparison between civil commitment practices in two common law nations (the United States and the UK), see Fennell & Goldstein, 2006; for a comparison between practices in multiple British Commonwealth jurisdictions, see Fistein et al., 2009; for a comparison between one state in the United States (California) and New Zealand (in the context of sex offender commitments), see Vess, 2005.

On how the differences between civil and common law systems may "play out" in the context of a regional tribunal or commission comprised of nations with both types of systems, see infra chapter 9.

[2] See, e.g., Gostin & Gable, 2004, p. 118 ("The enforcement of existing human rights instruments in the United Nations System has not measured up well to its regional counterparts"). On the role of the UN Human Rights Council, see Abudu et al., 2008.

[3] On their absolute obligation to do so, see Hunt, 2005.

[4] See Gostin & Gable, 2004, p. 117 ("The collective jurisprudence of the regional systems has established significant protections for persons with mental disabilities"). For an earlier global appraisal, see Weston, Lukes & Hnatt, 1987. On the value of "global governance institutions," see Buchanan & Keohane, 2006.

[5] On the significance of marginalization in this context, see Lord, 2004. On the question of the impact of national human rights institutions on the development of human rights in individual nations, see, e.g., deBeco, 2007; Reif, 2000; Dickson, 2003; Carver, 2010; Lynch, 2006; Kumar, 2006; Liddicoat, 2009; Osaka, 1997. See infra chapter 9.

[6] Beyond the scope of this book is the question of whether matters relating to commitment and release from psychiatric institutions should be heard in courts of general jurisdictions or in special mental health courts. For a sample of the extensive literature on the latter sort of tribunal, see, e.g., Goldkamp & Irons-Guynn, 2000; Lurigio et al., 2001; Winick, 2003; Poythress et al., 2002; Petrila et al., 2001 (all United States); Carney, 2003; Tait, 2003; Delaney, 2003; Williams, 2006; Carney & Beaupert, 2008; Carney, Tait & Beaupert, 2008; Carney, Beaupert, Perry & Tait, 2008; Beaupert, 2009 (all Australia); O'Brien et al., 1995; Diesfeld & McKenna, 2006; Diesfeld &

II. The United States

There is a remarkable overlap between the body of decisions that define U.S. constitutional mental disability law and the body of international human rights standards that mandate humane treatment of persons with mental disabilities (Perlin, 2007, p. 447).

The past forty years have witnessed a revolution in American mental disability law (id., p. 435). This revolution is one that largely constitutionalized virtually every aspect of the involuntary civil commitment and release process (see Perlin & Dorfman, 1996), as well as most "pressure points" in the course of institutionalization (the right to treatment, the right to refuse treatment, the right to the least restrictive alternative course of treatment). It saw the first broad-based, federal civil rights statutes enacted on behalf of persons with mental disabilities.[7] It witnessed the creation of a "patients' bar" to provide

---

McKenna, 2007 (all New Zealand); Ferencz & McGuire, 2000; Perkins, 2003; Sarkar & Adshead, 2005 (all United Kingdom). But see Rees, 2003, p. 40 (evaluating the Australian system from an international human rights law perspective, recommending "timely, external review" of Tribunal decisions.) I consider the relationship between mental health courts and the CRPD in Perlin, 2009. For a relevant analysis of psychiatric review boards, see Bauer et al., 2005 (Israel).

Also beyond the scope of this book is an inquiry into the different modes of commitment. See, e.g., Perlin, 2003 (discussing outpatient commitment in the United States); Dawson, 2008 (discussing same in Australia); Szmukler, Daw & Dawson, 2010 (same). On forensic commitment, see Gledhill, 2010 (Australia).

[7] See, e.g., *Olmstead v. L.C.* (1999) (under Title II of ADA nations are required to provide willing persons with mental disabilities community-based treatment when resources are available); *Kansas v. Hendricks* (1997) (statute is constitutional even though additional confinement follows prison time); *Godinez v. Moran* (1993) (defendant who waives right to counsel need not be more competent than a defendant who does not); *Heller v. Doe* (1993) (statute requiring different standards of proof for committal of persons with mental illness and persons with mental retardation is constitutional); *Riggins v. Nevada* (1992) (reversed conviction because trial court enforced administration of antipsychotic drugs during defendant's trial); *Zinermon v. Burch* (1990) (state is required to inquire into persons with mental illness request for admission to and treatment in mental hospital); *Washington v. Harper* (1990) (the right to be free of medication must be balanced against the state's duty to treat inmates with mental illness and run a safe prison); *City of Cleburne v. Cleburne Living Center* (1985) (mental retardation is a characteristic that the government may take into account); *Jones v. United States* (1983) (there is no correlation between severity of crime committed and time necessary for recovery); *Mills v. Rogers* (1982) (state may recognize greater liberty interests for persons with mental illness than U.S. Constitution); *Youngberg v. Romeo* (1982) (state is under duty to provide institutionalized individual with safe conditions, freedom from bodily restraint, and habilitation); *Vitek v. Jones* (1980) (inmate entitled to due process before he is found to be mentally ill and transferred to a mental hospital); *Addington v. Texas* (1979) (mental illness must be proven by more than a preponderance of evidence); *Parham v. J.R.*, (1979) (holding statute requiring

legal representation to such persons.[8] This revolution continues today, and there is no reason to expect any abatement in case law, statutory amendments, or advocacy initiatives in the coming years.[9]

But the revolution has largely been a parochial one. As I will discuss below, there have been important developments in other nations—both in common and civil law countries—but, by and large, with the partial exception of the jurisprudence of the European Court on Human Rights, until this point, it has been an American revolution. My expectation is that the ratification of the UN Convention has the capacity to radically alter this reality. See Weller, 2010 (on how the Convention reflects a "quiet revolution" in human rights/mental disability law).

III. Developments in Nations That Are Parts of Regional Human Rights Systems

A. Introduction

The prevailing human rights conventions—all linked to the UDHR—create judicial or quasi-judicial institutions that are given the responsibility of interpreting, administering, and applying "an entire regime of rules which each of

---

neutral fact finder to determine admission of children to state mental health hospitals comports with due process); *O'Connor v. Donaldson* (1975) (unconstitutional to confine a nondangerous person capable of surviving safely in freedom to a mental hospital); *Jackson v. Indiana* (1972) (statute that effectively condemned defendant to permanent institutionalization deprived him of equal protection and due process under the Fourteenth Amendment); *Rennie v. Klein* (1981) (patients with mental illness committed involuntarily retain their constitutional right to refuse antipsychotic drugs); *Rogers v. Okin* (1980) (psychiatrists are better suited than are judges to balancing interests of patients and public safety); *Wyatt v. Stickney* (1971); *Wyatt v. Aderholt* (1974) (persons with mental illness have constitutional right to adequate treatment in mental hospital); *Lessard v. Schmidt* (1972) (a statute that fails to provide person alleged to be mentally ill with adequate procedural safeguards is unconstitutional); *Rivers v. Katz* (1986) (persons with mental illness have right to control their own medical treatment). On the relationship between the *Wyatt* litigation and international human rights law developments, see Perlin, 2011.

[8] See 1 Perlin, 1998, §§ 2B-1 to 2B-15, pp. 191–292. Paradoxically, it also saw both a ferocious backlash against forensic patients (especially, but not solely, persons found not guilty by reason of insanity), and a "widening of the net," that, by "blurring" the boundaries of civil and criminal mental disability law, has increased the categories of persons subject to the involuntary civil commitment power (to now include those charged with certain sexually violent offenses and persons subject to "assisted outpatient commitment"). See id., § 2A-3.3, at 75-92; § 2C-7.3, pp. 491–499.

[9] Perlin, 2007, pp. 436–437.

these treaties embodies" (Wilner, 1995/1996, p. 408).[10] As will be discussed extensively below, the European system has been responsible for an amazingly robust body of mental disability law, informed by international human rights principles. There have been a few very significant cases from the Inter-American system and one from the African system.[11] As will be also be discussed infra chapter 9, there exists, at this point in time, no cognate Asian system. (See generally, Perlin, 2011.)

B. Europe

The European Convention on Human Rights (ECHR) presents a comprehensive statutory plan, and one that has been the subject of extensive scholarly commentary (see, e.g., Fennell, 1999; Amos, 2007; Wachenfeld, 1991; Bindman, Maingay & Szmukler, 2003; Palmer, 2009; Medda-Windischer, 2001; Defeis, 2004; Gostin, 2000; Wildhaber, 2007; Arold, 2007; Thorold, 1996; Richardson, 2005; Hewitt, 1998; Harding, 1989; Gostin & Gable, 2004; Kingdon et al., 2004; Prior, 2007).[12] Professors Laurence Helfer and Anne-Marie Slaughter have characterized it as a "remarkable success" (1997, p. 276).[13] Article 5 of the ECHR guarantees the right to liberty and security of the person, subject to limited circumstances in which governments may justifiably deprive persons "of unsound mind" of their liberty, mandating the provision of a "speedy" review of the detention by an independent court or tribunal, and the provision of an enforceable remedy in damages to those who are detained in a manner that contravenes the Convention (see Mackey, 2006; for a comprehensive evaluation of all ECHR case law as it applies to persons with mental disabilities, see Bartlett, Lewis & Thorold, 2007; see also, Niveau & Materi, 2006; on the Council of Europe's earlier recommendations on human rights and psychiatry from an equality perspective, see Jones & Kingdon, 2005.).

However, this Article is in no way a panacea to prevent all violations of human rights of persons with disabilities; by way of example, in a carefully nuanced article, Professors Gostin and Gable focus on two important problems that appear to fall outside of the scope of the Convention: confinement

---

[10] On how these regional human rights courts are a "tool" for better human rights, see Stacy, 2009, p. 55. On their value as an adjudicatory mechanism, see id., p. 144.

[11] On the role of a national judiciary in Africa in the promotion of human rights through judicial review, see Twinomugisha, 2009 (Uganda).

[12] On the need for mental health indicators as a part of a comprehensive health monitoring system in European Union states, see Korkeila et al., 2003. On issues of epidemiology of persons in European Union states institutionalized because of mental disability, see Salize & Dressing, 2004; Salize & Dressing, 2005.

[13] But compare, Robbins, 2005 (regionalization leads to marginalization of human rights). On the difficulties inherent in harmonizing regional disability policies, see Mablett, 2005. On the experience in one nation, see Cameron, 1999 (Sweden).

of nonprotesting patients and compulsory supervision in the community (Gostin & Gable, 2004, p. 59).[14] The ECHR also—in its prohibition against inhuman and degrading treatment (see Article 3)—sets into place "a mechanism for monitoring the conditions of confinement" (id., p. 78).[15]

As discussed earlier (see infra chapter 2), Professor David Hewitt has concluded that the European Court on Human Rights has interpreted the ECHR "very restrictively in psychiatric cases" (Hewitt, 2001, p. 1278),[16] considering specifically cases that characterized the handcuffing of patients as "therapeutically necessary" (id., discussing *Herczegfalvy v. Austria,* 1993), or sanctioned the use of seclusion for "disciplinary" purposes (id., discussing *Dhoest v. Belgium,* 1987).[17] Notwithstanding this gloomy analysis, Professor Gerard Quinn has concluded that the due process protections of the "negative right to liberty . . . are very robust under the Convention" (Quinn, 1992, p. 48; see also, Harding, 1989, pp. 260–262 [listing most important principles established in ECHR cases involving individuals being committed to psychiatric hospitals or institutionalized in such facilities]).[18] Professor Bruce Winick bridges the gap between Hewitt and Quinn by arguing that, even in the absence of case law, many of the ongoing "abusive practices [of commitment, treatment and institutional conditions]" still common in Eastern Europe (see infra chapter 5) "can be understood to violate the [ECHR] and other evolving

---

[14] Compare Richardson, 2005, p. 127, arguing that "mental disorder is a phenomenon requiring its own statutory framework" (see infra chapter 7, discussing the Convention on the Rights of Persons with Disabilities). For a comparative perspective on the different ways that European nations deal with issues of incapacity, see Dawson & Kämpf, 2006.

[15] In this context, on the recommendations of the Council for Europe on protecting the rights of persons with mental disabilities, see Kingdon et al., 2004. On the impact of European standards on practice in Canada, see Zuckerberg, 2007.

[16] For an analysis of ECHR jurisprudence in other human rights areas, similarly finding a "restrictive interpretation," see Orakhelashvili, 2003 (torture and wrongful death cases); see also, Bindman, Maingay & Szmukler, 2003, p. 91 (in treatment decision making, "patients' capacity . . . is essentially ignored").

[17] More broadly, compare Kamminga, 1994, p. 163, characterizing the European Court's record in dealing with "gross and systematic violations" of human rights as "unimpressive," to Hale, 2007 (ECHR better at protecting persons with disabilities from unwanted or unnecessary treatment than securing equal access *to* treatment), and see Ahmed & Butler, 2006 (EU should take positive measures to protect and fulfill human rights). See also, Dimopolous, 2009, p. 75, criticizing the European Court's decision in a case involving the treatment of children of intellectually disabled persons for its failure to "imbue [its judgment] with the claims of the social model of disability," discussing *Kutzner v. Germany* (2002).

[18] On the right to refuse treatment in this context, see Wicks, 2001. See generally, Lawson, 2006, p. 489 (ECHR jurisprudence offers "equivocal support" to litigants in its readings of the prohibition in Article 3 of "inhuman or degrading treatment or punishment").

principles of international human rights law" (Winick, 2002, p. 572), concluding that the remedy for these abuses is a "healthy dose of international human rights law and therapeutic jurisprudence" (id.; see infra chapter 10, arguing that Winick's insights must be taken seriously by scholars and policymakers in this area).

Several cases decided by the European Court of Human Rights illuminate some of this tension.[19] In *Winterwerp v. Netherlands* (1979), the Court found that in order to detain "persons of unsound mind" in accordance with Article 5 of the European Convention, there must be a finding that the disorder requires confinement and the disorder must be diagnosed using objective medical expertise. The ECHR also found that it is essential for the person concerned to have access to a court and the opportunity to be heard either in person or, where necessary, through some form of representation. In *Herczegfalvy v. Austria* (1993), the ECHR noted that the position of inferiority and powerlessness typical of patients confined to psychiatric hospitals calls for increased vigilance. Although ultimately the ECHR did not find a violation of Article 3 it noted that use of handcuffs and security bed were "worrying" (id., p. 1278). Professor Hewitt is especially critical of this decision: After *Herczegfalvy*, he charges, "it is hard to think of a single accepted psychiatric practice that might breach Article 3" (id.).

Other cases illuminate other aspects of the ECHR.[20] While the provision in Article 5(2) that everyone who is arrested has to be given the reasons "for his arrest and of any charge against him," appears to be self-limiting to the criminal setting, it was held in *Van der Leer v. Netherlands* (1990) that it applied to all detentions, and was thus breached when a patient was not informed that her stay in a hospital as a voluntary patient had been converted to a detention ordered by a court (see Gledhill, 2007, pp. 366–367, discussing *Van Der Leer*). The European Court has found that ordering detention in a psychiatric institution without prior medical opinion violates the European Convention, finding that mental disability must be of sufficient seriousness to justify deprivation of liberty (*Varbanov v. Bulgaria*, 2000),[21] and that

---

[19] On the European Court's jurisprudence in forensic cases involving insanity pleas, see Gearty & Sutherland, 1992. On that Court's "clarif[ication]" of issues applicable to a forensic population, see Prior, 2007, p. 555. For a broader consideration of this jurisprudence as it applies to the United Kingdom, see Curtice & Sandford, 2009. On forensic mental health services and psychiatric assessment in the European Union, see Salize, Lepping & Dressing, 2005 (urging the harmonization of legal frameworks); Dressing & Salize, 2006 (same). On the role of the writ of habeas corpus in the European Court's jurisprudence (and the implications for practice in the United States), see Shoenberger, 2006. On the redevelopment of forensic units in the former East Germany, see Konrad, 2001.

[20] On the court's decisions in right to treatment litigation, see Quinn, 1992.

[21] *Varbanov* is discussed extensively in Kanev, 2002. See also *Nowicka v. Poland*, 2002 (holding that two court-ordered detentions totaling 83 days violated Article 5(1) since

individuals have a right, under Article 5, to initiate review of detention (*Rakevich v. Russia*, 2004). In *E v. Norway* (1990), the European Court of Human Rights has found that a delay of eight weeks violates the right to speedy review by a court. And in *Megyeri v. Germany* (1992), the Court found that, for periodic review of commitment to be effective, there may need to be procedural safeguards present; in this case, a breach of the Convention was found where no lawyer was assigned to represent the patient in question. There must also be judicial process involved in determining whether detention, under Article 5, is lawful. (*X. v. UK*, 1981; for a helpful discussion of the *X* case, see Gostin, 1982).

In the most recent litigation, in a potentially enormously significant procedural decision, the ECHR agreed to hear on the merits the case of a Bulgarian citizen with a psychosocial disability. It found that the plaintiff, who was partially deprived of his legal capacity and placed into the Pastra Social Care Institution without his consent in 2002, and has never been evaluated to determine whether he was capable of living on his own, and who was placed in the guardianship of the institution's director (who thus controls his finances and identity papers and can decide his place of residence), could proceed with his case. In that case, the plaintiff alleges violations of his rights under the European Convention on Human Rights, including his right not to be subject to inhuman and degrading treatment under Article 3, his right to liberty under Article 5, to a fair hearing under Article 6, to respect for home and private life under Article 8, and to an effective remedy under Article 13 (*Stanev v. Bulgaria*, 2010).[22]

This litigation notwithstanding, it should not be presumed that the judicial process has served as a full palliative for conditions in European communities and psychiatric institutions.[23] A *New York Times* article from 2009, by way of example, concluded, "Across Central and Eastern Europe, many people with mental illnesses or disabilities are sequestered without rights or recourse under Communist-era rules that put their fates in the hands of legal guardians, often regardless of the severity of their disabilities, according to human rights groups" (Brunwasser, 2009).

---

the detentions were to conduct psychiatric examinations that normally took only a few hours and were based on a private dispute).

[22] See also, *Kiss v. Hungary* (2010) (indiscriminate removal of voting rights, without an individualized judicial evaluation and solely based on a mental disability necessitating partial guardianship, cannot be considered compatible with the legitimate grounds for restricting the right to vote).

[23] See infra chapter 4, discussing issues involving the use of state-sanctioned psychiatry as a tool of political suppression in the former Soviet Union and "Red Bloc."

C. Other Regions of the World[24]

Several important cases litigated in other parts of the world have had a tremendous impact on the relationship between international human rights law and mental disability law. Not only do these cases serve as an example for other nations to follow in assuring human rights to every person, but they also demonstrate the potential effectiveness of regional tribunals (see Cavallaro, 2002, p. 492, discussing how such litigation can be a vehicle "to mobilize the media and public opinion").[25]

1. South America[26]

One such case is *In the Matter of Victor Rosario Congo* (1999), involving a 48-year-old Ecuadorian who, as a result of the State's gross negligence and willful acts, died of malnutrition, hydroelectrolitic imbalance, and heart and lung failure. Specifically, Congo was beaten with a club on the scalp by a guard, deprived of any medical treatment, and placed in isolation naked and virtually incommunicado.

The Inter-American Commission on Human Rights (Inter-American Commission)[27] found that the State violated Congo's right to humane treatment under Article 5 of the American Convention on Human Rights (American Convention). The Commission determined that Article 5 of the American Convention must be interpreted in light of the Principles for the Protection of Persons with Mental Illness and for the Improvement of Mental Health Care (MI Principles):

> The Commission considers that in the present case the guarantees established under Article 5 of the American Convention must be interpreted in light of the Principles for the Protection of Persons

[24] Asia will be discussed separately infra chapter 9 in the context of the proposed Disability Rights Tribunal for Asia and the Pacific.

[25] On how advisory practice before the Inter-American Court contributes to the evolution of human rights law, see Pasqualucci, 2002.

[26] For a recent and helpful overview of mental health care reforms in this region, see de Almeida & Horvitz-Lennon, 2010. On the general inadequacies of mental health law in this region, see PAHO, 2008.

[27] But see, on the Inter-American Court in general, Goldman, 2009, p. 883, noting that most states in this region have "fail[ed] . . . to implement the [Operating Convention's] rights and guarantees." Compare Cavallaro & Brewer, 2008a, p. 827, offering prescriptions so that the Inter-American Court "can maintain and potentially increase its often-significant real-world impact on human rights issues"; Grossman, 2008, p. 1282 ("The Inter-American system has contributed significantly to the development of human rights in the region as well as to broader democratic values"). On the Court's effectiveness in general, see Basch et al., 2010.

> with Mental Illness and for the Improvement of Mental Health Care. These principles were adopted by the United Nations General Assembly as a guide to the interpretation in matters of protection of human rights of persons with mental disabilities, which this body regards as a particularly vulnerable group. (Id., para. 54)

In a subsequent footnote, the Commission underscored:

> The UN Principles for the Protection of Persons with Mental Illness are regarded as the most complete standards for protection of the rights of persons with mental disability at the international level. These Principles serve as a guide to States in the design and/or reform of mental health systems and are of utmost utility in evaluating the practices of existing systems. Mental Health Principle 23 establishes that each State must adopt the legislative, judicial, administrative, educational, and other measures that may be necessary to implement them. These Principles are also standards of assessment that makes international human rights monitoring by NGO's more possible. (Id., n. 8)[28]

Continuing, the Inter-American Commission found that the solitary confinement of Congo constituted inhuman and degrading treatment in violation of Article 5(2) of the American Convention; especially in light of the fact he was left in isolation unable to satisfy his basic needs. Thus, the State violated Congo's right to "be treated with respect for the inherent dignity of the human person" (id., para. 59). Further, the Commission found that the State is responsible for the physical assault committed by one of its agents and that there is a duty on the State to ensure the physical, mental and moral integrity of persons suffering from mental illness (id., para. 62).

The Inter-American Commission also found that the State violated Article 4(1) of the American Convention because the State failed to take measures in its power to ensure the right to life of a person who "partly because of his state of health and in part owing to injuries inflicted on him by a State agent, was defenseless, isolated and under its control" (id., para. 84). Finally, the Commission found that under Article 25(1) of the American Convention, Congo had a right to judicial protection, which the State violated since there were no judicial proceedings opened to investigate and establish the responsibilities for the injuries to and death of Congo (id., para. 97). As a result of this case, the Commission recommended that the persons responsible for the violations be punished, that the Congo's family be compensated, that medical and psychiatric care for persons suffering from mental illness be provided,

---

[28] This is of particular importance because it makes the MI Principles "hard law", or in other words, binding on the United Nations members who have signed it. See supra chapter 2. Thus, it guarantees more extensive rights for persons with mental disabilities.

and that specialists be assigned to penitentiary system to identify psychiatric disorders of those confined.[29]

Another success story of the effectiveness of litigation in this part of the world is the 2003 case in Paraguay where the Inter-American Commission granted immediate, life-saving measures to protect the lives and physical, mental, and moral integrity of 460 individuals detained in the state-run Neuro-Psychiatric Hospital (Hillman, 2005). Mental Disability Rights International (MDRI) investigated the abuses in Paraguay's Neuro-Psychiatric Hospital and documented the atrocious treatment and conditions for all 460 people. The investigation included two teenage boys, Julio and Jorge who had been detained in six-by-six foot isolation cells, naked and without access to bathrooms for over four years. The conditions were found to violate the right to community integration, the right to life, the right to humane treatment, the right to personal liberty, and the rights of the child.

As a result of this case, MDRI and the Center for Justice and International Law (CEJIL) worked through the Inter-American Commission to ensure that Paraguay develops a system of community-based mental health in order to prevent such abuses in the future. In late February 2005, MDRI and CEJIL signed a groundbreaking agreement with the Paraguayan government which "required the state to develop a plan for deinstitutionalization and creation of community-based mental health services, along with the guarantees of funding for such a plan by Paraguay's President and Minister of Health" (Hillman, 2005, p. 28). According to Professor Tara Melish (one of the counsel in the case), this is what happened subsequently:

> Consequently—triggered by the personal intervention of the President of Paraguay himself after visiting the hospital to observe the denounced conditions (as well as the credible threat of litigation if the precautionary measures were ignored)—the state took immediate responsive action, firing the hospital's director, reconstructing and modernizing patient facilities, reassessing intake procedures, and beginning a reform process aimed at providing community-based, rather than institution-based, care to persons with psychosocial and intellectual disabilities. A process of mediated supervision of the reform process has continued with the participation of the state, the Commission, and the petitioning parties. (Melish, 2006, p. 285)

Finally, in *Ximenes-Lopes v. Brazil* (2006), a man being held for psychiatric treatment at a private psychiatric clinic/rest home—operating as part of the Brazilian public health system—died while hospitalized. Responding to

[29] On why cases such as *Congo* should be the subject of judicial decisions, and not "friendly settlements," see King-Hopkins, 2000.

allegations that he was abused and tortured (and that these actions led to his premature death), the Inter-American Court stated that:

> [Brazil's duties] to respect and guarantee protection norms and to ensure the effectiveness of rights go beyond the relationship between their agents and the individuals under the jurisdiction thereof, since they are embodied in the positive duty of the State to adopt such measures as may be necessary to ensure the effective protection of human rights in inter-individual relationships. (Id., para. 85)

The Court concluded that Brazil was under a special duty to protect life and personal integrity, notwithstanding the fact that the facility was a private one, finding under the Convention that private entities acting in a state capacity in the provision of health care were under its jurisdiction, where, as in this case, the state failed to adequately regulate and supervise them (id., para. 89). It also required Brazil to establish educational programs for staff working in mental health institutions (id., para. 250).

This case—widely praised (see, e.g., Keener & Vasquez, 2009; Nolan, 2009; Pasqualucci, 2008)—stimulated fresh debate within Brazil about public health policy (Cavallaro & Brewer, 2008a, p. 791). Commentators characterized it as demonstrating "how an issue framed legally in terms of civil and political rights may serve to address questions of social justice that might also be framed in economic, social, and cultural terms" (Cavallaro & Schaeffer, 2006, p. 379). Anna Cabot and her colleagues concluded that it set "a vital precedent in the Inter-American System. It signifies a wave of change, characterized by the recognition and proper interpretation of human rights principles pertaining to persons with mental disabilities and the proper application of these principles" (2006, p. 45). In short, it guaranteed citizens the right to "a dignified life" (Keener & Vasquez, 2009, p. 624).[30]

2. Africa[31]

In *Purohit and Moore v. The Gambia* (2003), the African Commission on Human and Peoples' Rights (African Commission)[32] found that Gambia

---

[30] On how the *Ximenes-Lopes* case addressed "questions of social justice," see Cavallaro & Brewer, 2008b, p. 92.

[31] On the use of international law by domestic African courts in other aspects of human rights law, see, e.g., Mujuzi, 2009 (Uganda; death penalty); Moyo, 2009 (South Africa; racially discriminatory land reform programs); Kludze, 2008 (Ghana; multiple civil rights). Compare Gumedze, 2005 (international human rights instruments have had little impact in Swaziland). On its use in Africa in the interpretation of procedural doctrines that affect substantive human rights litigation, see, e.g., Taiwo, 2009 (Nigeria; standing doctrine). On the revival of constitutionalism in Africa in general, see Prempeh, 2006 2007; Christiansen, 2007. For a comparison of the African and European human rights systems, see Allo, 2009.

[32] In the years subsequent to the decision in *Purohit and Moore*, an African Court on Human Rights has been established. For a criticism of that court's first decision (a case

violated various provisions of the African Charter on Human and Peoples' Rights (African Charter) in the way persons with mental disabilities were treated in Gambia and by the Lunatic Detention Act of the Gambia (LDA).[33] Although communications are not received by the African Commission until local remedies are exhausted, in this case the Commission found that the existent remedies were not realistic for persons with mental disabilities.[34]

In determining the merits of *Purohit and Moore*, the African Commission found that when States ratify the African Charter they undertake a responsibility to bring its domestic laws and practice in conformity with the African Charter.[35] Further, the Commission found that Articles 2 and 3 guaranteeing equal protection and antidiscrimination are nonderogable rights. Thus, Gambia violated these rights through the implementation of LDA, which detained more people from poor backgrounds and provided only those charged with capital offenses with legal assistance.

The LDA was not in conformity with the African Charter by its classification of persons with mental disabilities as "lunatics" and "idiots." The African Commission found that these terms dehumanized and took away their inherent right to human dignity in violation of Article 5. Like the Inter-American Commission, the African Commission turned to the MI Principles in reaching this conclusion. In addition, the African Commission found that the LDA violated Article 6 of the African Charter because the LDA authorized detention on the basis of opinions by general medical practitioners, did not have

involving torture in Chad), see Murungu, 2009. On the question of court access, see Juma, 2007. On the need for institutional evolution of that Court, see Wright, 2006. For a predecessor analysis, see Udombana, 2000. On how the Court is a "landmark development in the field of international human rights," see Sinha, 2004, p. 160. For a slightly more skeptical view, see O'Shea, 2001.

33 On the question of whether the African regional human rights system is compatible with international human rights standards, see Mbaya, 1996. For historical perspectives, see Mutua, 1995; Mugwanya, 2003, and for suggestions for improvement, see id. On the role of human rights in "traditional Africa," see Khushulani, 1983, pp. 415–418. On the role of individual human rights in the African context, see Ajibola, 1998. On "Africanizing" human rights in Africa, see Ugochukwu, 2010.

34 There are clusters of other social and cultural issues that must be considered in the specific African context. On the "uniquely vulnerable nature" of the African continent in this context, see Allo, 2009, p. 21. Primary among these is the role that traditional healers and the "folk sector" plays in dealing with persons with mental illnesses, especially in the rural areas. See, e.g., Alem et al., 2008. On the importance of "spirits," see Behrend, 1999. On the role of "traditional healers," see Okasha, 2003. For an anthropological overview, see Ingstad & White, 1995. For a historical perspective, see Milner, 1966. On the role of "magio-religious traditions" *in place of* law, see Kelley, 2007 (Niger). On the significance of "African values" in the context of international human rights law, see infra chapter 9.

35 On early reporting problems under the African charter, see Gaer, 1992. See also, Amoah, 1992, p. 240, discussing "ineffectiveness" of the African Commission as "an effective weapon for human rights protection." For suggestions for improvement, see Mbondenyi, 2008.

fixed periods of detention, and did not provide for review or appeal. In *Purohit and Moore*, the Commission also found that the right to health is crucial and persons with mental disabilities, as a result of their condition and by virtue of their disabilities, should be accorded special treatment that would enable them to sustain the optimum level of independence in accordance with both the African Charter and MI Principles.

This case marked the first time that the African Commission had interpreted the African Charter as well as the first time it found a country's domestic law to be in violation of the regional human rights treaty (see Kanter, 2009, and Baderin, 2005, p. 132 [*Purohit* "a landmark case"]; but see Viljoen & Louw, 2007, p. 5, and id., n. 22, alleging that state parties did not implement any of the Commission's recommendations);[36] compare Hunt, 2005, p. 43 (finding a "clear obligation" for states to carry out regional tribunal judgments).

It would be overly optimistic to conclude that regionalism in Africa is a solution to all of the issues discussed in this book. In a parallel area of law and policy, scholars have praised the African Commission's interpretation of relevant human rights instruments as providing "an effective legal framework" for the protection of participants in HIV/AIDS clinical research (Nienaber, 2009, p. 544). This, however, is a decidedly more positive interpretation than offered by other commentators (see, e.g., Amoah, 1992, discussed supra note 35; see generally, Bondzie-Simpson, 1988).[37] It is likely that Professor Vincent Nmehielle's conclusion—that "this whole process is still part of the metamorphosis of African human rights consciousness—a point in time of African human rights history that is bound to lead to another era" (2003, p. 424)—still resonates. And it is difficult to disagree with Dean John Mubangizi that "there are still lots of pains to endure before the African system of human rights can compare favourably to its more advanced counterparts" (2006, p. 165).

---

[36] Substandard and repressive conditions continue to exist in Africa. On the history of mental health law in South Africa, see Kruger, 1980. See Walker, 2009, discussing the "hot as ovens and dirty beyond belief" facilities for "civil lunatics" in Nigeria. A recent World Health Organization study concluded that "progress toward community mental health care in most African countries is still hampered by a lack of resources (Alem et al., 2008). See also, Njenga, 2006, p. 97 ("The practice of forensic psychiatry in Africa is shrouded in both mystery and confusion"). For a comparison of forensic psychiatric services in one African nation (Malawi) and one European nation (Scotland), see Hayward, White & Kauye, 2010. For a contrasting view of the practice of forensic psychiatry in *Europe*, see Nedopil, 2009, p. 233, characterizing it as a "thrilling and growing field" of practice.

[37] See Nmehielle, 2003, pp. 423–424, n. 47, for a full range of commentary.

IV. Conclusion

A relatively recent review article, in discussing the human rights of persons admitted to psychiatric hospitals in South America, characterized the development of human rights protections for such individuals as "one of the great and continuing achievements of the latter part of the twentieth century" (Gable et al., 2005, p. 366). The same article, however, concluded somewhat glumly, noting that the countries of the region "have not satisfied their obligations to protect, respect and fulfill the human rights of persons with disabilities, despite human rights instruments, recognizing these obligations" (id., p. 370).

Three years ago, Professor Pauline Prior noted that "the countries with the worst human rights abuses are not highly visible in the case law of the [European Court on Human Rights]," noting that citizens in those nations often do not have the financial means to bring a legal challenge (2007, p. 556), but noting that recent developments in cases involving individuals from nations in that region with developed economies have "ensure[d] an international debate on the need for strong legal protection for this group of disempowered individuals" (id.). Since Professor Prior wrote her article, there have been some significant case-law developments (see, e.g., *Stanev v. Bulgaria*, 2010, discussed supra, p. [x]), and, more globally, the ratification of the CRPD should serve as impetus to the creation of counsel-appointment mechanisms (see infra chapter 8).

Like Prior's article, most of the other important scholarly commentary in this area (and most of the case law) predates Convention ratification. We can expect that future Court and Commission decisions will illuminate the extent of the "real life" impact of the Convention on practice before and the jurisprudence of these tribunals.

4

The Use of Mental Disability Law to Suppress Political Dissent

I. Introduction[1]

Writing about the need for enforcement of international human rights protections against political abuse, George Alexander concluded that "psychiatric incarceration may occasion a greater intrusion of the rights of the politically unpopular than mere jailing" (1997, p. 392). He came to this finding by way of his consideration of the "unique role" of state psychiatry "in discrediting opinion and dehumanizing those with whom one disagrees" (id.).

This is a powerful charge and is one that might, at first blush, appear puzzling. Because psychiatric intervention is medical treatment, it is generally assumed that it has been undertaken for benevolent purposes. Indeed, in rejecting the appellant's argument that the burden-of-proof in involuntary civil commitment cases should be "beyond a reasonable doubt" (the same standard used in criminal cases in the United States), the U.S. Supreme Court made it clear that it saw a significant difference between the loss of liberty in a criminal case, and the loss of liberty in a civil commitment case:

> Even though an erroneous confinement should be avoided in the first instance, the layers of professional review and observation of the patient's condition, and the concern of family and friends generally will provide continuous opportunities for an erroneous commitment to be corrected. It is not true that the release of a

[1] See generally, Perlin, 2006c.

> genuinely mentally ill person is no worse for the individual than the failure to convict the guilty. One who is suffering from a debilitating mental illness and in need of treatment is neither wholly at liberty nor free of stigma. . . . It cannot be said, therefore, that it is much better for a mentally ill person to "go free" than for a mentally normal person to be committed. (*Addington v. Texas*, 1979, p. 429–430; see generally, 1, Perlin 1998a, § 2C-5.1a, at 395–400 (discussing *Addington*), and Perlin, 2000c, pp. 95–96, critiquing the "pretextual assumptions" of *Addington*).

Yet, if we are to consider the well-documented history of the use of state psychiatry in the Soviet bloc and in China, we are forced to confront the reality that, for many years, procedural safeguards such as these were totally absent, and institutional psychiatry was a major tool in the suppression of political dissent. As Richard Bonnie has noted:

> Psychiatric incarceration of mentally healthy people is uniformly understood to be a particularly pernicious, form of repression, because it uses the powerful modalities of medicine as tools of punishment, and it compounds a deep affront to human rights with deception and fraud. Doctors who allow themselves to be used in this way (certainly as collaborators, but even as victims of intimidation) betray the trust of society and breach their most basic ethical obligations as professionals. (Bonnie, 2002, p. 136)

Moreover, it appears painfully clear that, while the worst excesses of the past have mostly (but decidedly not totally) disappeared, the problem is not limited to the pages of history. What is more, the revelations of the worst of these abuses (and the concomitant rectification of many of them) may, paradoxically, have created the false illusion that all the major problems attendant to questions of institutional treatment and conditions in these nations have been solved. This is certainly not so. (Perlin, 2007)

Remarkably, the issue of the human rights of persons with mental disabilities had been ignored for decades by the international agencies vested with the protection of human rights on a global scale (Perlin et al. 2006a, chapter 1). As discussed earlier (see supra chapter 1), Dr. Theresia Degener observed that "drafters of the International Bill of Human Rights [IHBR] did not include disabled persons as a distinct group vulnerable to human rights violations," and that "none of the equality clauses of any of the three instruments of [the IHBR] mention disability as a protected category" (Degener, 2000, p. 187).[2] Degener's writings reflect the change that has taken place in

[2] The three instruments are the Universal Declaration of Human Rights (1948; UDHR), the International Covenant on Civil and Political Rights (1966; ICCPR), and the International Covenant on Economic, Social, and Cultural Rights (1966; ICESCR). See supra chapter 3.

disability rights jurisprudence. In 2000, she stated further that "disability has been reclassified as a human rights issue," and that "law reforms in this area are intended to provide equal opportunities for disabled people and to combat their segregation, institutionalization and exclusion as typical forms of disability-based discrimination" (id., p. 181).[3]

For people with mental disabilities, in particular, the development of human rights protections may be even more significant than for people with other disabilities. Like people with other disabilities, people with mental disabilities face degradation, stigmatization, and discrimination throughout the world today. (See *City of Cleburne v. Cleburne Living Center*, 1985, p. 462 [Marshall, J., dissenting in part, arguing that "The mentally retarded have been subject to a 'lengthy and tragic history' of segregation and discrimination that can only be called grotesque," and describing "a regime of state-mandated segregation and degradation . . . that in its virulence and bigotry rivaled, and indeed paralleled, the worst excesses of Jim Crow"]). But unlike people with other disabilities, many people with mental disabilities are routinely confined, against their will, in institutions, and deprived of their freedom, dignity, and basic human rights. People with mental disabilities who are fortunate enough to live outside of institutions often remain imprisoned by the social isolation they experience, often from their own families. They are not included in educational programs, and they face attitudinal barriers to employment because they have not received the education and training needed to obtain employment or because of discrimination based on unsubstantiated fears and prejudice. Only recently have disability discrimination laws and policies in the United States and elsewhere focused on changing such attitudes and promoting the integration of people with disabilities into our schools, neighborhoods, and workplaces (Perlin, 2001–2002, 2000a, 2000b, 2000e, all discussing the Americans with Disabilities Act, see 42 U.S.C. §§ 12101 et seq.).

I believe that the omnipresent deprivations of freedom, dignity, and human rights are the product of what I have already referred to in this book as sanism and what I have already referred to as pretextuality (see supra chapter 2; see generally, Perlin, 1999, 2000c). I do not believe we can make any sense of the phenomena that are discussed in this chapter without seriously considering the pernicious impact of sanism and pretextuality on all of mental disability law (Perlin, 2003).

As discussed earlier (see supra chapter 1), within the past decade, there has been an explosion of interest in the area of human rights and mental

---

3 As noted earlier in this work (see supra chapter 1), within the legal literature, it appears that the first time disability rights was conceptualized as a human rights issue was as recently as 1993 when, in a groundbreaking article, Eric Rosenthal and Leonard Rubenstein first applied international human rights principles to the institutionalization of people with mental disabilities (Rosenthal & Rubenstein, 1993; see also, Kumar, 2003; Ramacharan, 1991).

disability law (Perlin, 2002–2003, p. 539).[4] Generally still unexplored, however, is the question of the extent to which this new interest has had any impact on the matter addressed in this chapter: how has institutional, state-sponsored psychiatry been used as a tool of political suppression, what are the implications of this pattern and practice, and does it continue today? Even though the worst excesses of Soviet-sanctioned political suppression came to an end with the dissolution of the Soviet empire, the problem remains a serious one in other nations (most importantly, China). Just as important, the pervasive impact of sanism and pretextuality continue to, globally, contaminate public psychiatric practice. This contamination is particularly corrosive because the dramatic and well-publicized cessation of the Soviet bloc's political abuses have lulled us into a false consciousness through which we inaccurately believe that the underlying problems have disappeared. They have not.

This chapter will proceed in the following manner. In part II, I will discuss the first revelations of the "dehumanization" referred to by Professor Alexander. In part III, I will discuss developments after these revelations were publicized. In part IV, I will weigh the extent to which the postrevelation reforms have been effective and meaningful. In part V, I will elaborate on the meanings of "sanism" and "pretextuality" in this context, and discuss how they relate to the topic at hand. Then, in part VI, I will raise questions that have not yet been answered, and that, I believe, should help set the research agendas of those thinking about these important issues.

II. The First Revelations

The history of the use of institutional psychiatry as a political tool was documented by Michel Foucault 40 years ago (Foucault, 1965). Foucault examined the expanded use of the public hospital in France in the 17th century, and concluded that "confinement [was an] answer to an economic crisis . . . reduction of wages, unemployment, scarcity of coin" (id. at 47). By the 18th century, the psychiatric hospital—a place of "doomed and despised idleness" (id. at 55)—satisfied "the indissociably economic and moral demand for confinement" (id.).

The first important modern revelations appear in Sidney Bloch and Peter Reddaway's shattering study, *Psychiatric Terror: How Soviet Psychiatry Is Used to Suppress Dissent* (1977). Bloch and Reddaway documented the cases of nearly 500 political dissenters forcibly hospitalized from 1950 to 1970 (Bloch & Reddaway, 1984). This was accomplished, in large part, by the Soviet

[4] See supra chapter 1, discussing Rosenthal, 2002–2003, p. 391 (referring to his early research and advocacy work); Kanev, 2002, p. 435 (noting that Amnesty International first involved itself in this issue in Bulgaria in 2001); Kanter, 2003, p. 268 ("the principle of non-discrimination and equality for people with disabilities has entered center stage in the international arena").

approach to diagnosis (and its uniquely broad formulation of "schizophrenia," "a critical factor in labeling dissent as 'mental illness'"; Bloch & Reddaway, 1985). Bloch and Reddaway revealed that Soviet forensic psychiatrists diagnosed dissenters as expressing "paranoid reformist delusional ideas" in case reports; the patient's conviction that "the state . . . must be changed" was seen as an indicia of mental illness (id.; see also, Bloche, 2001). This tactic served three interrelated ends: It allowed the government to avoid the sorts of procedural safeguards that are normally associated with criminal prosecution (Compare *Addington v. Texas*, 1979). Second, the stigma of a "mentally ill" label effectively discredits the politics of the person being so labeled.[5] Finally, because there were, at that time, no maximum terms to civil commitments (compare *State v. Fields*, 1978, establishing right to periodic review of commitments at which state bears burden of proof); see generally, 1 Perlin, 1998a, § 2C6.5c, at pp. 456–462), confinement to psychiatric hospitals was indefinite (Alexander, 1997, p. 391).

Studies such as the one done by Bloch and Reddaway awakened the West to the realities of the ways that psychiatry was being misused in the service of totalitarian political regimes, a misuse that continued until the 1990s. Of course, as Bonnie has noted, "The risks of mistake and abuse are further magnified, of course, in totalitarian societies, where the state has the power and inclination to bend all institutions to its will and, where the counterforces may be weak or nonexistent, depending on the country's pretotalitarian history" (Bonnie, 2002, p. 140). Not coincidentally, reports such as this provided activists with the first important evidence that international human rights law was potentially an important tool for countries "without democratic and constitutional systems because it may provide the only genuine safeguard against the abuse of persons with mental disabilities—abuse that may be based on political, social, or cultural grounds" (Gostin & Gable, 2004, p. 21; see also, Bonnie, 2002, p. 140: "The Soviet experience was significant because it provided a vivid illustration of the risks associated with unchecked psychiatric power, and the importance of erecting institutional safeguards to minimize these risks in the context of involuntary hospitalization and treatment").

By 1989, changes in the political climate in the Soviet Union led the Soviet government—over the objection of the psychiatric leadership[6]—to allow a

---

[5] On how it is socially acceptable to use pejorative labels to describe and single out persons with mental illness, see Perlin, 1998b, p. 786.

[6] Bloch and Reddaway (1977, p. 322) explain that Soviet psychiatrists who rendered such diagnoses (referred to as "core psychiatrists") received many contingent benefits for cooperating with the authorities:

> The rewards of the good life include access to a variety of privileges and benefits not available to ordinary Soviet citizens. The core psychiatrist is likely to travel abroad, as a tourist or as an attendant at a conference, to have access to stores selling luxury goods at moderate prices, to have a country cottage, and to take vacations at special sanatoria. Their salaries are about three times higher in real terms than those of ordinary psychiatrists.

delegation of psychiatrists and academics from the United States, representing the U.S. Government, to conduct extensive interviews of suspected victims of abuse and to make unrestricted site visits to hospitals selected by the delegation (Bonnie & Polubinskaya, 1999, p. 279; see also, Bonnie, 1990). Reporting on this issue in 1999, Professors Richard Bonnie (one of the members of the delegation) and Svetlana Polubinskaya explained:

> The investigation by the U.S. delegation provided unequivocal proof that the tools of coercive psychiatry had been used, even in the late 1980s, to hospitalize persons who were not mentally ill and whose only transgression had been the expression of political or religious dissent. Most of the patients interviewed by the delegation had been charged with political crimes such as anti-Soviet agitation and propaganda or defaming the Soviet state. Their offenses involved behavior such as writing and distributing anti-Soviet literature, political organizing, defending the rights of disabled groups and furthering religious ideas.
>
> Under applicable laws of Russia and the other former Soviet Republics, a person charged with crime could be subjected to custodial measures of a medical nature if the criminal act was proven and the person was found non-imputable due to mental illness.[7] Non-imputable offenders could be placed in maximum security hospitals (the notorious special hospitals) or in ordinary hospitals depending on their social dangerousness.[8]
>
> The delegation found that no clinical basis existed for the judicial finding of non-imputability in seventeen of these cases. In fact, the delegation found no evidence of mental disorder of any kind in fourteen cases. In all likelihood, these individuals are representative of many hundreds of others who were found nonimputable for crimes of political or religious dissent in the U.S.S.R., mainly between 1970 and 1990. (Bonnie & Polubinskaya, 1999, p. 280–282)

Glumly, Bonnie and Polubinskaya concluded that this repressive use of psychiatry in Russia was made "inevitable" (id., at pp. 283–284) by the "communist regime's intolerance for dissent, including any form of political or religious deviance, and by the corrosive effects of corruption and intimidation in all spheres of social life" (id.) On this point, they indicted "a subset of Soviet psychiatrists[9] [who] knowingly collaborated with the KGB to subject mentally

[7] See generally, Baker, 1987.

[8] RSFSR arts. 58–61 (Criminal Code) (1962) reprinted in *The Soviet Codes of Law*, 1980, pp. 88–89; RSFSR arts. 410–413 (Code of Criminal Procedure 1962) reprinted in id. at 315–316.

[9] These were ones who were associated primarily with Moscow's Serbskii Institute for General and Forensic Psychiatry.

healthy dissidents to psychiatric punishment, in blatant violation of professional ethics and human rights" (id.). In this respect, they concluded, "abuse of psychiatry in the Soviet Union had less to do with psychiatry per se than with the repressiveness of the political regime of which the psychiatrists were a part" (id.).[10] Indeed, "psychiatry was a state institution," and "the social prestige of psychiatrists lay almost entirely in their role as agents of social control, and psychiatrists were more closely aligned with the police than with other specialties in medicine" (id., pp. 287–288).

More recent studies of other Soviet bloc nations revealed similar patterns of behavior. Krassimir Kanev, Bulgaria's leading human rights activist, has noted, "Observations show that in the absence of an accurate definition of 'danger,'[11] Bulgarian psychiatry, as well as the Bulgarian judiciary, combine clinical criteria with the values of society in an astonishing way"(Kanev, 2002, p. 439). A review of civil commitment in Romania reveals a practice that can only be characterized as macabre:

> During the Ceaucescu regime, Article 114 was used in conjunction with Decree Law 12, On the Medical Treatment of Dangerously Mentally Ill Persons, to systematically confine dissidents, on the recommendation of the State Prosecutor or health authorities, as mentally ill persons. Dissent, often expressed through the propagation of anti-state propaganda or illegal departure from the country (Romania Decree Law, undated) was itself viewed as a symptom of severe mental illness.[12]

---

[10] See Bonnie & Polubinskaya, 1999, pp. 284–285:

> The roots of the problem lie much deeper in the attitudes and training of Soviet psychiatrists, and in the role of psychiatry in Soviet society. Repression of political and religious dissidents was only the most overt symptom of an authoritarian system of psychiatric care in which an expansive and elastic view of mental disorder encompassed all forms of unorthodox thinking, and in which psychiatric diagnosis was essentially an exercise of social power.

[11] On the multiple textures of the word "danger" in this context, see 1 Perlin, 1998a, § 2A-4.1, pp. 92–101. To be subject to involuntary civil commitment, one must be seriously mentally ill, and, as a result of that mental illness, a likely danger to self or others. See id. § 2A-4.2, pp. 101–104. On the relationship between involuntary civil commitment and the United Nations' Principles for the Protection of Persons with Mental Illness and the Improvement of Mental Health Care (MI Principles), see Winick, 2002; Rosenthal & Sundram, 2002. On the relationship between the new UN Convention and the provision of counsel in civil commitment cases, see infra chapter 8

[12] See generally *International Association on the Political Use of Psychiatry, Information Bulletin* No. 6 (Mar. 1983). Art. 166 stated:

> Propaganda of a Fascist nature and propaganda against the socialist state, committed by any means in public, is punished by a sentence of imprisonment from 5 to 15 years and the forfeiture of certain rights. Propaganda or the undertaking of any action with the aim of changing the Socialist system or

One psychiatrist in Romania, interviewed for the article just referred to, explained why, in his opinion, this had to be true:

> Under Ceaucescu, political opponents could not exist. . . . In Ceaucescu's time, there was a man who said in the street with a banner, "Down with Ceaucescu." Strictly professionally speaking, it was difficult to believe that this was a real political opinion because it was so obvious that no one would allow him to express himself, so he had to be delusional and couldn't adjust. Real political opposition [*sic*] were subversive. (Loue, 2002)

Romania's characterization of individuals attempting to flee as mentally ill criminals reflected the former Soviet view that crossing the border is a sign of mental illness, as is distributing religious leaflets (id., quoting Smith & Ouszreuk, 1996, p. 65). Reliance on such behaviors as the basis for a diagnosis of mental illness is problematic for both the patient and the psychiatrist. As Ochberg and Gunn have explained:

> The psychiatrist has a dilemma. If he accepts society's definition of madness without using his own separate criteria, he becomes a depository for all sorts of problems unrelated to medicine and he risks becoming an agent of society for the enforcement of contemporary mores. On the other hand, if he takes the opposite view to extremes, he ends up by refusing to treat any patient whose only symptoms are behavioral and who does not show organic changes. (1980)

This state of affairs is not and was not limited to Russia and the Soviet Bloc.[13] Robin Munro's monumental study of state psychiatry in China paints an equally bleak picture.[14] Munro charged that Chinese state psychiatry

---

> activities which could result in a threat to the security of the state will be punished by a sentence of imprisonment from 5 to 15 years and the forfeiture of certain rights.

Art. 245 provided:

> Entering or leaving the country through illegal crossing of the frontier will be punished by a sentence of imprisonment from 6 months to 3 years. The acquisition of means or instruments of the undertaking of measures from which it unequivocally follows that the offender intends to cross the frontier illegally will also be regarded as an attempt. (Loue, 2002).

[13] For a comparison between the two areas of the world in this regard, see van Voren, 2002.

[14] Munro updates his work and responds to critics in Munro, 2002. For one of those criticisms, see Lee & Kleinman, 2002.

engaged in what he characterized as hyperdiagnosis, or "the excessively broad clinical determination of mental illness" (pp. 26–27),[15] as reflected in:

> a tendency on the part of forensic psychiatrists to diagnose as severely mentally ill, and therefore legally non-imputable for their alleged offenses, certain types of dissident or nonconformist detainees who were perceived by the police as displaying a puzzling "absence of instinct for self-preservation" when staging peaceful political protests, expressing officially banned views, pursuing legal complaints against corrupt or repressive officialdom, etc. (Id., p. 26)

Munro characterized another category of politically motivated ethical abuse that he found in China as "severe medical neglect," described as "numerous mentally ill individuals being sent to prison as political 'counter-revolutionaries' and then denied all medical or psychiatric care for many years in an environment bound only to worsen their mental condition" (id., pp. 26–27). Here, he charged that China engaged in "the deliberate withholding of such care from political offenders whom the authorities had already clearly diagnosed as being mentally ill" (id.).

Munro drew on empirical studies showing that of 222 cases examined in which diagnoses of schizophrenia were made, there were 55 cases of a political nature, and 48 cases involving "disturbances of social order" (Id. at 84). From these statistics (comparing them to the cohort of those diagnosed with serious mental illness who had been charged with violent felonies), Munro concluded that "so-called political cases and also those involving disturbance of public order are evidently seen by China's legal-medical authorities as representing no less serious and dangerous a threat to society than cases of murder and injury committed by genuinely psychotic criminal offenders" (id., pp. 84–85).

III. Following the Revelations

As indicated above, the publicity that accompanied the exposés of conditions in Russian psychiatric hospitals led to teams of investigators visiting Russia to confirm the initial evidence. (See Bonnie, 2002, p. 138: "One of the important purposes of mental health law reform in the 1960s and 1970s was to bring coercive psychiatry within reach of the rule of law.") A 1989 U.S. delegation was followed by a review team sent by the World Psychiatric Association in 1991. At the same time, American representatives met with Soviet mental health professionals in the USSR Ministry of Foreign Affairs in

[15] As of the time of the writing of this chapter, Munro was director of the Hong Kong office of Human Rights Watch; he subsequently was appointed to be senior research fellow at the Centre of Chinese Studies of the University of London.

an effort to seek cooperative solutions to the underlying problems (Bonnie & Polubinskaya, 1999).

Soon thereafter, Russia adopted a new mental health law (id., p. 292; see Bonnie, 1994, reprinting English version of text of new law), and in the subsequent 2 years, 10 other former-Soviet bloc nations did the same (Bonnie & Polubinskaya, 1999, pp. 292–293). At the same time, responding to growing concerns of the United Nations Human Rights Commission on the question of the protection of those detained on the grounds of mental illness (concerns spurred in large part by the revelations discussed in this chapter),[16] the United Nations adopted the Principles for the Protection of Persons with Mental Illness and for the Improvement of Mental Health Care in 1991 (Principles for the Protection of Persons with Mental Illness and for the Improvement of Mental Health Care, G.A. Res. 119, U.N. GAOR, 46th Sess., Supp. No. 49, Annex, pp. 188–92, U.N. Doc. A/46/49 [1991] [the MI Principles]).[17]

---

[16] See Moncada, 1994, p. 591, n.5:

> The U.N. General Assembly acknowledged Human Rights Commission Resolution 10 A XXXIII (of March 11, 1977), requesting the Subcommission on Prevention of Discrimination and Protection of Minorities (Subcommission) study the problem of those detained on the grounds of mental illness with a view towards creating some guidelines for their protection. G.A. Res. 33/53, U.N. GAOR, 33d Sess., U.N. Doc. A/33/475, Dec. 14, 1978.

The study by the Subcommission's Special Rapporteur, Erica-Irene A. Daes, revealed that:

> (a) Psychiatry in some States of the international community is often used to subvert the political and legal guarantees of the freedom of the individual and to violate seriously his human and legal rights; (b) In some States, psychiatric hospitalization and treatment is forced on the individual who does not support the existing political régime of the State in which he lives; (c) In other States persons are detained involuntarily and are used as guinea pigs for new scientific experiments; and (d) Many patients in a great number of countries who should be in the proper care of a mental institution because they are a danger to themselves, to others, or to the public, are living freely and without any supervision. U.N. ESCOR, Comm'n on Hum. Rts., Sub-Comm'n on Prevention of Discrimination and Protection of Minorities, Report prepared by Erica-Irene A. Daes at 28, U.N. Doc. E/CN.4/Sub.2/17/Rev.1 (1983) (Daes Report).
>
> The Daes Report incorporates replies submitted by various governments and non-governmental organizations. . . . In this vein, the reply by Amnesty International underlined the abuse of psychiatry for political purposes and present[ed] concrete complaints concerning the treatment of prisoners of conscience and other persons inside psychiatric hospitals in the Soviet Union. (Daes Report, id., p. 16).

[17] On the significance of soft law in the development of international human rights, see Courtis, 2002–2003. Soft law may guide the interpretation, elaboration, or application of hard law; constitute norms that aspire to harden; serve as evidence of hard law; exist in parallel with hard law obligations and act as a fall-back; or serve as a source of

These Principles, establishing minimum human rights standards of practice in the mental health field, have been recognized as "the most complete standards for the protection of the rights of persons with mental disability at the international level" (*Congo v. Ecuador*, 1999, p. 475, para. 111), and they have been used by international oversight and enforcement bodies as an authoritative interpretation of the requirements of the ICESCR and the American Convention on Human Rights (Rosenthal & Sundram, 2002, p. 488).[18]

The MI Principles established standards for treatment and living conditions within psychiatric institutions, and create protections against arbitrary detention in such facilities. The MI Principles recognize that "[e]very person with a mental illness shall have the right to live and work, to the extent possible in the community." They have major implications for the structure of mental health systems since they recognize that "[e]very patient shall have the right to be treated and cared for, as far as possible, in the community in which he or she lives" (Rosenthal & Sundram, 2002, p. 489, citing MI Principles 3, 7(1), 8(2), 9(2), 9(4), 15-18 & 24).

The MI Principles also protect a broad array of rights within institutions, including protections against harm, "including unjustified medication, abuse by other patients, staff, or others," and require the establishment of monitoring and inspection of facilities to ensure compliance with the Principles. They require treatment "based on an individually prescribed plan," and they require that "[t]he treatment of every patient shall be directed towards preserving and enhancing personal autonomy." The MI Principles establish substantive standards and procedural protections against arbitrary detention in a psychiatric facility (id., citing MI Principles 9(2), 9(4), & 22).

Although the MI Principles do not speak specifically to the issue of psychiatry-as-a-tool of state oppression, the European Convention for the Protection of Human Rights and Fundamental Freedoms (ECHR, 1998) has been interpreted in that specific context (Rosenthal & Sundrum, 2002, p. 530).[19] Article 5(1) of the ECHR lists the circumstances in which governments may justifiably deprive persons of their liberty and includes a provision

relatively hard obligations through acquiescence or estoppel. See Alvarez, 2003, p. 421. See supra chapter 2.

[18] Of course, in those nations that have ratified the Convention on the Rights of Persons with Disabilities (see infra chapter 7), that convention now serves as the prevailing law. I discuss the MI Principles in this context here because there are still many nations that have not yet ratified this Convention. But see, Minkowitz, 2007, criticizing MI Principles for not being sufficiently protective of the rights of persons with psychosocial disabilities, especially in the context of the right to refuse treatment.

[19] Jurisprudence from the European Court of Human Rights demonstrates how similar many of the provisions of the MI Principles are to the requirements of convention-based law. In some cases, convention-based rights under the . . . ICCPR or the European Convention on Human Rights (ECHR) may provide greater protections than do the MI Principles . . . . The line of cases established under Article 5 of the ECHR

referring to "persons of unsound mind,"[20] requiring such a finding so as to justify confinement in a mental hospital, but leaving the term undefined (Gostin & Gable, 2004, pp. 65–66). In one of the leading European civil commitment cases, however, the European Court of Human Rights has said specifically this Article would not permit the detention of a person simply because "his views or behaviour deviate from the norms prevailing in a particular society" (*Winterwerp v. The Netherlands*, 1979, p. 16).[21]

In short, the promulgation of the MI principles and the CRPD have the potential to be an important bulwark against the sort of governmental misconduct that is exemplified by the Soviet experience. This does not answer the question, however, of whether that potential has been fulfilled.

---

helps clarify many points not specifically mentioned in the MI Principles. (id.). See generally supra chapter 3.

[20] Art. 5—Right to Liberty and Security:

> Everyone has the right to liberty and security of person. No one shall be deprived of his liberty save in the following cases and in accordance with a procedure prescribed by law:
> a. the lawful detention of a person after conviction by a competent court;
> b. the lawful arrest or detention of a person for non-compliance with the lawful order of a court or in order to secure the fulfilment (*sic*) of any obligation prescribed by law;
> c. the lawful arrest or detention of a person effected for the purpose of bringing him before the competent legal authority on reasonable suspicion of having committed an offence or when it is reasonably considered necessary to prevent his committing an offence or fleeing after having done so;
> d. the detention of a minor by lawful order for the purpose of educational supervision or his lawful detention for the purpose of bringing him before the competent legal authority;
> e. the lawful detention of persons for the prevention of the spreading of infectious diseases, of persons of unsound mind, alcoholics or drug addicts or vagrants;
> f. the lawful arrest or detention of a person to prevent his effecting an unauthorised entry into the country or of a person against whom action is being taken with a view to deportation or extradition.

See European Convention for the Protection of Human Rights and Fundamental Freedoms, 1988, reprinted in Perlin et al., 2006b, p. 161.

[21] Compare *O'Connor v. Donaldson*, 1975, p. 575:

> May the State fence in the harmless mentally ill solely to save its citizens from exposure to those whose ways are different? One might as well ask if the State, to avoid public unease, could incarcerate all who are physically unattractive or socially eccentric. Mere public intolerance or animosity cannot constitutionally justify the deprivation of a person's physical liberty.

IV. Law-in-Action vs. Law-on-the-Books: Have the Revelations Led to Meaningful Change?

The dichotomy between "law on the books" and "law in action" is a gap that has plagued American mental disability law since it began. Cases are decided on the Supreme Court level, yet are not implemented in the states. The United States Supreme Court has articulated sophisticated doctrine, for example, by mandating dangerousness as a prerequisite for an involuntary civil commitment finding, yet trial courts ignore that doctrine. The Supreme Court has issued elaborate guidelines to be used in cases of criminal defendants who will likely never regain their competence to stand trial, yet, nearly forty years later, half of the 50 states still ignore these standards (Perlin, 2002, pp. 428–429; 2000c, pp. 59–76; 2000d, pp. 1046–1047; Morris & Meloy, 1983).

To what extent does this same gap continue in the nations that are the subject of this chapter?[22] Regrettably, conditions in many eastern European facilities are still so substandard as to violate fundamental international human rights (Perlin, 2007, pp. 849–859, 859–863, & 873–886; see generally infra chapter 5). Consider first a report by Amnesty International condemning conditions in Romanian psychiatric hospitals:

> Many of the people placed in psychiatric wards and hospitals throughout the country apparently do not suffer an acute mental disorder and many do not require psychiatric treatment. Their placement in psychiatric hospitals cannot be justified by the provisions of the Law on Mental Health and they should also be considered as people who have been arbitrarily deprived of their liberty. They had been placed in the hospital on non-medical grounds, apparently solely because they could not be provided with appropriate support and services to assist them and/or their families in the community. Often, because of their disability they are more vulnerable to abuse, which apparently is not taken into consideration by hospital staff as in most places such residents were not segregated from people who have different needs for care. (Amnesty International, Romania, Memorandum to the Government Concerning Inpatient Psychiatric Treatment, 2004)

Similarly, when Amnesty International investigated conditions in Bulgaria, it documented cases of women locked in a cage outside one institution. The cage was full of urine and feces and the women covered in filth. One woman was unclothed on the lower half of her body and many sores were visible on her skin (Amnesty International press release, Bulgaria: Disabled Women Condemned to "Slow Death," 2001. On the perception of "persisting paternalistic and custodial attitudes towards patients" in Bulgaria, see

---

[22] On this issue in other nations, see, e.g., Kelley, 2007 (Niger); Hickling, (2002) (the Caribbean).

Boyadjiev & Onchev, 2007, p. 8). Other like conditions have been graphically and relentlessly documented throughout all of eastern Europe; Oliver Lewis's extensive investigations of a cluster of eastern European nations found, by way of example, persistent and unrelenting violations of Article 5 of the ECHR, noting that in many nations, public psychiatric hospital staff were not even aware of the existence of these international human rights provisions (Lewis, 2002, p. 294; see also Mental Disability Advocacy Center, 2004).[23]

Conditions in China's institutions continue to violate international law.[24] Writing soon after Munro's article was published, Dr. Paul Appelbaum, former president of the American Psychiatric Association, concluded that "At least some of the evidence cited by Munro suggests deliberate use by psychiatrists of diagnoses of mental disorders to facilitate the system's efforts to crush challenges to its social and political domination of the populace" (Appelbaum, 2001, p. 1297). Since that time, there has been much written about the treatment of persons adhering to the teachings of Falun Gong:[25]

> After 1999, Falun Gong members continued to protest as some of the more deplorable acts perpetrated against the group came to light and international attention focused on the group's plight. In addition to continuing reports that thousands of Falun Gong were being held in forced labor or "re-education" camps, it was revealed that stalwart Falun Gong members who had protested on numerous occasions were sent to a psychiatric hospital not due to mental illness, but for "re-education." The practice of imprisoning the more recalcitrant members of the Falun Gong in psychiatric hospitals has come under increased international scrutiny and criticism. (Leavy, 2004, pp. 760–761)[26]

---

[23] See Perlin, 2007, pp. 346–347:

> On a site visit to a Nicaraguan public hospital in 2003, I observed male patients walking in wards totally naked (with both male and female staff present). Female patients were brought outside the hospital for lunch. They were wearing "doctor's office" type gowns, exposing their breasts and buttocks. Food was passed around in large bowls, and there were no utensils. Each patient had to reach in and scoop out food (some sort of vegetable stew) with her hands.

[24] On the schism between law-on-the-books and law-in-action in China, see Chen, 2009, p. 109.

[25] Falun Gong is a movement that describes itself as emphasizing five sets of yoga-type exercises designed to "cultivate" one's mind, body, and spirit and thereby gain access to one's inner energy. See Jones, 2004, p. 132, n. 232.

[26] See Chaney, 2005, p. 4: "According to the Falun Gong, hundreds of its practitioners have been confined to psychiatric institutions and forced to take medications or undergo electric shock treatment against their will"; see also, Chu, 2005; Lu & Galli, 2002; Galli & Lu, 2004. On how the selection of Falun Gong as an "evil cult" reflects a

An exhaustive report by Human Rights Watch concludes that psychiatric incarceration is still used for political purposes in China, and that conditions parallel those found in the Soviet Union in the 1970s and 1980s (Dangerous Minds, 2002; see also, Dhir, 2008, p. 105 ["Psychiatric detention continues to be used as a tool of political oppression in China"]). Note the authors of the Human Rights Watch report:

> The challenge for the international psychiatric community now is to find ways of exerting its influence to ensure that China's secretive . . . system and other custodial psychiatric facilities around the country can no longer be used by the security authorities as a long-term dumping ground for political and religious nonconformists who, for one reason or another, they find it awkward or inconvenient to bring to criminal trial. . . . Advocacy efforts by local and international psychiatric bodies would also greatly assist in encouraging individual Western governments and the European Union to take up the issue, notably by placing the issue of political psychiatric abuse in China on the formal agenda of the various bilateral human-rights dialogue sessions that have become, in recent years, a central and regular feature of Sino-Western relations. (Id.; see also, Physicians for Human Rights, 2006)

Thus, although the use of psychiatry as a tool of political suppression may no longer be the problem that it was in the 1980s (but see Leavy, 2004; Chaney, 2005, and Finn, 2006 [citing to continued abuses in Russia], and Kahn, 2006, [discussing the institutionalization of members of the Falun Gong in China]), violations of international human rights laws continue unabated.[27] (See, e.g., Winick, 2002, p. 538, discussing current conditions in facilities in Hungary, and concluding that they are "reminiscent of the state of American mental health facilities thirty-five or more years ago," and see also id.: "many diagnosed as mentally disabled are permanently institutionalized in Hungarian psychiatric facilities, although perhaps 50% of them could live safely in the community with suitable care"; see generally, Perlin et al., 2006a, pp. 844–846.) Again, according to Richard Bonnie: "Notwithstanding the 1992 mental health legislation, coercive psychiatry remains largely unregulated and shaped by the same tendencies toward hyperdiagnosis and overreliance on institutional care that characterized the communist era" (Bonnie, 2002, p. 142).

"selective" process "mainly based on political consideration and administrative procedure," see Zhu, 2010, p. 499.

[27] See http://www.ukgaynews.org.uk/Archive/2005sept/2201.htm (finding that Russia discriminated against a potential employee by characterizing his homosexuality as a "mental disorder").

Subsequent revelations make clear that this is not simply a relic of the past (see Finn, 2006).[28]

V. Sanism and Pretextuality

We cannot underestimate the extent of our societal blindness to the ongoing violations of international human rights law in the context of the institutional commitment and treatment of persons with mental disabilities. Notwithstanding a robust set of international law principles, standards, and doctrines—most based on American constitutional law decisions and statutory reforms of the past three decades (Perlin, 2006a, chapter 2), and on the recent ratification of the CRPD (see infra chapter 7)—people with mental disabilities live in some of the harshest conditions that exist in any society (see, e.g., Mental Disability Rights International reports cited supra chapter 1; infra chapter 5; Rosenthal et al., 2002). As previously noted, these conditions are the product of neglect, lack of legal protection against improper and abusive treatment, and primarily, the social attitudes of sanism and pretextuality (see supra chapter 2).

As I will discuss in the next chapter, an examination of comparative mental disability law revealed at least five dominant, universal, core factors that reflect "the shame that the worldwide state of mental disability law brings to all of us who work in this field. Each is tainted by the pervasive corruption of sanism that permeates all of mental disability law. Each reflects a blinding pretextuality that contaminates legal practice in this area" (Perlin, 1999, p. 26). This same sanism is, in great part, to blame for the societal disinterest that allows the conditions discussed here to fester.[29]

The recently ratified United Nations Convention on the Rights of Persons with Disabilities (see infra chapter 7) gives, in those nations that have ratified it, "disability rights organizations a specific tool for promoting human rights for persons with disabilities in domestic contexts and to their own government" (Degener & Quinn, 2002, p. 18). That Convention may not necessarily be a full palliative for the problems discussed in this chapter, but it would certainly be a step in the right direction. See Perlin (2009, pp. 493–494):

---

[28] An Article published soon after the dissolution of the Soviet bloc had warned presciently that "it will be a long time before the modernization of psychiatric practice in Eastern Europe takes place." Neumann, 1991, p. 1386.

[29] (1) Lack of comprehensive legislation to govern the commitment and treatment of persons with mental disabilities, and failure to adhere to legislative mandates; (2) Lack of independent counsel and lack of consistent judicial review mechanisms made available to persons facing commitment and those institutionalized; (3) A failure to provide humane care to institutionalized persons; (4) Lack of coherent and integrated community programs as an alternative to institutional care, and (5) Failure to provide humane services to forensic patients. See Perlin, 2006a, chapter 8; see Chapter 5 infra.

> The convention opens up for reconsideration the full panoply of issues discussed in this article as they relate to persons with mental disabilities. If, by way of example, rules of evidence and procedure create an environment that perpetuates the sort of sanism and pretextuality that has had such a negative impact on the lives of persons with mental disabilities and that condones teleological judicial behavior through over-reliance on cognitive-simplifying heuristics, then a strong argument could be made that these rules must be recrafted in the context of the convention.

VI. Unanswered Questions

In their analysis of the Russian experience, Bonnie and Polubinskaya summed up their findings in this manner:

> At bottom, the human rights problem raised by these prosecutions is the criminalization of dissent; repression of dissent is problematic whether the dissenter is sent to jail or to a psychiatric hospital. However, it would be a mistake to regard the hospitalization of dissidents as only a derivative problem. To hospitalize a dissenter who is not mentally ill on grounds of non-imputability combines repression with moral fraud and magnifies the violation of human rights; it demeans the dissenter's dignity, devalues his or her message and establishes the legal authority for an indeterminate period of what can only be called psychiatric punishment. (Bonnie & Polubinskaya, 2002, p. 282)

What is clear now is that the heroic exposés discussed in this chapter—while having a major impact on the political use of psychiatry in Russia and the Soviet bloc nations—have not solved many of the underlying problems. As Robin Munro's work teaches us, political dissidents and outsiders in China still face punishment in the guise of psychiatric hospitalization. And, moreover, the amelioration of conditions in Russia, while certainly more than cosmetic, have done little or nothing to improve the plight of those persons institutionalized for nonpolitical reasons in many of the former Soviet bloc nations (Lewis, 2002, pp. 293–294). I believe that the universality of sanism is, in large part, responsible for this situation. In short, the publicity and attention that focused on the political misuses of state psychiatry resulted in discrete amelioration in one area (the treatment of psychiatric "political prisoners" in Russia). But this amelioration did not extend to: (1) "political prisoners" elsewhere, and, (2) nonpolitical residents of state psychiatric facilities in these same nations.

Having said this, I believe that this overview leaves many unanswered questions. I will briefly address them in the hopes that they will now be added to others' research agendas. First, has the political use of psychiatry been limited to nations with a history of totalitarian governments? It should not surprise anyone that there is also a history of such political use of psychiatry in the United States against important political and cultural figures. Ezra Pound, Alger Hiss, General Walker, and others were removed from public prominence through hospitalization (Alexander, 1993, p. 1475; Robitscher, 1980, pp. 104–109). Were cases like this sui generis, or are they more typical than might be expected? Notes Professor Alexander on this point: "There are a number of other cases of politically prominent figures who were disposed of behind the bars of institutions but, as in the other forms of alleged madness, the bulk of those disposed of have been relatively powerless" (Alexander, 1993, p. 1475). The hands of the authorities in the United States have, historically, been far from clean.

Second, If the excesses described by Professors Bonnie and Polubinskaya have substantially ceased, do admissions to psychiatric institutions in the former Soviet Union now comport with due process? A relatively recent case in the Soviet Republic of Karelia suggests that this is far from so (see http://www.mdac.info/news_reports/news_reports.htm, Perlin, 2006a, pp. 92–93 (discussing case)). There, a local court found that a patient, one who had spent nearly two months in the hospital after being coerced to sign a "voluntary" consent form,[30] had been denied her statutory right to appear before the court in person, contrary to local law (Article 34 of Law on Psychiatric Care; Article 304 of The Civil Code of the Russian Federation). A contemporaneous report of the Mental Disability Advocacy Center concluded that "people with mental health problems in Russia endure humiliating and degrading treatment regarding access to and use of toilet facilities in psychiatric institutions, [and that] facilities . . . provided to patients suffer such a lack of privacy that patients experience extreme anxiety and humiliation having to endure such conditions" (Perlin, 2006a, p. 93, discussing case). Lawyers from the Mental Disability Advocacy Center have appealed to the UN Special Rapporteur on Torture and the UN Working Group on Arbitrary Detention to intervene in the case of Pavel Shtukaturov, who, they allege, is being involuntarily detained, denied the right to meet with his attorney, and is apparently being punished and intimidated by hospital authorities for applying to the European Court of Human Rights (e-mail from Oliver Lewis, legal director, MDAC, February 28, 2006). The earlier problems, plainly, have not been resolved.[31] As Bonnie

[30] On the question of whether "voluntary" admissions are, in fact, voluntary, see 1 Perlin, 1998a, § 2C-7.2, pp. 482–483.

[31] See also, e.g., http://www.mdac.info/documents/PR_RuAppealCourt_20051216_eng.pdf, 2006 ("Russian Appeal Court Declares State's Denial to Provide Services to Children with Disabilities Unlawful"); http://www.mdac.info/documents/PR_SvRussia_20050804_eng.pdf, 2006 (challenge to Russia's guardianship system before European Court of Human Rights); http://www.mdac.info/MEDIA+RELEASE+06.11.2007 (how people in Russia considered incapable of making certain decisions have their right to make almost all decisions withdrawn by the

concludes, "The challenge of mental health reform in Russia and the other former Soviet states is a daunting one" (Bonnie, 2002, p. 142).

Third, each year, China becomes more and more important to the world's economy. What impact has that had—and will it have—on the conditions Professor Munro describes? Some of the serious problems raised in Munro's article still persist (see, e.g., LaFreniere, 2010, discussing the current state of conditions in Chinese institutions). Bonnie, for one, is pessimistic about the likelihood of ameliorative reform, in large part because of what he perceives as Western disinterest: "In the case of China, the international community does not appear to be willing to press the regime on human rights, and therefore the path toward ending political abuse will not be through political liberalization" (Bonnie, 2002, pp. 142–143).[32] An exposé in the *New York Times* tells us that the use of state psychiatry as a tool of political repression continues unabated in China (Kahn, 2006).[33] In short, this problem has not disappeared.

Fourth, if all nations provided top-flight legal services to persons institutionalized because of mental disability, would these problems disappear?[34] The development of mental disability law in the United States tracks—inexorably and almost absolutely—the availability of appointed counsel to persons facing commitment to psychiatric institutions, to those being treated in such institutions, and to those seeking release from such institutions (1 Perlin, 1998a, § 2B-1 to §2B-15, pp. 191–292). Without the availability of such counsel, it is virtually impossible to imagine the existence of the bodies of involuntary civil commitment law, right to treatment law, right to refuse treatment law, or any aspect of forensic mental disability law that are now taken for granted (see, e.g., Perlin, 2000e, chapter 3; 2006a, chapter 2). Similarly, especially in the area of involuntary civil commitment law, the presence of regular and ongoing judicial review has served as a bulwark of protection against arbitrary state action (1 Perlin, 1998a, § 2B-12, pp. 271–73, and see MDAC Report, 4.1.2 §. ii, Lack of Clear Procedures for Judicial Review of Involuntary Civil Commitment Applications ["reporting on lack of periodic review of commitment findings in Kyrgyz Republic"]).

---

imposition of guardianship); http://www.mdac.info/MEDIA+RELEASE+21.08.2007 (reporting on case involving the forcible detention and involuntary medication in Russia of journalist who had written story criticizing psychiatric treatment of children in that nation).

[32] Rather, he sees Chinese psychiatry as the key to amelioration: "Instead, the only available path, in the short term, is through, Chinese psychiatry, using the collegial pressure of international psychiatric and medical organizations." Id.

[33] "Dutch psychiatrists have determined that a prominent Chinese dissident who spent 13 years in a police-run psychiatric institution in Beijing did not have mental problems that would justify his incarceration, two human rights groups said Thursday." Id.

[34] I discuss this issue in more depth infra chapter 8.

Put simply, none of these protections—accessible, free counsel, and regular judicial review—is present in most of the world's mental disability law systems (see infra chapter 5). It is rare for even minimal access to counsel to be statutorily (or judicially) mandated, and, even where counsel is legislatively ordered, it is rarely provided (Perlin, 2007, 2008). Moreover, the lack of meaningful judicial review makes the commitment hearing system little more than a meretricious pretext. The task, as Professor Bonnie has indicated, is "daunting" (Bonnie, 2002, p. 142), and the absence of these safeguards suggests that promises of authentic reform may, in practice, still be largely illusory. The United Nations Convention on the Rights of Persons with Disabilities obligates all state parties "[t]o adopt all appropriate legislative, administrative and other measures for the implementation of the rights recognised [*sic*] in the present Convention" (Art. 12). The extent to which this obligation is honored will reveal much about the Convention's ultimate "real world" impact (Perlin, 2007, p. 339).

Fifth, to what extent do these issues "matter" to the political leaders of the nations in question, and to what extent is it likely that the attitudes of such leaders are likely to change? The revelations of the misuse of state psychiatry in Russia attracted local and world attention in the years soon after the dissolution of the former Soviet Union. The report by Mental Disability Rights International (2005) excoriating Turkey for its "barbaric" widespread use of electroconvulsive or "shock" treatment (ECT) on psychiatric patients—as young as 9 years old—without the accompanying use of anesthesia has come to be an issue the debate over that nation's application to become a member of the European Union (see "European Union Calls on Turkey to Improve Rights of People with Mental Disabilities," 2006), and that application has given some transitory leverage to those disability rights groups that seek to have such practices banned[35] (see infra chapter 5; on how desire to share in

---

[35] See http://www.mdri.org/projects/turkey/MDRI_EU_PressRelease.pdf, 2006:

> It is extremely important that the EU has raised concerns about the human rights of people with disabilities in Turkey," said Eric Rosenthal, Executive Director of Mental Disability Rights International. "Abuses that take place behind the closed doors of institutions are all too often overlooked by the public and international oversight bodies. By raising these concerns, the EU report ensures that egregious abuses against children and adults with mental disabilities will be taken into account as Turkey applies for EU accession.

See also, Smith, 2005, available at http://www.nytimes.com/2005/09/29/international/europe/29turkey.html?_r=1:

> The report, by Mental Disability Rights International, an advocacy group based in Washington, is likely to complicate the EU talks because many European officials are already wary of letting Turkey join the Union and will use any evidence that the country falls short of European standards to argue against its membership. But the authors of the report hope that the pressure will bring a quick end to the worst abuses. "We realized Turkey was a great opportunity for

EU economic incentives may lead to greater acceptance of human rights, see Stacy, 2009, pp. 118–123).

These examples aside, however, this issue certainly does not appear high on the agenda of the most pressing social issues in the nations discussed in this book, notwithstanding the fact that many of these practices (if not all) appear to be gross violations of international human rights (Perlin et al., 2006a, see infra chapter 8). The early works by Professor Alexander (Alexander, 1993, 1997), the exposés by Munro (2000) and by Bloch and Reddaway (1977, 1984, 1985), the research by Bonnie (alone [1990, 1994, 2002] and with Polubinskaya, 1999), and later work (still very much ongoing) by MDRI and MDAC have performed a remarkable public service in highlighting these abuses and carefully demonstrating how these nations in question, consistently and unremittingly, have violated (and continue to violate) international law.

VII. Conclusion

The two topics on which I have focused in this chapter—the political use of state psychiatry and the wretched conditions in which "nonpolitical" individuals are held and treated in state psychiatric facilities (see infra chapter 5)—cannot be understood as two discrete and unrelated issues. They are connected in very important ways, and it is critical that we understand that connection.

The Russian state (and other Soviet bloc nations) used (and China continues to use) state psychiatry as a means of silencing dissidents for multiple reasons: so as to allow the state to circumvent the (minimal) procedural safeguards that would have to attend a criminal trial; to allow for indefinite confinement, and to stigmatize and thus discredit potential political threats (Bloch & Reddaway, 1985, p. 152). The very same states treat patients in public psychiatric hospitals in ways that utterly fail to meet minimal standards of human decency, and that violate the MI Principles by means that avoid procedural safeguards (as to fair hearing and periodic review; see, e.g., cases cited in Gostin & Gable, 2004; Rosenthal & Sundram, 2002) and freely perpetuate these actions because the persons who are institutionalized are stigmatized as a result of their mental illness—the inevitable end-product of sanism—and are thus discredited as human beings.

Although these motivations may not be "political" (in the sense that—other than in China—those being mistreated are not necessarily identified as political dissidents or dissenters), the outcome of state action is political in

---

using that process to have some influence," said Eric Rosenthal, Mental Disability Rights International's founder.

that it reflects the state's failure to take seriously the human rights of persons whom it has institutionalized because of mental illness. The exposé of the unregulated use of ECT in Turkey (and the impact of that exposé on Turkey's aspirations to European Union membership) show us that mistreatment of the nonpolitical remains, at its core, a political act.[36]

[36] See Geisinger & Stein, 2008, p. 1136, n. 18 (citations omitted):

> For example, in response to a report from Mental Disability Rights International detailing Turkey's routine use of unanesthetized electroshock "therapy" on children with intellectual disabilities, the Council of Europe conditioned its future favorable view to Turkey's ascension to the European Union on compliance with Turkey's existing international obligations to refrain from torture.

5

The Universal Factors

An examination of comparative mental disability law reveals that there are at least five dominant, universal, core factors that must be considered carefully in any evaluation of the key question of whether international human rights standards have been violated (see Perlin, 2007). Each of these five factors is a reflection of the shame that the worldwide state of mental disability law brings to all of us who work in this field. Each is tainted by the pervasive corruption of sanism that permeates all of mental disability law. Each reflects a blinding pretextuality that contaminates legal practice in this area (See supra chapter 2).

In this chapter, I will discuss each of these universal factors, and offer examples from selected regions of the world. These examples will come primarily not from case law and sophisticated jurisprudential analyses as we might find in other substantive areas of the law (in good part, because there is so little case law and sophisticated analysis to be found), but from reports done by trailblazing advocacy agencies and NGOs that have done such heroic work in this area.

I. An Overview

The state of mental disability law in many parts of the world today[1] reveals a pattern and practice of ongoing abuses that is "reminiscent of the state of

[1] The situation is somewhat less problematic in parts of Western Europe and in Israel. See e.g., Heyer, 2002; Geist, Petermann & Widhammer, 2003; Rössler,

American mental health facilities 35 or more years ago" (Winick, 2002, p. 538). Early institutional rights cases in the United States revealed persistent and pervasive mistreatment of persons with mental disabilities (see generally, Perlin, 1999). As recently as 1958, state hospitals were characterized by the president of the American Psychiatric Association as "bankrupt beyond remedy" (Solomon, 1958, p. 7, as quoted in Perlin, 2007, p. 335). Three years later, a witness testified at a Congressional hearing that "[s]ome [state hospital] physicians I interviewed frankly admitted that the animals of nearby piggeries were better housed, fed and treated than many of the patients on their wards" (Constitutional Rights Hearing, 1961, pp. 40–42 [statement of Albert Deutsch], quoted in Perlin et al., 1995, p. 97). When the chairman of the legal action committee of the National Association of Retarded Children (now The ARC) characterized the Pennhurst State School[2] as "Dachau, without ovens" (Lippmann & Goldberg, 1973, p. 17, quoted in Perlin, 1991, p. 100 n. 215), there was never any accusation of exaggeration.

And so it is elsewhere today.[3] A 2002 report on conditions in social care homes in Hungary bears witness:

> These abuses include the use of locked bed cages in Hungarian psychiatric facilities, also known as net beds, in which patients are

---

Salize & Riecher-Rösser, 1996 (Germany); Ales, 2003; Burti & Benson, 1996 (Italy); Wallsten & Kjellin, 2004; Garpenby, 1993; Kjellin, Östman & Östman, 2008; Stefansson & Hansson, 2001 (Sweden); Fallberg, 2000 (Nordic nations); Puttkonen & Vollm, 2007; Hakkinen & Lehto, 2005; Kaltiala-Heino & Välimäki, 2002 (Finland); Bauer et al., 2007; Aviram, 2007 (Israel); Mulder et al., 2008 (Netherlands). For regional considerations, see, e.g., Dawson & Kämpf, 2006; Kallert, Rymaszewska & Torres-Gonzalez, 2007; Legemaate, 1995; Dressing & Salize, 2006. For a comparison of Sweden to Australia, see Sahlin, 2008.

It should be noted that these regions are not totally without problems. Finland, by way of example, has been studied extensively. See, e.g., Korkeila et al., 2002 (on heavy use of restraints in certain areas); Kartiala-Heino, 2000 (same); Kaltiala-Heino & Fröjd, 2007, p. 92 (in case of institutionalized juveniles, on need to balance "right to self-determination, right to be protected and cared for, and need for treatment"); Kokonnen, 1993 (on ways to improve legal protections); Välimäki et al., 2009 (on enforcement of patients' right to complain about their treatment). See also, Lindqvist, 2007 (on need for more training in dealing with substance abusers with mental disorder exhibiting violent behavior) (Sweden).

[2] *Pennhurst State Sch. & Hosp.* v. Halderman (1981)(Developmental Disabilities Bill of Rights Act [42 U.S.C. § 6010] merely a federal/state grant program; neither the right to treatment nor the least restrictive alternative sections of the bill of rights was enforceable in private action); *Pennhurst State Sch. & Hosp.* v. Halderman (1984) (Eleventh Amendment bars federal relief due to federalism concerns in right-to-community services case).

[3] See generally, WHO-AIMS, 2009a, p. 94 ("Perhaps partly due to the lack of updated mental health legislation, human rights activities are very limited in [low and middle income countries]."

> restrained at night, and perhaps for periods during the day. They include the use of unmodified electroconvulsive therapy administered for punitive purposes. They also include the isolation of patients in overcrowded social care homes located in rural areas, thereby cutting off patients from people in their communities. They include as well abusive practices by guardians, who instead of seeking to promote the best interests of their wards, commit them to these isolated social care facilities on a "voluntary" basis.
>
> Many facilities offer unsanitary living conditions containing rooms that smell of urine and feces. Patients lack privacy, living in rooms that are incapable of being locked. They lack conjugal rights. Their ability to communicate with those outside is highly restricted or forbidden altogether, and both incoming and outgoing mail is opened by facility staff. Phone calls are either limited or not permitted. These facilities do not offer adequate medical or dental care for their patients. Patients frequently remain uninformed concerning their rights and often lack the ability to complain about their treatment. (Winick, 2002, pp. 537–538)[4]

In some parts of the world, these conditions are fatalistically accepted (Alem, 2000, p. 94, as quoted in Fischer, 2005, p. 183). By way of further example, Uruguayan researchers were told by hospital officials that informing patients about their treatment would be logistically difficult and would actually worsen the patients' conditions (MDRI Uruguay Report, 1995, p. 41; Fischer, 2005, p. 184). Although the Iron Curtain has long ago fallen, "[i]n some countries, prosecutors still retain the Stalin-esque power to order detention in a psychiatric institution without prior medical opinion" (Lewis, 2002a, p. 295; see generally, chapter 4).[5]

Reflect again on the American experience. There has been a major revolution over the past 40 years that has, on many levels, transformed U.S.-based public mental health care (Perlin, 2002a, p. 423; see supra chapter 3). The question to consider is this: Can and will these transformational experiences be replicated elsewhere?[6] These are the five core factors that we must examine.

---

[4] A report on Argentina revealed a similar pattern of gross human rights abuses (MDRI Argentina Report, 2007).

[5] On practices in Lithuania, see Birmontiene, 1996. In Latvia, see Erdmane et al., 2009. In the Baltic States in general, see UNICEF, 2005· In Russia, see Jenkins et al., 2010b. In Ukraine, see Phillips, 2009. Practices in central and eastern Europe are compared to practices in Africa in Bartlett, 2010.

[6] Professor Winick believes that this replication has already begun:

> In some ways, the American experience is now being replicated in Eastern Europe. As discussed above, see supra chapter 1, organizations, such as Mental Disability Rights International and Mental Disability Advocacy Center are

II. The Core Factors[7]

A. Core Factor #1: Lack of Comprehensive Legislation to Govern the Commitment and Treatment of Persons with Mental Disabilities, and Failure to Adhere to Legislative Mandates

A relatively recent report by the World Health Organization (WHO) revealed that 25% of all nations in the world have no mental health law (Press Release, WHO, 2005, reprinted in Perlin et al., 2006a, p. 846; see also, de Almeida & Horvitz-Lennon, 2010 [same statistics for Latin America and Caribbean nations]). "In Ethiopia, for example, there is no mental health legislation and involuntary hospitalization and treatment only requires informed consent from the escort bringing the individual to the hospital" (Alem, 2000, p. 95).[8] A more recent study of 12 European and Western nations found that only half of those had a specific mental health act, and that none of the existing acts used "current psychiatric terminology" (Rymaszewska & Dabrowski, 2005, reprinted in Perlin et al., 2006a, p. 849). Before 1988, neither the USSR nor many of the other Soviet bloc nations had enacted any mental health laws (Appelbaum, 1998. See also, e.g., Policy Brief, 2008 [64% of African nations have no mental health legislation or have legislation that is outdated]; Okasha, 2003 [most African nations have no mental health policies]; Trivedi, Narang

---

> championing the rights of those with mental illness in these countries, dramatizing the existence of abuses and asserting their rights in the courts. Thus, we are seeing the beginning of a transformation of mental health law in Eastern Europe from a medical to a legal model. (Winick, 2002, p. 539. See also, Waterstone, 2004)

[7] It should be emphasized that there are many other issues beyond these "core factors" that are universal. One of these, otherwise beyond the scope of this book, is the issue of the treatment of persons with mental illness who are in immigration detention facilities, facing deportation, or asserting refugee status after displacement. See, e.g., Chacón, 2010; Phillimore & Goodson, 2008; Mahtani, 2003; Shivji, 2010; Watters & Ingleby, 2004.

[8] See also, Alhamad, 2006, p. 76 ("Most Arab countries have no clearly defined and written mental health act"); Connelly, 2009, p. 140 ("Cambodia has no legislation that addresses mental health or mental disability"). In Somaliland, there are no health statistics (or mental health statistics) available at all. Sheriff et al., 2010. Among WHO member states in Africa, 33 spend less than $50 per capita per year on *all* health care. Jenkins et al., 2010a. Issues are confounded by ongoing displacement and migration. See Stoll & Johnson, 2007. On the perception there of disability as an "incurable illness," see Helander, 1995 (Somalia). On the perception of epilepsy as "punishment for sin or the incarnation of an evil spirit or the result of witchcraft," see Whyte, 1995 (Tanzania).

On efforts to rebuild the mental health system in Iraq, see Kammel, 2008. On practices in India, see Babu, 2004; Reddy & Chandrasekhar, 1998.

& Dhyan, [one-third of South Asian nations have no mental health legislation]).[9]

On a site visit to Estonia, in December 2000, done in conjunction with the Estonian Psychiatric Patients Advocacy Association, I asked administrators of the psychiatric hospital in Tallinn (the nation's capital) for a copy of the Estonian mental health law. No one knew where it could be found.[10]

Other nations' mental health laws are incomplete, outmoded, or unclear.[11] The 1999 Psychiatric Care Law of the Kyrgyz Republic has no "definitions" section (Vardanyan et al., 2004, § 4.1.1).

> In a [WHO] study of Costa Rica, Honduras, Nicaragua, and Panama, researchers found that in practice most compulsory psychiatric hospitalizations had no approval by a judge regardless of the laws of the country and that no patient was entitled to refuse treatment" (Fischer, 2005, p. 183). In the Kyrgyz Republic, again, the 1999 law "lacks any provisions mandating the reporting and investigation of alleged patient abuse and/or neglect at psychiatric facilities. (Vardanyan et al., 2004, § 4.1.3)[12]

Elsewhere in the same law, the term "emergency case"—discussed in an article on psychiatric decision-making in cases—is never defined (Vardanyan et al., 2004, § 4.1. On a site visit to Nicaragua, a colleague and I were shown the Nicaraguan mental health law which, in its entirety, was one brief paragraph [Ley No. 202, 1995]).[13]

---

[9] For a radically different view, see Szmukler & Holloway, 1998› urging the elimination of mental health legislation in the United Kingdom, arguing that such legislation "reinforces discriminatory stereotypes" (id., p. 664). Although their arguments are powerful, I believe they fall short of the mark in any discussion of practices in nations with developing economies and nations with authoritarian regimes or heritages. See infra this chapter, and supra chapter 4.

[10] The Estonian Soviet Socialist Republic Mental Health Act can now be found online. Psühhiaatrilise abi seadus [Mental Health Act] (Est.), available at http://www.legaltext.ee/text/en/X1050K3.htm (last visited Jan. 25, 2007).

[11] On the exclusion of persons with disabilities from a role in making disability legislative policy, see Lang & Murangira, 2009) (discussing seven African nations).

[12] The law should be amended to include mandatory reporting and investigation of alleged patient abuse and neglect provisions. Reporting and investigating allegations of patient abuse and neglect is a key element in ensuring that abusive and/or negligent staff will be identified and disciplined or have their employment terminated, as is appropriate. These requirements also serve to stop and prevent patient abuse and neglect. Id.

[13] In Turkey, by way of another example, there are, in the Turkish Civil Code, several general principles concerning admission to psychiatric hospital and treatment of institutionalized persons with mental illness, but "everyday practice has been largely free of statutory regulation." See Arikan et al., 2007, p. 30.

The United Nations Convention on the Rights of Persons with Disabilities (CRPD) obligates all state parties "[t]o adopt all appropriate legislative, administrative and other measures for the implementation of the rights recognised in the present Convention" (CRPD, Art. 4.1(a)). See infra chapter 7. The extent to which this obligation is honored will reveal much about the Convention's ultimate "real world" impact.[14] This is especially pressing in nations, such as the Arab states, where "eminent psychiatrists believe Arab cultures do not need a mental health act" (Alhamad, 2006, p. 76).

Often, when there are laws on the books, they are simply ignored.[15] Jennifer Fischer, in her multination analysis of the global state of right-to-refuse treatment, reports: "Although some countries require consent to treatment, hospital staff routinely ignore it, and testimony from patients and former patients indicates that staff rarely provide adequate information about the treatment" (Fischer, 2005, p. 185; see also, Lewis, 2002a, p. 295). Consider this report by Amnesty International on conditions in Romania:

> Many of the people placed in psychiatric wards and hospitals throughout the country apparently do not suffer an acute mental disorder and many do not require psychiatric treatment. Their placement in psychiatric hospitals cannot be justified by the provisions of the Law on Mental Health and they should also be considered as people who have been arbitrarily deprived of their liberty. They had been placed in the hospital on non-medical grounds, apparently solely because they could not be provided with appropriate support and services to assist them and/or their families in the community. Often, because of their disability they are more vulnerable to abuse, which apparently is not taken into consideration by hospital staff as in most places such residents were not segregated from people who have different needs for care. (Romanian Memorandum, 2004, reprinted in Perlin et al., 2006a, p. 849)

Similarly, a study of conditions in Uruguay revealed that in practice, there appears to be little or no attention paid to the mental health law. "Many patients do not have a diagnosis in their chart, nor an explanation of why they were committed in the first place. Patient records do not contain individualized treatment plans nor any medical notes reflecting physical examination or psychiatric assessment" (Moncada, 1994, p. 617, citing MDRI Preliminary Uruguay Report, 1994, p. 32).[16]

---

[14] See, e.g., Connelly, 2009, p. 153: "Cambodia [a nation with no mental health law] should ratify the Convention to spur [domestic] policymaking and legislative action."

[15] See, e.g., Kelley, 2007 (Niger).

[16] For a comprehensive study of the provision of mental health services in Central America, see WHO-AIMS, 2009b.

These conditions continue (see Roberts, 2002). As recently as October 2006, the European Human Rights Court awarded a Hungarian man a verdict of two million Hungarian forint[17] following his illegal detention for three years in a Hungarian psychiatric hospital (in a case in which a local Hungarian court failed to offer any suggestions as the reasons for his detention; Press Release, MDAC, 2006a). These violations are clearly not a "thing of the past."[18] It was not until November 2006, by way of example, that an individual from a social care institution in Hungary litigated a case and appeared in person before the EHRC (see "Man Wins," 2006).http://www.mdac.info/en/european-court-human-rights-hears-first-social-car).

Such conditions clearly violate international human rights law. Prior to the ratification of the UN Convention, Amnesty International charged that the Romanian practice "amounts to arbitrary detention and denial of fair trial rights, including Articles 9 and 14 of the International Covenant on Civil and Political Rights (ICCPR) and Articles 5 and 6 of the European Convention for the Protection of Human Rights and Fundamental Freedoms (ECHR)" (Romanian Memorandum, 2007). Oliver Lewis's study of a cluster of Eastern European nations similarly finds persistent and unrelenting violations of Article 5 of the ECHR, and notes that in many nations, public psychiatric hospital staffs are not even aware of the existence of these international human rights provisions (Lewis, 2002a, p. 295). Such findings, sadly, reflect the norms in many areas of the world.[19]

B. Core Factor #2: Lack of Independent Counsel and Lack of Consistent Judicial Review Mechanisms Made Available to Persons Facing Commitment and Those Institutionalized

The development of mental disability law in the United States tracks—inexorably and almost absolutely—the availability of appointed counsel to persons facing commitment to psychiatric institutions, to those being treated in such institutions, and to those seeking release from such institutions (see 1Perlin, 1998, § 2B-2, pp. 192–195; see generally infra chapter 8). Without the availability of such counsel, it is virtually impossible to imagine the existence

---

[17] This is the equivalent of $8,805.91 (USD), as of June 21, 2010. See Quick Currency Converter, http://www.xe.com/).

[18] See also Press Release, Mental Disability Advocacy Center, EU Opens Door to Bulgaria, Disabled People Shut in Institutions, Victim Seeks Justice at European Court (Oct. 4, 2006), discussed in Perlin, 2007, p. 340, n. 38 (reporting on a case brought in the European Court of Human Rights by MDAC on behalf of a Bulgarian individual detained and medicated against his will in a local hospital notwithstanding the opinion of five psychiatrists who recommended outpatient treatment) [hereinafter Bulgarian Case]. See also supra chapter 4 (other references to MDAC cases in Russia).

[19] For a comprehensive survey of admission practices in European Union states, see Dressing & Salize, 2004.

of the bodies of involuntary civil commitment law, right to treatment law, right to refuse treatment law, or any aspect of forensic mental disability law that are now taken for granted (see 1 Perlin, 1998, chapter 2; 1999, 2 Perlin, 2000, chapter 3; 4 Perlin, 2002b, chapters 8–9). Similarly, especially in the area of involuntary civil commitment law, the presence of regular and ongoing judicial review has served as a bulwark of protection against arbitrary state action (see 1 Perlin, 1998, see supra chapter 2).

Put simply, neither of these protections—accessible, free counsel and regular judicial review—is present in most of the world's mental disability law systems.[20] It is rare for even minimal access to counsel to be statutorily (or judicially) mandated, and, even where counsel is legislatively ordered, it is rarely provided. Moreover, the lack of meaningful judicial review makes the commitment hearing system little more than a meretricious pretext. As recently as three years ago, the chair of the National Human Rights Commission on Korea was able to write, without fear of contradiction, that the Korean legal community "has not shown the slightest interests" in the pattern of "grave injustice [in the national psychiatric institutionalization] system" (Ahn, 2007, p. 1).

Again, the Kyrgyz Republic provides an instructive example. The 1999 Psychiatric Care Law of the Kyrgyz Republic does not specifically provide for appointing counsel in involuntary civil commitment proceedings (Vardanyan et al., 2004, § 4.1.2. i). As the Mental Disability Advocacy Center (MDAC) report on that nation indicates:

> The right to an attorney is essential to ensure that the rights of the patient are protected in the involuntary civil commitment process. It is not enough to have legislation that allows an individual to instruct an attorney to represent them, as many are simply unable to pay for an attorney. The law should be modified to clearly state that an individual who is subject to the involuntary commitment process has a right to representation by an attorney and if they cannot afford it, an attorney will be provided to them free of charge. (Id., § 4.1.2. i , footnote omitted)

---

[20] Writing about this topic two years ago, I noted: "The only non-U.S.-based evidence I could find in the literature, of a hospital administration urging the extended appointment of counsel in civil commitment cases, is from Israel" (Perlin, 2008, p. 251; see Bauer et al., 2005; Bauer et al., 2007). On "cause lawyering" in Israel, see Woods, 2005. On the implications of Israel's activist judiciary, see Salzberger, 2008. On the uniqueness of Israel's "mixed" legal system, see Kedar, 2007. On the need for participants in Israel's mental health system to "become more professional and better trained," see Toib, 2006, p. 204. Israel's mental health legislation is an amalgam of Ottoman, Turkish, British, and Jewish sources (Barak & Gordon, 2002).

See also Gostin, 1987, p. 360 ("It is a basic jurisprudential principle that all people are entitled to a full and impartial judicial hearing prior to a loss of liberty").

The UN convention mandates that "States Parties shall take appropriate measures to provide access by persons with disabilities to the support they may require in exercising their legal capacity" (CRPD, Art. 12.3).[21] The extent to which this Article is honored in signatory nations will have a major impact on the extent to which this entire Convention "matters" to persons with mental disabilities.

The absence of judicial review is stark, and it is here that the gap between law-on-the-books and law-in-action is the starkest. See supra chapter 4 (IV). Putting aside those jurisdictions in which there is not even a written promise of judicial review (see, e.g., Vardanyan et al., 2004, § 4.1.4, "There are simply no provisions in the 1999 Psychiatric Care Law for judicial review"), in many of those nations where judicial review appears to be mandated by statute, it in fact does not exist (Lewis, 2002a, p. 295).[22] Writing about this recently from the Uganda perspective, Professor Ben Twinomugisha concluded, "The power of judicial review not only fits into a democratic society but also helps protect democracy and human rights" (2009, p. 8).

Elsewhere, Oliver Lewis tells us that "[m]ainstreaming 'mental disability rights' into our regular human rights agenda is a crucial step towards thinking seriously about protecting the rights of people with mental disabilities" (Lewis, 2002b, p. 316). It is impossible to fulfill this aspiration unless counsel is regularly provided and meaningful judicial review is instituted.[23]

C. Core Factor #3: A Failure to Provide Humane Care to Institutionalized Persons

The justification for the entire enterprise of inpatient psychiatric hospitalization rests on one thin reed: that meaningful, ameliorative individualized

---

[21] Elsewhere, the Convention commands:

> States Parties shall ensure effective access to justice for persons with disabilities on an equal basis with others, including through the provision of procedural and age appropriate accommodations, in order to facilitate their effective role as direct and indirect participants, including as witnesses, in all legal proceedings, including at investigative and other preliminary stages. (CPRD, Art. 13.1)

[22] And see id.:

> After a person has been detained by a psychiatrist, most countries' legislation provide for a review by a judge, as required by Article 5(4) ECHR, which provides that "[e]veryone who is deprived of his liberty . . . shall be entitled to take proceedings by which the lawfulness of detention shall be decided speedily by a court and his release ordered if the detention is not lawful." However, no country in the region is in compliance with Article 5(4).

[23] For a survey of litigation in the ECHR under the UK's Human Rights Act (a universe of 192 cases at the time of the conclusion of the research), see Bindman, Maingay & Szmukler, 2003.

treatment is available at the facility to which the individual has been committed, and that that treatment is logically geared to improving the individual's condition so that optimally he can be released (*Wyatt v. Stickney*, 1972).

The international record of providing such treatment is, to be charitable, abysmal. Nearly 30 years ago, researchers noted that deinstitutionalization, outside the United States, "has proceeded considerably more slowly" (Goldman, Morrisey & Bachrach, 1983, p. 154). The examples discussed later in this section underscore that, in much of the world, there has been little improvement since then (see WHO-AIMS, 2009a, p. 94, [majority of nations participating in World Health Organization study reported having no inspection of their mental hospitals or community-based inpatient units]).

The CRPD furthers the human rights approach to disability, and recognizes the right of people with disabilities to equality in most every aspect of life (Dhir, 2005). It calls for "respect for inherent dignity" (CRPD, Art. 3(a)), and "non-discrimination" (id., Art. 3(b)). The quality of services made available to persons in psychiatric hospitals in much of the world is so substandard as to easily meet the "shock the conscience" standard often employed in U.S. courts in determining whether specific conditions of institutionalization violate due process and/or the cruel and unusual punishment clause of the Eighth Amendment (see, e.g., *Rochin v. California*, 1952, p. 172).[24]

Investigators discovered these "critical" conditions at Romanian hospitals:

> The majority of the patients in the women's psychiatric ward of the Tarnaveni general hospital were accommodated in 2003 in two large rooms which were kept constantly locked. There were around 100 patients in the so-called "upper locked ward" and about 50 patients in the "lower locked ward." Adjacent to the latter was the "lower locked side ward" where about 10 women with very severe disabilities were held with no access to running water and the toilet had no plumbing. Patients did not have access to basic toiletries and had only one opportunity a week to shower. All women on the wards were expected to shower within two hours when hot water was available on Fridays and no towels were provided. Staff did not ensure that women in the "lower locked ward" and "lower locked side ward" were appropriately dressed. Patients often walked around scantily clothed or naked and very few had shoes. The hospital floor was often cold and wet. In the "lower locked side ward" the floor was often covered in faeces and urine because many patients held there were incontinent. Some patients spent the entire day in urine-soaked or faeces-covered clothing and bedding. Patients did not have an adequate and varied diet. In the

[24] On the misuse and overuse of seclusion and restraint (with prevalence rates of as high as 66% in some institutions), see Sailas & Wahlbeck, 2005).

> "lower locked ward" and "lower locked side ward" the patients were made to take their meals in the dormitory area, although there was a dining area close by. They were served through a small opening in the door and were not supervised by the staff during the meal. They were not provided with cutlery and ate using their hands. Metal bowls used at mealtimes were often thrown by patients at each other, frequently resulting in injuries. (Romanian Memorandum, 2004, p. 4)

What is more, conditions continued to get worse. "Also in January 2004 the conditions had reportedly deteriorated in the psychiatric hospital in Turceni, which cares for 105 patients and residents in a crumbling, damp building, smelling of urine and filth. The patients were suffering from lice and wore pajamas that were dirty and tattered" (id., p. 5). Consider here Article 22 of the UN Convention: "No person with disabilities, regardless of place of residence or living arrangements, shall be subjected to arbitrary or unlawful interference with his or her privacy." What impact will this article have on cases that might be brought in the future to ameliorate conditions such as those described here?

Elsewhere, "cage beds" are routinely used to house patients in spite of the fact that such "treatment" (the word must be placed in quotations)[25] has been roundly condemned by the United Nations Human Rights Commission and the European Committee for the Prevention of Torture and Inhuman or Degrading Treatment or Punishment (CPT) (Press Release, 2004).[26] In the Czech Republic, researchers—led by officials of the MDAC—found "cases of individuals, including young children, kept in cage beds for practically the entire day—every day—except when they needed to use the toilet" (Press Release, 2003). These practices were subsequently decried by a member of the European Parliament who demanded abandonment of the use of such beds as a prerequisite for the Czech Republic's admission to the European Union (id., quoting Member of Parliament John Bowls. Compare Mossialos, Murthy & McDaid, 2003 [expressing fear that interests of persons with disabilities will not be given proper consideration in European Union expansion]).[27]

The use of cage beds is not limited to the Czech Republic (see Lewis, 2002a, p. 299 [discussing use of such beds in Hungary, Slovakia, and Slovenia]; see also, Gombos, 2002, pp. 363–364). The justification for their continued use is a textbook example of the way that pretextuality dominates this entire

[25] John Russell's characterization of these beds as "horrendous" (2008, p. 202) is, if anything, understated. See also, Yamin, 2003, p. 345, discussing their use in cases of children with epilepsy.

[26] See, e.g., Nowak, 2006 (on what practices constitute torture).

[27] On the issue of EU constitutionalism in the context of state constitutional traditions, see Walker, 2006.

subject matter area (see supra chapter 2; Perlin, 2007, 2009. Oliver Lewis describes an experience in Slovakia:

> The author observed the long-term use of caged beds in one Slovak home: seven women were each placed in a caged-bed for most of the day. The reasons given for using a cage bed on a 21-year-old woman with intellectual disabilities was that "she is aggressive." When asked whether it was surprising that a person caged for long periods of time would become aggressive, staff maintained that in any case she was easier to handle. The reason given for another woman's placement in a cage bed was that she had high blood pressure: "she might fall out of bed." (Lewis, 2002a, pp. 299–300; see also Goldsmith, 2004)

Conditions in South America are not so different.[28] These are the findings of Mental Disability Rights International (MDRI) on a recent investigation of the Neuro-Psychiatric Hospital of Paraguay:

> The [hospital] cells are completely bare, save for a wooden platform jutting out from the cell wall. Holes in the cell floors that should function as latrines are crammed and caked over with excrement. The cells reek of urine and feces, and the walls of the cells are smeared with excrement. Each boy spends approximately four hours of every other day in an outdoor pen, which is littered with human excrement, garbage, and broken glass. . . . [Other] conditions included:
>
> - unhygienic conditions, including the presence of open sewage, rotting garbage, broken glass, and excrement and urine on sidewalks, patios, and in wards throughout the institution;
> - sub-custodial and dangerous levels of staffing;
> - an absence of almost any treatment interactions of any kind;
> - frequent shortages of food and medicines; [and]
> - lack of medical, dental, and psychiatric support on a timely basis. (MDRI Paraguay Report, 2007)

More recently, the Inter-American Court on Human Rights granted MDRI's latest petition for emergency intervention, which exposed a series of deaths and allegations of sexual abuse occurring within the psychiatric institution. The petition cataloged egregious abuses, including four unexplained

---

[28] On the role of the Peruvian Truth and Reconciliation Commission in "put[ting] mental health on Peru's national agenda," see Laplante & Holguin, 2006, p. 137. But see, Getgen, 2009, p. 1 (exclusion of cases of forced sterilization from the Commission's scope of investigation "effectively erases State responsibility and decreases the likelihood for justice and reparations").

On the need to restructure psychiatric care in Latin America, see Levav, Restrepo & de Macedo, 2004.

deaths, numerous complaints of sexual abuse, and serious physical injuries including a castration, all within the previous six months. The IACHR decision called on the Paraguayan government to take immediate measures to protect the lives and physical safety of the persons detained in the institution and to investigate the deaths and allegations of abuse. The IACHR also called on the government to report on actions taken to investigate these abuses toward preventing reoccurrences (MDRI Paraguay Report Update, 2010; see supra chapter 3). These findings substantially track other findings made by the same NGO in Mexico five years earlier:

> At Ocaranza [a psychiatric hospital], people were penned into small areas of residential wards where they were left to sit, pace, or lie on the concrete floor all day. Without activities or attention, they rocked back and forth or self-stimulated in other ways. Some patients regularly urinated or defecated on the floor, in areas where others often sit or walk through with bare feet. Residents of Ocaranza were brought straight from this ward to the dining area without an opportunity to wash their hands or clean themselves. Those able to get to a bathroom did not have access to toilet paper. People on the ward were given medications with water from a common bucket, using one cup passed from one person to another.
>
> The children's ward at the Jalisco psychiatric facility was even worse. Children were left lying on mats on the floor, some covered with urine and feces. During both MDRI's 1998 and 1999 visits, flies were everywhere and the smell was overwhelming. Self-abuse was common and basic medical care was lacking.[29] Without adequate supervision, children were observed eating their own feces and physically abusing themselves without attention from staff. The institution does not have the behavior programs necessary to prevent children's self-abusive behavior. According to staff, some children were left completely without habilitation, self-care skills training, or activities to keep them busy. (MDRI Mexico Report, 2000)[30]

Cages, astonishingly, are also used outside of institutions. An Amnesty International investigation in Bulgaria documented women locked in a cage outside one institution. "The cage was full of urine and [feces] and the women covered in filth. One woman was unclothed on the lower half of her body and many sores were visible on her skin" (Press Release, 2001). And, on a visit to Nicaragua in 2003, I visited a home in which two mentally disabled persons

---

[29] On the right of access to medication under international law, see Yamin, 2003.

[30] See supra, Perlin, 2007, pp. 346–347, discussing my observations at a Nicaraguan mental hospital. It should be noted that hospital officials had advance knowledge that we were coming. This was in no way a surprise visit.

(aged 23 and 32) were permanently confined to outdoor rooms that were built as cages to prevent them from leaving the premises. At the time, in an interoffice memorandum, I characterized that visit as "the saddest sight of my professional life" (Perlin, 2007, p. 347).

The conditions discussed in this section "eerily reflected the conditions at Willowbrook State School in New York City when they were exposed to a stunned nation some 30 years ago by the then-fledgling investigative reporter Geraldo Rivera" (Perlin, 2002a, pp. 424–425). But it is not sufficient to say that Central and Eastern Europe, and Central and South America are simply "thirty years behind" the United States. Consider what has transpired during those 30 years:

- the United Nations General Assembly adopted the "Mental Illness Principles" (MI Principles, 1991);
- the European Court on Human Rights (ECHR) decided multiple cases reaffirming basic and fundamental rights in the commitment and institutionalization process (see Perlin et al., 2006a, pp. 451–782, discussing ECHR case law);
- mental disability–focused NGOs such as MDRI and MDAC called the world's attention to the examples of inhumane treatment discussed above (Mental Disability Advocacy Center, 2007; MDRI Paraguay Report, 2007; MDRI Argentina Report, 2007; MDRI Paraguay Report Update, 2010);[31]
- "global" NGOs such as Amnesty International have, finally (albeit tardily, and perhaps, in some cases, reluctantly) acknowledged that violations of the rights of persons institutionalized because of mental disability are, indeed, international human rights violations (e.g., Press Release, AI, 2004, 2002a, 2002b);
- The World Health Organization has published a resource book on mental health, human rights, and legislation (Perlin et al., 2006b, pp. 63–105; for criticisms of this document, see Perlin et al., 2006a, pp 891–894);[32]
- Academics and activists have begun to create theoretical frameworks through which these problems can be addressed (e.g., Lord & Stein, 2008); and
- Most recently, and most importantly, the UN Convention has been ratified. (http://www.un.org/disabilities/default.asp?id=150).

Yet, until governments of all nations authentically commit themselves to ameliorate—with transparency—conditions in public institutions, all that

[31] There are other such NGOs as well. See, e.g., "Newsletter Zelda," 2010, reporting on activities of the Resource Centre for People with Mental Disability in Latvia.

[32] For an extensive history of the World Health Organization's neglect and rediscovery of human rights, see Meier, 2010.

has transpired in courtrooms, legislatures, international human rights bodies, and the writings of scholars will amount to little more than "paper victories" (Perlin, 2002c, p. 246, quoting Lottman, p. 93, in Bradley & Clarke, 1976).[33] The extent to which these new rights are given authentic life will significantly determine whether the "victories" just referred to are more than "paper" ones (See also infra chapter 8 [on role of counsel]).

D. Core Factor #4: Lack of Coherent and Integrated Community Programs as an Alternative to Institutional Care

In 1999, the U.S. Supreme Court held, in the case of *Olmstead v. L.C.*, that the Americans with Disabilities Act (ADA, 1990) entitled plaintiffs—residents of Georgia Regional Hospital—to treatment in an integrated community setting as opposed to an unnecessarily segregated state hospital. In writing the majority opinion, Justice Ginsburg stressed that "[u]njustified isolation . . . is properly regarded as discrimination based on disability," and ordered that states be required to maintain "a comprehensive, effectively working plan for placing qualified persons with mental disabilities in less restrictive settings" (id., p. 597, pp. 605–606), thus explicitly endorsing the ADA's "integration mandate" (Perlin, 2000).

For years, U.S. litigators had sought the creation of constitutional rights to community treatment and/or aftercare, but these efforts were, ultimately, uniformly unsuccessful (Klapper, 1993),[34] although courts were not reluctant to enforce statutory provisions mandating such care (see, e.g., *Dixon v. Weinberger*, 1975, pp. 979–980 [a statutory-based decision], requiring a hospital to develop a plan for treatment of plaintiff patients in "suitable residential facilities under the least restrictive [alternative] conditions"], as discussed in Warren & Moon, 1994). The ADA, however, offered advocates new tools to use in these efforts. Although early descriptions of the ADA as an "Emancipation Proclamation" for persons with disabilities (Perlin, 2000, p. 1028) were probably overstated (see Perlin, 2007, pp. 350–51), the Supreme Court's decision in *Olmstead* did make it clear that—under U.S. federal statutory law, at least—the community integration principle was now part of the American legal fabric.[35]

---

[33] It should be clear that the vast global disparities in access to health services in general have a disproportionate impact on persons with mental disabilities. See Gostin, 2008a.

[34] But compare Ferleger, 2010 (urging a resuscitation of strategies calling for a constitutional right to community care and services).

[35] But see, Bagenstos, 2004, pp. 69–70:

> [T]he fact that disability rights activists have placed such a high priority on the enactment of legislation expanding the Medicaid program is itself telling. It reflects a recognition by disability rights activists that the ADA alone is not sufficient to achieve community integration for people with disabilities. Social welfare law remains important as well.

It is not the same everywhere.[36] The Kyrgyz investigation, again, revealed that, in that nation, there were only "three instances of out-patient care" (Vardanyan et al., 2004, § 7.2.2). Hospital authorities in Uruguay told researchers that "between one third and two thirds of the total inpatient population need not be committed but are held because they have nowhere else to go" (Moncada, 1994, p. 617).[37] In other nations, "[h]undreds of thousands of people with mental health problems, intellectual disabilities, alcohol problems, drug addiction (and people with no health problems at all, so-called 'social cases') are housed together in [large residential institutions that] have become known as 'social care homes.' . . . These are institutions from which residents are rarely discharged" (Lewis, 2002, p. 297).[38] Professors Lance Gable and Larry Gostin charge: "Many countries did not create community mental health systems to support persons who had been deinstitutionalized. In jurisdictions that have established community services, these services often remain chronically under-funded, fragmented, and punitive (2009, p. 252).[39]

Most recently, a student article has argued carefully and thoughtfully that states should abandon their current *Olmstead* implementation plans and, instead, adopt new broader strategies to provide persons with disabilities the "superior community-based care for which the Convention calls." Flynn, 2010, p. 437.

[36] For earlier considerations of the parallels between the U.S. and European experiences, see Wachenfeld, 1991, p. 131; Hollingsworth, 1992; see also Bottomley, 1987, discussing the Australian experience. For a more recent comparative approach (considering Canada, the United States, Great Britain, and Australia), see Shera et al., 2002. For a comparative approach to the concept of "reasonable accommodation," see Waddington, 2008. On the reasonable accommodation mandate and the CRPD, see e.g., Lawson, 2008; Lord & Brown, 2010. For examples of innovative Japanese community programs, see Sukegawa, 1993; Yanaka, 1993. For a consideration of conditions in India, see Cremin, 2007.

[37] These issues remain unresolved in many areas of Latin America. See PAHO, 2008'. quoting Dr. Javier Vasquez:

> "The Region laws and policies have not led to hospitalization procedures consistent with international human rights standards and conventions, and with them, the periodic review of hospitalizations by multidisciplinary bodies guaranteeing the freedom of movement and other health-related rights," Dr. Vásquez said. "In many countries, these institutions [psychiatric hospitals] continue to house large numbers of people whose freedom of movement and other rights are constrained." This is the crux of the problem," he said, since "without the exercise of personal freedom we cannot even begin to speak of other fundamental freedoms and rights.

[38] On the inadequacy of community mental health services in South Africa, see Lund et al., 2010. On the perceptions of African mental health workers of the quality of mental health services provided, see Alem, Jacobson & Hanlon, 2008. On the extreme lack of mental health resources in all South Asian nations, see Kala, 2008.

[39] See, e.g., Salize, Schanda & Dressing, 2008 (discussing potential trend toward reinstitutionalization); see also, WHO-AIMS, 2009a, p. 94 (involuntary admissions to mental hospitals more frequent than to community-based inpatient units).

When persons with disabilities are in the community, they continue to face discrimination in the job market (Tuen, 1999). Remarkably, a Hong Kong case reflected the government's position that it could lawfully reject an applicant for a public job because that person was *related to* a person with mental illness (on the theory that "such applicants cannot be trusted to perform the job safely" (Petersen, 2006, p. 249, discussing *K., Y, and W. v. The Secretary for Justice*, 2000; Perlin & Ikehara, 2010; on the potential impact of the CRPD on disability discrimination law in Hong Kong in general, see Byrnes, 2008).

There may, however, be some modest cause for optimism. First, activists and advocates have begun to sketch out legal theories through which the right to community integration may be located in international human rights law (see, e.g., Rosenthal et al., 1999 [sketching out a human rights framework for integrating children with disabilities into the community in Russia]). In their report excoriating conditions in mental institutions in Kosovo, Eric Rosenthal and Eva Szeli emphasized:

> In addition to protecting rights within institutions, international law recognizes a right to community integration. Policies that promote community integration are not just good practice to promote mental health; they have also been recognized as a right under international human rights law. Under the MI Principle 3, "[e]very person with mental illness shall have the right to live and work, as far as possible, in the community." For people in need of mental health treatment, Principle 7 recognizes that "[e]very patient shall have the right to be treated and cared for, as far as possible, in the community in which he or she lives." The right to community integration can only be limited where a person meets the formal standards for civil commitment, as set forth in Principles 15–17.
>
> The right to community integration has recently been recognized as a legal obligation under the International Covenant on Economic, Social, and Cultural Rights (ICESCR). The United Nations Committee on Economic, Social, and Cultural Rights has adopted General Comment 5, which describes the obligations of governments to protect against discrimination under the covenant. To protect against discrimination, the General Comment 5 recommends that governments adopt legislation and policies that "enable persons with disabilities to live an integrated self-determined and independent life." The General Comment goes on to make clear, by citing the U.N.'s World Programme of Action concerning Disabled Persons, that anti-discrimination laws should not only require social policies that promote community integration but that these are individual rights. Governments are required to allocate resources accordingly. Thus, the right to protection [against discrimination] implies that the needs of each

> and every individual are of equal importance, that these needs must be made the basis for the planning of societies, and that all resources must be employed in such a way as to ensure, for every individual, equal opportunity for participation. Disability policies should ensure the access of [persons with disabilities] to all community services. (Rosenthal & Szeli (2002), reprinted in Perlin et al., 2006a, pp. 874–875)

At about the same time, Eric Rosenthal and Arlene Kanter looked specifically to *Olmstead* as a source for such rights, arguing that failing to provide opportunities for people with disabilities to live in the community, rather than in institutions, may violate a broad array of recognized human rights (Rosenthal & Kanter, 2002, reprinted in Perlin et al., 2006a, pp. 875–876).[40] Drawing on the *Olmstead* reasoning, they concluded that "governments that provide services to people with disabilities exclusively in institutions, without providing meaningful alternatives in the community, may be found to violate international human rights law by providing services in a discriminatory manner" (id., p. 876).

Indeed, a wide range of international human rights documents beyond the ICESCR and the MI Principles may offer additional support of these theoretical arguments. Again, in urging that a right to community integration be articulated under international human rights standards, Rosenthal and Kanter draw on:

> References to community integration [found, variously,] in Article 23 of the Convention on the Rights of the Child, and in instruments and documents of the U.N. General Assembly such as the Declaration on the Rights of Mentally Retarded Persons, the 1991 Principles for the Protection of Persons with Mental Illness, the 1993 Standard Rules on Equalization of Opportunities for Persons with Disabilities, and General Comment 5 to the International Convention on Economic, Social and Cultural Rights, as well as in the Charter of Fundamental Rights of the European Union. (Id., p. 877).[41]

---

[40] Beyond the scope of this book are the human rights issues raised when, in the community, children are removed from the homes of adults with mental illness. See Prior, 2003.

[41] Another more recent example of an international instrument recognizing a right to community integration is the Inter-American Convention on the Elimination of All Forms of Discrimination against Persons with Disabilities, adopted by the Organization of American States (OAS). This Convention contains many important provisions, including the explicit recognition of a right to community integration. However, unlike other general human rights conventions, the OAS Convention does not create an immediate obligation on states to enforce the rights it establishes. (id., p. 879).

The time is right, they argue, for the broader application of the U.S. Supreme Court's community integration mandate, together with rights recognized in various international human rights conventions and interpretations, concluding, "[p]erhaps the time has come" (id., p. 881).

As discussed earlier (see supra chapter 3), in at least one remarkable example, the theoretical arguments discussed above appear to have been successful. MDRI and the Center for Justice and International Law (CEJIL) have signed an historic settlement with the Paraguayan government aimed at ending the improper detention of hundreds of people in the country's state-run psychiatric hospital. Filed with the Inter-American Commission on Human Rights of the Organization of American States (OAS), the settlement is the first agreement in Latin America to guarantee the rights of patients to live and receive mental health services in the community (Paraguay Settlement, 2007; see generally, Hillman, 2005).

Under the terms of this settlement,

> Paraguay must now produce a mental health reform plan to create community-based services for people who have been left to languish for decades in the locked institution. The plan will require the government to transition more than 400 patients detained in the hospital back into the community. (Paraguay Settlement, 2007)

There is an authentic concern that, unless meaningful and broad-based community-based services are established in a comprehensive manner, the litigation that has been undertaken to reform institutional conditions can not possibly have long-term value (for later developments in Paraguay, see Press Release, MDRI, 2008 [reporting on subsequent litigation]).

Consider here again Article 22 of the UN Convention: "No person with disabilities, regardless of place of residence or living arrangements, shall be subjected to arbitrary or unlawful interference with his or her privacy." What impact will this Article have on cases that might be brought in the future to ameliorate conditions such as those described here? As the above section should make clear, virtually all nations are deficient in providing community services. Think about the potential application of Article 19:

> States Parties to the present Convention recognize the equal right of all persons with disabilities to live in the community, with choices equal to others, and shall take effective and appropriate measures to facilitate full enjoyment by persons with disabilities of this right and their full inclusion and participation in the community, including by ensuring that:
>
> (a) Persons with disabilities have the opportunity to choose their place of residence and where and with whom they live on an equal basis with others and are not obliged to live in a particular living arrangement.

Professor Frederic Megret focuses on the Convention's reference to "full and effective participation and inclusion in society" as one of its main focal points (2008, p. 508). Professor Anna Lawson considers the "reasonable accommodation" mandate of the CRPD a major factor in the inclusion of persons with disabilities in "the mainstream of society" (2008, p. 80). Professor Bernadette McSherry (2008) concludes that "the Convention must be read to make available to all persons—in the community and in institutions—the highest attainable standard of mental health." Certainly, such participation and inclusion is regularly and globally denied to persons with disabilities (cf. Waterstone, 2004 [right of persons with disabilities to vote]).[42]

E. Core Factor #5: Failure to Provide Humane Services to Forensic Patients

Virtually all studies and reports referred to in this article have focused on the status (and plight) of civil patients: those whose commitments to the mental health system were not occasioned by arrest or other involvement in the criminal court process.[43] Depressingly, persons in the forensic system (see generally, Perlin & Dlugacz, 2008, 2009) receive—if this even seems possible—less humane services than do civil patients. In Australia, Professors Boyd-Caine and Chappell conclude that there is "simply no scrutiny of the [decision-making] process" (2005, p. 26 [New South Wales]; see also, Daffern, Mayer & Martin, 2003, p. 67 ["no published research on aggression in an Australian forensic psychiatric hospital exists"]; see generally, Chappell, 2004.[44] See Gostin, 2008b, pp. 911–912, discussing the "inhuman and degrading" treatment of forensic patients.[45] On the rights of persons in correctional and penal institutions under international human rights law, see Fellner, 2006;

---

[42] See, e.g., http://www.mdac.info/en/european-court-human-rights-upholds-right-vote-per (reporting on decision in which European Court of Human Rights upheld the right to vote of persons with disabilities).

[43] There is a paucity of research about forensic patients in many nations. See Njenga, 2006, p. 97 ("The practice of forensic psychiatry in Africa is shrouded in both mystery and confusion"); for a comparative consideration of sociodemographics of forensic patients in Zimbabwe and the United Kingdom, see Menezes, Oyebode & Haque, 2007; see also, e.g., Daffern, Mayer & Martin, 2003 (discussing Australia); Müller-Isberner et al., 2000 (discussing Germany). For a European overview, see Nedopil, 2009.

[44] For a rare ray of optimism, see Tellex et al., 2004 (penal reform in Chile and its impacts on forensic psychiatry have generated an increased awareness of the field and given impetus to academic development of the study and research into forensic psychiatry issues).

[45] In many nations, there are no forensic psychiatry departments in any medical school. See Alhamad, 2006.

Turner, 2008; Prior, 2007; see generally, infra chapter 6.[46] On the expected future "mushroom[ing]" of this population, see Weisstub & Carney, 2006).

Some examples are, for want of a better word, stupefying.[47] In Hungary, until relatively recently, convicted prisoners from Budapest Prison were used to "keep an eye on" patients in IMEI (Hungary's only high security forensic psychiatric institution) "with high suicide risk" (Press Release, WHO, 2005). In Albania, persons with mental disabilities who have been charged with a criminal offense reside in a prison unit and must comply with prison rules while institutionalized. "Although Albanian law stipulates one year of treatment to be followed by a re-evaluation, the average length of stay is five years" (Weinstein, 2001).

In Kyrgyz, there are no statutory provisions to deal with cases of persons who are potentially incompetent to stand trial (Vardanyan et al., 2004, § 4.2.1). As a result, persons with severe mental illness who are charged with crime have no opportunity to be treated in an effort to improve their condition so as to become competent to stand trial (compare *Jackson v. Indiana*, 1972 [unconstitutional to retain untried defendant indefinitely in maximum security forensic hospital if it is not probable he will regain his competency to stand trial in the foreseeable future]). In insanity cases, although Kyrgyz law allows for an independent evaluation of a defendant prior to trial, "legal aid attorneys [said] that they have never retained an independent expert because they have no money to do so" (Vardanyan et al., 2004, § 6.2). This right thus becomes illusory.[48]

Although, in Hungary, patients have the right to a retention hearing following a finding of nonresponsibility for a criminal act (insanity), such "[p]roceedings are over in less than 5 minutes, and the issues remain untested: similar to detention hearings under civil law, lawyers do not meet their clients or take instructions" (Lewis, 2002, p. 297). Such hearings, again, reflect the endemic pretextuality of the Hungarian mental health delivery system.[49]

---

[46] Scholars have also begun to turn their attention to comparative questions of substantive criminal law and procedure as they relate to persons with mental disabilities, especially, though not exclusively, in cases involving the death penalty. See, e.g., Guo, 2010, and Lu & Zhang, 2005 (China); Novak, 2009 (Malawi & Uganda); Fisherow, 2005 (Japan); Clack, 2003 (same); Tittemore, 2004; Morrison, 2006 (the Caribbean); Browne et al., 2006 (global considerations). These issues are generally beyond the scope of this book.

[47] In addition to the examples discussed below, see also, e.g., Menezes, Oyebode & Haque, 2007 (Zimbabwe); Nyanguru, 2000 (Lesotho); Weisstub & Carney, 2006; Nakatani et al., 2010 (Japan).

[48] On the right of a criminal defendant to an expert witness in an insanity case in the United States, see *Ake v. Oklahoma* (1985).

[49] Other examples are readily available. See, e.g., Global Initiative on Psychiatry, 1997 (Serbia).

Conclusion

To be sure, this is a bleak picture. I do not believe that the examples offered here are either unique or exceptional. Rather, I believe they are endemic to institutional mental health care around the world. There are, however, some rays of light that may lead to at least a measure of optimism in the future—the fact that groups such as Amnesty International have (albeit tardily) entered the fray, the publication of the WHO manual, the settlement of the Paraguay case, and the ratification of the UN Convention. Yet, all in all, the "bankrupt without remedy" descriptor used by the president of the American Psychiatric Association in 1958 (Solomon, 1958, p. 7, as quoted in 3 Perlin, 2002c, p. 252) could still be used to describe the state of mental disability law treatment in many countries of the world.

There is some important increased interest in this area of law and social policy. It is important to keep in mind that MDRI's and MDAC's excoriating reports, in addition to drawing the attention of scholars and policymakers to these issues, have even intruded into the political process of European Union accession.[50] By way of example, practices discovered in the Czech Republic by researchersled by officials of the MDAC (keeping children caged nearly the entire day, see supra pp. 91–92, Press Release 2004, were subsequently decried by a member of the European Parliament who demanded abandonment of the use of such beds as a prerequisite for the Czech Republic's admission to the European Union (Id., quoting Member of Parliament John Bowls; see also Press Release, MDAC, 2006; see supra chapter 4). And in the past several years, they have also been covered extensively in the mainstream media (Smith, 2005, 2006). Again, the recent publication of the UN Convention cannot help but draw political attention to these issues.[51] From the perspective of legal education, the publication of the first casebook in this area of the law (Perlin et al., 2006) will likely lead to courses about this topic being offered at more law schools, reaching future potential public interest/human rights lawyers.[52] These circumstances and combinations of factors may well lead to ameliorative changes in the nations discussed here, as well as elsewhere in the world.

---

[50] On related accession issues, see Hugg, 2010.

[51] For a recent thoughtful analysis of Uganda's mental health law from the perspective of the UN Convention, see Moses, 2007.

[52] On the relationship between international human rights law and forensic *evaluations* in the context of cultural competency, see Perlin & McClain, 2009.

6

The Application of International Human Rights Law to Mental Disability Law: Specific Contexts

Until this point in this volume, I have looked mostly at the broad, overarching issues that are relevant to the inquiry I have undertaken: a brief overview of international human rights law, a consideration of the role of regional human rights courts and commissions, the use of state psychiatry as a tool to suppress political dissent, and the universal factors present worldwide in institutional law.

At this point, I am narrowing in my focus a bit, and will examine four separate substantive issues, all of which lead us to consider the intersection between international human rights law and mental disability law through varying perspectives: law school education, the limits of expert testimony, the private law question of a psychotherapist's duty to warn, and correctional law. Although these issues appear to have little in common, my conclusion is that the same overarching factors that I have discussed previously and that I will return to in subsequent chapters—the role of sanism and pretextuality, and the importance and promise of therapeutic jurisprudence—play a major role in any analysis of these disparate issues. Although—with the modest exception of corrections law—there has been very little scholarly literature about the intersection between international human rights law and these substantive legal questions, I believe that, as time goes on (and especially in light of the ratification of the Convention on the Rights of Persons with Disabilities, see infra chapter 7), we will come to more readily see the significance of this intersection.

Chapter 6A. Law School Pedagogy

I. Law Schools, International Human Rights, and Mental Disability Law

In order for there to be any meaningful and long-lasting change in the relationship between international human rights and mental disability law, law schools throughout the world must understand the essentiality of this connection, and must adapt their curriculum so that the ideas discussed in this book become a basic part of law students' education. There has been substantial academic literature in recent years about comparative pedagogy (e.g., Manteaw, 2008), but there has been little focusing on this specific issue.

In this section, I will discuss (1) how law school pedagogy can have an ameliorative impact on the acceptance of and the application of international human rights in general, (2) the criticism of legal education for its failure to focus on the relationship between international human rights and mental disability law, (3) efforts that have been made to bridge this gap, and (4) a blueprint for further developments in this area of law and policy.

II. An Ameliorative Impact?

There can be little question that legal education can have a positive impact on the promotion of human rights (Yeh, 2008), political freedoms (Irish, 2007), and a mission of social justice (Phan, 2005; see also, Note, 2006; Skrodzka, Chia & Bruce-Jones, 2008; Ordor, 2007; Hovhannisan, 2006). Some scholars have labeled this "justice education" (Barry et al., 2008). Professor Philip Iya has gone so far as to urge that "human rights issues should form part of *every* law school course taught to all law students" (Iya, 2005, p. 26, emphasis added).[1] There are two primary ways this can be done: in traditional doctrinal courses and seminars, and in law school–sponsored clinics.[2]

---

[1] On the specific issues raised in nations where legal education is not traditionally a *graduate* program, see, e.g., Joy et al., 2006 (Japan); Nottage, 2006 (same). On the pressures to create a new law school pedagogic structure in Japan, see Saegusa, 2009. On issues related to Japanese legal education in general in this context, see, e.g., Haley, 2010; Hasegawa, 2006; Riles & Uchida, 2009; Grondine; 2001; Nottage, 2001; Ashley, 2001. On issues related to the Japanese court system in this context, see, e.g., Miyazawa, 2001; Martin, 2010. On issues related to the teaching of disability law in Japan, see Klein, 2008.

[2] Scholars have also begun to consider how clinical programs can be used as a vehicle through which to infuse the practice of law with therapeutic jurisprudence principles, see, e.g., Brooks, 2005; Cooney, 2005; Gould & Perlin, 2000; Ronner, 2008), and how this could be done outside of the United States as well. See Olowu, 2010 (Africa). See generally infra chapter 10. On how clinical programs must be vigilant to avoid sanism in the representation of persons with mental disabilities, see Perlin, 2003, 2008.

A. In the Traditional Classroom

In 2004, American University Law School Dean Claudio Grossman laid down the gauntlet: "Law schools play a vital role in establishing legitimate expectation for behavior in societies. Therefore, human rights education is crucial in the promotion of important values" (2004, p. 20).[3] Soon thereafter, law schools began to think about the impact that globalization would have on pedagogy,[4] and the "the powerful role that legal education can play in preparing lawyers for a practice that operates at the intersection of public interest law, human rights, and development" (Cummings & Trubek, 2008, p. 52).[5] Even if the assertion that globalization has "radically changed the nature of legal education" (Chesterman, 2008, p. 66) is slightly overstated, the reality is that global law is now being used to teach domestic advocacy (Mitchell, 2007), that international law is being more fully integrated into the first-year curriculum (Grossman, 2006), and, at the least, globalization has had—and continues to have—a significant impact on legal education (Dunham & Friedland, 2009; see also, Spiro, 2000).[6]

B. In Clinics and Skills Settings

Professor Deena Hurwitz has envisioned how international human rights law clinics "offer enormous potential, for students to experience the integration of law and policy, the dynamic nature of international law, and the possibilities for participating in its development and enforcement" (Hurwitz, 2003, p. 548; see also, Carrillo, 2004; Stuckey, 2002).[7] Progressive scholars now also realize that clinical education is critical globally in training a cadre of lawyers to engage in progressive political reform (Joy et al., 2006), to provide legal services for disadvantaged persons (Wortham, 2006), and to engage in humanizing the

---

[3] See Kumar, 2008, pp. 556–557:

> Human rights education needs to go beyond the frontiers of academic learning or, for that matter, professional pursuit. Human rights education should aim to forge social transformation and promote a worldview based upon respect for the rights and freedoms of humanity.

[4] See, e.g., Merisotis & Phipps, 1999; Mohamedbhai, 2002; Pachnowski & Jurczyk, 2010; Owens, 2010.

[5] For a strong criticism of the job done by American law schools in this regard, see Backer, 2002.

[6] On globalization and the teaching of jurisprudence, see, e.g., An-Na'im, 2005. On the relationship of globalization to human rights, see Bruun & Jacobsen, 2006; Cheah, 1997. On the internationalization and globalization of legal education, see Del Duca, 2000; Dunham & Friedland, 2009.

[7] On the role of legal aid clinics in the representation of persons with disabilities, see Liebman, 1999, p. 232. On the role of such clinics in the representation of other underrepresented minorities (e.g., indigenous persons in developed nations), see Cody & Green 2007.

law (Olowu, 2010) and in the teaching of justice (Wilson, 2004; Barry, 2007; Grosberg, 2001),[8] especially in nations where the academic establishment has traditionally frowned on any skills-based education (Bryxová, Tomoszek & Vlkcová, 2006 [Czech Republic]; Blomquist, 2004 [Lithuania]; Skrodzka, Chia & Bruce-Jones, 2008 [Poland]; Oke-Samuel, 2008 [Nigeria];[9] Jessup, 2002 [African nations]).[10] This dovetails with Professor Benjamin Liebman's observation that "the importance of legal aid to human rights protection is central to arguments in its favor" (1999, p. 273; see also, Fu, 2009, [on the importance of access to legal aid in China]; Choate, 2000 [same].[11] Compare Uphoff, 1999 [arguing why live client clinics could not work successfully in Romania]. Uphoff is responded to in, inter alia, Wortham, 2006, and Phan, 2005).

Over the past several years, scholars have turned their attention in this context to China, to the nascent reform and professionalization of the provision of legal services there (see generally, Fu & Cullen, 2008; Kong, 2009; Haicong, 2009; Lo & Snape, 2005) in both civil (Woo, Day & Hugenberger, 2007) and criminal (Lu & Miethe, 2002; Guo, 2010) areas of the law, and especially to the growth (and the need for greater growth) of legal aid programs (Liebman, 2007; Xu, 2005), in legal skills programs (Zhu, 2009; Landsbery, 2009), clinical legal education programs (Pottenger, 2004; Ling, 2007; Tan et al., 2006; Zhou, 2009 Milstein, 2009), and in experiential learning in general (Chavkin, 2009) in that nation (on the absence of a "constitutional jurisprudence" in China, see Tong, 2009, p. 105. See also, Caplow, 2006 [discussing Hong Kong in this context]).[12] In a recent article about the need for procedural safeguards in cases involving defendants with mental disabilities facing the death penalty, Professor Zhiyuan Guo has argued forcefully that such defendants be afforded the same rights to expert psychiatric assistance at state expense to which defendants are entitled—see *Ake v. Oklahoma*, 1985—in the United States, concluding that rationales "similar to those justifying the legal aid system, i.e. equal protection, due process, and meaningful access to justice" support that conclusion (Guo, 2010, pp. 50–51). Professor Benjamin Liebman's observation that the development of legal aid has been a step toward judicial equality in China (1999, p. 281; see also, Phan, 2005)[13] should be considered in this context, an observation particularly

---

[8] On the role of nonlawyers in the provision of justice services, see Maru, 2006.

[9] On clinical legal education developments in Nigeria, see Ordor, 2007.

[10] On the differing responses to clinics in formerly Communist nations, see Schnasi, 2003, comparing success in Moldova with lack of success in Serbia.

[11] On the need for international human rights advocacy to be client-centered, see Haynes, 2006.

[12] On the impact of the U.S. law school education model on these developments, see Erie, 2009.

[13] Compare Joyce & Winfrey, 2004, p. 898, discussing Dowdle, 2000 (arguing that programs modeled on U.S.-based legal aid initiatives can be "suppressive," because they may "undermine indigenous programs . . . better suited to the domestic culture").

striking in the context of the assertion by Professors Fu and Cullen that such legal aid offices are beginning to take on cases involving the rights of persons with disabilities (Fu & Cullen, 2008, p. 8).[14]

III. Failure to Focus

There has been little attention paid in the law school curriculum to the relationship between international human rights and mental disability law (see generally, Perlin, 2007). Although scholars have begun to explore the need for fundamental international/transnational pedagogic reform both in the United States (Reimann, 2004) and abroad (Maisel, 2008; Maisel & Jones, 2008; Juwana, 2006), both in clinical and doctrinal settings, and have begun to explore the need for such educational reforms to be responsive to the needs of other important legal minorities (e.g., indigenous persons, see Cody & Green, 2007), the topic of mental disability law has remained "under the radar" (compare Zhengzi et al., 2004, p. 78, noting that no advanced degree in any aspect of health law is available in China). A relatively recent survey of clinical law teachers with international teaching or consulting experience by Professor Roy Stuckey, by way of example, reveals only *one* non-U.S.-based professor involved with this enterprise in mental disability law contexts in other nations (Stuckey, 2005).

Recently, Professor Frances Gibson of LaTrobe University in Australia has proposed a series of guidelines that law school clinics should follow in aiding in the implementation of the UN Convention on the Rights of Persons with Disabilities:[15]

1. Clinics should adopt a universal approach aimed at providing conditions in their education, employment, and service programs that will work effectively for all people regardless of personal characteristics.
2. All clinical staff and students should undergo mandatory, skills-based disability awareness training.

---

[14] On changes in the structure of legal education in Japan, see Lubbers, 2010; Saegusa, 2009; Riles & Uchida, 2009; Aizawa, 2006; Foote, 2006; Kawabata, 2002; Feldman, 1993. On changes in China, see Tong, 2009. On changes in Korea, see Jeong, 2010. On changes in Australia, see, e.g., Giddings, 2008; Evans & Hyams, 2008. On the contrast between American and Russian legal education, see Lempert, 1999. On the application of American methods to Korea and Japan, see Wilson, 2009. On the "Americanization" of Israeli law faculties, compare Lahav, 2009, to Sandberg, 2009. On the need for Western academic visitors to "immerse themselves" in "local context and culture" as part of international collaborations, see Maisel, 2008, p. 504.

[15] For examples of law school clinical work in the sphere of international human rights in the United States in general, see, e.g., http://www.law.cuny.edu/clinics/clinicalofferings/IWHRC/skills.html; http://www.law.columbia.edu/focusareas/clinics/humanrights

3. Clinical staff should work with Faculty on policies for getting more students with disabilities into law schools and encouraging colleagues to consider disability issues. The legal profession and the community needs lawyers with all types of disabilities. Legal educators are the gatekeepers to the profession for students with disabilities.
4. Clinics have an important role for students with disabilities and clinical staff should encourage students with disabilities to enrol in clinics. Clinical lecturers should publicize the essential functions required of student lawyers in the clinic so that staff and students with disabilities can make informed decisions about their work.
5. Clinical lecturers should adopt a critical analysis of the law's approach to questions of disability.
6. Clinical staff should serve as a model for promoting diversity in law practice and the community including employment of staff with disabilities.
7. Clinical staff should advocate to make the justice system accessible. (Gibson, 2010, p. 5)

It is still premature to determine whether clinical programs have chosen to follow Professor Gibson's recommendations.

IV. Bridging the Gap: The Use of Online Education[16]

A. Introduction

Over the past ten years, I have created a program of online mental disability law courses for attorneys, activists, advocates, important stakeholder groups (consisting of consumers and users of psychiatric services, sometimes referred to as "survivor groups"), mental health professionals, and governmental officials in an effort both to teach participants the bases of mental disability law and to encourage and support the creation and expansion of grassroots advocacy movements that may optimally lead to lasting, progressive change in this area.[17] This is especially timely in light of recent research demonstrating how the Internet has already become an important provider of advocacy services and advocacy information to many persons with disabilities (see Blanck et al., 2003; Blanck & Ritchie, 2003), and how inaccessible most current websites are to many persons with disabilities.

In this section, I will first discuss the use of distance learning in a law school environment, and will briefly consider the special implications of

[16] See Perlin & Ikehara, 2010.

[17] The course was developed at the suggestion and urging of Dean Richard A. Matasar, an early visionary in computer-based legal education. See, e.g., Matasar, 1998, 2002–2003; Matasar & Shiels, 1995.

The oldest and most established human rights online program is that established by Human Rights Education Associates. See http://www.hrea.org/index.php.

distance learning for persons with disabilities. Following that, I will talk about our prior work in Japan and in China and our hoped-for expansion in Japan that will help support the Disability Rights Tribunal that I discuss subsequently (see infra chapter 9).

B. Distance Learning in Law Schools[18]

Distance learning is generally defined as "communication which connects instructors and students who are separated by geography and, often, by time," or as "the electronic connection of multiple classrooms" (Leskovac, 1998). Distance learning courses enable students to share different perspectives, and provide an new environment for teaching law students to collaborate with other types of professionals (Berg, 2003), a characteristic "increasingly essential to the effective practice of law" (Berg, 2003, p. 34). Distance learning—the use of computers, telecommunications, and digital networking to permit learning outside the boundaries of the classroom—"holds the potential to expand the availability of cross-listed courses by reducing these barriers . . . [and] can provide professors of cross-listed courses with pedagogical tools for enhancing interdisciplinary communication and collaboration, and circumventing some of the problems inherent in teaching students from different disciplines" (Berg, 2003, p. 35). This is a pivotal development in the history of American legal education, and it is essential that it be acknowledged by those committed to social change (especially in the context of the relationship between the methodologies of legal education and the substance of what is being taught). It is mandatory that we look to new means for providing legal education—in economic, efficient and interdisciplinary ways—to our students in innovative ways that demonstrate the linkage between education and social change.[19]

Self-evidently, distance learning has great implications for international legal education as well as for domestic legal education. A report in the *Fletcher Forum of World Affairs* concluded: "[T]here is no doubt that ICTs [Information and Communication Technologies], if properly adopted and implemented, can bring economic and cultural opportunities to developing countries. Education facilities may be greatly improved through distance learning and Internet access" (Cukor & McKnight, 2001, p. 47).

1. THE SPECIAL IMPLICATIONS OF DISTANCE LEARNING EDUCATION FOR PERSONS WITH DISABILITIES

One of the specific challenges in creating a distance learning pedagogy in mental disability law is the need to provide a program that can also be

---

[18] See Perlin, 2010, 2011.

[19] On technology and legal education in Japan and Australia, see Ibusuki & Nottage, 2002.

meaningfully accessed by persons with disabilities.[20] By way of example, a recent study by the UK-based Disability Rights Commission showed that 81% of British websites are inaccessible to persons with disabilities.[21] Scholars have begun to explore how the Internet can provide individuals with disabilities the tools to enable them to live independently and "to gain greater independence and social integration" (Rich, 2002), and have thus begun to call for a coordinated program of study to examine the extent to which Internet sites are accessible to persons with disabilities (Blanck & Sandler, 2000). A study of 200 websites affiliated with Centers for Independent Living concluded:

> Accessible technology for persons with disabilities has the potential to enhance independence in life. Its future development hold promise for a wide range of persons with disability . . .
>
> The commitment to digital equality as a civil right must be founded in policy that incorporates accessibility and universal design in public and private programs providing technological access to all. (Blanck & Ritchie, 2003, p. 24)[22]

V. NYLS's Work in Asia

New York Law School has taught sections of two of its courses in Japan[23]: In 2002, a section of *Survey of Mental Disability Law* in conjunction with the Tokyo Advocacy Law Office, the Association for Better Mental Health, and with Zenkanren; and in 2004, a section of the *Americans with Disabilities Act* in conjunction with the same groups (see Perlin 2006, 2007).[24]

This program has also done extensive work in China with the American Bar Association's Rule of Law–Asia office where, in conjunction with the All China Lawyers' Association, and the Northwest University of Politics and Law, it conducted "Training the Trainers" workshops in Xi'an, China to teach experienced death penalty defense lawyers how to train inexperienced lawyers, employing the online distance learning methodologies used in our online

---

[20] On the "ghettoization" of mental disability law, see Perlin, 2010.

[21] See http://www.drc-gb.org/newsroom/newsdetails.asp?id=805&section=4. See also, Axel Schmetzke, *Online Distance Education—"Anytime, Anywhere" but Not for Everyone*, manuscript p. 12, available online at http://www.rit.edu/~easi/itd/itdv07n2/axel.htm (in a study of the 24 most highly ranked schools of library and information science, only 59% of main campus library Web pages were accessible).

[22] For a discussion of the courses offered as part of this program, see Perlin & Ikehara, 2010.

[23] It has also taught a section in Nicaragua. See Perlin, 2007.

[24] As of the time of the writing of this volume, plans are underway to expand the NYLS-Japan partnership further in the coming academic year.

Mental Disability Law curriculum just discussed (Perlin, 2009).[25] Also, related to this topic, I have worked with lawyers and activists in Taiwan in an effort to create a Pan-Asian mental health advocacy network to be built on the framework of the online courses (Perlin, 2007).

There is no question that one of the most critical aspects of law reform is the presence of dedicated and knowledgeable counsel (see infra chapter 8). Without the assignment of such counsel, meaningful and ameliorative change is almost impossible to achieve (Perlin, 2008). With this in mind, NYLS is planning on creating a "triangulated" partnership with a law school in Japan and a law school in China, through which students will also take the course in *Advocacy Skills in Cases Involving Persons with Mental Disabilities: The Role of Lawyers and Expert Witnesses.* As I discuss subsequently (see infra chapter 9), it is hoped that these students will be among those who eventually provide quality representation at the Disability Rights Tribunal for Asia and the Pacific, once that body is created.

VI. Conclusion

Via traditional classrooms and seminars, in clinics and in online courses, law schools have the opportunity to teach students about the relationship between international human rights law and mental disability law, both in theoretical and experiential frameworks and settings. The ratification of the CRPD makes it even more essential that courses in this area—skills and doctrinal—be added to curricula without delay.

Chapter 6B. Expert Evidence Law[26]

I. Introduction

Trial issues may turn on questions beyond the common knowledge of judges or juries, and in such cases, evidence from expert witnesses may be admitted into the court process. The question of how courts assess expert evidence—especially where mental disability is an issue—inevitably raises the corollary question of whether courts actually evaluate its content, or, whether, teleologically, they consider only the conclusion and/or recommendations? If so, do courts privilege certain testimony (because the conclusion serves what are perceived as socially desirable aims) and subordinate other testimony (because the conclusion serves what are perceived as socially undesirable aims)? If this privilege/subordinate pattern is found, is this a result of pretextuality or sanism (see supra chapter 2), or is it something else?

[25] As of the time of the writing of this volume, plans are also underway to create partnerships with Chinese law schools in the coming academic year.
[26] See generally, Perlin, Birgden & Gledhill, 2009.

This section will consider these questions in a comparative disability law context in both common and civil law systems. First, it considers the professional standards that govern the behavior of forensic psychologists[27] and discuss the relevant ethical issues. Then, it considers these questions in the contexts of expert testimony in some common law jurisdictions and civil law jurisdictions. Finally, it speculates as to whether the United Nations Convention on the Rights of Persons with Disabilities is likely to have any impact on practices in this area, and offers some modest conclusions.

II. Professional Standards in Psychology

A. Professional Codes

The recent adoption of the *Universal Declaration of Ethical Principles for Psychologists* (International Union of Psychological Science, 2008)[28] provides a set of moral principles to guide psychological associations in codes of ethics and a universal standard against which to evaluate the ethical and moral development of psychological progress, reflecting the moral principles and values that are expected in both common law and civil law systems. The *Declaration* describes ethical principles based on shared human values "to build a better world where peace, freedom, responsibility, justice, humanity, and morality prevail" (International Union of Psychological Science, 2008, p. 1).

The *Declaration* is underpinned by four principles. *Respect for the Dignity of All Human Beings* recognizes the inherent worth of all individuals (Principle I). *Competent Caring for the Well-Being of Persons and People* maximizes therapeutic effects and minimizes antitherapeutic effects while being cognizant of psychologists' values, culture, and social context (Principle II). *Integrity* includes open, honest, and accurate communication and recognizes potential biases that could result in the harm and exploitation of others (Principle III). *Professional and Scientific Responsibilities to Society* recognizes psychology as a science and a profession that increases knowledge of human behavior, maintains the highest ethical standards, and contributes to social structures and policies that benefit all human beings (Principle IV). Adhering to Principle I ensures that individuals with disability are included, adhering to Principles II and III optimally avoids sanism, adhering to Principle III minimizes the potential harm of teleological thinking, and adhering to Principles III and IV minimizes the potential deleterious impact of pretextuality.

---

[27] Forensic psychologists, of course, are not the only expert witnesses who testify in mental disability law cases. This chapter focuses on this subset of professionals because of the robust body of literature that relates to the questions at hand.

[28] The *Declaration* was adopted unanimously by the General Assembly of the International Union of Psychological Science and the Board of Directors of the International Association of Applied Psychology in Berlin in July 2008.

The principles that underpin the *Declaration* are supported in common law countries by the Code of Ethics and Conduct of the British Psychological Society (BPS, 2006), the Code of Ethics for the American Psychological Association (APA, 1992), and the Code of Ethics of the Australian Psychological Society (APS, 2007). All three Codes address potential issues regarding pretextuality by ensuring integrity (e.g., psychologists do not engage in intentional misrepresentation, APA, 2002) and competence (e.g., psychologists remain abreast of scientific innovations and practice within the boundaries of their competence, BPS, 2006). All three Codes warn against unfair discrimination or prejudice against people with disability (Standard 3.01: Unfair Discrimination in the APA, 2002; Ethical Principle 1.1: Standard of General Respect in the BPS, 2006; and Standard A.1: Justice in the APS, 2007). In addition, the Australian Code addresses the pitfalls of sanism in that Standard A.1 stipulates "psychologists demonstrate an understanding of the consequences for people of unfair discrimination and stereotyping related to their . . . disability" (APS, 2007, p. 11) and General Principle C: Integrity stipulates "psychologists are aware of their own biases, limits to their objectivity" (APS, 2007, p. 26).

B. Expert Testimony by Psychologists

Compared to standards set by codes of conduct, expert testimony by psychologists can be, variously, ethical, incompetent, and/or biased.

1. ETHICAL EXPERT TESTIMONY Competent psychologists do not go beyond the limits of their competence—they provide expert opinion based on special knowledge and expertise, clearly describe generalizability and limitations of findings, consider the court or justice system to be the client, and communicate the limitation of their role to all participants (Haas, 1993). Principles of ethically sound psychological conduct have been listed by Dickey (2008) as

- beneficence (acceptance of responsibility to do good);
- non-malfeasance (do no harm);
- autonomy (respect for freedom of thought and action);
- justice (basing actions on fairness between individuals);
- fidelity (trustworthiness to commitments), and
- generally respect for a person's rights, dignity, competence, responsibility, and integrity.

However, such principles are difficult to apply within the legal system as it currently operates (McGuire, 1997). Nevertheless, if the court admits evidence that does not support codes of conduct, ethical psychologists can decline to appear while knowing that "the judge would instead send the case to Jones [an unethical psychologist], who, unlike you, is of doubtful character and capability" (Faust, 1993, p. 362).

2. INCOMPETENT EXPERT TESTIMONY There are times when expert testimony can be incompetent—"the seductive power of the courtroom and the subtle gratification of being on stage as the expert can sometimes blind the psychologist to the need for particular skills and particular frames of mind necessary to both serve the court system and do justice to the complexity and integrity of the psychological profession" (Haas, 1993, p. 259). Haas indicated that incompetent practice can be demonstrated in various ways:

1. Failing to understand the justice system includes testifying about the facts or providing a legal opinion, and relying on persuasion rather than content (i.e., style over substance);
2. Exhibiting professional arrogance includes overconfidence, inadequate assessment, inappropriate use of third-party reports, etc.;
3. Advocating rather than testifying (including scenarios in which psychologists believe they best understand the legal outcomes required; see Haroun & Morris, 1999);
4. Failing to keep abreast of a rapidly changing field results in out-of-date empirical knowledge;
5. "Burning out" and/or becoming impaired through psychopathology and substance abuse (on how these issues affect lawyers, see Perlin, 2008a); and
6. Overservicing clients for financial gain, leading to exaggerating credentials and findings.

These obstacles to competency can be overcome through a combination of adequate forensic supervision and less professional hubris.

3. BIASED EXPERT TESTIMONY There are times when expert testimony can be biased (or even dishonest, see supra chapter 2, discussing pretextuality). Most recently, Dvoskin and Guy (2008) have maintained that

> The most egregious errors by expert witnesses are almost always attributable to narcissistic needs, including the need to be praised, to make money, to be right, and to win . . . it feels good to have so many people care what one thinks and says about the case. But yielding to those needs is a dangerous and slippery slope . . . attempted to embellish the evidence . . . enhance their credentials . . . tempted to tell prospective clients what they want to hear, thus landing in positions that do not fit the evidence." (p. 203; see also, Perlin, 2008b)

If the court rejects evidence that supports professional standards (i.e., scientific evidence is excluded because it is new and relatively unknown), the psychologist is then placed in direct opposition to the legal system and so experiences an ethical dilemma (Faust, 1993). The unethical psychologist (as described above) may try to circumvent the legal system through deception—exaggerating the quality or certainty of particular evidence—because other options are limited, the chances of detection are small, the likelihood of achieving the desired outcome are good, and the lawyer's desire to "put the best case forward" is compelling (id.). Faust has argued that "inadvertent misrepresentation" is more common than "intentional distortion"; "...sometimes those who will enter the courtroom to opine about a particular issue are there mainly because they hold erroneous beliefs or possess a greater faith in some method than warranted" (id., p. 363). Haas (1993) provided an example where a forensic psychologist offered opinions without adequate data, used strong language to cover up the lack of scientific evidence, and "there was no indication that the psychologist was alert to pressure that could have led to the misuse of his influence" (p. 258). In an earlier work, I provided starker examples of experts who may be described pejoratively as defendant or prosecutor "whores" and who may profess neutrality but are in fact biased (see Perlin, 2008b).

In summary, expert testimony ought to be ethical but at times can be incompetent or biased (or even dishonest). In addition, Haas (1993) noted that competence is a necessary, but not a sufficient, condition for expert testimony. Expert witnesses also require professional virtues such as fidelity, prudence, discretion, integrity, public-mindedness, benevolence, and hope. That is, high quality and competent forensic practice draws on scientific underpinnings *and* promotes human welfare. Competent forensic practice is therefore influenced by the values of the profession, which are then played out through expert testimony in legal jurisdictions.

III. Expert Testimony in Legal Jurisdictions

How is expert evidence—especially in cases involving mental status issues—dealt with in different jurisdictions? Research suggests a significant split between common law jurisdictions (those whose legal systems have been influenced primarily by British law) and civil law jurisdictions (those whose systems were similarly influenced by continental law). This section will consider the differences in the treatment of expert testimony, broadly, as between civil and common law jurisdictions, and, within these two overarching categories, how such testimony is considered in specific civil and common law nations (for a helpful comparison of the common law and civil law systems see Barnes, 2005).

A. Common Law

The fundamental aspect to the common law tradition is the adversarial system, in which opposing lawyers control the testimony through the questions they pose and thereby only aspects of the evidence that support their respective arguments are presented (Haas, 1993). Therefore, the central feature of this system places almost total responsibility on the parties for bringing suit, developing legal theories, producing evidence, and deciding which witnesses to call; no investigation or witness-selection is actioned by the judge (Cound, Friedenthal, Miller, & Sexton, 2007).[29] As the common law depends on the parties, rather than a "neutral" observer, to gather and present evidence, it "relies at least as much on the power of persuasion and rhetoric than on a formal, scientific-like investigation" (Slobogin, 2003, p. 285). Deferring to professional standards can result in expert testimony being admitted if it meets the court's standards, while simultaneously the court relies on expert testimony to convince it that the evidence meets the court's standards (a pragmatic approach, see Slobogin, 2003). Faust (1993) argued that the role of psychologists in the courtroom requires interaction between legal standards (whether the court accepts or rejects the evidence) and professional standards (according to codes of conduct as discussed above).

There are rules about the circumstances in which a court may allow expert evidence to be admitted; and what is to be considered expert evidence. These questions may overlap. Using the example of the New Jersey Evidence Code (see N. J. Evid. R. 104),[30] expert testimony is admissible if: (1) the intended testimony concerns a subject matter that is beyond the ken of the average juror; (2) the field testified is based on state-of-the-art evidence such that an expert's testimony could be sufficiently reliable; and (3) the witness has sufficient expertise to offer the intended testimony). For another example using

[29] There are some significant differences *within* common law systems between the United States model and the model in other common law nations. The United States model is unique in its: (1) reliance on jury trials, (2) use of discovery rules giving wide latitude for exploration of all issues (including oral depositions), (3) far greater latitude in case presentation, and (4), in most cases, an each-party-pays-its-own-costs rule (Rowe, Sherry, & Tidmarsh, 2008). In England, for example, jury trials in civil matters are limited to matters involving fraud, defamation, or "prescribed matters," which has been limited to false imprisonment and malicious prosecution actions: see Supreme Court Act 1981 (UK), § 69, and County Courts Act 1984 (UK), § 66; disclosure of documents is usually limited to documents on which reliance is placed or which undermine the party's case, and there is only a limited duty to search for documents, which is what is reasonable in circumstances, including the complexity of the proceedings, the significance of the document, and the ease and expense of any retrieval of documents (Civil Procedure Rules, Part 31.6 and Part 31.7; trials—and all other aspects of civil proceedings—are subject to the "overriding objective" as set out in the Civil Procedure Rules, namely of dealing with cases "justly," an aspect of which is the saving of expense and another aspect of which is the proportionality of steps in light of matters such as the importance and complexity of the case and the financial position of the parties (Civil Procedure Rules, Part 1); the Court has to bear this in mind whenever making decisions, and the parties are under a duty to assist the court. The English approach to costs is also different: generally, the losing party pays the reasonable costs incurred by the winning party: see Civil Procedure Rules Part 44.3(2).

[30] A typical set of state evidence rules.

a slightly different definition, see the Evidence Act 2006 (New Zealand), which defines expert evidence as evidence "based on the specialised knowledge or skill of that expert" and expert is defined as "a person who has specialised knowledge or skill based on training, study or experience" (section 4). Although this suggests that the evidence is limited to specialized situations, i.e., those beyond the ken of most people, section 25 of the Act conditions admissibility on the ability of the evidence to provide "substantial assistance" to the fact finder in either understanding other evidence or making a finding of fact, and it is expressly provided that it is not inadmissible because it is a matter of common knowledge.

In the United States, the definition of "expert testimony" was clarified in *Daubert v. Merrell Dow Pharmaceuticals* (1993) and *Kumho Tire Co. v. Carmichael* (1999) (see Slobogin, 2003). *Daubert* established that expert evidence must comprise information that is based on scientifically valid reasoning, is reliable, and was obtained through sound scientific methods; in effect the court is asking two questions: (1) "Why should we believe the expert?" (i.e., the credibility, reliability, and validity of the expert opinion in terms of fact and logic) and (2) "Why should we care?" (i.e., the relevance of the opinion to the specific issue) (Dvoskin & Guy, 2008). Six years later, *Kumho* established that expert testimony captures scientific, technical, and other specialized knowledge and should be considered on a case-by-case basis (id.). In other words, expert evidence is contextualized rather than being based on hard and fast rules. Concern for credibility and relevance means that "this reification of the trial judge as gatekeeper is of paramount importance to expert witnesses" (id., p. 204). Under this general framework, psychologists' evidence is used in the courts on the basis of claims to use scientific and professional knowledge and skills to "make better-than-chance assessments of an individual's fitness to stand trial, possession of mental competence, degree of psychopathology, fitness to care for a child, likelihood of acting in a violent manner, and so forth . . . accomplished by reviewing existing scientific literature, performing scientific research, and conducting sound psychological assessments" (Haas, 1993, p. 257).

The scientific method requires valid information that has incremental validity (or predictable validity), and surpasses base rates (Faust, 1993). However, the scientific criteria of reproducibility and ecological validity in the behavioral sciences are difficult to achieve in applying laboratory data to the "real world" (Orne, 2002). Surpassing base rates in, for example, risk assessments, is difficult to attain, as base rates for reoffending of 30% to 60% are required for predictive accuracy (Andrews, Bonta, & Hoge, 1990). Meanwhile, sexual and violent offenders have low reoffending rates. In sex offenders, the reoffending rate is 13% and rarely exceeds 40% at 15 to 20 years follow-up (Hanson, 1998). Slobogin (2003) warned that psychological testimony based on the behavioral sciences may ultimately be unacceptable to the courts (although this does not appear to have been the case to date). An empirical analysis of how judges carried out *Daubert*'s "gatekeeping" function in cases involving different sorts of expert testimony has been conducted (see Merlino, Murray, & Richardson, 2008). Here, it is obligatory to note the *disparity* in decision making in *Daubert* cases; the prosecutor's position is sustained (either in support of questioned expertise or in opposition to it) vastly more often than is that of the defense counsel's position (Risinger, 2000).

Writing about the role of experts in common law cases involving testamentary capacity, Champine (2006) concluded that "concerns about the (mis)use of mental health experts are widespread" (p. 83 n. 273). Professor Champine surveyed the leading authorities, noting that they extensively discussed inaccuracies in decision making by mental health professionals in forensic contexts (see Bersoff, 1992), explained the difficulties that clinicians had in applying legal standards (see Lambie, 2001), considered the assumptions about expert knowledge that were implicit in the standards governing admissibility of expert testimony (see Sanders, Diamond, & Vidmar, 2002), and compared the limitations of clinical decision-making against statistical decision-making (see Mossman & Kapp, 1998; Redding, Floyd, & Hawk, 2001; Shuman & Sales, 1998).

Beyond this, we have known for years of the meretricious power of *heuristics*—intuitive decision-making influencing judgment, which, although reducing the complexity of the task at hand, may lead to severe and systematic errors (see Kruglanski & Ajzen; 1983; Tversky & Kahneman, 1993; Perlin, 2000b; see supra chapter 2). The use of heuristics leads to distorted and systematically erroneous decisions and causes decision makers to "ignore or misuse items of rationally useful information" (Perlin, 1990, p. 966, n. 46) leading to the problem that:

> One single vivid, memorable case overwhelms mountains of abstract, colorless data upon which rational choices should be made. Through the availability heuristic, individuals judge the probability or frequency of an event based upon the ease with which they recall it, leading generally to demands for harsher punishment in all cases. Through the typification heuristic, people characterize a current experience via reference to past stereotypic behavior. Through the attribution heuristic, they interpret a wide variety of additional information to reinforce pre-existing stereotypes. (Perlin, 1997, p. 1417)

Scholars have considered the pernicious impact of these devices on the admissibility of expert testimony and other related issues such as psychotherapy and medical practice. Several studies have concluded that clinical assessments of the likelihood of dangerousness are clouded by bias (Bersoff, 1992), that expert testimony by physicians and psychologists will be affected by hindsight bias (Anderson, Lowe, & Reckers, 1993; Arkes, Wortmann, Saville, & Harkness, 1981; Arkes, Faust, Guilmette, & Hart, 1988; Jolls, Sunstein, & Thaler, 1998; McNeil, Pauker, Sox, & Tversky, 1982), and that expert testimony is often the product of cognitive errors and erroneous beliefs

(Chapman & Chapman, 1969; Meadow & Sunstein, 2001; Rachlinski, 2003). Plous (1993) concluded that "several studies have found that experts display either roughly the same biases as college students or the same biases at somewhat reduced levels" (p. 146).

Expert witnesses are not the only individuals vulnerable to heuristics. Judges can be susceptible to overuse of the availability heuristic (Schauer, 2006), may idealize science (Hans, 2007; Mnookin, 2007), and "like other people, judges rely on simple decision rules, or heuristics, to make decisions" (Rachlinski, Guthrie, & Wistrich, 2006, p. 1229). A recent study of magistrates that tested for several common heuristics (or "cognitive illusions") in different litigation settings showed "statistically significant biasing effects, with the strongest for anchoring, hindsight, and egocentric [overconfidence] biases" (Bone, 2007, p. 1987, quoting Guthrie, Rachlinski & Wistrich, 2007, pp. 787–816). As I wrote a decade ago, "Judges' predispositions to employ the same sorts of heuristic bias as exhibited by expert witnesses further contaminate the process" (Perlin, 2000a, p. 33).

In a consideration of the potential biases of expert testimony, which may result in dishonesty, how do these biases "play out" in the context of experts' purported neutrality—to what extent are experts neutral, and to what extent do we expect that they will be neutral? (Deason, 1998; Mnookin, 2008; Perlin, 2008b.) Some expert bias is intentional, and some expert bias is unintentional (Beckham, Annis, & Gustafson, 1997), but it is still a "real risk" even if unintended (Haroun & Morris, 1999). Dvoskin and Guy (2008) warned that in considering whether to accept a case, potential experts must evaluate their limitations and biases and "realize that not all referrals will be a good fit with their expertise" (p. 205). Paul Appelbaum (1987) noted the "frequency with which highly respected [psychiatric] experts arrive at conclusions favorable to the side for which they are working or to which they have been assigned," p. 21), and this bias is inevitable (Marcus, 1985, cited by Prentice, 2000). Stephen Morse (1982) said, flatly: "Mental health professionals, like all other citizens, have social and political biases that extend to their views of criminal justice" (p. 1057). Randy Otto (1989) identified examples of both sorts of bias: intentional (financial incentives, desire to promote a particular viewpoint on a social issue, and the desire to please one's employer) and unintentional (empathy or identification with a litigant or a side; "unwitting involvement in the adversarial process . . . the need to defend one's position in the face of a hostile opposing attorney" (p. 268). David Bernstein (2008) concluded that because of conscious, unconscious, and selection biases, expert testimony is "uniquely vulnerable to 'adversarial bias'" (p. 453).

An awareness of bias in expert testimony has been present for some time. In 1959, Bernard Diamond, reporting on results from an empirical study on criminal cases, argued (persuasively, to my mind) that bias may be inevitable. I first discussed this issue in 1993:

> I begin with the proposition that the phrase "neutral expert" is an oxymoron. Bernard Diamond, for one, believed that a witness'

> unconscious identification with a "side" of a legal battle or his more conscious identification with a value system or ideological leanings may lead to "innumerable subtle distortions and biases in his testimony that spring from this wish to triumph."
> (Perlin, 1993, p. 641)

Elsewhere, I have written about the impact of sanism on expert witnesses (see Perlin, 2008b), concluding that this impact is "profound . . . at all 'pressure points' at which experts interact with litigants," and that sanist attitudes "will inevitably distort and bias all . . . aspects of the expert's work" (id., p. 243). I think it is essential that this bias be kept in mind as these topics are considered. It is also critical to consider the interplay between therapeutic jurisprudence principles (see generally infra chapter 10) and the role of expert testimony. See, e.g., Perlin (2000a, p. 417): "Therapeutic jurisprudence will also restructure the contours of forensic testimony and of the relationship between fact-finders and expert witnesses"; see also, Arenas and Romey (1999, pp. 161–162): "Therapeutic jurisprudence, by focusing on social-legal-psychological interactive systems between experts, expert testimony, and the courts, becomes a lens and a methodology for the study of the operant rules, role imaging and role expectations, applicable to the introduction of scientific or expert knowledge into the courtroom."

B. Civil Law

I will next consider the roles of in expert testimony civil law jurisdictions. In such jurisdictions, the "inquisitorial system" model places far greater responsibility on the judge. In civil law nations, the court conducts an "active and independent inquiry into the merits of each case," (Cound, Friedenthal, Miller, & Sexton, 2001), p. 2) and this inquiry may include the judge calling and questioning witnesses and ordering specific fact-finding.[31]

Civil law considerations lead to the next inquiry: to what extent do judges in nations other than those in the common law tradition have expectations of neutrality in this subject matter? What follows is not meant to be an exhaustive study, but a sampling of certain specific relevant jurisdictions. However, a closer examination reveals important differences even within these two gross categories (see Legrand & Machado 1998, on the differences in legal cultures in common law and civil law nations).

First, it is important to note that many countries that currently have no regulation of the psychology profession. This should not be a surprise, as 25% of all nations in the world have no mental health law (Perlin, 2007; see supra chapter 5). Recently, the United Kingdom had transferred regulation of the profession from the British Psychological Society to legal regulation through

[31] On the question of the use of precedent in civil law systems, see Fon & Parisi, 2006.

health care legislation, while Ireland, Portugal, Malta, and Switzerland were working toward licensing legislation (Tikkanen, 2004).

An examination of the law of expert testimony in civil law nations reveals some important commonalities, and many individual variations (note that Taylor, 1996, provides a helpful and comprehensive history of the origins of expert testimony in France). First, in a significant number of these jurisdictions, there is only one expert involved in cases, and that expert is appointed by the court (see, for example, Schmidt, 2003 (China); Pradel, 1993; Taylor, 1996 (France); Browne, Williamson & Barkacs, 2002; Lee, 1997 (Korea); and Timmerbeil, 2003 (Germany).[32] Second, experts are not paid by the parties. For example, in France "the expert may not accept any remuneration . . . from the parties" (Taylor, 1996, p. 206), and in Germany the losing party must pay the reasonable expenses of the winning party's expert (Timmerbeil, 2003). Third, most expert reports are submitted to the court in writing and there is often no oral testimony (see Greve, 1993), although courts often have the option of requiring the expert to make an oral presentation to the parties (Taylor, 1996). Fourth, at least in cases involving evaluation of mental state in criminal cases, experts have a long period of time in which to examine the defendant in Germany (Kühne, 1993) and Greece (Mylonopoulos, 1993). There is a plethora of other individual variations. In at least one nation (Israel), the forensic witness has an expanded role; in insanity defense cases, for example, s/he can furnish the court with information about diagnosis, prognosis, and treatment possibilities as well (Simon & Ahn-Redding, 2006). In Nigeria, Bienen (1976) noted that a judge is free to deny the defendant's use of expert testimony (see also, Simon & Ahn-Redding, 2006). In China, Munro (2000) describes psychiatric appraisals conducted by committees "at different echelons of the government" consisting of "responsible officials and experts" from "courts, procuracy, and public security, judicial administration, and health departments" (cited in Simon & Ahn-Redding, 2006, p. 170). In Italy, an expert *must* accept a court appointment and neither psychological not behavioral tests are allowed as parts of psychiatric examinations (Corso, 1993). In Japan, Satsumi and Oda (1995) found that experts can be retained by the prosecution, the defense, or by the court (Simon & Ahn-Redding, 2006). In Germany, although court-chosen witnesses may be called to testify, party-selected witnesses cannot testify at all (Timmerbeil, 2003). In South Africa, the use of experts is mandatory in potential death penalty cases if the issue of mental illness is raised (Simon & Ahn-Redding, 2006).

Perhaps most interestingly, in Korea, the expert takes a different oath than does the lay witness (Lee, 1997). Expert witnesses take the following oath: "I swear that I will give my opinion faithfully in accordance with my conscience and will be subject to the penalty of false expert testimony in case

[32] There, however, parties can also hire their own experts (id.).

of any falsehood in my opinion."[33] This oath differs from the oath for all other witnesses, which reads: "I swear that I will conscientiously speak the truth without concealing or adding anything and will be subject to the penalty of perjury in case of false statement."[34] In that nation, the court decides whether the witness may attend court proceedings or review the evidence presented (Lee, 1997).

In summary, there is no "one size fits all" answer to the question of how courts assess expert evidence in cases involving questions of mental disability. What is clear, though, is that, putting aside the extensive range of variations—both as between civil and common law systems and within *different* civil and common law systems—the same attitudinal barriers of sanism and pretextuality, reflected in false "ordinary common sense" and teleological reasoning have a significant impact on the ways that such testimony is constructed (see supra chapter 2).

IV. International Human Rights Law and Disability

It is necessary to turn next to questions of *international law*. This has been a neglected area for decades (Perlin et al., 2006), but has been significantly rejuvenated by the ratification of the United Nations Convention on the Rights of Persons with Disabilities (United Nations, 2006); see infra chapter 7; see generally, Melish, 2007; Stein & Stein, 2007. This treaty furthers the human rights approach to disability and recognizes the right of people with disabilities to equality in most every aspect of life (see Dhir, 2005).[35] I have elsewhere noted:

> The new United Nations Convention on the Rights of Persons with Disabilities obligates all state parties "[t]o adopt all appropriate legislative, administrative and other measures for the implementation of the rights recognized in the present Convention." The extent to which this obligation is honored will reveal much about the Convention's ultimate "real world" impact. (Perlin, 2007, p. 339)

The Convention leaves open many important questions in many areas of law and policy. Its focus—and the focus of the scholarly debate now taking place—has certainly been more on questions of empowerment than on questions of trial procedure,[36] and includes, for example, the relationship between

[33] Korea Code of Civil Procedure, Art. 311, translated in *Current Laws of the Republic of Korea*, 2, 753–743 (Korea Legislation Research Inst. ed., 1992).

[34] Korea Code of Civil Procedure, Art. 292(2) translated in *Current Laws of the Republic of Korea*, 2, 753–741 (Korea Legislation Research Inst. ed., 1992).

[35] See supra chapter 7, discussing specific Articles.

[36] On the "procedural innovations" of the CRPD, see Lord & Stein, 2009, p. 277; see also, Stein & Lord, 2008.

the Convention and the International Classification of Functioning, Disability, and Health (Kayess & French, 2008). Yet, it is clear that it opens up for reconsideration the full panoply of issues discussed in this chapter as they relate to persons with mental disabilities. If, by way of example, rules of evidence and procedure create an environment that perpetuates the sort of sanism and pretextuality that has had such a negative impact on the lives of persons with mental disabilities, and that condones teleological judicial behavior through overreliance on cognitive-simplifying heuristics (see Perlin, 2008b), then, a strong argument could be made that these rules must be recrafted in the context the Convention. Certainly, this question *must* be "on the table" for lawyers and for advocates in the coming years.

V. Conclusion

There is little question that, internationally, courts interpret expert evidence in cases in which mental disability is an issue in ways that track preexisting pretextual attitudes toward mental disability and persons with mental disabilities. Much of the judicial decision-making in this area is pretextual, and those pretexts flow from sanist roots. Although there are significant differences within legal systems and on jurisdiction-by-jurisdiction bases, the underlying attitudinal factors continue to infect and affect jurisprudence throughout the world. The United Nations Convention on the Rights of Persons with Disabilities—and its potential impact on this jurisprudence—remains a "wild card" with regard to future developments, but it is still far too early to speculate as to its ultimate impact.

Chapter 6C. Psychotherapist-Patient Law[37]

Little attention has been paid to the relationship between private U.S.-based mental disability law and international human rights law. To the best of my knowledge, the first consideration was a presentation at the 2005 International Academy of Law and Mental Health Congress by Professor Colin Gavaghan on *The Development of the Tarasoff Principle and Its Application in Europe*, which first demonstrated—in the context of tort law as it relates to the existence of a psychotherapist's duty to protect/duty to warn (*Tarasoff*, 1976)—that there were significant connections between international human rights law and "private law" and that those connections were definitely worthy of future study (see Gavaghan, 2007). This section seeks to build on Professor Gavaghan's initial research and to answer these questions: (1) What is the status of *Tarasoff* abroad? (2) What are the implications of the answer to this question? and (3) How does this relate to international human rights law?

[37] See generally, Perlin, 2006.

It will proceed in this manner: Part I discusses briefly the standard American psychiatric interpretations of *Tarasoff*, and asks whether this "take" reflects primarily American values or whether it is more universalist. Part II briefly looks at how related confidentiality issues are looked at outside the United States. Part III considers how the United Kingdom's Human Rights Act—an important factor in UK "duty to protect/duty to warn" law—relates to international human rights law in a "dualist" system (see generally, Hill, 2005). Part IV considers the (still modest) case law that broadly applies *Tarasoff* in an international context. Part V concludes and offers some modest predictions for future developments in this area of tort law in this context.

I. Mental Health Professionals' Reaction to the *Tarasoff* Opinion[38]

Tarasoff unleashed a "torrent" of commentary, and the initial professional reaction to the case was, to understate it, "severely critical" (see Perlin, 1992, pp. 35–36; George, 1983).[39] Some advocated for civil disobedience; others advocated for a lawsuit to be brought by the University of California against the California State Supreme Court in federal court (Fulero, 1988). The criticism focused mostly on the unwarranted judicial intrusion into the private sphere of psychotherapeutic practice. (3 Perlin, 2002, § 7C-2.3, p. 457). The major arguments put forth in academic circles included these:

- A mandatory disclosure of confidential information would ultimately harm the public because it would discourage patients from revealing violent tendencies to therapists and discourage them from entering therapy altogether if they were aware of the disclosure procedures (Fulero, 1988).
- Therapists may become highly oversensitive to dangerous information, overreact, and take action too often. (Id.).
- The decision was premised on the "false view" (Givelber et al., 1985, p. 37) that therapists would be able to predict future dangerousness with accuracy through professional standards (3 Perlin, 2002, § 7C-2.3, p. 457).
- Prioritizing the public good over the individual needs of the patient violated central ethics of the practice. (Givelber et al., 1985, p. 37).

---

[38] *Tarasoff* held that, in certain limited circumstances, when a therapist determines (or should have determined) that her patient presents a "serious danger of violence to another, she incurs a duty to use reasonable care to protect the intended victim against such danger." If she fails to do this, she may be liable for tort damages (pp. 340–342; see generally, Perlin, 1992).

[39] See also, Perlin, 1992 (exploring the therapeutic jurisprudence dimensions of *Tarasoff*).

- The *Tarasoff* duty compromised the confidentiality essential to successful psychotherapy. (Dubey, 1974).

An empirical survey revealed that, in the immediate aftermath of *Tarasoff*, a majority of respondents reported "increased anxiety when the subject of dangerousness arose during therapy" (Wise, 1978, p. 181). Over half reported an increased fear of legal liability because of the newly recognized duty to warn; almost a fifth reported feeling tempted to avoid probing into some sensitive areas of therapy, including matters of dangerousness, and over one quarter indicated that *Tarasoff* had led them to change their methods of keeping records, mostly with the goal of seeking to avoid future legal liability (id., pp. 181–182). However, later surveys concluded that the "data does not support the view that *Tarasoff* represents psychiatric Armageddon," but that what *Tarasoff* has done is to "crystallize and shape beliefs concerning a therapist's obligation to protect those at risk from a patient" (Givelber et al., 1985, p. 56).

Nearly two decades ago, these were my conclusions:

> Surveys suggest that therapists have overstated both the *Tarasoff* prescription (as to ways of effectuating the duty) as well as its national precedential applicability. Furthermore, they frequently misstate its holding, construe it to require accurate predictions, and others believe the duty to be triggered by utterance of any threat. Also, it has been argued that professionals have been misled by associational newsletters that have distorted or misstated the holdings of *Tarasoff*'s progeny, and that these misunderstandings serve to further alienate law and psychotherapy.
> (Perlin, 1992, p. 57)

At the same time, I encouraged researchers and scholars to explore the therapeutic jurisprudence dimensions of *Tarasoff*:

> *Tarasoff*, therefore, should be the source of a variety of therapeutic jurisprudential inquiries. First, what impact will the need to comply with *Tarasoff* have on clinical practice? Second, will courts' construction of empirical evidence that is developed about such impact take into consideration therapeutic jurisprudential values? Third, what impact will *Tarasoff* litigation have on clinical practice? (Id., p. 55)

To what extent will the experience in other nations replicate these American findings, and how might these questions be answered in the context of other nations' case law?

II. Does Confidentiality Matter?

Even without a specific *Tarasoff* obligation, the expectation of confidentiality is regularly qualified in other circumstances (e.g., when a patient puts her mental state at issue in litigation, or when there is conflict between confidentiality and a police power statute; Perlin, 2002, § 7A-5, vol. 3, pp. 333–334). The psychotherapist-patient privilege dates only to the 1950s, and "has not produced the expectations of confidentiality created by the long history and deep cultural roots of the other privileges" (Cantu, 1998, p. 376).

And so is the expectation of confidentiality or of privilege qualified in other nations. For example, in Hong Kong, the privilege is qualified where the maker of the statement has a duty (whether legal, social, or moral) to make the statement and the recipient has a corresponding interest to receive it. (*Li Suk Han Hana v. Sun Tien Lun Catherine*, 2005). In India, the privilege will only be recognized if the benefit to society outweighs the costs of keeping the information private (*Sharda v. Dharmpal*, 2003). In New Zealand, the privilege does not apply on a blanket basis to all information disclosed to a psychotherapist (*Ross v. Fryer*, 2003). In short, we should not expect that the degree to which other jurisdictions were receptive to *Tarasoff*-type arguments should hinge on concerns about potentially breaching absolute confidentiality.

III. The Nature of Dualist Systems

There are basically two European jurisprudential models: nations with monist systems and nations with dualist systems (SEE Wildhaber, 2007).[40] Nations such as the Netherlands, for example, are considered "monist," where their constitutions expressly provide that certain treaties are directly applied and that in such cases these treaties are deemed superior to all laws, including local constitutional norms (Jackson, 1992). On the other hand, the United Kingdom is generally considered the "prime example" (id., p. 319) of a dualist system, in which treaties must be implemented through separate legislation in order to have the effect of domestic law (Templeman, 1991; see also, van Dijk & van Hoof, 1990).[41] If domestic law cannot be construed in accordance with Convention law, then the latter overrides domestic law (*R. v. Sec'y of State for Transp., ex parte Factortame Ltd (No. 2)*, 1991).

IV. *Tarasoff* in a Comparative Law Context

The most important developments abroad have come in the United Kingdom, a dualist system. There, the Human Rights Act (HRA) mandates that domestic law must be read and given effect "in a way which is compatible with the [European] Convention [of Human Rights]" (Human Rights Act § 3, 1998), that it is "unlawful for a public authority to act in a way which is incompatible with a Convention right" (id., § 6(1)), and that domestic courts must "take into account" the jurisprudence of the European Human Rights Courts in

[40] I consider this issue in the context of the potential creation of an Asian disability rights tribunal infra chapter 9.

[41] On the impact of this jurisprudence on litigation related to forensic patients and prisoners in the UK, see Curtice & Sandford, 2009.

deciding cases under the HRA (id., § 2(1); see generally, Slynn, 2005; Johnston & Kaye, 2004). Explicitly, passage of the HRA was evidence of Parliament's determination "to give further effect to ECHR rights in domestic law so that people can enforce those rights in the United Kingdom courts" (Gearty, 2001, p. 159). The HRA is thus seen as a mechanism, not solely for the "maintenance" of Convention rights, but also for the "further realization of human rights and fundamental freedoms" (Masterman, 2005, p. 910). Unquestionably, then, the ECHR applies to cases involving residents of the United Kingdom (Alter, 2001; Kwiecien, 2005).

Beyond this, section 2(1) of the HRA allows for the consideration of jurisprudence from other jurisdictions (Masterman, 2005, p. 921). So it should not be surprising that European courts have cited *Tarasoff* (and other American duty to protect cases) on several occasions (see *Palmer v. Tees Health Authority*, 2000, citing, inter alia, *Tarasoff*). Also, in parallel developments, international and comparative law scholars have been urging the creation of a legally integrated body of tort law among European nations (van Gerven, 2002). The emergence of such law will "guarantee . . . individual plaintiffs to have full access to domestic courts in the Contracting States" (id., p. 146). Interestingly, in a paper urging support for such a body of law, Professor Stathis Banakas focused specifically on its potential application to cases in which "a psychiatrist assumes responsibility to a patient that he leads into an emotional or sexual relationship" (2002, p. 370).

The key variable in any consideration of the *Tarasoff* doctrine abroad is the weight given to international human rights documents such as the European Convention of Human Rights (the Convention), and especially Article 2, which reads, in relevant part, "Everyone's right to life shall be protected by law." This raises the question: is there a duty to warn or protect in other nations?

Unquestionably, Article 2 is considered "one of the most fundamental provisions in the Convention" (*Osman v. United Kingdom*, 1998, p. 297), and "enshrines one of the basic values of the democratic societies making up the Council of Europe" (id). There is no originalist argument to be made: the European Court of Human Rights has consistently stated that the Convention is a "living instrument which . . . must be interpreted in the light of present day conditions" (Masterman, 2005, p. 911, citing *Tyrer v. United Kingdom*, 1979–80, p. 1); what is more, the Convention itself assumes that "domestic courts will also take a progressive approach to the rights and fundamental freedoms it contains" (Masterman, 2005, p. 911). Beyond this, it is clear that the potential use of the HRA as a "tool for the development of domestic common law standards is not in doubt" (id., p. 913).

The first, and by far most important, case to consider is *Osman v. United Kingdom* (1998).[42] There, Mrs. Osman sued a local police force for failure to protect her husband (who had been shot by Paget-Lewis, their son's teacher

---

42 The HRA did not incorporate the ECHR until 2001, three years after the Osman case was decided.

who had formed an obsessive attachment to the son; id., pp. 252–256, recounting incidents in which Paget-Lewis photographed the Osmans' son, stalked him, left obscene graffiti about him on multiple occasions around the school, stole files that contained the son's new address, and changed his name to Osman), notwithstanding ample communication between the Osman family, the police, school officials, and a school psychologist (id., p. 257).[43] Mrs. Osman argued that the police had been put on adequate notice of Paget-Lewis's danger to their family, but that they had failed to adequately protect the family. The Court of Appeals struck the action (on the grounds that the police could not be found negligent for failure to investigate a crime; id., pp. 263–264). Subsequently, Mrs Osman—as she was allowed to do in a dualist system—petitioned the European Court of Human Rights on the grounds, inter alia, that the appellate court's decision violated Article 6 of the Convention, providing that "[i]n the determination of [one's] civil rights and obligations . . . everyone is entitled to a . . . hearing . . . by [a] . . . tribunal" (id., p. 285).

In a fractured decision, the European Court of Human Rights rejected the plaintiff's argument under Article 2, concluding that the plaintiff had "failed to point to any decisive stage in the sequence of the events leading up to the tragic shooting when it could be said that the police knew or ought to have known that the lives of the Osman family were at real and immediate risk from Paget-Lewis" (id., p. 308). According to the court:

> For the Court, and bearing in mind the difficulties involved in policing modern societies, the unpredictability of human conduct and the operational choices which must be made in terms of priorities and resources, such an obligation must be interpreted in a way which does not impose an impossible or disproportionate burden on the authorities. Accordingly, not every claimed risk to life can entail for the authorities a Convention requirement to take operational measures to prevent that risk from materialising. Another relevant consideration is the need to ensure that the police exercise their powers to control and prevent crime in a manner which fully respects the due process and other guarantees which legitimately place restraints on the scope of their action to investigate crime and bring offenders to justice, including the guarantees contained in Articles 5 and 8 of the Convention.
>
> In the opinion of the Court where there is an allegation that the authorities have violated their positive obligation to protect the right to life in the context of their above-mentioned duty to prevent

[43] The school psychologist noted that the teacher "must indeed give cause for concern," and did have "personality problems," but recommended he remain as a teacher at the school. Id.

> and suppress offences against the person, it must be established to its satisfaction that the authorities knew or ought to have known at the time of the existence of a real and immediate risk to the life of an identified individual or individuals from the criminal acts of a third party and that they failed to take measures within the scope of their powers which, judged reasonably, might have been expected to avoid that risk. (Id., p. 305)

The court also rejected the plaintiff's application under Article 8 ("Everyone has the right to respect for his private . . . life . . ."), concluding that there was no breach of any "positive obligation" under this Article (id., pp. 309–311). However, the Court ruled further that the plaintiff's rights under Article 6 were violated:

> [T]he Court considers that the applicants must be taken to have had a right, derived from the law of negligence, to seek an adjudication on the admissibility and merits of an arguable claim that they were in a relationship of proximity to the police, [and] that the harm caused was foreseeable . . . In the view of the Court the assertion of that right by the applicants is in itself sufficient to ensure the applicability of Article 6(1) of the Convention. (Id., p. 313)

There were multiple concurrences and dissents. In one, three judges argued that there was enough evidence that for several months, authorities were "well aware of the strange and worrying behaviour of Mr Paget-Lewis," and that "they could have had hardly any doubts that further, more serious, harm was to be foreseen" (id., pp. 324–325, DeMeyer, Lopes Rocha, and Casadevall, JJ.s, partially dissenting and partially concurring). These judges suggested a remedy that would have fit within the dictates of *Tarasoff*: "[The police] should have taken Mr Paget-Lewis into custody before it was too late in order to have him cared for properly. Instead they let things go until he killed two persons and wounded two others" (id., p. 325).

Importantly, the holding of *Osman* focused on the issue of immunity-from-suit, and not on the substantive law of negligence, and the court ultimately concluded that the Osmans had the right, under the ECHR, to proceed with their case. Nonetheless, the case became a barometer for public attitudes about the substantive expansion of negligence-based liability. It thus quickly inspired a cottage industry of commentary (English, 2001, p. 305). One analysis characterized *Osman* as "extraordinary" (Hickman, 2002, p. 253), seeing it as having "alerted tort lawyers to the potential significance of the HRA, [and as a potential] springboard for broader common law development" (id., p. 261). On the other hand, in a lecture to the Common-Law Bar Association, Lord Hoffmann candidly admitted *Osman* filled him with "apprehension" (1999, p. 164), and served to "reinforce the doubts I have had for a long time about the suitability, at least for this country, of having questions of human rights determined by an international tribunal made up of judges from many countries" (id.). Indeed, one British review article concluded that *Osman* "mystified many members of the senior judiciary in this country" (Gearty, 2001, p. 184), noting that one judge of the House of Lords characterized the *Osman* case as "extremely difficult to understand" (id., citing *Barrett v. London Borough of Enfield*, 1999 [scope of duty owed to child in foster placement]).[44]

The year after *Osman* was decided, in *Palmer v. Tees Health Authority* (2000) the British Court of Appeals rejected a plaintiff's claim in a case in which the plaintiff's daughter was abducted, sexually assaulted, and murdered—and her body mutilated—by Armstrong. Plaintiff had sued a hospital where Armstrong had been previously psychiatrically treated, and alleged that defendants '"failed to diagnose that there was a real, substantial and foreseeable risk of Armstrong committing serious sexual offences against children and of causing serious bodily injury to any child victims," and consequently failed to provide him with adequate treatment to reduce the risk of him committing such offences" (id., p. P1). The Court of Appeal distinguished *Osman* because there was no relationship between the perpetrator and the victim. Although Armstrong had said during treatment that he had "sexual feelings towards children and that a child would be murdered after his discharge" (id., p. P3), there was no relationship between Armstrong and the specific victim, so the requisite proximity was absent (id., p. P11).

Interestingly, *Palmer* distinguished *Tarasoff* "where the court [had] held that there was a duty to warn an identified victim" (id., p. P12). The court elaborated:

> An additional reason why in my judgment in this case it is at least necessary for the victim to be identifiable . . . to establish proximity, is that it seems to me that the most effective way of providing protection would be to give warning to the victim, his or her parents or social services so that some protective measure can be made. . . . [T]he ability to restrict and restrain a psychiatric patient is subject to considerable restriction under the Mental Health Act 1985 . . . and are not unlimited in time. . . . It may be a somewhat novel approach to the question of proximity, but it seems to me to be a relevant consideration to ask what the defendant have done to avoid the danger, if the suggested precautions, i.e. committal under section 3 of the Mental Health Act or treatment are likely to be of

---

[44] Subsequently, in *Z v. United Kingdom,* 2002, a case involving actions by abused children against local authorities who allegedly owed them a duty of care breached by their failure to prevent the abuse (at the hands of the children's parents), based on legal arguments characterized as "novel and entirely speculative," the European Court of Human Rights narrowed the range of circumstances in which decisions to strike claims could be seen as breaching Article 6. See generally, Mullender, 2003, p. 307. Nonetheless, *Osman* is still seen as the leading case in this area of the law.

> doubtful effectiveness, and the most effective precaution cannot be taken because the defendant does not know who to warn. This consideration suggests to me that the Court would be unwise to hold that there is sufficient proximity. (Id., pp. P12–P13)

Tarasoff has been cited in a bare smattering of other occasions in British cases. In *W. v Egdell* (1990), for example, the plaintiff, who had pled guilty to manslaughter in a multiple homicide case and was subsequently institutionalized in a secure hospital, retained a psychiatrist to submit a report supporting the plaintiff's petition for transfer to a regional facility. When the psychiatrist indicated he could not support the transfer, the plaintiff withdrew his application to the tribunal and refused to consent to the defendant's disclosing the report to the medical officer at the secure hospital. The doctor disclosed the report, and the plaintiff subsequently sued him for breach of confidentiality. The trial judge found that the duty of confidence owed by the defendant to the plaintiff not to divulge the contents of the report was overridden by the public interest in protecting the public by placing the report before the proper authorities, and he dismissed the actions (id., p. 364).

The plaintiff's appeal was dismissed, the appellate court, citing *Tarasoff*, holding that "[t]he balance of public interest clearly lay in the restricted disclosure of vital information to the director of the hospital and to the Secretary of State who had the onerous duty of safeguarding public safety" (id., p. 416). In language that tracks the "public peril begins" language from *Tarasoff*, the court concluded on this point:

> Although it may be said that Dr Egdell's action in disclosing his report . . . fell within the letter of paragraph 81(b) [of the Medical Council's confidentiality rules], the judge in fact based his conclusion on what he termed "broader considerations"—that is to say, the safety of the public. I agree with him. (Id.)

Then, in *D v. East Berkshire Community Health NHS Trust* (2005), the parents of young children brought actions for negligence against health care authorities, claiming damages for alleged psychiatric harm caused by unfounded allegations made by health care and child care professionals that the parents had abused their children. The House of Lords affirmed the dismissal of the parents' case, noting:

> In some American jurisdictions it has been accepted that a doctor may owe a duty to a person who is not his patient [citing, inter alia, *Tarasoff*, and *Sullivan v. Moody* (2001), an Australian case]. . . . In the present case acceptance of that proposition is implicit in acceptance of a potential duty to the child. So the question is whether, in diagnosing the child's condition in a case of possible abuse, the position of the child is so different from that of the parent that a duty may sensibly be owed to the one but not to the other. (*East Berkshire Cmty Health NHS Trust*, p. 397)

Neither of these cases, however, has been the subject of commentary that *Osman* has. And it is clear that *Osman* did lead to a "serious reappraisal of public . . . negligence claims" (Lidbetter & George, 2001, p. 605); that it required courts to "attach more weight to the interests of claimants" (id., p. 606); that "there are fewer policy arguments against liability available to public bodies than there were before *Osman*" (id., p. 615); and that courts are "now more favourably disposed to claimants in such cases" (id., p. 599). After *Osman*, English courts will be more reluctant "to dispose of negligence" claims prior to a hearing on the merits (Davies, 2001, p. 524), as a result of *Osman*'s "pushing back the boundaries of public authority liability" (van Gerven, 2002, p. 146).[45]

Of course, *Osman* was not, strictly speaking, a "*Tarasoff* case." But there is no question in my mind that it helped create a judicial environment that will be more sympathetic to such claims. One commentator has observed:

> What Article 2 may now do . . . is to require judges now to take the decision whether the care and treatment provided was adequate or proper . . . rather than to decide . . . solely whether it was treatment which a responsible body of doctors would have provided. (Havers, 2001, p. 68)

Notwithstanding the rejection of the plaintiffs' claim in the *Z* case, *Osman*'s language as to risk, identifiably, and foreseeability remains viable (cf. Wright, 2001, p. 145 [after *Z*, focus in *Osman*-type cases likely to shift to other Convention Articles]).

Also important to note are recent tort decisions from the continent on duty of care and other issues that may also give rise to *Tarasoff*-like obligations.[46] By way of examples, an Austrian court has found (in a contractor's accident case) that an individual may owe a duty of care to specified third parties (European Tort Law, 2001, p. 68, citing [2001] J.B.L. 525); a Swiss court has found (in a ski accident case), that a party had no duty to provide safety measures against "unpredictable behavior" (id., p. 466, citing [2000] Pra. 89, no. 185 (Switz.); a Greek case (involving an attack in a business's parking lot) mandated a duty to protect the company's clientele (id., p. 272, citing [2001] ChrID A', 310, 311), and a Finnish case (involving the need to warn as to the hazards of smoking tobacco) found a potential duty of care (id., p. 184, citing [2002] LM 100). In the one case more factually connected to the issues under consideration here (albeit tangentially), another Swiss court, in denying recovery in a suicide case, framed the question as to whether the doctor acted according to general standards of medical expertise (id., p. 468,

---

[45] One commentator has grumpily criticized *Osman* as paving the way for subsequent cases that he characterized as potential "compensation-seeker's charter[s]." Mullis, 2000.

[46] Beyond the scope of this work is the question of how the entire issue of medical malpractice is dealt with in civil law nations, especially those without a "litigation tradition." See, e.g., Feldman, 2009 (discussing Japan).

citing [2000] Pra. 89, no. 155 (Switz.). These and other cases led an editor of a yearbook edited by the European Centre of Tort and Insurance Law to conclude that "there is a growing tendency to accept duties of the public authorities to become active for the protection of the citizens" (id., p. 522 [remarks of Helmut Koziol]).

V. Conclusion

Why is this important in the context of this volume? Even though *Tarasoff* has been cited only a handful of times in nondomestic contexts, the idea of a duty to warn or to protect does have legitimacy outside America's borders. The issue that was the immediate flashpoint of the *Tarasoff* case and its immediate progeny—the concern that lack of absolute confidentiality might do irreparable harm to the patient-psychotherapist relationship—does not appear to even be a consideration outside of the United States.[47]

Contrarily, the underlying issues of public agency liability—especially as articulated in *Osman*—are the central issues abroad. Perhaps most significantly, the European court system appears to have no problem whatsoever in intertwining what American jurisprudence sees as "private law" issues (even if, as in *Tarasoff*, the party defendant is a public entity) with what we see as public law issues (which we often treat as "civil rights cases"). The reliance on the ECHR as the lynchpin for the *Osman* decision tells us that the potential deprivation of a forum in a *Tarasoff*-case is seen as a violation of international human rights. This conclusion may have profound implications for future developments in this area.

Most of the new attention on the intersection between international human rights law and mental disability law has focused on the wretched institutional care to which persons with mental disabilities are subjected around the globe (see supra chapter 5). But some has also begun to focus on community issues (See Kanter, 2003; Flynn, 2010). It is not particularly provocative to predict that there is a good chance that this will lead to a greater focus on this entire related area of law and on the legal regulation of psychiatric practice (which remains at the heart of the *Tarasoff* decision).

Chapter 6D. Corrections Law[48]

I. Persons with Mental Disabilities in Jails and Prisons[49]

Millions of people are released each year from our nation's jails and prisons, many of whom require linkages to an already inadequate and overtaxed

---

[47] On the relationship between *Tarasoff* and pretextuality (see supra chapter 2) and the way courts often fail to consider relevant social science data in the decisions in "*Tarasoff* cases," see Perlin, 1990, p. 62.

[48] See generally, Perlin & Dlugacz, 2008, 2009.

[49] See id.

public mental health system.[50] Jamie Fellner estimates that more than half of jail and prison inmates have mental health problems (2006a, p. 135; see also, Rich, 2009). Gail Wasserman and her colleagues estimate that, among incarcerated juveniles, the rate rises to as high as 65% (McReynolds & Wasserman, 2008, p. 1175; Wasserman, 2002). The rate of mental illness among prison inmates is three times higher than that of the general population (Marschke, 2004). Prisoners with mental illness—as a result of their mental illness—are statistically more likely to violate certain prison rules, making it resultantly more likely that they face segregation and thus exacerbation of their mental illness (Nilsen, 2007; Haney, 2003; see generally, Mauer & Chesney-Lind, 2002).

Such prisoners are "considerably" more likely than non–mentally ill inmates to be victimized by physical or sexual assault while incarcerated (Marschke, 2004, p. 496), and serve, proportionately, longer terms of imprisonment (id., p. 497; see generally, Talvi, 2007). In the context of the unprecedented increase in the overall prison population during the past three decades, these factors have combined with the erratic access of persons with mental disabilities to adequate screening and treatment during incarceration, and inconsistent efforts at promoting successful reentry upon release to create a major challenge on the national scale (Rich, 2009).[51]

II. Human Rights and Corrections Law[52]

Human rights are necessary for all individuals; human rights violations occur when persons are treated as objects or as a means to others' ends (Ward & Birgden, 2007). Offenders have enforceable human rights (Birgden & Perlin, 2008, 2009). The Vienna Declaration and Program of Action (http://www.unhchr.ch/huridocda/huridoca.nsf/(Symbol)/A.CONF.157.23.En) and the Universal Declaration of Human Rights (Perlin et al., 2006, pp. 27–33) recognized that inherent dignity and inalienable rights of all individuals is the foundation of freedom, justice, and peace. Through global covenants, individual rights regarding offenders are safeguarded against cruel, inhuman, or degrading treatment or punishment (International Covenant on Civil and Political Rights [ICCPR], 1966, Art. 7);[53] prisoners should be treated with humanity and dignity, and provided with reformation and social rehabilitation

[50] This, of course, is not a problem endemic to the United States. See, e.g., Farmer, 2003, discussing Russian conditions; Alexander, 2009, discussing African conditions. I focus solely on the United States experience here because of the abundance of accessible research findings.

[51] See id., p. 115: "Failure to prepare inmates for reentry, and failure to provide supervised medication, trained staff and related housing, and social services to paroled inmates almost assures repetition of the cycle of crime and punishment."

[52] See generally, Birgden & Perlin, 2009.

[53] See generally, Neziroğlu, 2007.

(id., Art. 10); individuals are guaranteed the right to the highest attainable standard of physical and mental health (International Covenant on Economic, Social and Cultural Rights [ICESCR], 1966, Art. 12); individuals are guaranteed respect for human rights and fundamental freedoms in forensic and correctional systems (Vienna Declaration on Crime and Justice, 2001); and prisoners should be treated in a humane manner and with dignity (United Nations Body of Principles for the Protection of all Persons under Any Form of Detention or Imprisonment, 1988; see generally, Birgden & Perlin, 2009).[54]

Although scholars have considered the general question of the human rights of correctional inmates under international law (see, e.g., Hresko, 2006; Vasiliades, 2005; Geer, 2000), little attention has been paid to the specific question of how these standards affect correctional inmates with mental illness (Perlin & Dlugacz, 2009; Fellner, 2006b). It is that question that is next addressed.[55]

III. Application of International Human Rights Law Doctrines to Incarcerated Persons with Disabilities[56]

Many obstacles to the enforcement of UN human rights conventions have been identified in the decades since the entry into force of the ICCPR and the ICESCR. These include concerns that (1) there is limited enforcement machinery;[57] (2) the existing machinery is understaffed, underfunded, and may not have the authority to compel compliance with—or to punish violations of—human rights standards; (3) ultimately, human rights enforcement may be viewed as a State function ("the fox guarding the henhouse" syndrome); and (4) the general lack of accountability that results from some of these issues ("Enforcing Human Rights," 1993).[58]

The United States' track record with regard to such Conventions has been mixed. Courts in the United States have been inconsistent in their enforcement of and adherence to UN Conventions (Bronstein & Gainsborough, 2004).[59] In *Lareau v. Manson* (1980, pp. 1187–1189, n. 9) a federal district court cited to the United Nations Standard Minimum Rules for the Treatment of Prisoners standards in cases involving, the "double bunking" of inmates

[54] For a comparative law perspective on sentences of life imprisonment, see van Zyl Smit, 2006. For a consideration of the changing role of prisons, see Liebling, 2006.

[55] On the specific issues raised by detainee interrogations in military contexts, see Pope & Gutheil, 2009.

[56] See generally, Perlin, 2009.

[57] See Helfer, 2005, p. 1622, n. 103: "Many human rights conventions also have weak monitoring and enforcement mechanisms."

[58] Also, note that even with the general human rights instruments, the lack of universal consensus about the rights to be protected creates a considerable sticking point in enforcement.

[59] For a survey of all relevant issues, see Henkin, 1999.

(compare *Bott v. DeLand*, 1996, overruled on other grounds in *Spackman ex rel. Spackman v. Bd. of Educ.*, 2000 [Utah's unnecessary abuse standard based on "internationally accepted standards of humane treatment"]). But on the other hand, in *Flores v. Southern Peru Copper Corp.* (2003, p. 259), the Second Circuit found that the United Nations' Convention on the Rights of the Child (CRC) did not convey a private right of action to plaintiffs as a matter of law. In at least one case, however, while noting that the nonratified Convention was not binding on U.S. courts, the Massachusetts Supreme Judicial Court "read the entire text of the convention" and "conclude[d] that the outcome of the proceedings in this case are completely in accord with principles expressed therein" (*Adoption of Peggy*, 2002, p. 38).

Most significantly and more recently, in *Roper v. Simmons*(2005),[60] in the course of striking down the juvenile death penalty,[61] the Supreme Court (per Justice Kennedy) acknowledged that the United States had not ratified the CRC, but added:

> It is proper that we acknowledge the overwhelming weight of international opinion against the juvenile death penalty, resting in large part on the understanding that the instability and emotional imbalance of young people may often be a factor in the crime. See Brief for Human Rights Committee of the Bar of England and Wales et al. as *Amici Curiae* 10–11. The opinion of the world community, while not controlling our outcome, does provide respected and significant confirmation for our own conclusions. (Id., p. 578)[62]

Since *Roper*, the U.S. Supreme Court has returned to this issue in *Graham v. Florida*, a 2010 opinion striking down "life without parole" sentences for juveniles not directly involved in homicides. The Court's opinion, again per Justice Kennedy, makes the same point, perhaps more clearly:

> There is support for our conclusion in the fact that, in continuing to impose life without parole sentences on juveniles who did not commit homicide, the United States adheres to a sentencing practice rejected the world over. This observation does not control

---

[60] See also, *State v. Romano*, 2007, p. 1114, n. 14 (relying, in part, on the UN Convention for the Traffic in Person and the Exploitation of Others, in opinion affirming a prostitution conviction, and citing approvingly *Almeida v. Correa*, 1970, pp. 570–71, for its citations to a UNESCO document in its resolution of a paternity case).

[61] On the special issues related to the relationship between the death penalty, mental illness, and international human rights law, see Jubilut, 2007.

[62] Soberingly, a recent survey by Professor Jean Koh Peters (2006, pp. 968–969) found that almost three-quarters of children worldwide live in countries where CRC is not observed or where evidence as to observance is inconclusive, despite CRC's widespread ratification.

our decision. The judgments of other nations and the international community are not dispositive as to the meaning of the Eighth Amendment. But "[t]he climate of international opinion concerning the acceptability of a particular punishment" is also "not irrelevant."

Today we continue that longstanding practice in noting the global consensus against the sentencing practice in question. . . .

Thus, as petitioner contends and respondent does not contest, the United States is the only Nation that imposes life without parole sentences on juvenile nonhomicide offenders. We also note, as petitioner and his *amici* emphasize, that Art. 37(a) of the United Nations Convention on the Rights of the Child, Nov. 20, 1989, 1577 U.N.T.S. 3 (entered into force Sept. 2, 1990), ratified by every nation except the United States and Somalia, prohibits the imposition of "life imprisonment without possibility of release . . . for offences committed by persons below eighteen years of age."

The State's *amici* stress that no international legal agreement that is binding on the United States prohibits life without parole for juvenile offenders and thus urge us to ignore the international consensus. . . . These arguments miss the mark. The question before us is not whether international law prohibits the United States from imposing the sentence at issue in this case. The question is whether that punishment is cruel and unusual. In that inquiry, "the overwhelming weight of international opinion against" life without parole for nonhomicide offenses committed by juveniles "provide[s] respected and significant confirmation for our own conclusions." . . .

The debate between petitioner's and respondent's *amici* over whether there is a binding *jus cogens* norm against this sentencing practice is likewise of no import. The Court has treated the laws and practices of other nations and international agreements as relevant to the Eighth Amendment not because those norms are binding or controlling but because *the judgment of the world's nations that a particular sentencing practice is inconsistent with basic principles of decency demonstrates that the Court's rationale has respected reasoning to support it.*

(pp. 2033–2034, emphasis added).[63]

[63] On the Supreme Court's application of international human rights norms in this context, see Perlin & McClain, 2009. On the way the *Roper* decision was based, in a human rights context, on "a broad understanding of the role of public reasoning in the contemporary world," see Sen, 2006, p. 2926.

There is some important literature that suggests that, in other nations, in other contexts, ratification of a UN Convention *has* had a salutary impact on domestic law.[64] Writing about the ratification in the UK of the CRC, Professor Adrian James has written:

> There have been significant changes in the environment within which children's issues are addressed in both private and public law cases in the family courts; in addition, it is also clear that at an organizational level, major strides have been taken in embracing the provisions of the [CRC] and in making children's rights, especially those of participation, meaningful. (James, 2008, p. 61)[65]

Although this has rarely been the subject of scholarly consideration in this context, it appears that these developments, in way, can be seen as "closing the loop"; that is, mutually reenforcing phenomena of early forays into the tentative acceptance of international human rights law principles are seen as reinforcing the norms that underlay them, and that acceptance then leads to stronger iterations of these principles—in conventions, treaties, etc.—that then help entrench the standard—as a best practice or eventually as a standard of care—that eventually works its way back into domestic constitutional law.

IV. The Specific Application of International Human Rights Law to Correctional Law

International human rights law and standards specifically address the full range of issues that affect prisoners with mental illness (Fellner, 2006a, p. 140).[66] A "white paper" prepared by the American Friends Service Committee reveals how documents such as the ICCPR, the ICESCR, and the Convention against Torture all contain significant protections to persons in correctional institutions (American Friends Service, 2003; on the parallel European Convention's provisions, see Harding, 1989). In this context, recently, Professor Eva Nilsen (2007) has written persuasively that global human rights standards should be relied on as a source of legal protections for persons in correctional settings, arguing that international courts—in their interpretations of such standards—"give a robust interpretation to claims of

---

[64] On the impact of this jurisprudence on litigation related to forensic patients and prisoners in the UK, see Curtice & Sandford, 2009.

[65] In a relatively recent filing with the U.S. Supreme Court, *amicus* Disability Rights Legal Center of Los Angeles, CA, has relied on a Submission to the Special Rapporteur on the Right to Education of the UN Human Rights Council in support of its arguments on behalf of number of students with disabilities eligible for special education in adult correctional facilities. See *Forest Grove School District v. T.A* (2009) (decided on other grounds).

[66] For a comparative study of treatment standards for this population in the United States, the UK, and Australia, see Turner, 2008.

degrading treatment that violates human dignity" (id., p. 160, and see pp, 160–161, nn. 246–250, citing sources); see also Konrad et al., 2007; Labelle, 2008).[67] Alvin Bronstein and Jenni Gainsborough (2004, p. 814, emphasis added) similarly argue that "the U.S. *unquestionably* has a moral responsibility to accept as binding [international] human rights standards."[68] Further, it is clear that prisoners with mental disabilities should be entitled to expect the same standard of health care as those "with unrestricted freedom" (Abramowitz, 2005, p. 525). Rick Lines of the International Harm Reduction Association has similarly argued that expanded mechanisms should be created under the Convention against Torture to ensure such adequate health care (2008; on how one Swiss Canton has creatively used Council of Europe standards to bring about this end, see Elger, 2008).[69] Jamie Fellner, again, concludes that the systems of discipline and segregation in U.S. prisons violate prisoners' human rights (2006b).

The next question to consider is the impact that the new CRPD will have on these arguments. As discussed extensively in earlier chapters (and see infra chapter 7), the Convention sets out a broad array of human rights available to all persons with mental disabilities (see supra chapter 5, p. [15], and chapter 3, p. [17]). Self-evidently, these Convention Articles, on their face, have a significant impact on the conditions of confinement of institutionalized jail and prison inmates with mental disabilities (see Perlin & Dlugacz, 2009).

By way of example, a recent proposal seeking to reform correctional law and practices as they affect persons with mental disabilities recommends that prisons be required to adopt procedures guaranteeing systematic screening for mental illness (see, e.g., Nicholls et al., 2005), and that in cases involving allegations of violations of the Eighth Amendment, the current subjective standard be replaced with an objective standard (see Marschke, 2004).[70]

---

67 See also, e.g., Neziroğlu, 2007 (discussing how the fact of mental and psychological *suffering* in prison is attracting more attention on the part of human rights advocates and correctional reformers). On dignity issues in this context in general, see Turner, 2008; see generally, supra chapter 2.

68 Compare Kosak, 2005, pp. 399–400: "Prisons in the United States do not provide all aspects of an effective mental health care system. In most prison systems, what is provided is ineffective due to lack of funding, inadequate staffing to meet the needs of the entire prison population, lack of training for the health care and security staff, and lack of procedures to identify and track the needs of prisoners."

69 On the application of international human rights standards to women in prison, see Gainsborough, 2008.

70 See, e.g., *Farmer v Brennan*, 1994, pp. 837–838:

> We reject petitioner's invitation to adopt an objective test for deliberate indifference. We hold instead that a prison official cannot be found liable under the Eighth Amendment for denying an inmate humane conditions of confinement unless the official knows of and disregards an excessive risk to inmate health or safety; the official must both be aware of facts from which the

The drafter of this proposal also considers the lack of trust typically accorded to inmate complaints (id., p. 538; and see Rich, 2009, p. 118, discussing this observation), a concern significantly abetted by sanism (see supra chapter 2). The new UN Convention is entirely in accord with these recommendations, and its potential use as an antistigma tool (see infra chapter 7) may also potentially, to some extent, alleviate this situation.

V. Conclusion and Potential Future Developments

The CRPD has not yet been ratified in the United States. Nonetheless, its principles should serve as a model of "best practices," in the same way that the Convention on the Rights of the Child served as such a model in the Massachusetts case discussed earlier (see *Adoption of Peggy*, 2002, p. 38) for all future inquiries into the rights of prisoners to adequate mental health care and treatment. It is not an exaggeration to say that it provides a potential blueprint for litigators looking for fresh approaches to the seemingly intractable constellation of legal and behavioral issues faced by prisoners with mental disabilities.[71]

The U.S. Supreme Court—albeit by the most slender of majorities—has made it clear in a series of criminal law and procedure cases that international human rights law is a legitimate source of rights in any determination of appropriate domestic constitutional standards. Although lower courts have, in the past, incorporated UN Standards, Covenants, and Conventions in decisions dealing with prisoners rights' issues, the Supreme Court has never, to this date, had the occasion to construe this body of law in a correctional conditions case.

---

inference could be drawn that a substantial risk of serious harm exists, and he must also draw the inference. This approach comports best with the text of the Amendment as our cases have interpreted it. The Eighth Amendment does not outlaw cruel and unusual "conditions"; it outlaws cruel and unusual "punishments." An act or omission unaccompanied by knowledge of a significant risk of harm might well be something society wishes to discourage, and if harm does result society might well wish to assure compensation. The common law reflects such concerns when it imposes tort liability on a purely objective basis. See Prosser and Keeton §§ 2, 34, pp. 6, 213–214; see also Federal Tort Claims Act, 28 U.S.C. §§ 2671–2680; *United States v. Muniz,* 374 U.S. 150, 83 S.Ct. 1850, 10 L.Ed.2d 805 (1963). But an official's failure to alleviate a significant risk that he should have perceived but did not, while no cause for commendation, cannot under our cases be condemned as the infliction of punishment.

[71] On the relationship between correctional litigation, international human rights law, and therapeutic jurisprudence, see Birgden & Perlin, 2009, p. 257: "TJ legal theory can assist forensic psychologists to balance offender rights and community rights without trumping the law."

The CRPD is a beacon to those who advocate for persons with disabilities. Lawyers representing plaintiffs in institutional conditions cases should turn to the Convention as a potential affirmative source of rights on behalf of their clients, and as a strategy for offering "redemption" to this population. In arguing in support of the United States' ratification of the Convention, Tara Melish recently wrote that "Ratification will allow us simultaneously to serve as a model for the rest of the world, projecting our commitment to the rights of persons with disabilities outward, while ensuring that we are in fact living up to that projection as a nation and social community of equals at home" (Melish, 2007, p. 47). For now, however, lawyers in ratifying nations representing the population discussed in this chapter need to begin to assess the Convention in the context of their clients' conditions of confinement in an effort to offer some ameliorative prospects.

7

The UN Convention: The Impact of the New UN Convention on the Rights of Persons with Disabilities on International Mental Disability Law

In this chapter, I will discuss the text of the Convention, the first case law that has discussed the Convention, and some initial criticisms of the Convention.

I. Introduction

There is no question that the most significant development in the relationship between international human rights law and mental disability law has been the ratification of the Convention on the Rights of Persons with Disabilities (CRPD).[1] As previously discussed, the "wide scope" (Carver, 2010, p. 26) of the "holistic" (Stein, 2007a, p. 679; Megret, 2008b, p. 261) CRPD furthers the human rights approach to disability and recognizes the right of people with disabilities to equality in most aspects of life (Perlin, 2010). "The Convention responds to traditional models and situates disability within a social model framework and sketches the full range of human rights that apply to all human beings, all with a particular application to the lives of persons with disabilities"

[1] For pre-CRPD articles urging the adoption of a social model and repudiating the medical model, see, e.g., Hendricks & Degener, 1994; Rosenthal & Rubenstein, 1993; Quinn & Degener, 2002. For a related pre-CRPD article discussing how enforcement of the UN Mental Illness Principles (see supra chapter 4) would provide basic procedural protections in the civil commitment context in Japan, see Cohen, 1995. On how the CRPD rejects the medical model, see Kampf, 2008. On the application of the social model to questions of mental illness in general, see Andersen-Watts, 2008.

(Lord & Stein, 2009, p. 256; see also, McCallum, 2010). It provides a framework for ensuring that mental health laws "fully recognize the rights of those with mental illness" (McSherry, 2008, p. 8). It categorically affirms the social model of disability (see, e.g., Gustavsson & Zakrzewska-Manyerys, 1997) by describing it as a condition arising from "interaction with various barriers [that] may hinder their full and effective participation in society on an equal basis with others" instead of inherent limitations (id., citing Art. 1 and Pmbl., para. e.), reconceptualizes mental health rights as disability rights (Fennell, 2008), and extends existing human rights to take into account the specific rights experiences of persons with disabilities (Megret, 2008a).

Professor Gerard Quinn characterizes it as a "moral compass" for social change, reflecting a "paradigm shift" in the way we think about and treat persons with disabilities (2009, p. 41), characterizing it as a "beacon for an international consensus on justice and disability" (id., p. 52). Professor Lisa Waddington says it ushers in a "new era in human rights protection" (2007). Professor Jacqeline Laing says it "brings hope to the vulnerable" (2008, p. 22). Professor Penelope Weller argues that it illustrates "profound shifts both in the conception of human rights and the implementation of human rights in public policy domains" (2009, p. 90). Professor Annegret Kampf simply labels it "remarkable" (2008, p. 26), and prophesizes that it will now be "much harder to ignore persons with disabilities" (id., p. 21). The International Disability Alliance characterizes it as the "universal standard" for the human rights of all persons with disabilities. (2008, p. 1).[2]

In this chapter, I will first discuss what I see as the most important provisions of the Convention. Next, I will look at some of the scholarly literature evaluating the impact that the CRPD might have locally as well as the still-meager case law that considers the CRPD. Then, I will briefly look at some of the criticisms of the Convention, and will finally conclude with some thoughts as to the most likely "pressure point areas" in which future developments will give us clues as to the Convention's ultimate impact on the population in question.[3]

II. The Convention

The CRPD makes clear that persons with disabilities have the same human rights as all other persons (Stein, 2007b). As indicated earlier, see supra chapter 5, the CRPD calls for, among other rights, "respect for inherent dignity" and "nondiscrimination" (Art. 3), "freedom from torture or cruel, inhuman or degrading treatment or punishment"(Art. 15), "freedom from

[2] On the obligations imposed by the Convention, see Allain, 2009.

[3] See Gunn, 2009, p. 359, characterizing persons with disabilities as "the most fragile in any society."

exploitation, violence and abuse" (Art. 16), a right to protection of the "integrity of the person" (Art. 17), "equal recognition before the law" (Art. 12),[4] and equal "access to justice" (Art. 13).

Along with the Convention is an "optional protocol"[5] that provides mechanisms for individual and group communications and an inquiry procedure (Lord & Stein, 2009). The Optional Protocol is also an international treaty that establishes two procedures aimed at strengthening the implementation and monitoring of the Convention: an individual communications procedure allowing individuals to bring petitions to the Committee claiming breaches of their rights, and an inquiry procedure giving the Committee authority to undertake inquiries of grave or systematic violations of the Convention.

The CRPD is unique because it is the first legally binding instrument devoted to the comprehensive protection of the rights of persons with disabilities. It not only clarifies that States should not discriminate against persons with disabilities, but also sets out explicitly the many steps that States must take to create an enabling environment so that persons with disabilities can enjoy authentic equality in society. (On "authentic equality" in a related context, see United Nations, 1986.) By way of example, States are required to take measures to ensure accessibility of the physical environment and information and communications technology, and States have obligations in relation to raising awareness, promoting access to justice, ensuring personal mobility, and collecting disaggregated data relevant to the Convention. By measures such as these, the Convention goes into much greater depth than other human rights treaties in setting out the steps that States should take to prohibit discrimination and achieve equality for all.[6]

Also, employing a social development perspective,[7] the CRPD recognizes the importance of international cooperation and its promotion to support

---

[4] On the relationship between Article 12 and supported decision making, see Salzman, 2010, p. 181:

> [S]upported decision making and its recognition of universal (or near universal) capacity helps correct for the frequent underestimation of the abilities of persons with intellectual, psychosocial, and other conditions affecting mental functioning. Accordingly, supported decision making enables each individual to realize his or her fullest capabilities.

[5] On Optional Protocols in UN human rights instruments in general, see Mahon, 2008; see also, supra chapter 2.

[6] On the relationship between the CRPD and the Americans with Disabilities Act (see supra chapter 5), see Salzman, 2010; Lawson, 2008 (both focusing on requirements for reasonable accommodations); see also, Lord & Brown, 2010.

[7] Social development programs and policy innovations aim to integrate citizens into society through investments in individual capabilities, improvement of individual well-being, and promotion of participation in economic, social, and political systems (Midgley, 1993, 1995; see generally, McBride, Benitez & Danso, 2003).

national implementation efforts. It enumerates certain actions that the international community could take to promote international cooperation such as:

- ensuring that international development programs are inclusive of and accessible to persons with disabilities;
- facilitating and supporting capacity-building;[8]
- facilitating cooperation in research and access to scientific and technical knowledge; and
- providing technical and economic assistance as appropriate.

An examination of the CRPD needs to start with the Preamble, which gives a general context to the Convention and identifies important background issues. In the "purpose" section (see Art. 1), it sets out the goal of the Convention—to promote, protect, and ensure the full and equal enjoyment of all human rights and fundamental freedoms of all persons with disabilities, and to promote respect for their inherent dignity (see supra chapter 2).[9]

The key terms in the Convention are defined: communication,[10] discrimination on the basis of disability,[11] reasonable accommodation,[12] and universal design.[13] General principles are set out, identifying the standards or imperatives that apply to the enjoyment of all rights in the Convention, such as the principle of nondiscrimination and the principle of equality. It underscores the obligations that ratifying nations have, clarifying the steps that States must take to promote, protect, and ensure the rights in the Convention. Measures

---

[8] On the significance of capacity-building in the international human rights endeavor, see Liu & Halliday, 2009.

[9] On the specific significance of dignity in this Convention, see e.g., Hendriks, 2007; Kayess & Fogarty, 2007.

[10] "Communication" includes languages, display of text, Braille, tactile communication, large print, accessible multimedia as well as written, audio, plain-language, human-reader and augmentative and alternative modes, means and formats of communication, including accessible information and communication technology. (Art. 2)

[11] "Discrimination on the basis of disability" means any distinction, exclusion or restriction on the basis of disability which has the purpose or effect of impairing or nullifying the recognition, enjoyment or exercise, on an equal basis with others, of all human rights and fundamental freedoms in the political, economic, social, cultural, civil or any other field. It includes all forms of discrimination, including denial of reasonable accommodation. (Id.)

[12] "Reasonable accommodation" means necessary and appropriate modification and adjustments not imposing a disproportionate or undue burden, where needed in a particular case, to ensure to persons with disabilities the enjoyment or exercise on an equal basis with others of all human rights and fundamental freedoms. (Id.)

[13] "Universal design" means the design of products, environments, programmes and services to be usable by all people, to the greatest extent possible, without the need for adaptation or specialized design. "Universal design" shall not exclude assistive devices for particular groups of persons with disabilities where this is needed. (Id.)

that interfere with an individual's exercise of capacity must be carefully restricted (see Salzman, 2010; see generally, Kayess & Fogarty, 2007).

Specific rights are enumerated, identifying the existing civil, cultural, economic, political, and social human rights, affirming that persons with disabilities also hold those rights. Further, the Convention lists enabling measures, identifying the specific steps that States must take to ensure an environment for the enjoyment of human rights (awareness-raising, ensuring accessibility, ensuring protection and safety in situations of risk and humanitarian emergencies, promoting access to justice, ensuring personal mobility, enabling habilitation and rehabilitation, and collecting statistics and data).

The Convention also stresses the need for international cooperation (see Skogly, 2009), recognizing the importance of the international community working together to ensure the full enjoyment of the rights of persons with disability (see Fritsch, 2009). In its implementation and monitoring Article, it requires States to establish national frameworks for monitoring and implementing the Convention (see Stein & Lord, 2010, manuscript, pp. 7–10, discussing the Convention's "innovations" in this context),[14] and establishes a Conference of States Parties to consider any matter in relation to implementation of the Convention, as well as, significantly, a Committee on the Rights of Persons with Disabilities to monitor the Convention (see Quinn, 2009). Finally, in its final clauses, it sets out the procedures for signature, ratification, entering into force, and other procedural requirements relevant to the Convention.

Consider the major principles of the Convention, providing for:

- equality before the law without discrimination;
- right to life, liberty, and security of the person;
- equal recognition before the law and legal capacity;[15]
- freedom from torture, exploitation, violence, and abuse;
- right to respect physical and mental integrity;
- freedom of movement and nationality;
- the right to live in the community;
- right to education,[16] to health,[17] to work, to an adequate standard of living, to participate in political and public life[18] and in cultural life;[19]

---

[14] On monitoring of human rights instruments in general, see Mahon, 2008.

[15] See Lawson, 2007, p. 595 (legal capacity "lies at the very heart of the Convention").

[16] See generally, Petersen, 2010; see also, Hernandez, 2008 (CRPD can be a tool to provide inclusive education to students with disabilities in India and China).

[17] On the relationship between the right to health, international human rights law, and mental disability law in general, see supra chapter 1. On the relationship in the particular context of the CRPD, see Hunt & Mesquita, 2006; Gable, 2007.

[18] See e.g., *Kiss v. Hungary* (2010) (blanket voting disenfranchisement of persons with disabilities violates European Convention on Human Rights); see supra chapter 5, p. 50, n. 22.

[19] On the significance of the right to participate in sports, recreation, and play, see Lord & Stein, 2009. On the significance of access to the environment, see von Benzon, Makuch & Makuch, 2008.

- respect for inherent dignity[20] and individual autonomy,[21] including the freedom to make one's own choices and the independence of persons;
- nondiscrimination;
- full and effective participation and inclusion in society, and in political, cultural, and public life;
- respect for difference and acceptance of persons with disabilities as part of human diversity and humanity;
- equality of opportunity;
- accessibility;
- equality between men and women;
- respect for the evolving capacities of children with disabilities and respect for the right of children with disabilities to preserve their identities;
- freedom of expression and opinion;
- respect for privacy;
- respect for home and the family; and
- right to an adequate standard of living.

As I have discussed previously (and will discuss in depth subsequently, see infra chapter 8), one of the most critical issues in seeking to bring life to international human rights law in a mental disability law context is the right to adequate and dedicated counsel. The CRPD mandates that "States Parties shall take appropriate measures to provide access by persons with disabilities to the support they may require in exercising their legal capacity" (see Perlin, 2008, pp. 252–253, quoting Art. 12).[22] Elsewhere, the convention commands:

> States Parties shall ensure effective access to justice for persons with disabilities on an equal basis with others, including through the provision of procedural and age appropriate accommodations, in order to facilitate their effective role as direct and indirect participants, including as witnesses, in all legal proceedings, including at investigative and other preliminary stages. (Art. 13)

I have previously written that "The extent to which this Article is honored in signatory nations will have a major impact on the extent to which this entire Convention affects persons with mental disabilities" (Perlin, 2008, p. 253).

---

[20] On how States' responses to this section may determine whether local laws are violative of the CRPD, see Petersen, 2008.

[21] On the significance of the principle of autonomy in the CRPD, see Parker, 2008; Donnelly, 2008.

[22] On the significance of this statement of capacity, see Hessel, 2008.

If and only if, there is a mechanism for the appointment of dedicated counsel,[23] can this dream become a reality.[24]

In addition, the Convention sets out obligations on the part of ratifying States, including the requirement to adopt legislation and administrative measures to (1) promote the human rights of persons with disabilities; (2) abolish discrimination; (3) protect and promote the rights of persons with disabilities in all policies and programs; (4) stop any practice that breaches the rights of persons with disabilities; (5) ensure that the public sector respects the rights of persons with disabilities; (6) ensure that the private sector and individuals respect the rights of persons with disabilities; (7) undertake research and development of accessible goods, services, and technology for persons with disabilities and encourage others to undertake such research; (8) provide accessible information about assistive technology to persons with disabilities; (9) promote training on the rights of the Convention to professionals and staff who work with persons with disabilities; and (10) consult with and involve persons with disabilities in developing and implementing legislation and policies and in decision-making processes that concern them.

Monitoring issues are critical to Convention enforcement.[25] The CRPD establishes a Committee on the Rights of Persons with Disabilities, which has the role of reviewing periodic reports submitted by States on the steps they have taken to implement the Convention (Art. 36).[26] The Committee also has authority to examine individual communications and conduct inquiries in relation to those States that have recognized the Committee's authority to do so by ratifying the Optional Protocol. The Committee on Rights of Persons with Disabilities is a body of independent experts tasked with reviewing States' implementation of the Convention, serving in their personal capacities. The Committee is made up of 18 independent experts (Art. 34). State parties are to choose experts on the basis of their competence and experience in the field of human rights and disability, and also in consideration of equitable geographic representation, representation of different forms of civilization and legal systems, gender balance, and participation of experts with disabilities.[27]

---

[23] On the significance of "cause lawyers" in the development of mental disability law in the United States, see Stein, Waterstone & Wilkins, 2010. On the role of "cause lawyering" in other public interest law areas in a civil law nation with an authoritarian history, see Munger, 2007, 2008/2009.

[24] On the need for vigorous clinical legal education programs to best ensure a cadre of dedicated lawyers, see supra chapter 6.

[25] On the role of national human rights institutions in doing this monitoring, see infra chapter 9, and see supra chapter 3, n. [5] see Carver, 2010.

[26] On the significance of periodic review in the enforcement of human rights instruments in general, see Bernaz, 2009.

[27] On gender issues related to the CRPD in general, see Sandoval, 2009.

The Committee is mandated to periodically examine reports that are prepared by States, on the steps they have taken to implement the Convention. For those States party to the Optional Protocol, the Committee has authority to receive complaints from individuals of alleged breaches of their rights and to undertake inquiries in the event of grave or systematic violations of the Convention.

The CRPD provides an explicit reporting mechanism. Each State party to the Convention must submit to the Committee on the Rights of Persons with Disabilities an initial comprehensive report on measures taken to implement the Convention within two years after the Convention enters into force for that State. The initial report should:

- establish the constitutional, legal, and administrative framework for the implementation of the Convention;
- explain the policies and programs adopted to implement each of the Convention's provisions; and
- identify any progress made in the realization of the rights of persons with disabilities as a result of the ratification and implementation of the Convention.[28]

This latter right "clearly requires Governments to do much more than merely abstain from taking measures which might have a negative impact on persons with disabilities" (Kanter, 2009, p. 537).

Each State must submit subsequent reports at least every four years or whenever the Committee requests one. Subsequent reports should respond to the concerns and other issues highlighted by the Committee in its concluding observations to previous reports, indicate progress made in the realization of the rights of persons with disabilities over the reporting period, and highlight

---

[28] This is not the first time that the United Nations has considered the significance of progressive realization in the context of persons with disabilities. See Flynn, 2010, pp. 435–436, quoting UN Econ. & Soc. Council [ECOSOC], Comm. on Econ., Soc. and Cultural Rights, General Comment No. 5, Persons with Disabilities, P 9, U.N. Doc. No. E/1995/22 (Sept. 12, 1994):

> The obligation of States Parties to the Covenant to promote progressive realization of the relevant rights to the maximum of their available resources clearly requires Governments to do much more than merely abstain from taking measures which might have a negative impact on persons with disabilities. The obligation in the case of such a vulnerable and disadvantaged group is to take positive action to reduce structural disadvantages and to give appropriate preferential treatment to people with disabilities in order to achieve the objectives of full participation and equality within society for all persons with disabilities. This almost invariably means that additional resources will need to be made available for this purpose and that a wide range of specially tailored measures will be required.

any obstacles that the Government and other actors might have faced in implementing the Convention over the reporting period (Art. 35).

Complaints can be made to the Committee, per the Optional Protocol. That document establishes an individual communications procedure that permits individuals and groups in a State party to the Protocol to complain (in what is known as a "communication") to the Committee on the Rights of Persons with Disabilities that the State has breached one of its obligations under the Convention. The Committee examines the complaint and the observations of the State, and, on this basis, formulates its views and recommendations, if any, forwards them to the State, and makes them public.

The Committee can also undertake inquires via an inquiry procedure established by the Optional Protocol. If the Committee receives reliable information indicating grave or systematic violations by a State party to the Optional Protocol of any of the provisions of the Convention, the Committee may invite the State in question to respond to such information.

After considering the State party's observations and any other reliable information, the Committee may designate one or more of its members to conduct an inquiry and issue a report "urgently." If the State agrees, the Committee may visit the country in question. After undertaking the inquiry, the Committee transmits its findings to the State, which has 6 months to submit further observations. The Committee eventually summarizes its findings, which it makes public. However, a ratifying State may "opt out" of this inquiry procedure.

Critical to the structure of the CRPD is the monitoring role of "civil society." The Convention expressly stipulates that civil society, in particular persons with disabilities and their representative organizations and NGOs, shall be involved and participate fully in the monitoring process (see Art. 33.3). In this context, the Convention commands State parties to "in accordance with their legal and administrative systems, maintain, strengthen, designate or establish within the State Party, a framework, including one or more independent mechanisms, as appropriate, to promote, protect and monitor implementation of the present Convention" (Art. 33.2). Such "independent mechanisms" may include local national human rights institutions.[29]

In relation to international monitoring, States Parties are invited to give due consideration to consulting with and actively involving persons with disabilities and their representative organizations when nominating experts for the treaty body (see Art. 34.3). Experience from other international human rights treaty monitoring bodies highlights the critical role that civil society can play in the periodic reporting process, in supporting individuals in bringing

---

[29] Article 33 makes "indirect although not explicit reference" to the Paris Principles on the status of national human rights institutions (NHRIs). See de Burca, 2010, p. 185, n. 38, discussing those Principles; see Quinn, 2007. On the relationship between the CRPD and NHRIs in general, see Carver, 2010; Quinn, 2009.

individual communications, and in providing reliable information to the Committee on grave or systematic human rights violations as a basis for an inquiry. (See infra chapter 9, discussing the role of NGOs in the proposed Disability Rights Tribunal for Asia and the Pacific.)

Finally, States may enter reservations to conventions or treaties they choose to sign. See http://www.un.org/disabilities/default.asp?id=475 (listing all reservations to the CRPD). Under the rules governing treaty reservations introduced by the Vienna Convention (1969), after a treaty has been signed, states have an opportunity to attach reservations to it before ratification "whereby it purports to exclude or to modify the legal effect of certain provisions of the treaty in their application to that State" (Art. 2(1)(d)). (But see id., Art. 19(c): if a "reservation is incompatible with the object and purpose of the treaty" it may be invalid.)[30]

Last year, in discussing the CRPD, I stated: "I believe that this convention has the potential to create the most significant tectonic plate shift in mental disability law since the United States Supreme Court, finally, in 1972, agreed that the Due Process Clause of the U.S. Constitution applied to persons institutionalized because of mental disability" (Perlin, 2009, p. 484). I expect that the coming years will determine the accuracy of this prediction.

III. Local Issues and Litigation

Scholars have begun to assess the status of disability rights law in individual nations, and speculate as to the potential impact of the CRPD on local residents. (For a comparative consideration, looking at its likely effects in Finland and Uganda, see Kumpuvuori & Katsui, 2009). By way of example, Professor Michael Schwartz has written extensively about the conditions faced by persons with disabilities in Vietnam, and concludes that "the human values expressed in these laws give rise to the hope that Vietnam will work to conform

---

[30] By way of example, Thailand's reservation to the CRPD states "The Kingdom of Thailand hereby declares that the application of Article 18 of the Convention shall be subject to the national laws, regulations and practices in Thailand" (http://www.un.org/disabilities/default.asp?id=475). Article 18 guarantees that "States Parties shall recognize the rights of persons with disabilities to liberty of movement, to freedom to choose their residence and to a nationality, on an equal basis with others." It is not clear *why* Thailand entered into this reservation, but, if it is used in an effort to thwart previously institutionalized persons from relocating in community residences (see supra chapter 5), one could argue that one of the major raisons d'être of the Convention has been vitiated. Malaysia's reservations on Article 18 and Article 15 (prohibition of torture) have been specifically criticized by Human Rights Watch (see http://www.hrw.org/en/news/2010/08/16/malaysia-disability-rights-treaty-ratification-important-step [2010]).

The issue of incompatible reservations to the CRPD is discussed in Allain, 2008.

its policies and practices to reflect the high aspirations and ideals of the U.N. Convention" (2007, p. 514). Professor Andrew Byrnes argues that the CRPD mandates "a thorough review of Hong Kong law, policy and practice in the light of the Convention's framework" (2008, manuscript, p. 15). More globally, looking at sub-Saharan nations in the context of a different UN Convention (the Conventional on the Elimination of All Forms of Discrimination against Women), Professor Angela Banks determines that such Conventions "encourage states to undertake reforms that will facilitate and strengthen domestic enforcement" (2009, p. 782).[31] There is no question that much of this will be more challenging and difficult in nations where individuals with disabilities have traditionally been taught to "cherish their dependence on the care they receive from parents and institutions" (Heyer, 2000, p. 17; see also, Perlin, 2008a, pp. 500–501, discussing Heyer's article in this context).[32]

There has been remarkably little litigation yet based on the CRPD.[33] In one case before the European Court of Human Rights, *Glor v. Switzerland* (2009), a person with diabetes had been excluded from the armed forces because of that disability. The Court suggested that the CRPD served as the basis of what Professor Jill Stavert has characterized as "a European and universal consensus on the need to prevent discriminatory treatment of persons with disabilities" (2010, p. 143, relying on *Glor*, para. 53), relying on the concept of reasonable accommodation in the CRPD (Kanter, 2009, p. 556). In a case from India, a woman with mental disabilities was raped by security guards in a government-run orphanage, the rape leading to her pregnancy. Over her wishes, the State government sought a ruling to abort the pregnancy. The Supreme Court held that the woman be allowed to continue the pregnancy, and that the pregnancy could not be terminated without her consent, invoking the national Maternal Termination of Pregnancy Act to rule that the Act

---

[31] See also id., pp. 790–791: "Implementing the reforms necessary for effective domestic enforcement does require the structural reforms that are part of traditional rule of law initiatives."On the need for a strong local judiciary to promote human rights through judicial review, see Twinomugisha, 2009.

[32] On the specific issues endemic to Asia and the debate over so-called Asian values, see infra chapter 9; see generally, Thio, 1999.

[33] See also, e.g., *Governors of X Endowed Primary School v Special Educational Needs and Disability Tribunal* (2009) (CRPD did not provide support for claim under disability discrimination in United Kingdom); *AM (Somalia) v Entry Clearance Officer* (2009) (CRPD did not require preferential treatment for person with disability in asylum application); *The Queen on the Application of Cardiff County Council v Welsh Ministers* (2010) (CRPD did not support applicant's claim involving funding arrangements on behalf of person with disability in care home); *The Queen (on the application of Steven Harrison) v The Secretary of State for Health* (2009)(CRPD does not require the making of direct cash payments to individuals receiving health care services under the United Kingdom National Health Service Act).

clearly respects the personal autonomy of persons with mental disabilities who are above the age of majority (www.un.org/disabilities/documents/events/csw54_side-event_rangtadasilva.doc), and urging the need to "look beyond social prejudices" to ensure the best pre- and postnatal care and supervision of the mother and child. Professor Rangita de Silva de Alwis, director of the International Human rights Policy at the Wellesley Centers for Women, has written that this case reflects "a conceptual framework on the intersectionalities" of the Convention on the Elimination of all Forms of Discrimination against Women and the CRPD (id.).

In a recent domestic Australian case (involving an application to set aside wills because of testamentary incapacity) the Supreme Court of the State of Victoria, in the course of its decision, had this to say about the CRPD:

> The CRPD marks a paradigm shift in approaches to persons with disabilities. It reflects a movement from treating persons with disabilities as objects of social protection towards treating them as subjects with rights, who are capable of claiming and exercising those rights and making decisions based on free and informed consent as active members of society. (*Nicholson v. Knaggs*, 2009, para. 13)

This decision, according to Professor Ron McCallum, demonstrated the ability of the CRPD to "influence the growth of . . . Common Law" (2010, p. 10).

Perhaps most interestingly, in the course of a New York State case finding that guardianship appointments need be subject to requirements of periodic reporting and review, Surrogate Judge Kristen Booth Glen relied on the CRPD in support of her decision, reasoning that international human rights norm were relevant to the case before her, and "more broadly, [to] the situation of persons with intellectual disabilities, by virtue of the Supremacy Clause" (*In the Matter of Mark C.H.*, 2010, p. *9). In addition, whatever treaty obligations the United States might eventually assume, "international adoption of the protection of the rights of persons with intellectual and other disabilities, including the right to periodic review of burdens on individual liberty, is entitled to 'persuasive weight' in interpreting our own law and constitutional protection" (id., p. *11, citing, inter alia, *Lawrence v. Texas*, 2003 [see supra chapter 6]).

She referred here to Article 12 of the Convention, concluding that "state interventions, like guardianships, pursuant to parens patriae power, must be subject to periodic review to prevent the abuses which may otherwise flow from the state's grant of power over a person with disabilities such as those covered by [state law]" (id., p. *10).[34] In addition, she noted that, besides

---

[34] On the importance of a careful reading of Article 12, see Dhanda, 2007 pp. 460–461:

> The text of Article 12 does not prohibit substituted decisionmaking and there is language which could even be used to justify substitution. Under the circumstances, it could well be argued that the article would be a stranglehold of the past on the Convention. However, such a contention can be made only if the

Article 12, other Articles provided persons with disabilities with a "plethora of rights" in this regard (id., and see n. 47, listing relevant articles).[35]

As, at the time of the writing of the opinion, the United States had signed but not yet ratified the Convention,[36] she located the state's obligation in the Vienna Convention on the Law of Treaties, that required signatories to "refrain from acts which would defeat [the CRPD's] object and purpose" (id., citing Vienna Convention, Art. 18). "Arguably," she continued, granting guardianships (especially plenary guardianships) over persons with mental retardation and developmental disability with absolutely no review provisions defeats the "object[s] and purpose" of a Convention intended to "protect against the injustice . . . and violation of rights" confronting persons with intellectual disabilities (id.).

IV. Some Criticisms[37]

There are those who believe the Convention does not go far enough.[38] Tina Minkowitz, an attorney and psychiatric survivor, argues that that it should

---

> universal reach of the capacity formulation is diluted or ignored and the article is read divorced from the process of advocacy and negotiation. [E]very effort at keeping legal capacity shackled to the past has been challenged and fought. When viewed in the light of these processes, then the paradigm shift made by the article can be seen and appreciated.

See also, *Nicholson v. Skaggs*, 2009, paras. 69–70 ("The Article recognises that some people with disability need support to make decisions in the exercise of their legal rights"); Lord, Suozzi & Taylor, 2010, p. 573 (Article 12 acknowledges "that some disabled people require no support in making decisions, while others may need intensive support").

[35] E.g., Art. 22 (right to privacy); Art. 16 (freedom from exploitation); Art. 15 (right to freedom from degrading punishment). "Unsupervised, unreviewed guardianships of persons with mental retardation and developmental disability may, sadly, result in violations of any or all of these protected rights" (id.).

At the time of the writing of this volume, the CRPD has only been cited in one other case in the United States. See *Townsend v. Calderone* (2010) (dismissing complaint on unrelated grounds; CRPD issue not reached).

[36] See http://www.usun-ny.us/press_releases/20090730_156.html (United States signed CRPD, July 30, 2009). On the reasons why the Bush administration had refused to sign the CRPD, see Melish, 2009, discussing http://archive.usun.state.gov/press_releases/20061213_396.html. On why the United States should ratify the CRPD, see Melish, 2007. On the need for the United States to "restor[e its] human rights reputation," see Koh, 2007, p. 659.

[37] For a global critique of human rights Conventions, see Dillon, 2008, p. 154 ("A specialized human rights convention does not in itself guarantee substantial change").

[38] A psychiatric survivor group from Germany has recently called for the exclusion of Dr. Theresia Degener (see supra chapters 1 & 2) from the CRPD Committee on the Rights of Persons with Disabilities because of her position that psychiatric facilities,

have banned institutionalization entirely (Minkowitz, 2007).[39] Minkowitz contends that forced psychiatric interventions violate the prohibition against torture (id., p. 405; see also, Gottstein, 2008, p. 101 ["forced drugging is experienced as torture by those forced to endure it"]), "necessitating criminalization of perpetrators and reparations for victims and survivors" (Minkowitz, 2007, p. 405), concluding that, with "the advent of the CRPD, a new era is in the making" (id., p. 427).[40] In her consideration of Minkowitz's position, Professor Arlene Kanter points out that the Convention is, nevertheless, "stronger" than any prior UN document and views institutionalization only "as a last resort" (2009, p. 565). Writing contemporaneously with Minkowitz, Anna Lawson summed the issue up this way:

> According to Article 14.1, disabled people must be granted the right to liberty and security of person on an equal basis with others. It provides very clearly that "the existence of a disability shall in no case justify a deprivation of liberty." Thus, it will never provide adequate grounds for detention in a prison, hospital or other residential institution that a person simply has a particular physical, intellectual or psycho-social condition. (2007, p. 612)[41]

Coming from another perspective, Mary Donnelly warns that the right to autonomy—one of the bedrock principles of the CRPD—"is limited in what it can deliver in the context of treatment for a mental disorder," and that it must be seen as "part of a broader human rights framework, [including] delivery on the rights to dignity, privacy and bodily integrity" (2008, p. 57).[42]

---

in se, do not violate the CRPD. See e-mail from Rene Talbot (August 26, 2010), on file with author, and see also e-mail from Rene Talbot (July 22, 2010), on file with author (CRPD monitoring agency "turns into an organization for the perpetuation of illegal psychiatric power").

39 Minkowitz was a member of the UN Working Group that produced the first draft text of the Convention. Id., p. 405.

40 For a call for further research on questions of coercion and involuntary treatment, see Selize & Dressing, 2005.

41 I do not believe that the CRPD requires the abolition of all involuntary civil commitment. I believe, however, that it demands that such commitment—whether it be premised on the police power or on the *parens patriae* power—be absolutely the last resort, that such commitments be based on a finding of serious mental illness (and significant dangerousness to self or others as a result of that mental illness) by the "beyond a reasonable doubt" commitment standard, and that adequate and effective counsel (and expert assistance) be provided for each person facing such commitment. Such commitments must be time limited, and the same body of rights must apply at all subsequent periodic review hearings. See generally Perlin, 1998.

42 See also, Lord, Suozzi & Taylor, 2010, p. 576 (weaknesses in Convention are consequence of "unresolved tension between the medical and charity model of

Another issue to consider is this: To what extent will signatory nations actually *enforce* the Convention that they ratified? This is an issue that scholars have addressed in a variety of fact settings involving other social and economic rights (see, e.g., Lyon, 2010 [migrant workers]; Piccard, 1010 [women], Kenney, 2009 [investment treaties]; Pauwelyn, 2005 [world trade]), but it has not yet been addressed in the literature in this context. The most cynical view is the one expressed by Goldsmith and Posner, as construed by Eric Neumayer (2007):

> International human rights treaties do not exert any independent effect on the behavior of countries. If governments respect human rights, they do so because it coincides with their interests. The coincidence of interest can be a result of domestic political pressure (as is the case in liberal democracies), the consequence of cooperation (as might be the case when two states have each other's ethnic groups residing in their territories as minorities), or the consequence of external coercion, which will occasionally be applied by powerful states if human rights abuse in less powerful countries threatens their interests. Importantly, so the argument goes, countries never respect human rights simply because they feel obliged to comply with international law.
>
> . . . Authoritarian states typically ignore human rights norms codified in international treaties, unless they are coerced or find it otherwise in their interest to respect human rights, which is rarely the case. (pp. 400–401, citing Goldsmith & Posner, 2005)

It is no secret that some nations are known to deviate from international human rights standards and ignore other international human rights norms (Totah, 2003), especially when they are perceived as constraining "national interests" (Katz, 2003, p. 92), and that other states may use the ratification of a treaty as a ploy to offset external or internal pressure for policy change (Adams, 2005). Yet, especially when human rights treaties are interpreted in a political environment that recognizes the "interconnectedness of identity, interests, dignity and access to . . . resources" (see Andrews, 2006, p. 712), such treaties have the power to truly transform society. Professor Elizabeth Defeis has written eloquently about how the Universal Declaration of Human Rights was central in the struggle in South Africa against apartheid, and how it provided "a focus and rallying point for those seeking to overturn the system" (2004, p. 265). There is no reason why the CRPD cannot serve a similar function.

---

disability and the social model of disability"), and id., p. 577 (agenda that led to the drafting of the Convention "is as yet unfinished").

V. Conclusion

The ratification of the CRPD is the most important development—ever—in institutional human rights law for persons with mental disabilities. The CRPD is detailed, comprehensive, integrated, and the result of a careful drafting process. It seeks to reverse the results of centuries of oppressive behavior and attitudes that have stigmatized persons with disabilities. Its goal, set out in Article 1, is clear: to promote, protect, and ensure the full and equal enjoyment of all human rights and fundamental freedoms of all persons with disabilities, and to promote respect for their inherent dignity. Whether this will actually *happen* is still far from a settled matter. In the next chapter, I argue why the presence of dedicated and regularized counsel is the single most important reform to have a chance of making the aspirations of the CRPD a reality.

8

The UN Convention: The Role of Counsel

I. Introduction

If there has been any constant in modern mental disability law in its near-forty-year history, it is the near-universal reality that counsel assigned to represent individuals at involuntary civil commitment cases is likely to be ineffective (Perlin & Sadoff, 1982; Perlin, 2008). It is well known in virtually all American jurisdictions (Perlin, 1998, chapter 2B; Perlin, 1992), and internationally as well. As discussed earlier (see supra chapter 5), in many nations, there simply is *no* mental disability "law" (Perlin, 2007, and see id., p. 337 ["A recent report by the World Health Organization revealed that 25% of all nations in the world have no mental health law"]), and that, even where there is such a law "on the books," the promise of counsel was little more than an illusion (see id., p. 341 ["It is rare for even minimal access to counsel to be statutorily (or judicially) mandated, and, even where counsel is legislatively ordered, it is rarely provided. Moreover, the lack of meaningful judicial review makes the commitment hearing system little more than a meretricious pretext"]). See Perlin, (2008, p. 242: in many nations, "promise of counsel was little more than an illusion").[1]

[1] This should not be read as a blanket endorsement of the way counsel is often provided in American jurisdictions. See Perlin, 1992, p. 404 (footnotes omitted):

> Traditionally, sporadically-appointed counsel . . . were unwilling to pursue necessary investigations, lacked . . . expertise in mental health problems, and suffered from "rolelessness," stemming from near total capitulation to experts,

Blanket pessimism, however, may not be the appropriate response. Encouragingly, a variety of interrelated factors may shed some light on this scandal and lead to positive social change in this area: the new, robust case law from the European Court on Human Rights on virtually all aspects of mental disability law (see Perlin et al., 2006a, pp. 451–789);[2] the ratification of the United Nations Convention on the Rights of Persons with Disabilities, and the publication of the World Health Organization *Resource Book on Mental Health* (see Perlin et al., 2006b, pp. 63–105), both of which will eventually attract international attention to this issue (e.g., Gable, 2007; Kanter, 2007); the focus by mental disability law–specific NGOs (e.g., Mental Disability Rights International; Mental Disability Advocacy Center) on institutional conditions in central and eastern Europe and in Central and South America, calling attention to this issue (see generally, Perlin, 2007), and greater interest globally in what can broadly be called "access to justice" issues (e.g., Chan, 2007; Woo, 2007; see supra chapter 5, p. 88, n. 22).

Is this modest optimism justified? Are there, in reality, any glimmers of hope that might lead us to expect that, globally, there will be some point in the future when lawyers who represent persons facing civil commitment will no longer be, in Judge David Bazelon's memorable phrase, "walking violations of the Sixth Amendment"? (Bazelon, 1973, p. 2.)

In part II of this chapter, I will survey an array of international jurisdictions (common law, civil law, and mixed) and consider the range of findings (from nations in which there is no counsel, to perfunctory-at-best counsel, to almost-adequate counsel). In part III, I will consider other major legal, political, and social developments that might, it is hoped, illuminate these issues.[3] In part IV, I will consider the impact of sanism and pretextuality on these developments. Finally, I will offer some modest conclusions.

II. A Global Consideration

Globally, there is little good news.[4] In many nations, there is no mental health law at all (see Perlin, 2007, pp. 337–340, listing multiple examples). In others, there is simply no provision for counsel (id., pp. 340–342, listing examples).

---

hazily defined concepts of success/failure, inability to generate professional or personal interest in the patient's dilemma, and lack of a clear definition of the proper advocacy function. As a result, counsel . . . functioned "as no more than a clerk, ratifying the events that transpired, rather than influencing them."

[2] On the right to counsel in ECHR proceedings, see Bartlett, Lewis & Thorold, 2007, pp. 242–252.

[3] See supra chapter 6 for a discussion of the impact of clinical legal education on these developments.

[4] For a particularly pessimistic view of the state of affairs in the former Soviet bloc nations, see Lewis, 2002.

In others, counsel appears to be present in name only, what is referred to disparagingly in the literature as the "warm body" problem (see Metzger, 2007, p. 1198 ["This right to counsel is not satisfied by the mere appearance of a warm body wearing a business suit and holding a copy of the [statute book]"]). In only a few instances does counsel appear to be doing a remotely adequate job.[5] Persons with mental disabilities are a paradigmatic example of the individuals—in Frank Bloch's words—"deprived of basic rights and needs [who] are unable to benefit from relief that might be available through their local legal system and legal regime" (Bloch, 2007, p. 8).

In some areas of the world, the picture is especially dismal. On the African continent, South Africa is apparently the only nation that provides counsel prior to civil commitment (Mental Health Act of 2002, s. 15).[6] A recent comprehensive study of access to justice in Africa does not reveal any other example of the existence of such a right (see Penal Reform Int'l & Bluhm Legal Clinic, 2007). A recent comprehensive analysis of the law in Uganda, in fact, focuses on that legislation's failure to provide counsel as one of its major "human rights gaps" (Moses, 2007, pp. 12–13). Although there is a right to counsel in India (India Mental Health Act § 91, 1987), research has revealed no such right in a range of other Asian nations including, inter alia, Afghanistan, China, Indonesia, Pakistan, South Korea, Sri Lanka, Thailand, and Vietnam;[7] similarly, no such right appears to exist in a range of South American nations, including Argentina, Peru, and Venezuela. The only non-U.S.-based evidence of a hospital administration urging the extended appointment of counsel in civil commitment cases is from Israel (Bauer et al., 2005, p. 668: ["[I]t seems advisable that all persons hospitalized compulsorily . . . be legally represented at RPB [Regional Psychiatric Board] hearings, in order to ensure the greatest possible protection for their rights, first and foremost their liberty"]; see also Bauer, 2007, p. 67, speculating that amendment to national mental health law

---

[5] There has been significant litigation in western Europe on matters involving, e.g., involuntary civil commitment and institutional rights, stemming largely from the promulgation of the Human Rights Act of 1998, which brought certain rights articulated in the European Convention of Human Rights into domestic law. See Bindman et al., 2003; Kingdon et al., 2004; Perlin, 2007; Gledhill, 2007; Smith, 2007; Williams, 2006. Also, there has been significant scholarly attention paid to these issues by scholars in the United Kingdom and Australia. See Beaupert, 2009; Carney & Beaupert, 2008; Carney et al., 2007; Pearson, 2004; Bisogni, 2002 (all Australia); Gledhill, 2007 (UK), but these appear to be the stark exceptions.

[6] For a recent article mapping out theoretical and doctrinal foundations for an indigenous model of conceptualizing disability rights in South Africa, see Bhaba, 2009.

[7] On how a Disability Rights Tribunal for Asia and the Pacific could significantly ameliorate this issue, see infra chapter 9.

providing for counsel in all RPB proceedings "will bring about a diminution in the number of involuntary hospitalizations").[8]

This is troubling for many reasons, not the least of which is that, without the availability of such counsel, it has been "virtually impossible" to imagine the existence of the bodies of involuntary civil commitment law, right to treatment law, right to refuse treatment law, or any aspect of forensic mental disability law that are now taken for granted in the United States (Perlin, 2007, p. 341).[9] Without the presence of counsel, legal reform—in nations with developing economies, at least—"will all too often be a hollow shell" (Golub, 2007, p. xviii, in Penal Reform Int'l & Bluhm Legal Clinic, 2007).[10]

I also believe it necessary that a "coherent network" of culturally competent advocacy services be built into any advocacy program to work with lawyers in any dedicated advocacy system (see Beaupert, 2009, p. 103, and see Van Ness & Perlin, 1977, p. 63, discussing the equal mix of lawyers and nonlawyers providing advocacy services in New Jersey's Division of Mental Health Advocacy, one of the first U.S.-based statewide programs providing legal advocacy for persons with mental disabilities).[11] This integration of legal and advocacy services is an essential predicate to meaningful legal reform.[12]

---

[8] Bauer works for the Forensic Psychiatry Unit of the Mental Health Services Division of the Israel Ministry of Mental Health.

[9] The development of organized and regularized counsel programs has given rise to the supposition that such counsel is regularly available to persons with mental disabilities in individual matters involving their commitment to, retention in and release from psychiatric hospitals. But, this appearance of general availability is largely illusory. Moreover, such representation is rarely available in a systemic way in law reform or test cases and is rarely provided in any systemic way in cases that involve counseling or negotiating short of actual litigation. (Perlin, 2003b, pp. 707–708, footnotes omitted)

[10] On the relationship between the access to counsel and access to justice, see Zimerman & Tyler, 2010. On the question of effectiveness of counsel in civil commitment matters, see Perlin, 2003b, pp. 691–694, discussing *In re Mental Health of K.G.F.* (2001).

[11] On the different structures of mental disability law delivery systems, see 1 Perlin, 1998, chapter 2B. On the significance of advocacy offices having the capacity to engage in law reform, test case litigation (as well as individualized casework), see id., § 2B-4.2, pp. 208–214.

[12] On developments in public law litigation in one civil law jurisdiction (Brazil), see McAllister, 2008, in a common law jurisdiction, see Yew, 2008 (Singapore), and in a comparative law context in two common law jurisdictions (India and Australia), see Forster & Jivan, 2008. On specific issues faced in other legal contexts in mixed systems, see Himonga, 2010; Fombad, 2010. On the "amalgam" system in Israel, see supra chapter 5, p. 88, n. 20.

III. Other Major Legal, Political and Social Developments

There is an important paradox here that needs to be highlighted. At the same time that these nondevelopments have taken place, there have been many important and overlapping positive developments, which, when considered together, shine new light on the underlying issues and promise to focus new attention on them in the near future.

First is the first international case law that begins to articulate a broad right to counsel in all cases. Decisions such as *Airey v. Ireland*, 1979, and *Currie v. Jamaica*, 1989, as discussed in Paoletti, 2006, p. 655 n. 32 (both concluding that a litigant's right to effective access to the courts may sometimes require the state to provide for the assistance of a lawyer) have begun to give litigators the tools through which they can seek to "craft arguments supporting the right to counsel in civil proceedings under international law" (Paoletti, 2006, p. 651). For mental disability law to flourish, it is essential that advocates bring cases in international courts to articulate this specific right in the specific context of involuntary civil commitment.

Second, again, is the ratification of the United Nations Convention on the Rights of Persons with Disabilities (see supra chapter 7). As discussed previously, the UN Convention mandates that "States Parties shall take appropriate measures to provide access by persons with disabilities to the support they may require in exercising their legal capacity" (GA Res. 61/106, P 12.3, U.N. Doc. A/RES/61/106; Dec. 13, 2006; see generally Stein, 2007; for a thoughtful and comprehensive predecessor article, see Dhir, 2005).[13] Elsewhere, the convention commands:

> States Parties shall ensure effective access to justice for persons with disabilities on an equal basis with others, including through the provision of procedural and age appropriate accommodations, in order to facilitate their effective role as direct and indirect participants, including as witnesses, in all legal proceedings, including at investigative and other preliminary stages. (GA Res. 61/106, P 13.1, U.N. Doc. A/RES/61/106; Dec. 13, 2006)

---

[13] On the potential international law bases of a global right to counsel in all civil cases, see Paoletti 2006; Lidman, 2006; Engler, 2006; Kaufman, 2008; Davis, 2009. For a stark example of the need for the articulation of this right, see Sesickas, 2000 (Lithuania). For an analysis of the efforts of the judiciary in one nation to ensure such access to justice, see Yew, 2008 (Singapore). In the United States, at least, civil commitment cases—for purposes of such matters as burden of proof—occupy a space between civil and criminal cases. See, e.g., *Addington v. Texas*, (1979) (finding that an intermediate burden of clear and convincing evidence is required, explaining why neither the traditional criminal nor civil burden is appropriate in such a case); see 1 Perlin, 1998, § 2C-5.1a, pp. 395–400.

The extent to which this Article is honored in signatory nations will have a major impact on the extent to which this entire Convention affects persons with mental disabilities (see Perlin, 2008, 2009).

Distinguished commentators have raised important, but still unanswered, questions:

- To what extent will the Convention, in fact, *truly* be a "human rights convention for the 21st century"? (See, e.g., Waddington, 2007.)
- Will the convention be a "clear moral compass"? (See, e.g., Quinn, 2007. Keynote Speech at the European Conference on the Integration of Persons with Disabilities: The UN Convention on the Human Rights of Persons with Disabilities 3 (June 10, 2007), discussed in Perlin, 2008, p. 253 n. 79).
- Is there a human right to legal aid? (See Rice, 2007.)
- To what extent must any advocacy system include an authentic consumer voice? (See Carney et al., 2008.)
- To what extent will the advocacy system be culturally competent? (See Beaupert, 2009.)
- To what extent will skills training be an essential component of any advocacy program? (See Banks & Kayess, 2007.)
- What are the benchmarks for designing and implementing supported decision making, and what benchmarks exist for support networks, community services, policies/programs, and constitutional/legislative provisions? (See Bach, 2007.)

Not until there is a body of law construing the Convention will these questions be answered.

The third development is the focus by mental disability law-specific NGOs (e.g., Disability Rights International; Mental Disability Advocacy Center) on institutional conditions in central and eastern Europe and in Central and South America, calling attention to this issue. Recent years have seen the emergence of two important NGOs, one based in Washington, DC, and one based in Budapest, both of which have done a heroic job (Perlin, 2007, p. 334) by calling the world's attention to worldwide conditions in psychiatric institutions and to the inhuman and degrading treatment of persons institutionalized by reason of mental disability.[14] It is not an exaggeration to say that, together, these two groups have done more than all the "traditional" human rights offices combined to call the world's attention to these issues (Perlin & Szeli, 2011). And the lack of counsel available to persons institutionalized because of mental disability is one of those issues emphasized in their

[14] For discussions of the work done by MDRI and MDAC, see Perlin, 2007, p. 337; Gable, 2007, p. 540; Kanter, 2007, 316; Geisinger & Stein, 2007, pp. 107–109; Hortas, 2004, pp. 181–182; see generally Perlin et al., 2006a, pp. 803–809, 855–57, 862–863, 867–869, 872–881. See generally supra chapter 1.

reports and other documents (Lewis, 2002, pp. 195–96. See also Mental Disability Rights International, 1995, 2000, 2008).

The fourth is the inspiring work done by human rights advocates and professors focusing on the need for clinical programs as a part of a comprehensive human rights legal education to best prepare of their students to focus on global justice issues when they enter law practice (Perlin, 2008; Stuckey, 2002; Iya, 2005; McQuoid-Mason, 2000; see supra chapter 6).

Individuals with mental disabilities—people who are largely "voiceless" and "traditionally isolated from the majoritarian democratic political system"—are frequently marginalized to an even greater extent than are others who fit within the definition of "discrete and insular minorities" (Perlin, 2003b, p. 687;[15] see also, Lawson, 2008; Kampf, 2008). As scholars begin to explore the human right of "access to justice" in Western (see Smith, 2007), eastern European (see Sesickas, 2000), and Asian (see Kumar, 2008; Chan, 2007) nations, it becomes even more critical that we turn our attention to the specific question of the access to justice of *this* population.[16]

IV. The Meaning and Significance of Sanism and Pretextuality in This Context

I have previously discussed the significance of sanism and pretextuality in this area of law and social policy (see supra chapter 2). It is especially significant in matters involving the assignment of counsel and the quality of counsel. Writing about this topic seven years ago, I alleged:

> Sanism permeates the legal representation process both in cases in which mental capacity is a central issue, and those in which such capacity is a collateral question. Sanist lawyers (1) distrust their mentally disabled clients, (2) trivialize their complaints, (3) fail to forge authentic attorney-client relationships with such clients and reject their clients' potential contributions to case-strategizing, and (4) take less seriously case outcomes that are adverse to their clients. (Perlin, 2003b, p. 695, see supra chapter 2, p. 35)

Although there is a robust "psychiatric survivor" movement both in the United States and elsewhere (Honig & Fendell, 2000; Margulies, 1992; see

[15] The "discrete and insular minorities" phrase is found in *United States v. Carolene Products Co.*, 1938, p. 152, n. 4.

[16] See Carney et al., 2008: "Nowhere is [the risk of loss of liberty] more evident than in mental health tribunal review hearings about detaining a person against their will" (Australia). See also, Pearson, 2004, on the need for "zealous advocacy" in such cases (Australia).

supra chapters 1 & 7), this voice is typically ignored.[17] For more than 25 years, formerly hospitalized individuals and their supporters have performed an important role in the reform of the mental health system and in test case litigation. "Yet, there is little evidence that these groups are taken seriously either by lawyers or academics" (Perlin, 2007, pp. 699–700; see supra chapter 1).

As I discussed earlier (see supra chapters 1 & 2), sanism-inspired errors by lawyers can easily be fatal to the client's chance of success in the civil commitment context, and elsewhere in the legal process (e.g., right to refuse treatment; deinstitutionalization). If a lawyer rejects the notion that his client may be competent (indeed, if he engages in the not-atypical "presumption of incompetency" that is all too often de rigueur in these cases, Perlin, 2003a p. 193),[18] the chances are far slimmer that he will advocate for such a client in a meaningful way. In nations with no tradition of an "expanded due process model" (Perlin, 1997, p. 971), in cases involving persons subject to commitment to psychiatric institutions or those already institutionalized, a lawyer's sanism can kill his client's chance for release or for a judicial order mandating amelioration of conditions of confinement, or access to or freedom from treatment (see generally, Perlin, 2003b).

V. Conclusion

The legislative and judicial creation of rights—both positive and negative—is illusory unless there is a parallel mandate of counsel that is (1) free and (2) regularized and organized. Without the presence of such counsel, any rights articulated by a court, human rights commission, or legislature become merely "paper victories" (Perlin, 2002, p. 246, quoting Lottman, 1976, p. 93).[19]

Further, to be authentically effective, counsel needs to be available both for individual cases (in which commitment of the patient is being sought) and in "affirmative" cases—that is, cases consciously thought of as "public interest" or "law reform" cases in which persons with disabilities file suit as plaintiffs seeking variously to have courts articulate procedural or substantive

---

[17] One important exception is Imai, 2002, p. 199 (discussing Osgoode Hall Law School's clinic's collaborative work with Parkdale Community Legal Services in representing one such group).

[18] Id.:

> In short, the presumption in which courts have regularly engaged—that there is both a de facto and de jure presumption of incompetency to be applied to medication decision making—appears to be based on an empirical fallacy: psychiatric patients are not necessarily more incompetent than nonmentally ill persons to engage in independent medication decision making. (citation omitted).

[19] Compare, on access to justice in the United States in general, Johnson, 2000; to access in Asia, Kumar, 2008.

due process rights in the commitment process (e.g., *Lessard v. Schmidt*, 1972), or to have courts articulate such rights with regard to conditions of confinement, the latter encompassing both positive rights, e.g., a right to treatment services (e.g., *Wyatt v. Stickney*, 1971, affirmed, 1974) and negative rights, e.g., the right to refuse treatment, e.g., *Rennie v. Klein*, 1981).

An argument certainly can be made that the presence of sanism and the technical complexity of involuntary civil commitment cases (involving, necessarily, expert testimony by mental health professionals and subtle predictions about "future dangerousness," see generally, 2 Perlin, 1998, chapter 2A), augment the necessity and importance of adequate representation in such cases. In arguing why the United States should ratify the new UN Convention, again, as noted earlier (see supra chapters 1 and 2), Tara Melish focused on the "deeply entrenched attitudes and stereotypes about disability that have rendered many of the most flagrant abuses of the rights of persons with disabilities 'invisible' from the mainstream human rights lens" (2007, p. 44). These stereotypes are the essence of sanism; vigorous, advocacy-focused counsel is needed to answer and rebut them.

9

A Disability Rights Tribunal for Asia and the Pacific

Introduction[1]

There can be no question that the existence of regional human rights courts and commissions has been an essential element in the enforcement of international human rights in those regions of the world where such tribunals exist.[2] In the specific area of mental disability law, there is now a remarkably robust body of case law from the European Court on Human Rights, some significant and transformative decisions from the Inter-American Commission on Human Rights, and at least one major case from the African Commission on Human Rights (see supra chapter 3).[3]

[1] See generally, Perlin, 2010a, 2010b; Ikehara, 2010; Perlin & Ikehara, 2010a, 2010b.

[2] For an earlier assessment, see Weston, Lukes & Hnatt, 1987. On the multiplicity of international courts and tribunals, see Tiba, 2006. On the legitimacy of such institutions, see Buchanan & Keohane, 2006. The authors conclude that such institutions are valuable "because they create norms and information that enable member states and other actors to coordinate their behavior in mutually beneficial ways" (id., p. 408).

[3] In an earlier chapter, I discussed cases litigated in other parts of the world that have had a tremendous impact on the human rights for persons with disabilities (see supra chapter 3). Not only do they serve as an example for other nations to follow in assuring human rights to every person, but these cases also demonstrate the potential effectiveness of regional tribunals.

In Asia and the Pacific region, however, there is no such body (see Campbell & McDonald, 2006; on the "iron[y]" of Asia's "imperviousness" to international human rights law in this context, see Durbach, Renshaw & Byrnes, 2009, p. 212).[4] The tradition of human rights protection in this region has never been "enviable" (Diokno, 1980, p. 43; see also, Yamane, 1982, p. 18, noting "It would seem difficult if not impossible to establish a regional mechanism in Asia for safeguarding human rights on the basis of regional law"). Although the Association of Southeast Asian Nations (ASEAN) charter refers to human rights (see "Selected Human Rights Documents," 2000), that body cannot be seen as a significant enforcement tool in this area of law and policy.[5] Some of the antipathy flows from past colonialism, and the feeling that "human rights values" are "Western values" (Engle, 2000).[6] Some of it comes from the attitude that "Human rights mechanisms, enhanced by international instruments, are seen as a threat to national sovereignty" (Mohamad, 2002, p. 247).[7] Many reasons have been offered for the absence of a regional human rights tribunal in Asia;[8] the most serious of these are the perceived conflict between what are often denominated as "Asian values" and universal human rights,[9] and Asian nations' "staunch adherence to the principle of non-interference in the domestic affairs of another state" (Yee, 2004, p. 163). What is clear is that the lack of such a court or commission has been a major impediment in the movement to enforce disability rights in Asia.[10]

---

[4] Compare Iwasawa, 1997, p. 264 (discussing reluctance of domestic judges in Japan to adjudicate claims based on international human rights law).

[5] By way of example, although the Asian Human Rights Charter calls for the right of "differently abled persons" to "live in dignity, with security and respect," see Shelton, 2010, p. 1083 (quoting Charter, para. 11.1), it is clear that this aspiration is not realized in most Asian nations. On whether ASEAN even "exists" as an "international legal person," see Chesterman, 2010/

[6] See Kausikan, 1995–1996, p. 277: "Asian values have been a balm for the cultural wounds inflicted by western colonialism"; see also, Moyle, 1997; Gervais, 2003. But see, Ghai, 1999 (arguing that effect of colonialism was less in Asia than in Africa or Latin America); Friedman, 1999, p. 63 (Asian values argument, authoritarian at its core, "reproduce[s] the self-blinding imperialist argument"). On postcolonial conceptions of international law in South and Southeast Asia in general, see Desierto, 2008.

[7] But see, Stacy, 2009, p. 166 (on the *relationality* of sovereignty). The reasons that states may voluntarily sign away a portion of their sovereignty are explored carefully and thoughtfully in Munro, 2009.

[8] See also, Nakamura, 2009, discussing the demand on the part of Asian nations for state sovereignty, and the view on the part of many in East Asia that public law is a "coercive tool for social and economic regulation" (id., p. 202).

[9] For the most pessimistic view, see Jones, 2006, p. 269 ("Why regional intergovernmental institutions won't work"). See infra pp. 189–191.

[10] See Yee, 2004, pp. 162–164 (listing reasons for lack of Asian system). Some long-term measures to ameliorate this situation are offered in Mauzy & Milne, 1995.

The absence of such a body has become even more problematic since the Convention on the Rights of Persons with Disabilities (CRPD) has been ratified (see supra chapter 7). Finally, there is now "hard law" clearly establishing the international human rights of persons with disabilities, but, without a regional enforcement body, it is impossible to be overly optimistic about the "real life" impact of this Convention on the rights of Asian and Pacific region persons with disabilities.[11] This lack of optimism is furthered by the general lack of consumer involvement in mental disability treatment issues in Asia, where "the medical profession has an unquestionable right over the consumer" (Shinfuku, 1998, p. 273). There is also no questioning the serious mental health resource deficiencies in many Pacific Rim nations (Tasman, Sartorius & Saraceno, 2009).

As it is unlikely that an Asian regional human rights commission or court will be created in the near future,[12] the creation of a Disability Rights Tribunal for Asia and the Pacific (sometimes DR-TAP) would be a bold, innovative, progressive and important step on the path toward realization of those rights. It would also, not unimportantly, be—ultimately—a likely inspiration for a full regional human rights tribunal in this area of the world.[13]

As discussed extensively in earlier chapters, in all regions of the world, persons with mental disabilities—especially those *institutionalized* because of such disabilities—are uniformly deprived of their civil and human rights (see supra chapter 5; Perlin, 2007b). The creation of a DR-TAP would be the first necessary step leading to amelioration of this deprivation.

In this chapter, I will first briefly discuss the absence of human rights tribunals in Asia. I will then consider the "Asian values" dispute, and conclude that that leads to a false consciousness (since it presumes a unified and homogeneous multiregional attitude toward a bundle of social, cultural, and political issues), and that the universality of human rights must be seen to predominate here.[14] I will then look at China as a case example. After that, I will offer a structural outline of a Tribunal, and finally will explain why the

---

[11] Compare, Hay, 2008 p. 200 (footnotes omitted):

> In many Pacific countries the majority of citizens have little knowledge of what the term "rights" means and therefore the concept of having human rights or knowing what these might be is "interminably foreign." Merelyn Tahi, co-ordinator of the Vanuatu Women's Centre, commented, "you know the big question would be what is a right anyway? And I think that's the basic thing that we have to answer."

[12] See, e.g., Gotanda, 1995, p. 475, quoting Sidney Jones, of Human Rights Watch in Asia ("the possibility of agreement in Asia . . . on a . . . court is nil").

[13] Compare Leary, 1987, p. 339: "The worldwide movement for human rights protection and promotion can expect to be enriched as Asians take a more active role in the movement."

[14] For an earlier overview of the different perspectives on human rights in different East Asian nations, see Hsiung, 1986.

creation of the DR-TAP is timely, inevitable, and essential, if the UN Convention on the Rights of Persons with Disabilities is to be given true life. Here I align myself with Professor Helen Stacy: "Legal institutions are needed more than ever to formalize social politics into legal rules. . . . Legal institutions can mediate disputes in ways that neither social nor political institutions are able to do" (2009, p. 31).

I. Absence of Such Bodies in Asia and the Pacific

The creation of any effective human rights mechanism in Asia and the Pacific presents a bundle of key challenges (Hay, 2009). Professor Tom Ginsburg has said flatly that Asian regionalism remains in its "infancy" (Ginsburg, 2010a, p. 36). Southeast Asian governments regard human rights as an "ambivalent subject" in national development (Mohamad, 2002, p. 230). The harshest critique was leveled nearly 30 years ago by Professor Hiroko Yamane: "What is lacking in the field of human rights in Asia is that *moral conscience* which prompts individuals to resist repression and arbitrary disciplinary action taken by the government in power" (1982, p. 22, emphasis added). Asia and the Pacific have not established a regional human rights court so far, though there have been some historical attempts to establish a regional human rights body in this region (see generally, Hashimoto, 2004).[15]

These actions preliminarily addressed the need for a human rights body in this region, but no movements in this field of law during the 1980s and 1990s achieved significant success (see generally, Jalal, 2009; Campbell & McDonald, 2006).[16] It needs to be stressed that disability rights have *not* been traditionally recognized by most Asian governments (Harris, 2000). Professor Carole Petersen has concluded, in a similar vein, that the first Asian and Pacific Decade of Disabled Persons "has had little impact upon national legislation and policies" (Petersen, 2008, p. 614).[17] As indicated above, more recently,

[15] For example, a "Seminar on Human Rights in Developing Countries" was held in 1964, and a "Southeast Asia & Pacific Conference of Jurists" was held in 1965. On the role of NGOs in this process—see generally infra, pp. 191–193. see Wilde, 1998. And some resolutions on a human rights regional body in Asia this region were consecutively adopted by the General Assembly of the UN beginning in the late 1970s. The "Colombo Seminar on Human Rights" was held in 1982. On how this seminar was a hiatus in the movement toward the development of a regional human rights body, see Leary, 1990.

[16] In 1985, the Law Association for Asia and the Pacific (LAWASIA) proposed a Pacific Charter that would set forth wide ranging civil, political, social, and cultural rights. It would also include mechanisms for enforcing the Charter and dealing with complaints of human rights violations. Ultimately it failed due to political, social, cultural, and practical issues (Hyndman, 1992).

[17] On how the second Asian and Pacific Decade of Disabled Persons reflected a "fundamental shift in thinking" in the context of the CRPD, and a "philosophical change in looking at the rights of persons with disabilities," see Fritsch, 2009, p. 404.

ASEAN has adopted a "Charter of ASEAN" (2008) providing for the establishment of a human rights body (Cohen, 2010).[18] But critics have dismissed the mandate for this body as "essentially promotional," as it lacks the power to conduct independent fact-finding missions or to consider communications from state or individuals (Heyns & Killander, 2010, manuscript, p. 30), or as "aspirational" (Nakamura, 2009, p. 204).[19] Also, ASEAN only includes a handful of nations in this region.[20] Scholars have concluded that this body is "toothless" (Ginsburg, 2010a, p. 32; compare Kelsall, 2010, questioning whether body is "toothless tiger or tentative first step"; see also, Byrnes, Durbach & Renshaw, 2008),[21] and "not on a par with other regional systems" (Heyns & Killander, 2010, manuscript, p. 31).[22] See also, Nakamura, 2009, p. 197 (on the "non-legally binding nature" of ASEAN and other multilateral agreements in East Asia).

Gamely, Professor Richard Carver suggests that the global trend to protect internationally guaranteed human rights "is most marked in Asia" (2010, p. 9), but the gap between aspiration and enforcement in the area of disability rights remains a wide one.[23] (On issues specific to the South Pacific, see Farran, 2009, and on the specific needs for a regional commission in that area, see Jalal, 2009.[24] On the "mixed record" of national human rights commissions in

---

[18] ASEAN's regionalism is primarily "security-reinforcing" (Ginsburg, 2010a, p. 38). On its relationship to security and economic stability, see Jones, 2008; Lim, 1998. On its role in economic development, see Honghua, 2010; Banyan, 2010. On its failure to stem the growing sex-trafficking trade in this region, see Wuiling, 2006; on the need for international human rights law in the combating of sex trafficking in Asia generally, see Yun, 2007. See Petersen, 2007, p. 53, ("The ASEAN Declaration demonstrates little real commitment to the human rights dimension of trafficking by its members"). But see Desierto, 2010, manuscript at 46 (discussing ASEAN's "revolutionary potential"); Desierto, 2009 (on ASEAN's constitutionalization of international law).

[19] For a new strategy, suggesting that ASEAN members "globalize" the issue of liberal reforms by openly assessing their human rights record in global settings, see Katsumata, 2009.

[20] The Member States of the Association are Brunei, Cambodia, Indonesia, Laos, Malaysia, Myanmar, Philippines, Singapore, Thailand, and Vietnam. On the dilemmas raised by Mynamar's ratification of the ASEAN charter, see Arendshorst, 2009.

[21] The Asia and Pacific region is not only geographically vast but also has social, cultural, political, religious, and economic diversity. This is a main region why this region has not yet established a regional human rights court. See Phan, 2009.

[22] See also, Ghai, 2009b, noting how ASEAN nations have refused to criticize other ASEAN nations for ongoing human rights abuses.

[23] On the lack of legislation governing the employment of persons with disabilities in Singapore, see Tuen, 1999.

[24] Some of the excitement about a regional human rights tribunal in the Pacific is tempered by that region's history of colonization. See Toki & Baird, 2009. That history has been explicitly suggested as the cause of Asian states' refusal to allow for interference in what is perceived as "essentially a domestic issue" (Yee, 2004, p. 163).

Asia, see Peerenboom, 2006, p. 32, but see, Renshaw, Byrnes & Durbach, 2009, p. 251 [presence of national human rights institutions [NHRIs] "essential to creating and maintaining independent and effective national institutions"]; Durbach, Renshaw & Byrnes, 2009, p. 238 [an Asia Pacific Forum "can cultivate an environment which may increasingly become more amenable to the creation of a strong regional human rights institution"]; Durbach, 2010, manuscript, pp. 26–27 [concluding, in a discussion of Nepal, that, in the absence of a commitment to building political enterprises "receptive and respectful of NHRI objectives . . . [NHRIs] risk being set up to fail"]).[25]

II. The "Asian Values" Debate

The "Asian values" (see supra chapter 2) debate began in the early 1990s as a challenge from the States themselves, in particular Singapore (Emmerson, 1995), Malaysia (Lawson, 1996), and Indonesia (Asplund, 2009), which argued that international human rights law should not necessarily be applied to them because it was Western and did not conform to Asian culture (Engle, 2000; for a historical overview, see Bell, 1996).[26] "Asian values" generally refer to Confucianism, respect for elders, emphasis on order and social harmony, group orientation, and the collective interests of the society and State (Varayudej, 2006, p. 13).[27] "The implication is that not to share these values is to be less than 'Asian,' to have lost one's bearings and to become 'Westernized'" (Tay, 1996).[28]

---

[25] On NHRIs in Africa, see Dinokoplia, 2009 (such institutions empower civil society participation and advocacy on human rights protection).

[26] Albert Chen (2006) argues that these arguments flowed from Malaysia and Singapore in an effort to secure political and social stability and economic development. On why it is a "disservice" to characterize human rights as "Western," see Deng, 2009, p. 44.

For a careful analysis of how Japan's Psychiatric Review Board system faced "widespread antagonism as the product of foreign interference in Japanese life," see Cohen, 1995, p. 74.

[27] "Confucius is . . . not the only intellectual influence in [Asia]" (Sen, 1999, p. 14). Compare Svensson, 2006, p. 201 ("It is unclear what Confucian values actually are"); Englehart, 2000, p. 560 ("Confucianism . . . is not a simple tradition with a single dominant strain"). At least one commentator has argued that there are more similarities than disparities between human rights and Confucianism. See Williams, 2006.

[28] For parallel discussions of so-called African values, see Howard, 1986; Shivji, 1989; Cobbah, 1987. See Oloka-Onyango, 2000, p. 50 ("In most instances, relativists are politicians from the south whose human rights practice are at a minimum questionable, and often extremely violative on a number of fronts").

The "Asian values" debate is a form of cultural relativism.[29] However, cultural relativism should not and cannot be used as a defense in ignoring human rights. "Cultural relativism is not [a] sufficient justification for the denial of the universal application of human rights standards" (Hui, 2002, p. 1999; see also, Paul, 2000, p. 13, n. 51, citing, inter alia, Davis, 1998 [criticizing cultural relativism as deterministic and tautological], and Tay, 1996, examining the problematic character of the cultural argument in the context of Asian human rights; Engle, 2000 [same]), nor does the universality of human rights reject the significance of culture (Deng, 2009).[30] There is a difference between "adhering less to some global standard of human rights in order to promote overall human rights in socioeconomic realms and not adhering to certain rights because of a lack of political will or hiding behind the mask of cultural relativism" (Monshipouri, 2001, pp. 25–27).[31]

It has been persuasively argued that the Asian values debate "clearly concerns power as much as culture, involving issues of representation and authority more than cultural essences" (Gammeltoft & Hernφ, 2006, p. 161).[32] As Arati Rao has stated (see supra Chapter 2):

> The notion of culture favoured by international actors must be unmasked for what it is: a falsely rigid, ahistorical, selectively chosen set of self-justificatory texts and practices whose patent partiality raises the question of exactly whose interests are being served and who comes out on top. (1995, p. 174)[33]

---

[29] On how these views were reflected in the "profoundly undemocratic" Bangkok Declaration of 1993, see Loh, 1995, p. 159. That declaration has been characterized as "symboli[zing] the threat to the universality of human rights" (Brehms, 2001, p. 55).

[30] See id., p. 45 ("Every culture has its humanitarian ideals").

[31] On the relationship between culture and law in this context, see Haley, 2006.

[32] See Diokno, 2006, p. 81 ("The Asian-values-human-rights debate is primarily a power play between states"); Marks, 2009, p. 219, quoting South Korean President Kim Dae Jung: "The biggest obstacle [to establishing democracy and strengthening human rights in Asia] is not its cultural heritage but the resistance of authoritarian rulers and their apologists"; Ghai, 2009a, p. 110 (Asian values argument forwarded to "legitimize authoritarianism"); Muntarbhorn, 1998, p. 413, quoting Asian Human Rights Charter, para. 1.5 ("Instead, there is the exhortation of spurious theories of 'Asian values,' which are a thin disguise for their authoritarianism").

[33] On how "Asian values" reflect the policies of the "elites," see Bruun & Jacobsen, 2006, p. 5; Wilde, 1998, p. 142; see also, Ghai, 2009b, p. 123 (attitudes toward rights are located in "class and social structure"). Maria Diokno notes that "nearly all" statements made on behalf of Asian values "have come from heads of Asian states" (2006, p. 85); see also, Langlois, 2001, p. 44 (Asian values discourse "demonstrably politically self-interested"). On whether such statements are at all representative of regional opinion, see Stokke, 2006.

See also, from an anthropological perspective, Preis, 1985 rejecting cultural relativism (compare Renteln, 1985, 1990); on deploying cross-cultural perspectives in this inquiry, see Lee, 2008.

While it is important to take cultural differences into consideration when involved in international relations, in practice, cultural relativism rarely is a sincere call for tolerance (Sloane, 2001, p. 545); rather, it is often "intellectually shallow" (Sen, 1997, p. 31), evidence of "moral nihilism" (Svensson, 2002, p. 48), "a powerful tool of social control" (Diokno, 2006, p. 78), a justification for nations to "shirk their duty to respect human rights" (Chen, 2008, p. 56), "a means of justifying the status quo, particularly of power relations," Langlois, 2001, p. 25, or an "alternative to liberal government" (id., p. 29).[34]

Proponents of "Asian values" argue that if "Western" human rights treaties are respected in a given situation, "the public will be worse off—thrown into civil war, vulnerable to insurgents, or, alternatively, unable to engage in the practices they value" (Posner, 2008, p. 1771).[35] In other words, having human rights obligations interferes with the government's welfare promoting activities, and these welfare promoting activities should take precedence (id., p. 1771). Many Asian countries, in a justification of their claim that economic rights are more important than political rights, argue that, at different stages of a country's development, it is necessary to focus on different rights (Klein, 2001). In addition, many Asian governments complain "vehemently that international human rights should not be an excuse for strong-arm politics and interference in the domestic affairs of a country" (Peerenboom, 2003, p. 41).

Some scholars argue that the better Interpretation of the "Asian values" debate is not an assessment of a philosophical debate about the universality of human rights.[36] Rather, the better interpretation is that "virtually all governments concede that they have a 'universal' obligation to advance the welfare of their populations, but, given local conditions and traditions, they cannot advance the welfare of their populations if they are constrained by human rights treaties" (Posner, 2008, p. 1771). Regardless of how the "Asian values" debate is interpreted, the crux of the argument is whether "Asian values" really do exist and if so, whether they can be an excuse to disregard universal human rights. (See Lynch, 2009, p. 573: "Since the 1990s, a doctrine of exceptionalism based on 'Asian values' has been used to excuse many human rights violations in Southeast Asia"; *Human Rights in Asian Cultures*, 1997, p. 17: "The recognition of cultural diversity is not a justification . . . to totally discard the applicability of human rights to peoples with differing cultures."[37]

[34] On cultural relativism and state power, see Pollis, 1996. On how regional courts can "adjudicate culture," see Stacy, 2009, pp. 176–179.

[35] On how Western neoconservatives support the "Asian values" model, see Robison, 1996.

[36] On the artificiality of the dichotomy between Asian and Western values in this context, see Svensson, 2006; for a consideration of this question in an African context, see Shivji, 1989.

[37] On cultural issues in mental health, see Helman, 2001. On the specific cultural issues related to perceptions of mental illness and mental health care in Thailand, see Burnard et al., 2006.

On how the "Asian values" view of human rights in consonant with the view that the West was "morally decadent because of the growth of gay rights and relative success of the women's movement," see Chiam, 2009, p. 145, quoting Brown, 2001 [remarks attributed to Mahathir Mohammed, the former prime minister of Malaysia].)[38]

In fact, the "Asian values" debate leads to false consciousness, because it presumes a unified and homogeneous multigenerational attitude toward a bundle of social, cultural, and political issues.[39] This "monochrome picture" is a "gross over-simplification of reality" (Owada, 2009, p. 202; see also, Mauzy, 1997, p. 229, "Simplifications fail to convey the complex roots of the debate"; Tyagi, 1981, p. 137, "one must take into account the heterogenous character of [nations with developing economies in Asia and Africa]").[40] Jean-Pierre Cabestan goes so far as to say that "Asia is a complex and somewhat 'artificial' historical, religious, cultural and political entity" (2009, p. 716). There is no reason to assume that the Asian state "speaks with a monolithic cultural voice" (Sloane, 2001, p. 585).[41]

The "Asian values" argument fails to account for "the richness of values discourse in Asia" (Davis, 1998, p. 148), and the fact that "even more Asians have internalized . . . universal [human rights values and . . . the pendulum is

---

On the related questions of the impact of culture on custody decision-making, see Liu, 2004 (Taiwan); on accessible birth control, see Hui, 2002 (China); and on access to land, see Butegwa, 1994 (Africa). Dr. Worrawat Chanpattana, a Thai physician, argues that "Confucian cultures are loath to confront mental illness" (2010, p. 2). On how cultural exceptionalism operates "at the expense of gender equality," see Paul, 2000, p. 83; compare Wang, 2009 (criticizing Confucianism on gender issues).

38 On the authoritarian basis of the Malaysian Asian values argument, see Langlois, 2001. On the institutionalization of human rights in Malaysian law in general, see Whiting, 2003. For a critique of Malaysia's social policies on mental health, see Mubarak, 2003.

39 "Neither Asian culture nor Asian realities are homogenous throughout the continent." Ghai, 1994, p. 6. See also, Hoang, 2008, manuscript, p. 33:

> The "Asian values" perspective is based on Confucianism, and does not represent the region's rich, diverse religions and cultures. Furthermore, Asian values are neither static nor monolithic, but rather changeable and adaptive to real conditions of life.

On the question of cultural values in this context in Korea, see Byuing-Sun, 1997. On the role of Korean cultural values in the legal *negotiations* process, see Ko & Koo, 2010.

40 On how contemporaneous anthropologists seek to "skirt" the universalism-relativism debate, see Merry, 2006, p. 39.

41 On the question of whether proponents of the "Asian values" argument are guilty of constructing an overly unified and idealized "West," see Peerenboom, 2003, arguing that the "Asian values" debate is no longer fruitful. On the "myth" of Asia's antidemocratic values, see Jung, 1994.

swinging [further in that] direction" (Cabestan, 2009, p. 730).[42] Ole Bruun and Michael Jacobsen conclude that Asian culture is "too dynamic and creative to allow [for] stereotyped constructions" (2006, p. 7; see also, Patten, 1992). For these reasons, some argue that there is no such thing as an "Asian value" (Engle, 2000, p. 313; see also, Svensson, 2006).

Further, assuming that there are uniform "Asian values" leads to generalizations and stereotypes of what is "Asian" (Tay, 1996, p. 758).[43] One such generalization is that Asian countries favor the community over the individual. Nghia Hoang notes that "collectivism has however been invoked *selectively* by Asian leaders, politicians and scholars, to justify the neglect of human rights in practice" (2009, manuscript, p. 33; emphasis added). Opponents of the "Asian values" debate question whether Asian governments are really interested in promoting communities (Peerenboom, 2003, p. 39).[44] The broad state sovereignty claims of Asian governments are undermined, given the "increasing reach of international law and the participation of all countries in

[42] On ways that Buddhist thought is universalist and fully consonant with expanded human rights, as "an integral part of the spiritual tradition of Asia," see Mautner, 2008, p. 628; see also, Inadam, 1986, and as a vision that seeks to liberate Asia from totalitarian and authoritarian rule, see Vo, 2006. On Buddhism and human rights in general, see Keown, Prebish & Husted, 1998. On the relationship between the Buddhist principle of "transformative universalism" and social action, see Thurman, 1988, p. 127. On Buddhism and social action in general, see Jones, 1988. Influential spiritual leaders such as the Dalai Lama emphasize the importance of human rights and dignity in Buddhist thought. See Mahlmann, 2010, p. 17, citing Keown, 1998; Sloane, 2001, p. 584; Traer, 1995: Perera, 1991; Dalai Lama, 1999. Damien Keown has written that Buddhism locates "human rights and dignity within a comprehensive account of human goodness, and . . . sees basic rights and freedoms as integrally related to human flourishing and self-realization" (1998, p. 29).

On ways that Buddhist concepts have been used successfully by NGOs in Cambodia to increase the cultural currency of notions of "universal human rights," see Ledgerwood & Un, 2003, p. 546. On how Buddhism is "the only popular force constantly struggling for the defense of human rights in Vietnam," see Vo, 2006, p. 107. On Buddhism and human rights in the context of Thailand, see Harding, 2007, 1987.

On the compatibility of Hindu thought and practice with universal human rights, see generally, Persaud, 2009, Khushalani, 1983, pp. 406–408; and see Subedi, 1999 1999, p. 45:

> Hindu scriptures written at the advent of Hindu civilization embody the idea of universal fraternity and the equality of all living human souls.

On the ways that the Islamic traditions differ from Western traditions in this context, see Khushalani, 1983, pp. 408–413. On the compatibility of the mystical tradition of Sufism within Islam and human rights, see Muedini, 2010.2010.

[43] On the reluctance of many Japanese citizens, e.g., to comply with cultural ideology, see Marfording, 1997. On the relationship between human rights and Japanese culture, see Se & Karatsu, 2004; Bloise, 2010.

[44] See Campbell & McDonald, 2006, p. 264 (rejecting argument that there are "pan-Asian values").

the international legal order" (id., p. 41).[45] In addition, the "Asian values" debate assumes that culture is static, rather than something that varies generation to generation (Tay, 1996, p. 759). Given "the rich diversity within Asia [of] religions, political systems, levels of economic development, and historical experiences," Marina Svensson questions the assumption that Asian-specific values exist (2006, p. 201).[46]

The universalist position consists of two main variants: extreme moral universalism and moderate moral universalism (Peerenboom, 2003, p. 12; on moral relativism and human rights, see Spaak, 2007; on the difference between the extreme cultural relativism position and the moderate cultural relativism position, see Ghai, 2009). Extreme moral universalism is the concept that moral issues do not depend on culture or the views of any group or individual. Moderate moral universalism holds that "culture is irrelevant to the correctness of some, but not necessarily all, issues" (id.; compare Millner, 2000, p. 62, concluding "culture still matters"). Both variants underscore the importance of basic human rights that must be universally applied irrespective of cultural differences (compare Al-Emadi & Al-Asmakh, 2006, p. 810: "The analysis of the impact of culture should move beyond the relatively simplistic categorization of Eastern, Asian or Western countries").

The universality of human rights must predominate (Cerna, 1994).[47] "Individuals everywhere want the same essential things: to have sufficient food and shelter; to be able to speak freely; to practice their own religion or to abstain from religious belief; to feel that their person is not threatened by the state; to know that they will not be tortured; or detained without charge, and that if charged, they will have a fair trial" (Higgins, 1994; see also, Obiora, 1997, on the inalienability of human rights).[48] To deny persons with mental disabilities these basic human rights on the basis of "Asian values" is an attempt to hide behind the mask of cultural relativism (see, e.g., Tesón, 1984, p. 898: "Cultural relativism is not, and ought not to be, the answer to human rights concerns"; see also, Johnston, 2005, p. 52: "Cultural relativist arguments

[45] Compare Torok, 2005, discussing the need for law schools to teach courses in "Asian American jurisprudence."

[46] On how such cultural diversity "require[s] the robust implementation" of human rights, see Freeman, 2006, p. 49. On the relationship between this cultural diversity and the protection of indigenous persons, see Meijknecht & de Vries, 2010.On how cultural diversity can be "a rich foundation for human rights," see Murumba, 1998, pp. 239–240; Donders, 2010 (same).

[47] Compare, Yamaga-Karns, 1995, p. 569, "Universalism and cultural relativism may in fact serve as ideological checks and balances upon each other."

[48] My citation here to Higgins's well-known articulation of the universal desire for human rights is not to be construed as a position endorsing natural law interpretations of these issues. See, e.g., Zechetner, 1997, p. 320 (discussing the roots of universal human rights in three jurisprudential theories—natural law, rationalism, and positivism).

are difficult for many to accept when they are used to justify dangerous and life threatening practices, such as genital mutilation, or when men rely on them to maintain traditional practices that worsen the position of women"; Zechetner, 1997, on the corrupting influence of arguments supporting cultural relativism; Svensson, 2002, p. 48: "Cultural relativism ignores the voices of the oppressed and reveals an utter disrespect for the victims of practices and policies [of repressive practices").[49] Elizabeth Zechetner concludes: "Although human rights relativism has its flaws, universalism often provides *the only avenue available* to individuals in their intracultural struggle for fairness, justice, and equality" (1997, p. 341).

III. The Case of China: A Gap between Domestic Law and Reality

There are gaps between domestic law in China and the most recent and important UN document, the CRPD (Guo, 2009),[50] gaps that may be magnified, given what Professor Benjamin Liebman has characterized as a "lack of public confidence in the legitimacy of legal procedures" in China in general (2009, p. 28). China's record on providing rights to persons with disabilities is, to be charitable, spotty. Although the Protection of Disabled Persons Law purports to prohibit discrimination against persons with disabilities ((Petersen, 2008) see also Information Office, 2009, p. 772: "The state has made great efforts to develop undertakings relative to the disabled"),[51] its medically focused definitional section[52] reveals that it is far removed from the social rights manifesto of the CRPD (Kayess & French, 2008; Perlin, 2009). The law also includes what commentators have characterized as "charter-like moral instructions": "Handicapped people should be optimistic, . . . improve themselves, rely on themselves, and contribute to socialist construction" (see Keith & Lin, 2001, p. 67, discussing the Protection of Disabled Persons Law,

---

[49] Daniel Bell (2008, p. 83) is mildly skeptical about this enterprise: "The aspiration to develop values of more universal scope with substantive content may not be realizable."
[50] On the lack of comprehensive disability laws in most nations in the region, see Perlin & Ikehara, 2010 ; Perlin, 2010.
[51] On how this law flowed from "an uninhibited display of legislative idealism," see Keith & Lin, 2001, p. 67.
[52] "Disability" is defined as "one who suffers from abnormalities or loss of a certain organ or function, psychologically, physiologically or in anatomical structure, and who has lost wholly or in part the ability to engage in activities in a normal way." Law on the Protection of Disabled Persons (promulgated by the Standing Comm. Nat'l People's Cong., Dec. 28, 1990, effective May 15, 1991) 14 P.R.C. Laws & Regs V-03–00-101, available at http://www.chinacourt.org/flwk/show1.php?file_id=11967, Art. 2.

Art. 10).[53] It is no wonder that Professor Carole Petersen characterizes it as "patronizing" (Petersen, 2010b, p. 93).

A Hong Kong case[54] reflected the government's position that it could lawfully reject an applicant for a public job because that person was *related to* a person with mental illness on the theory that "such applicants cannot be trusted to perform the job safely" (Petersen, 2006, p. 249, discussing *K., Y, and W. v. The Secretary for Justice*, 2000; see supra chapter 5).[55] In discussing this case, Professor Carole Petersen concluded—accurately, in my mind—that it showed "at best, a careless disregard for the law" (Petersen, 2002, p. 116), and that it reflected "precisely the kind of stereotyping that needs to be publicly discussed and condemned" (Petersen, 2008, p. 636).[56]

Consider China's laws as they apply to persons with mental disability and sexuality (see generally, Perlin, 2009). In the 1980s, laws were passed in Gansu province: first, forbidding individuals with "hereditary retardation" from having children (Johnson, 1997, pp. 221–222) then, mandating sterilization for such individuals (Gewirtz, 1994). Similar laws were enacted in other provinces, and within a few years, there were parallel laws in five other sectors, some forbidding marriage, some forbidding childbearing, and some mandating sterilization (id., p. 149; Martin, 2007). These laws, which apply to one-third of China's population, flowed in significant part from the predominant Chinese notion that mental disabilities were "inherited" diseases (Gewirtz, 1994, p. 149 [mental retardation perceived to be inherited]; Johnson, 1997, p. 226 n. 38 [schizophrenia and manic depression presumed to be inheritable diseases]).

---

53 On the negative attitude in China toward persons with disabilities, focusing on the perception that the employment of persons with disabilities will "damage [employers'] image," the perception that persons with disabilities are "unhealthy" people, and the feeling that dealing with persons with disabilities is "unlucky," see Yu'e, 2009, pp. 89, 110–111. On the ways that mental illness constitutes a "catastrophic" event for caregivers in China, see Ramsay, 2010 p. 83. The research on caregiving in Chinese families is reviewed critically in Hsiao & Van Riper, 2010.

54 China applies the CRPD to Hong Kong (Petersen, 2008, pp. 624–625). Under the Basic Law of Hong Kong, China remains sovereign, but "the capitalist system and way of life [in Hong Kong] shall remain unchanged for 50 years" (Basic Law, Art. 42). The Basic Law of Hong Kong is often referred to as its constitution (Petersen, 2006; Chen, 2000). The phrase "one country, two systems" is often used to describe the governing principles (Chan, 1996; Lanfang, 2009). On the relationship between Hong Kong and China in general, see also, Davis, 1999. On the impact of Hong Kong governance on human rights policies, see Davis, 1996.

55 See Tsang et al., 2007 (Chinese employers significantly more likely than U.S. employers to perceive persons with mental illness as possessing a weaker work ethic and less loyalty to the company).

56 See also, id., pp. 629–630, speculating that the Hong Kong Disability Discrimination Ordinance (Cap. 487, Laws of Hong Kong) violates the CRPD. Compare Yu'e, 1999, p. 90 ("Disabled people . . . have absolutely no control over seeking employment").

China's 1994 Law on Maternal and Infant Health Care requires premarital checkups to determine the presence of "relevant mental diseases" (Maternal and Health Care Law, Art. 8(3)), defined as mental diseases that "may have an adverse effect on marriage and child-bearing" (id., Art. 7(3)).[57] The Chinese Marriage Law of 2001 forbids marriage if either individual "is suffering from any disease that is regarded by medical science as rend[er]ing [*sic*] a person unfit for marriage," (Marriage Law, Art. 7(b)), a category regularly construed to include mental disabilities (Feng, 2002). Beyond that, the law adds that a marriage is invalid "if any party has suffered from any disease that is held by medical science as rend[er]ing [*sic*] a person unfit for getting married and the disease has not been cured after marriage" (Marriage Law, Art. 10(c)). If it is appears that a baby will be born with a disability, China actively encourages the mother to abort (Maternal and Health Care Law, Art. 18; see generally, Petersen, 2010b).

These experiences remind us that realization of the rights set out in the Convention will not come easily. Advocates and activists in this area face barriers when seeking to articulate and implement an array of sexual autonomy rights for persons with mental disabilities (see generally, Perlin, 2008a). The difficulties posed by this backdrop make it even more imperative that a tribunal such as the one suggested here be created.

Beyond all of this, it is important to remember that the use of institutional, state-sanctioned psychiatry as a tool of political suppression is not completely a historical artifact in China (see supra chapter 4; Perlin, 2006b; see also, Munro; 2000; Peerenboom, 2006b).[58] Yet, China ratified the CRPD in August 2008; that ratification demonstrates a national commitment to the rights of persons with disabilities—in the community, in psychiatric institutions, and in correctional facilities.[59] Professor Ming Wan has written that the

---

57 On how marriage laws elsewhere in Asia reflect Confucian values, see Chaibong, 2003.

58 Professor Petersen also questions whether Hong Kong's civil commitment law (Cap. 136, Laws of Hong Kong) violates the CRPD (Petersen, 2008, p. 642).

59 Compare Petersen, 2010b, p. 109:

> It appears that the government wanted to be viewed as a leader in this field of human rights and believed that early ratification of the CRPD, without reservations, would promote that image. However, when China's initial report under the treaty is due, the Committee [on the Rights of Persons with Disabilities] will want to know whether ratification has brought about meaningful reforms for the more than 80 million people with disabilities in China.

China's official position is that it "cherishes the important role played by international instruments on human rights in promoting and protecting human rights" and that it will "earnestly fulfill its obligations to [the human rights] conventions [it has ratified]" Information Office, 2009, p. 775. Compare Guo, 2009, pp. 163–164: " Unlike other countries, China's Constitution is silent on the general domestic status of treaties, making the status of treaties unclear in the Chinese legal system. Some scholars regard

adoption of international human rights law in China "matters" (2007, p. 753; see also, Guo, 2009, on implementation of human rights treaties in China in general); as I will discuss below, I believe that it is important—both to China's citizens and to citizens of the other Asia/Pacific nations—for China to participate in this Tribunal.[60]

IV. Structural Issues[61]

In this section, I sketch out a blueprint for the DR-TAP (see Perlin, 2010; Perlin & Ikehara, 2010; Ikehara, 2010).[62] At the time of the preparation of this volume, this is still very much work in progress.[63] I share this here so that reader has at least a preliminary sense of some of the efforts I believe are necessary to remediate the underlying problems.[64] Certainly, if an ASEAN human rights mechanism is a "step in the right direction in the quest for an

---

this silence as excluding treaties as part of Chinese law, while most Chinese international lawyers agree that the Constitution should expressly clarify the issue and its silence does not mean the rejection of direct effect of treaties in domestic law."

[60] Professor Yuval Shany adopts this definition of international tribunals: "permanent judicial bodies made up of independent judges which are entrusted with adjudicating international disputes on the basis of international law according to a pre-determined set of rules of procedure and rendering decisions which are binding on the parties" (2010, p. 2, n. 2, quoting Tomuschat, 2008).

[61] See Shany, 2010, p. 37, on the "structural attributes" a successful tribunal must have (including legal powers, personnel capacity, resources, structural independence, and usage potential).

[62] On why international tribunals are necessary, see Guzman, 2008.

[63] This is a topic that cries out for substantial sociolegal scholarship, especially in the context of what Terence Halliday and his colleagues characterize as "global normmaking." Halliday, 2009; Halliday & Carruthers, 2007; Halliday & Osinsky, 2006. On the relationship between such normmaking and Chinese law, see Liu & Halliday, 2009.

In her recent article on Article 24 of the CRPD (right to inclusive education), Professor Carole Petersen discusses the proposed DR-TAP:

> It has been proposed that the Asia-Pacific region establish a Disability Rights Tribunal, which would have the capacity to hear complaints, issue decisions and provide remedies for violations of the rights of persons with disabilities. This idea is certainly worth pursuing. However, given the historic reluctance of governments in the Asia Pacific to create a regional mechanism with enforcement powers, it might be wise to include a voluntary mediation program under the auspices of the proposed tribunal. (2010a, p. 511) See footnote 69, infra, this chapter.

[64] On Asia's mental health crisis, see Chanpattana, 2010. On how much of Asian mental health law is based on "outdated knowledge," see Trivedi, Narang & Dhyani, 2007.

Asian human rights mechanism," (Chiam, 2009, p. 48), a DR-TAP would be a definite quantum leap in that direction.

Although it is still inchoate,[65] the incorporating Tribunal documents will include sections covering at least these issues:[66]

- General Structure:
  - Hybrid tribunal benefits—flexibility
    - Collaboration with nation-states
  - Composition—number of nations to be involved
  - Rules of procedure and pleading[67]
  - Voluntariness of tribunal
  - Language—all languages of each Asia-Pacific country
    - Official language(s) to be determined
  - Location—to be determined
  - Competency—jurisdiction to hear any matter relating to a State
  - Coordination with other international and regional bodies
  - Coordination with other Asian bodies
  - Relationship between nations that have signed the CRPD and those that have not
  - Legitimacy—independence from national oversight
    - General sense of accountability, respect
    - Fair procedures
- Judges
    - Designated seats for specific nations
    - Persons with disabilities to be determined
  - Backgrounds—lawyers, advocates, judges
    - Known and respected by national judges
    - Awareness of audience
    - Autonomy from political interests, impartial
    - Expertise in disability law
- Lawyers—trained in disability rights
  - Court-appointed if client indigent

---

[65] An additional regional planning meeting was held in Bangkok, Thailand, in October, 2010 under the auspices of the Asia-Pacific Development Center on Disability and UN ESCAP. See footnote 78, *infra*.

[66] See Helfer & Slaughter, 2005, p. 906 (factors that contribute to Tribunal's effectiveness include judicial independence, composition of the tribunal, the court's caseload or functional capacity, independent fact-finding capability, formal authority, awareness of audience, instrumentalism, quality of legal reasoning, judicial cross-fertilization and dialogue, form of opinion, nature of the violations, the existence of autonomous domestic institutions, and the relative cultural and political homogeneity of member states).

[67] Compare Shelton, 2010, pp. 582–596 (discussing jurisdiction issues in other regional human rights bodies), id., pp. 713–734 (discussing exhaustion issues in such bodies).

- Funding—government
  - UN funding
  - Voluntary contributions
  - NGOs
    - Standing
- Reporting—precedent from other transnational tribunals
  - Use of advisory opinions[68]
  - Free access to cases online
- Remedies—sanctions, reparations, injunctions
  - Enforcing compliance—binding authority not necessary
  - The role of mediation[69]
- Including Persons with Physical Disabilities
  - Already included in the CRPD
  - Do not alienate—address discrimination
- Nongovernmental Organizations ("NGOs")
  - Members should not serve on tribunals
  - Ability to bring claims before tribunal
    - Ability to request advisory opinions
  - Amicus briefs (see Weinstein, 2010).

---

[68] See, e.g., Schmid, 2006 (discussing use of advisory opinions in International Court of Justice and Inter-American Court of Human Rights).

[69] Professor Carole Petersen (2010) argues vigorously in support of mediation as a tool for CRPD enforcement in the context of cases seeking to enforce a right to an inclusive education.

There is decided ambivalence about mediation in other international human rights courts. The Inter-American court engages in "active" mediation (see Godshall, 2003, p. 527), a procedure that is alleged to be "consistent with African customs and traditions" (see Defeis, 1992, pp. 114–115); on the other hand, it has been argued that compulsory mediation would violate a litigant's right to a fair trial (Halevy, 2008, discussing the European Convention on Human Rights). More forcefully, Patricia Standaert has argued that a power imbalance between parties may make the use of mediation in international human rights tribunals "inappropriate and even destructive to the promotion of human rights" (1999, p. 528). On how mediation is employed in the European Court on Human Rights, see Splittgerber, 1996. On the potential use of mediation by indigenous communities as a means of locally "appropriating and deploying international human rights norms," see Toufayan, 2010, p. 372; see generally, Sarfaty, 2007. On the danger that mediation may not result in equal outcomes for the socially marginalized, see Cohen, 2006. On the Confucian view of mediation, see Chen, 2003, p. 276 ("mediation is much more consistent with Confucian philosophy than [is] litigation"). On the role of mediation in Asia and the Pacific in particular, see Barnes, 2007.

Below, I discuss some of these issues in some detail:

✓ Can a Voluntary Tribunal Be Successful?

Nongovernmental tribunals are tribunals of conscience, and their legitimacy depends on public reaction (Blaser, 1992). However, the mere fact that a tribunal is voluntary—meaning that a state has to be willing to subject itself to its jurisdiction—does not necessarily make it any less effective. A tribunal without mandatory jurisdiction may operate as effectively as one with mandatory jurisdiction (Guzman, 2008). Even without rules that require compliance with the decisions of a transnational tribunal, past agreements between nations, linked to reciprocity, may create strong political pressures of compliance (Borgen, 2007).[70] When a state refuses to submit to the jurisdiction of a voluntary tribunal it can signal to others in the international community that its actors are in violation of international law standards (Guzman, 2008).[71] Suzannah Linton puts it starkly by quoting Andrew Moravcsik: "States accept binding human rights treaties mainly as a means of political survival" (2008, p. 442).

Voluntary tribunals without mandatory jurisdiction have been successful, both internationally—see, e.g., the International Commission on Holocaust Era Insurance Claims (Delehunty & Perez, 2005; Kreder, 2007); the International Tribunal for the Law of the Sea (Rosenne, 1995; Clote, 2008; Linnan, 1995; Ndiaye, 2010)—and domestically, see, e.g., the South African Truth and Reconciliation Commission (Carter, 1997); the International Criminal Tribunal of Rwanda ("ICTR") (Sosnov, 2008; on hybrid courts in this context in general, see Dickinson, 2003; see also, Higonnet, 2006). If voluntary tribunals can exist in these incredibly charged areas of the law (see Raub, 2009), involving genocides, torture, and inhumane treatment, then voluntary tribunals can work in the issue of disability rights.

✓ Will the Judges Be Independent?

Judges directly influence the effectiveness of an international tribunal by compelling national actors to listen and respond.[72] For judges in a tribunal such as the one under discussion to be effective, they must be autonomous from political interests, making it more likely that the tribunal will be independent from national oversight (Helfer & Slaughter, 1997, p. 309), and must be willing to "brave political displeasure" (id., p. 315). It should go without saying

[70] On how transnational tribunals "affect the normative development of domestic legal systems," see id., p. 673.

[71] On this question in an Asian-specific context, see generally, Munro, 2009, and see id., p. 25 (nations may "fear a 'pariah' status and even sanctions if they do not participate in the established discourse on human rights").

[72] On the question of the selection process for judges to the International Court of Justice, see Keith, 2010.

that judges must remain independent (Brown, 2003; Yamane, 1982).[73] This need for independence cuts against arguments that there should be permanent seats for the DR-TAP judges from certain countries like Thailand, South Korea, Japan, and China, as the judges in such permanent seats could be viewed as lacking impartiality.[74]

As judgments of a voluntary international tribunal only affect domestic judgments to the extent that domestic courts are persuaded by the tribunal's reasoning, higher quality judges will lead to greater legitimacy (Weisburd, 2002, p. 44). If domestic judges respect international judges then there will be greater deference to the decisions of international tribunals (Guzman, 2008, p. 205).

Another consideration is whether there should be designated seats for judges with disabilities. By way of comparison, the Committee on the Elimination of Discrimination against Women ("CEDAW") consists of 23 experts, of which 21 are female (Committee on the Elimination of Discrimination against Women, http://www2.ohchr.org/english/bodies/cedaw/membership.htm [last visited May 8, 2010]). Art. 34(4) of the CRPD states that the Committee on the Rights of Persons with Disabilities ("Committee") should be elected by State parties with consideration given to equitable geographic distribution,[75] representation of different forms of civilization and of the principal legal systems, balanced gender representation, *and participation of experts with disabilities* (emphasis added). While having designated seats for judges with disabilities may not be necessary, experience with persons with disabilities including both work and personal should be key factors in determining judicial eligibility.

Most importantly, the judges of the DR-TAP must be trained in disability rights. This training may be difficult when many nations do not offer any courses in disability rights in any law schools.[76] It may fall to the DR-TAP

---

[73] On the question of the actual independence of the Japanese judiciary, see Levin, 2010.

[74] On the related question of the role of Taiwan as an unrecognized state in international tribunal jurisprudence, see Hsieh, 2007. On the question of the independence of Chinese judges in general, see Peerenboom, 2010. On the question of whether democracy is a prerequisite for judicial independence, see Ginsburg, 2010b (arguing that it is not), and see id., p. 258 ("authoritarian governments have some incentive to empower judiciaries and grant them genuine independence").

[75] Geography is a potentially significant issue. See Renshaw, Byrnes & Durbach, 2009, p. 252 ("In a region such as the Pacific, geographic separation with disparate cultures, languages and traditions, [the benefits of embedding dedicated human rights institutions into state governance] have the potential to contribute to a national institution that could effectively, inclusively and gradually inform the human rights culture of a Pacific nation's government and executive").

[76] On lack of counsel available to represent persons with mental disabilities in general, see infra chapter 8; Perlin, 2008b). See infra pp. 196–198 on appointment of counsel in the specific DR-TAP context.

itself to provide training to judges. Expertise in human rights law enhances the prestige of international human rights tribunals (Helfer & Slaughter, 1997, p. 301). Such expertise in disability law will inevitably enhance the prestige of the DR-TAP. This includes not only a deep understanding of the CRPD, but also awareness of the prejudice, hidden and overt, that persons with disabilities face in their everyday lives (Perlin & Ikehara, 2010; Perlin, 2010).[77]

✓ How Will the Tribunal Be Funded?

Many international tribunals successfully rely only on voluntary contributions, e.g., the Extraordinary Chambers in the Courts of Cambodia and the Special Court for Sierra Leone, both hybrid tribunals (Higonnet, 2006 p. 427). Hybrid tribunals, which often rely solely on voluntary contributions for funding, are substantially less expensive, in significant part because of their independence from the United Nations. Other international tribunals rely on the UN for funding. The International Criminal Tribunal for Yugoslavia (ICTY) and the International Criminal Tribunal for Rwanda (ICTR) are financed through assessed contributions (Panel, Discussion, 2007).

However, even if a tribunal is voluntary, and relies on voluntary contributions, the tribunal is still eligible for UN funding. By way of example, the International Tribunal for the Law of the Sea (ITLOS) is a voluntary tribunal that relies both on UN funding and voluntary contributions. The expenses of ITLOS, including expenses incurred on account of cases submitted to it are borne by the parties to the UN Convention on the Law of the Sea (UNCLOS; International Tribunal for the Law of the Sea website, 2010). Thus, State parties are not required to pay any additional fees for bringing a case to ITLOS. Non–state parties to UNCLOS do have to pay additional expenses. In addition, there is a voluntary trust fund established by the UN to assist states, particularly developing states, in the settlement of disputes through ITLOS (id.).

For the DR-TAP, a potential specific source of funding besides voluntary contributions is the UN Economic and Social Commission for Asia and the Pacific (ESCAP). ESCAP has 62 members and carries out work in the areas of macroeconomic policy and development, statistics, subregional activities for development, trade and investment, transport, environment and sustainable development, information and communications technology and disaster risk reduction, and social development, and focuses on issues that are most effectively addressed through regional cooperation (UNESCAP website, 2010).[78]

---

[77] On how online distance learning education can economically and efficiently accomplish this task, see Perlin & Ikehara, 2010 and Perlin, 2010. See supra chapter 6.

[78] UNESCAP funded the DR-TAP planning conference held in Bangkok in October 2010. At this conference, the question was raised as to whether it was politically more prudent to launch the Tribunal in the image of a *Commission* rather than of a *Court*, with the Court functions being created subsequently (as was done with the regional omnibus human rights courts). See Seymour, 2003.

✓ How Many Nations Will Be Involved (Initially and Eventually)?

Asia is the only continent on which there is no regional human rights enforcement agency (see generally, Klein, 2001). There are 4 billion people and 70 nations in Asia, and another 33 nations in Oceania. By way of example, there are currently ten nations in ASEAN and seven in the Asia/Pacific Forum of National Human Rights Institutions. One of the questions to be faced initially is the question of how many nations can be realistically expected to join this enterprise, and of these, how many are industrial, how many are heavily populated, how many are involved with other international law frameworks, etc.

Professor Li-Ann Thio has argued persuasively, to my mind, that human rights regimes in Asia should begin as subregional ones, "given Asia's geographical breadth, lack of shared historical past (even from the colonial era), and its varied political ideologies, legal systems, cultural-religious traditions, and levels of economic development" (1999, p. 5).[79] In light of the vast differences between different regions in Asia (see e.g., Tkatova, 2010, considering the application of international law in the Central Asian states of the former Soviet Union), and the reality that the entire Asian land mass "has not witnessed any homogenized culture or tradition" (Yee, 2004, p. 161), it is probably prudent to launch the DR-TAP as a subregional entity (see also, Shelton, 2010, p. 1055, stressing diversity of language, culture, legal systems and religious traditions, as well as "unclear" and "vast" geographical limits of region).[80]

✓ Will the Tribunal's Jurisdiction Extend to Private and Public Cases?

Human rights charters and human rights conventions typically speak to both private and public sectors (Lee, 2009; Sossin, 2009), but international human rights tribunals typically "can only address state responsibility, not individual liability, and thus cannot consider violations by private actors unless those persons are acting under color of law" (Van Schaak, 2001, p. 164). The exception here flows from an Inter-American Court of Human Rights decision, holding that the international responsibility of a state may arise "[N]ot because

[79] On the way that ASEAN has made has made "halting progress" toward the creation of a subregional human rights structure, see Romano, 2009, p. 264. For a strong endorsement of subregional bodies, see Saul, Mowbray & Baghoomians, 2010. Compare Sengupta, 2010, charging that ASEAN "lack[s] the political will" to establish a subregional human rights mechanism.

[80] In writing in support of a regional Asian human rights court, Professor Helen Stacy concludes that "the time is ripe" for such an institution to be comprised of the ASEAN nations, adding that, "Over time, it might also incorporate Australia and New Zealand" (2009, p. 160). I envision a more comprehensive tribunal in this book.

of the act itself, but because of a lack of due diligence to prevent the violation or to respond to it as required by [the human rights treaty] . . . If the state apparatus acts in such a way that the violation goes unpunished and the victim's full enjoyment of such rights is not restored as soon as possible, the state has failed to comply with its duty to ensure the free and full exercise of those rights to persons within its jurisdiction. The same is true when the state allows private persons or groups to act freely and with impunity to the detriment of the rights recognized in the Convention" (*Vélásquez Rodriguez v. Honduras*, 1989, as discussed in McCorquodale, 2006).[81]

✓ Will There Be Coordination with Other International Bodies?

One scholar has written that "the most significant impact of regional courts of human rights will be to play a coordinating role in harmonizing the dominant standards of human rights observance within the community of member states, and, more importantly, prevent regression from these standards" (Burstein, 2006, p. 425).[82] We know that, outside regional systems, judicial coordination and cooperation among international courts, as well as among national courts, to avoid inconsistent decisions—even on the legality of the same government measures—remains rare (Petersmann, 2006) And we know that a regional system of human rights protection requires authentic coordination (Trincade, 2000). So this becomes very important.

✓ Will There Be Coordination with Other Asian/Pacific Tribunals?

This is an extraordinarily difficult question. As previously discussed, Asian governments are often ambivalent (at best) toward international human rights standards (Muntarbhorn, 1998), and that may be the initial reason that there have been multiple suggestions for the creation of *subregional* human rights regimes (Harris, 2000; Thio, 1999). There is some evidence that disability rights has been taken seriously by at least one *national* human rights commission in this region (Whiting, 2003). These issues must also be given serious attention.

✓ What Will the Relationship Be between Those Nations That Have Signed the CRPD and Those That Have Not?

As of the preparation of this volume, 13 of the 90 nations that have ratified the CRPD are ESCAP members in the Asia/Oceania region ("Disability at

---

[81] On the application of human rights standards to private corporations, see Wood & Scharffs, 2002.

[82] See also, Duxbury, 2007, noting the move *toward* the creation of international organizations in this area of the world.

a Glance," 2009; http://www.un.org/disabilities/countries.asp?id=166). It is not clear at all whether others will, though 13 others have signed the Convention, which is often the first step to ratification (id.). Again, Professor Duxbury's conclusion that "there has been a growing move towards the institutionalization of international cooperation in Asia and the Pacific" (2007, p. 192) may lead to some optimism here. In a parallel context, Christina Cerna's study of the Inter-American system—concluding that State parties have generally accepted monitoring and supervision (2004, p. 2020)—should be kept in mind as we proceed; see also, Hernandez (2008, p. 526), studying the CRPD in the contexts of India and China, and concluding that the Convention has "galvanized" disability rights advocates in those nations. It is hoped that the creation of this Tribunal will have the same impact here.

✓ What Will the Standing Be of NGOs before the Tribunal?

This is a critical issue.[83] NGOs have exerted a "profound influence" on the scope and dictates of international law (Charnovitz, 2006b, p. 348; see also, Stacy, 2009).[84] Recognizing the legal personality of NGOs may help prevent interstate conflicts and encourage the development of nonprofit international organizations.[85] However, some states are concerned that granting such recognition may reduce governmental control, and NGOs are concerned it may entail a loss of autonomy (Charnovitz, 2006a).[86]

Professors James Cavallaro and Emily Schaffer firmly link the promotion of regional human rights to the presence of "vigorous advocacy movements and effective advocacy strategies" (2004, p. 219, and see id., p. 281 [litigation should be tied to "vigorous social movements"]). NGOs have the ability to

---

[83] NGOs are "instigators and enforcers" of international law (Alvarez, 2006, p. 333). They are groups of persons, freely created by private initiative, that cross or transcend national borders and are not profit-seeking (Charnovitz, 2006a). NGOs can also help support the growth of civil society, sponsor education, and raise awareness at the grassroots level (Phan, 2009). On whether NGOs reflect the democratization of the political process or are simply a bundle of political and social pressures brought to bear on outcomes of the democratic process, see Anderson, 2000. For an assessment of the effectiveness of NGOs in the enforcement of human rights law in general, see Edwards, 2010. On their role in global human rights activism, see Schoener, 1997.

Understanding how NGOs interact with local communities is important in order to increase the effectiveness of the local discussion that is generated by a tribunal (Pentelovitch, 2008, p. 489). On the relationship between national and international NGOs, see Blaser, 1985. On the related question of the role of the *media* in the international human rights process, see Hakimi, 2006.

[84] On the ethical challenges faced by NGOs in this context, see Bell, 2008.

[85] For a helpful earlier overview, see Weissbrodt, 1977; for a more recent survey, see Olz, 1997; for the most recent survey, see Simon, 2010.

[86] On the specific issues related to the role of NGOs in the South Pacific, see Farran, 2009.

raise issues and make requests for opinions that otherwise would not be raised by member states or organs controlled by member states (Pasqualucci, 2002, p. 258). Professor Li-Ann Thio argues that, for social change to be meaningful, "NGO activism in the region is crucial to the task of popularizing human rights consciousness and drawing attention to abuses"(1999, p. 83; see also, Armstrong, 1986, p. 258: "there are many grounds for believing that NGOs do make a significant contribution to the furtherance of human rights"). Looking at Africa, Frans Viljoen and Lirette Louw report that compliance with Commission orders is enhanced when the initial petition to the Commission was part of a broader social movement (2007, pp. 28–31).[87] Professor Cavallaro and Stephanie Brewer set out the issue clearly:

> We begin with the assertion that in states where respect for human rights is not entrenched, supranational tribunals are unlikely to enjoy the automatic implementation of their decisions, particularly when these decisions call for a significant political or financial commitment or implicate endemic human rights problems. As a result, supranational courts will often lack the power to trigger lasting improvements in the protection of human rights simply by directing governments to change their practices. Rather, the primary actors who provoke such improvements are generally the social movements, human rights activists, members of the media, members of government with progressive views on human rights, and others carrying on long-term advocacy campaigns or pushing for better policies on a given issue. We therefore maintain that supranational tribunals are most likely to be effective when their procedures and jurisprudence are relevant to such actors' long-term efforts to advance human rights.
>
> A corollary of our argument is that supranational courts should view individual cases that are emblematic of persistent or structural human rights problems as opportunities to stimulate broader change on the relevant issues. Thus, we contend that courts should follow procedures that increase the relevance of court cases to domestic (and in some cases, international) movements working to eliminate the structural causes of the violations in question. Without this broad strategic focus, supranational litigation (which affords access to only a tiny fraction of victims) will function as a lottery in which the handful of petitioners whose cases reach a court will obtain benefits not available to the vast majority of similarly situated victims. (2008, p. 770)

[87] On why standing may be the "key" to successful litigation before the African Court, see Weldehaimanot, 2009.

There are important limitations on NGOs in other interregional tribunals (see, e.g., Mohamed, 1999); I believe it is critically important that the drafting process that precedes the creation of this Tribunal explicitly allow for a broad NGO standing status. (On the standing of NGOs in general in such situations, see Charnovitz, 2006a.) Although NGOs *may* have such standing, it is by no means assured. So this must be made explicit. This is especially important in Asia where, the evidence suggests, "at the *non-governmental* level . . . , there has been an acceptance of the concept of the universality of human rights" (Klein, 2001, p. 40, emphasis in original). As Emilie Hafner-Burton and Kiyoteru Tsutsui have noted, "the growing legitimacy of human rights ideas in international society . . . provides much leverage for nongovernmental actors to pressure rights-violating governments to change their behavior" (2005, p. 1441).

There is already *some* evidence that NGOs in *some* Asian nations have taken a first step toward the acknowledgment of the universality of human rights via the creation of the nongovernmental Asian Human Rights Commission, that has called for an examination of "the circumstances of specific groups whose situation is defined by the massive violation of their rights," targeting *specifically* the rights of persons with disabilities (Muntarbhorn, 1998, pp. 413–414).[88]

✓ What Is the Expected Scope of the Remedies Available to the DR-TAP?

One of the major aims of international human rights litigation is to offer a vehicle that affords redress to petitioners (Shelton, 2010, p. 793). A remedy issued by an international tribunal increases the defendant's cost of complying with the ruling, and promotes democracy (Twinomugisha, 2009).[89] Any regional tribunal must have the capacity to enforce remedies, including injunctions, sanctions, and reparations (Guzman, 2008; on the question of reparations by *non-state* actors, see Rose, 2010, p. 343, conceding that the body of practice that provides for such reparations is "small and tenuous"). Such remedies may be pecuniary or nonpecuniary (Shelton, 2010, pp. 842–843). The remedial powers of human rights courts do vary according to the express provisions of the relevant treaties (Shelton, 2009, p. 555, n. 82).

---

[88] Perhaps the Japanese Law on the Promotion of Human Rights Education—specifically focusing on the rights of persons with disabilities—will have some impact on this venture (see Yun, 2007, on how recent efforts to reduce sex trafficking in Japan could be improved through international human rights enforcement mechanisms).

[89] For a consideration of Hong Kong's disability discrimination law, concluding that that law is "unlikely to bring about significant change until the enforcement model can be strengthened," see Petersen, 2005, p. 33.

Writing about the Inter-American Court, Professor Thomas Antkowiak said this:

> The Inter-American Court is no longer shy about requiring society-wide reparations, including legislative and institutional reform, even in cases involving a sole litigant. These orders have generally been issued in two circumstances: a) when a national law violates the American Convention; or b) when illegal practices of state agents or institutions are proven before the Tribunal. Such an approach seems justified, as remedies with a national reach are proportional to a systemic domestic problem or impermissible legislation. (2008, p. 394)[90]

The question to be addressed here is whether or not this Tribunal will be vested with similar powers. The DR-TAP should have the ability to provide any remedy deemed necessary (Weinstein, 2010).[91]

✓ Will There Be a Difference In the Way Such a Tribunal Would Operate in Monist and Dualist Nations?

There are basically two jurisprudential models: nations with monist systems and nations with dualist systems (see generally, Perlin, 2006; see also supra chapter 6). Nations such as the Netherlands, for example, are considered "monist," where their constitutions expressly provide that certain treaties are directly applied and that in such cases these treaties are deemed superior to all laws, including local constitutional norms (Jackson, 1992). On the other hand, the United Kingdom is generally considered the "prime example" (id., p. 319) of a "dualist" system, in which treaties must be implemented through separate legislation in order to have the effect of domestic law. (Templeman, 1991). If domestic law cannot be construed in accordance with Convention law, then the latter overrides domestic law (*R. v. Sec'y of State for Transp.*, ex parte *Factortame Ltd.*, 1991).

Korea and Japan, by way of example, are examples of monist nations (VanGrasstek & Sauvé, 2006; Lee, 1993); Singapore is a dualist nation (Thio, 1997). If some of the nations that participate in DR-TAP are monist and some are dualist, there will be other issues in need of resolution.

---

[90] But see Goldman, 2009, p. 884 ("no [Inter-American] state has yet put in place internal legal mechanisms and procedures that mandate *full* compliance with the decisions and orders of the Commission and the Court") (emphasis in original).

[91] Most regional courts defer to a home state, requiring domestic remedies be exhausted or unavailable before other options may be utilized. See Thorp, 2001/2002, p. 172; Shelton, 2010, p. 734 (exceptions to exhaustion rule in regional human rights commission jurisprudence).

✓ Will There Be a Difference in Nations That Have Common Law and Civil Law Traditions?

Although there have been significant developments in mental disability law jurisprudence in certain civil law nations (see supra chapter 3), by and large, the transformative changes in this area of the law have come from common law countries (Perlin, 2007a; for a comparison of the ways that expert testimony is treated in mental disability law cases in common and civil law jurisdictions, see Perlin, Birgden & Gledhill, 2009, and supra chapter 6). By way of example, of the four nations in the region that have successfully operative antidisability discrimination laws, three have common law systems (Akiyama, 2010).[92]

In an article I wrote recently with two colleagues, I concluded that there was no "one size fits all" answer to questions of how courts in varying common and civil law jurisdictions assess expert testimony in mental disability law cases (Perlin, Birgden & Gledhill, 2009, p. 81; see supra chapter 6). This finding must be kept in mind when a DR-TAP is created.[93]

✓ What Sanctions Are There if a Defendant Refuses to Comply?

Enforcement remains "the weakest component of the international human rights system" (Donoho, 2006, p. 52; see Nmehielle, 2004, p. 11, concluding that it was the lack of an effective enforcement mechanism under the African Human Rights Charter that led to the adoption of the Protocol on the African Human Rights Court).[94] The power of the Court to supervise compliance with its judgments raises the question of "how the Court will effectively determine whether sufficient efforts have been made to identify human rights violators and sanction them" (Wilson & Perlin, 2002, p. 666). In at least one Inter-American case, the Court reiterated [an] order that the State investigate the facts underlying these human rights violations, identify those responsible and sanction all of them appropriately, "*noting that leaving those violations unpunished promotes impunity and represents a failure of the State's obligation to guarantee the full and free exercise of rights under the Convention*" (id., discussing the *Cantoral Benavides Case*, 2001, available at http://www1.umn.edu/humanrts/iachr/C/88-ing.html (Emphasis added)). This language is critical for the future of a disability rights tribunal.[95]

---

[92] The four are New Zealand, Australia, Hong Kong, and the Republic of Korea.

[93] On how common law/civil law choices are factored into analyses of economic development, see Mancuso, 2009.

[94] But see Hunt, 2005 (on the obligations of nations to enforce judgments of human rights tribunals).

[95] Writing about the move *toward* new institutions in Asia and the Pacific, Alison Duxbury (2007) has noted the decision within those regions to create third-party

✓ How Will the Issue of Appointment of Counsel Be Handled?

In many ways this is the most critical question to consider. As I discuss elsewhere in this volume, without the assignment of dedicated, knowledgeable counsel, meaningful and ameliorative change is almost impossible to achieve (Perlin, 2008b; see supra chapter 8).[96] Without such counsel, no judicial system can work effectively to protect human rights for a person when his/her human rights are infringed.[97] It is obvious that persons with disabilities strongly need adequate counsel to protect and realize their rights, because of their powerlessness and vulnerability. A regional human rights court/tribunal must provide adequate counsel to help persons with disabilities to file his/her case (see generally, Perlin, 2008b).[98]

In Asia as elsewhere, public interest litigation has had a transformative impact as an "effective tool for the enforcement of fundamental rights, as well as for creating a legal and social environment in which justice could be made available to [the marginalized]" (Islam, 2007, p. 142;[99] see also, Forster & Jivam, 2008). In the context of a regional human rights tribunal, such litigation also, in the words of Cavallaro and Brewer, is more likely to "translate into substantive improvements in the lives not only of petitioners to their systems, but of the far larger universe of individuals who will never see the inside of a supranational court" (2008a, p. 770).

Litigation such as this requires dedicated counsel, a circumstance that is rare at an international level:

> Globally, there is little good news. In many nations, there is no mental health law at all. In others, there is simply no provision for counsel. In others, counsel appears to be present in name only, what is referred to disparagingly in the literature as the "warm body" problem. In only a few instances does counsel appear to be

---

dispute resolution procedures. See also Cardenas, 2007, p. 135 ("International actors should reinforce processes of conflict resolution"). This decision needs to be kept in mind in this context as well.

96 On the significance of access to justice in this region of the world, see Chan, 2007; Kumar, 2008.

97 For consideration of this issue in the specific context of the South Pacific, see Farran, 2009.

Professor Terry Carney has taken issue with this position, concluding that he would "put [more] lawyers last on the 'wish list' of needed reforms" (Carney, 2010, p. 14). I disagree with him profoundly, based on 40 years of evidence from the United States (see supra chapter 3) and more recent evidence from other regions. I believe that, without such counsel, any long-lasting efforts at ameliorative reform are doomed to failure. See generally, Perlin, 2008b.

98 On the special issues endemic to the lawyer-client relationship in litigation before regional human rights commissions and court, see Crow, 2005.

99 On the role of the courts in the protection of marginalized groups in Europe, see Guarnieri, 2007.

> doing a remotely adequate job. . . . Although there is a right to counsel in India, research has revealed no such right in a range of other Asian nations including, inter alia, Afghanistan, China, Indonesia, Pakistan, South Korea, Sri Lanka, Thailand, and Vietnam. (Perlin, 2008b, p. 251).

Importantly, however, the CRPD mandates that "States Parties shall take appropriate measures to provide access by persons with disabilities to the support they may require in exercising their legal capacity" (Perlin, 2008b, pp. 252–253, quoting Art. 12). Elsewhere, the convention commands:

> States Parties shall ensure effective access to justice for persons with disabilities on an equal basis with others, including through the provision of procedural and age appropriate accommodations, in order to facilitate their effective role as direct and indirect participants, including as witnesses, in all legal proceedings, including at investigative and other preliminary stages. (Art. 13; see supra chapter 7)

The extent to which this article is honored in signatory nations will have a major impact on the extent to which this entire Convention affects persons with mental disabilities (Perlin, 2008b, p. 253). If and only if, there is a mechanism for the appointment of dedicated counsel, can this dream become a reality.[100]

Internationally, law schools must commit themselves to the creation of clinical programs to train lawyers to provide legal representation to indigent persons facing involuntary civil commitment (see supra chapter 6, and supra chapter 8). It is also critical that lawyers understand the full textures of sanism (see supra chapters 1 & 2):

> In the civil commitment context, any sanism-inspired blunders by lawyers can easily be fatal to the client's chance of success. If a lawyer rejects the notion that his client may be competent (indeed, if s/he engages in the not-atypical "presumption of incompetency" that is all too often de rigueur in these cases), the chances are far slimmer that s/he will advocate for such a client in the way that lawyers have been taught—or, at the least, should be taught—to advocate for their clients. In nations with no traditions of an "expanded due process model" in cases involving persons subject to commitment to psychiatric institutions or those already

---

[100] Although the common assumption is that Asian citizens—especially those with a Confucianism background prefer "a conciliatory approach to the settlement of disputes" (Wong, 2000, p. 304), this conclusion has been sharply questioned in an empirical study that concludes "there is nothing immoral in turning to a more coercive forum" (Peterson, 2005, p. 13).

> institutionalized, sanism in lawyers can be fatal to an individual's chance for release or for a judicial order mandating amelioration of conditions of confinement and/or access to treatment and/or to be free from unwanted treatment interventions. (Perlin, 2008b, p. 262)

In short, the presence of counsel is the lynchpin to authentic change in this area of the law.[101]

Earlier (see supra chapter 6), I discussed the global role of online, distance learning education in training cadres of lawyers to represent persons with mental disabilities. It is essential that such cadres be created if there is to be meaningful representation before the DR-TAP; online education offers the promise of an economic and efficient way of providing this level of high-quality legal training (see e.g., Perlin, 2007a).

V. A Question of Timing

A recent law review article urging the creation of a Southeast Asian Court of Human Rights, concludes, "It is about time that the region moved ahead and acted towards that goal" (Phan, 2009, p. 431). Until such a court is created, activists and advocates have begun work on efforts to create a court focused on the sole subtopic of disability rights, the Disability Rights Tribunal for Asia and the Pacific, or DR-TAP (see Perlin & Ikehara, 2010a, 2010b; Ikehara, 2010; Perlin, 2010). For multiple reasons, the creation of a DR-TAP would be the single best way to ensure that the Convention on the Rights of Persons with Disabilities (CRPD) be given authentic life.

First, experiences in other regions show that similarly situated courts and commissions have been powerful forces in mandating the practical implementation both of other UN Conventions and treaties, and even of "soft law."[102] Cases decided by regional courts and commissions in Latin America and Africa, by way of example, have decided cases in which they have granted broad rights to institutionalized persons (see, e.g., Perlin, 2008a, p. 489, n. 37,

---

[101] Therapeutic jurisprudence is a school of legal analysis that seeks to determine whether legal rules, procedures, and lawyer roles can or should be reshaped to enhance their therapeutic potential while not subordinating due process principles (Perlin, 2005, 2008a; see generally, e.g., Wexler & Winick, 1996; Winick, 2005; Wexler, 2008). Skilled and advocacy-focused counsel can also import principles of therapeutic jurisprudence into client representation. In this context, see Petersen, 2000, discussing the possible impact of court-ordered apologies in a disability discrimination case. I discuss the concept of therapeutic jurisprudence and its potentially redemptive role in assuring the enforcement of international human rights law for persons with mental disabilities at length infra chapter 10.

[102] On how African human rights institutions have had to "reconcile divergent traditions, relying on a blend of traditional African values and more Western ideals of modernity," see Udombana, 2004, p. 141.

discussing *Congo v. Ecuador*, 1999)[103]; Kanter, 2009, p. 547, discussing *Purohit and Moore v. The Gambia*, 2003[104]; see generally, Perlin, 2009; see generally supra chapter 3). It strains credulity to suggest that the high courts of Ecuador or Gambia would have decided the *Congo* or the *Purohit* cases the way that the interregional bodies did (compare Jarmul, 1995–1996, discussing effect of decisions of regional human rights tribunals on national courts).[105]

Second, those of us who believe in the universality of human rights—and who recognize the false consciousness of the specious "Asian values" arguments [106] (and the false premises on which the "Asian values" debate rests, see Freeman, 1996) that seek to reject that universality (see, in this context, Perlin & Ikehara, 2010; see generally, Jacobson & Bruun, 2006)[107]—understand that a DR-TAP that spans multiple nations (in diverse geographic regions, with diverse populations comprised of diverse ethnicities, races, religions, and cultures) will make the enforcement of these human rights far more likely than reliance on state-by-state enforcement.[108] The false consciousness of the "Asian values" argument cannot be sustained over the long term. (Marsh & Payne, 2007).[109] See supra, this chapter, part II.

Third, the *language* of the Convention—the invocation of a social model and the repudiation of a medical model (see Hendriks & Degener, 1994; see also, Lawson, 2006); the empowering of people with disabilities to be the masters of their own fates; the focus on dignity and nondiscrimination—tells us that the time is especially right for such a Tribunal. Just as the African Charter on Human and Peoples' Rights (1986) calls for a pledge to achieve a better life for the peoples of Africa, to recognize that human rights stem from attitudes

---

[103] See supra chapter 3.

[104] See id.

[105] Professor Sienho Yee speculates that a regional system to protect human rights may happen "once the Asian states feel more secure about themselves" (2004, p. 164). This observation leaves an open question: do many of the African states that participate in the African Court actually feel "more secure" about themselves than do, say, Japan or Korea or China?

[106] See supra pp. 174–180.

[107] "Cultural relativism is not [a] sufficient justification for the denial of the universal application of human rights standards." Hui, 2002, p. 199. See generally, Perlin, 2010b, rejecting the culturally relativistic basis of the Asian values argument.

[108] See Lo, 2010, p. 23:The more appropriate idea of sovereignty today is that it refers to the state that "'possesses the totality of international rights and duties recognized by international law' as long as it has not limited them in particular terms by concluding a treaty." (citation omitted).

[109] See Svensson, 2006, p. 201 ("Asia is much too heterogeneous [an] area to be ascribed any common values"); Friedman, 2006, p. 39 ("The East is not a homogenous monolith"). See also, Byung-Sun, 1997, p. 247:

> still what is lacking is [the] effective implementation [of human rights] through the establishment of appropriate mechanisms for the protecting of human rights.

of human beings, to imply duties on the part of everyone, so would a DR-TAP similarly recognize these important principles necessary to achieve human rights (compare Goldman, 2009, p. 887, discussing the Inter-American human rights system: "[I]t is highly desirable for a region . . . to have all its states be bound by the same legal obligations and their peoples have the same rights"). On how ratification of human rights treaties "generally strengthens the hand of domestic and international rights advocates," see Peerenboom, 2006, p. 56 n. 14).

As the European Convention on Human Rights (1950) aims at "securing the universal and effective recognition and observance of the Rights therein declared," so too would the DR-TAP seek universal human rights (compare Asplund, 2009, p. 47, discussing how constitutional theory may have detached human rights "from a moral sphere"). The Inter-American Convention on Human Rights recognizes that "the essential rights of man are not derived from one's being a national of a certain state, but are based upon attributes of the human personality, and that they therefore justify international protection in the form of a convention reinforcing or complementing the protection provided by the domestic law of the American states" (1969, Preamble). The DR-TAP would accomplish the same goal.

Fourth, without establishing the DR-TAP, persons with mental disabilities will continue to suffer severe violations of their human rights by the States as there is no way to feasibly or realistically enforce these rights nor any way for persons with mental disabilities to meaningfully address these violations.[110]

Fifth, from a perspective of economics, the timing is right (see Peerenboom & Chen, 2008). If Asian nations want to demonstrate their commitment to human rights as other major nations around the world have, one way would be to support the establishment of the DR-TAP as a means of fostering and promoting better international relations. In Suzannah Linton's words, it is a "signaling device" that may eventually lead to substantial material benefits from the international community (2008, p. 443).

Sixth, the creation of partnerships to offer distance learning courses in mental disability law—ones that focus both on international human rights issues and on lawyering skills—will best provide a cadre of committed lawyers to provide the essential representation that is so needed at this Tribunal. This is the key to authentic change in this area of the world in this area of the law.

Conclusion

For the reasons discussed above, I believe that creation of the DR-TAP will be the best way of ensuring that persons with disabilities can exercise their civil

110 By way of example, for a consideration of the "problematic" way that persons with mental illness are treated in Japan, see Mandiberg, 1993, p. 27.

rights and become full members of the community. Professor Helen Stacy concludes—and I agree—that "Courts provide the connection between politics and practice, the bridge between the formal words of a treaty and the concrete changes necessary once a country has signed on to it" (2009, p. 125).[111] I believe further that it is only through the provision of vigorous and dedicated advocacy that the CRPD's promise can be fulfilled. DR-TAP—in conjunction with the expansion of law-student training and lawyer training in mental disability law studies—is the best way of achieving that promise.

---

[111] And see id.:

> Judges are a conduit of human rights acculturation. Judicial decisions spell out the rights of politically powerless people and groups. . . . Courts apply abstract human rights principles to the peoples' everyday lives.

10

Therapeutic Jurisprudence

I. Introduction

One of the most important legal theoretical developments of the past two decades has been the creation and dynamic growth of therapeutic jurisprudence (TJ) (see, e.g., Wexler 1990; Wexler & Winick, 1996; Winick, 2005; Wexler, 2008). Initially employed in cases involving individuals with mental disabilities, but subsequently expanded far beyond that narrow area, therapeutic jurisprudence presents a new model for assessing the impact of case law and legislation, recognizing that, as a therapeutic agent, the law can have therapeutic or antitherapeutic consequences.[1] The ultimate aim of therapeutic jurisprudence is to determine whether legal rules, procedures, and lawyer roles can or should be reshaped to enhance their therapeutic potential while not subordinating due process principles (Perlin 2003, 2005a, 2008; 2011b).

Therapeutic jurisprudence "asks us to look at law as it actually impacts people's lives" (Winick, 2009, p. 535), and focuses on the law's influence on emotional life and psychological well-being (Wexler, 2000, in Stolle et al., 2000). It suggests that "law should value psychological health, should strive to avoid imposing anti-therapeutic consequences whenever possible, and when consistent with other values served by law should attempt to bring about healing and wellness" (Winick, 2003, p. 26). By way of example, therapeutic jurisprudence "aims to offer social science evidence that limits the use of the incompetency label by narrowly defining its use and minimizing its

[1] For a transnational perspective, see Diesfeld & Freckelton, 2006.

psychological and social disadvantage" (Steinberger, 2003, p. 65). In recent years, scholars have considered a vast range of topics through a therapeutic jurisprudence lens, including, but not limited to, all aspects of mental disability law, domestic relations law, criminal law and procedure,[2] employment law, gay rights law, and tort law (Perlin, 2002–2003).[3] As Ian Freckelton has noted, "it is a tool for gaining a new and distinctive perspective utilizing socio-psychological insights into the law and its applications" (Freckelton, 2008, p. 582). It is also part of a growing comprehensive movement in the law toward establishing more humane and psychologically optimal ways of handling legal issues collaboratively, creatively, and respectfully (Daicoff, 2000). These alternative approaches optimize the psychological well-being of individuals, relationships, and communities dealing with a legal matter, and acknowledge concerns beyond strict legal rights, duties, and obligations. In its aim to use the law to empower individuals, enhance rights, and promote well-being, therapeutic jurisprudence has been described as "a sea-change in ethical thinking about the role of law . . . a movement towards a more distinctly relational approach to the practice of law . . . which emphasises psychological wellness over adversarial triumphalism" (Brookbanks, 2001, p. 329–330). That is, therapeutic jurisprudence supports an ethic of care.

One of the central principles of therapeutic jurisprudence is a commitment to dignity (see supra chapter 2; see generally, Winick, 2009). Ronner describes the "three Vs": voice, validation, and voluntariness (2008, p. 627), arguing:

> What "the three Vs" commend is pretty basic: litigants must have a sense of voice or a chance to tell their story to a decision maker. If that litigant feels that the tribunal has genuinely listened to, heard, and taken seriously the litigant's story, the litigant feels a sense of validation. When litigants emerge from a legal proceeding with a sense of voice and validation, they are more at peace with the outcome. Voice and validation create a sense of voluntary participation, one in which the litigant experiences the proceeding as less coercive. Specifically, the feeling on the part of litigants that they voluntarily partook in the very process that engendered the end result or the very judicial pronunciation that affects their own lives can initiate healing and bring about improved behavior in the future. In general, human beings prosper when they feel that they are making, or at least participating in, their own decisions. (2002, pp. 94–95; see generally, Ronner, 2010)

[2] E.g., sentencing (Kirchengast, 2007); sex offender laws (Birgden, 2007). On criminal law issues in general, see Wexler, 2008.

[3] On its potential application to international law issues in general, see Aponte Toro, 1999, and to international criminal justice, see Olowu, 2007, 2010.

I believe that TJ has the best capacity to rid the law of sanism and pretextuality. Elsewhere, in a book-length treatment of the insanity defense, I have written:

> [W]e must rigorously apply therapeutic jurisprudence principles to each aspect of the insanity defense. We need to take what we learn from therapeutic jurisprudence to strip away sanist behavior, pretextual reasoning and teleological decision making from the insanity defense process. This would enable us to confront the pretextual use of social science data in an open and meaningful way. (Perlin, 1994, p. 443)[4]

I believe the same principles apply to the subject matter of this volume as well.

What is the impact of TJ on the relationship between international human rights principles and mental disability law developments? As I will discuss below, I believe that applying therapeutic jurisprudence can assist both lawyers and mental health professionals in addressing and resolving human rights issues (see Birgden, 2009; Carasik, 2006).[5] In this chapter, I will first consider the TJ/international human rights intersection in the context of the forensic mental health system, focusing specifically on the role of forensic mental health professionals. Next, I will consider that intersection in the context of some of the issues that I have focused on in this work (specifically, the use of state-sanctioned psychiatry as a tool of suppression of political dissent, the "universal factors," the need for dedicated counsel, the enforcement of the CRPD, and the creation of a Disability Rights Tribunal for Asia and the Pacific). I will conclude with some recommendations for future action.

II. The Interplay between the Forensic Mental Health System, International Human Rights and Mental Disability Law[6]

A. Introduction

The professional literature is "strangely silent" on whether forensic psychology practice meets human rights standards (Perlin, 2005b), a silence that is

[4] See also, Perlin, 2010, p. 876:

> To teach mental disability law meaningfully, it is necessary to teach about the core characteristics that contaminate it (sanism and pretextuality), to teach about the cognitive approaches that distort it (false ordinary common sense and cognitive-simplifying heuristics), and to teach the school of jurisprudence that can optimally redeem it (TJ).

[5] On the increasing turn by lawyers and law clinical professors toward international human rights models, see Volpp, 2000; Hurwitz, 2003.

[6] See generally, Birgden & Perlin, 2008, 2009.

both shameful and baffling (Perlin, 2006).[7] Fellner (2006) estimates that in the United States 16 percent of adults in prisons and jails have a mental illness, this rate is two to four times the general population, and there are three times as many individuals incarcerated in prison as in mental health hospitals. Ogloff (2002) reviewed available data in Australia and New Zealand and concluded that the prevalence of mental illness amongst prisoners is significantly higher than the general population. In both countries, the rate of prisoners with mental illness is also increasing. Prisoners with mental illness are more likely to violate prison rules, leading to disciplinary hearings, inappropriate sanctions, and segregation (Fellner, 2006). In this section, I will consider the relationship of TJ to the application of international human rights principles to prisoners and detainees with a mental illness (see generally supra chapter 6).

Might therapeutic jurisprudence assist forensic psychologists and other mental health professionals to actively address human rights? Therapeutic jurisprudence, human rights, and forensic psychology can intersect in terms of therapeutic jurisprudence and human rights (Ward & Birgden, 2007), therapeutic jurisprudence and forensic psychology (Birgden & Ward, 2003), and human rights and forensic psychology (Perlin, 2005b, 2006). In common, therapeutic jurisprudence, human rights, and forensic psychology rights are normative, humanistic (with a concern for well-being), and interdisciplinary. A normative approach conceptualizes problems, seeks solutions, and specifies values that are foundational for a particular profession (Madden & Wayne, 2002). Therapeutic jurisprudence provides a useful interdisciplinary discourse—combining political theory and science, sociology, law, philosophy, biology, cultural studies, anthropology, and psychology—on human rights (Ward & Birgden, 2007). Both therapeutic jurisprudence and human rights can guide forensic psychologists in a normative approach (e.g., under what circumstances involuntary psychological treatment may be acceptable), a humanistic approach (forging a therapeutic alliance based on an ethic of care), and an interdisciplinary approach (a collaborative approach with other disciplines).

In relation to prisons, Zinger (2006) states that the best approach to ensure that the rule of law is upheld is to view corrections as being in the human rights business:

> The best argument for observing human rights standards is not merely that they are required by international or domestic law but that they actually work better than any known alternative—for offenders, for correctional staff, and for society at large. Compliance with human rights obligations increases, though it does not guarantee, the odds of releasing a more responsible citizen. In essence, a prison environment respectful of human rights is conducive to positive change, whereas an environment of abuse,

[7] But see, Pope & Gutheil, 2009 (American Psychological Association ethics code runs counter to Nuremberg Ethic).

> disrespect, and discrimination has the opposite effect: Treating prisoners with humanity actually enhances public safety. Moreover, through respecting the human rights of prisoners, society conveys a strong message that everyone, regardless of their circumstance, race, social status, gender, religion, and so on, is to be treated with inherent respect and dignity. (p. 127)

B. A Human Rights Model

Virtually no attention has been paid by forensic psychologists to the violation of human rights in institutions. Ward and Birgden (2007) have proposed a human rights model to be applied by forensic psychologists in offender rehabilitation (see also, Birgden, 2004). The proposed model is the only one known to be based on human rights principles.[8] Based on the work of Gewirth and consequential and deontological justifications, Ward and Birgden argue that the individual has the right to core values of freedom and well-being in order to function as an autonomous and dignified agent (Ward & Birgden, 2007).[9] The core value of freedom entails noncoerced situations and internal capabilities (e.g., the capacity to formulate intentions, to imagine possible actions, and to form and implement valued plans). Freedom is made up of personal freedom and social recognition. The core value of well-being entails meeting physical, social, and psychological needs. Well-being is made up of personal security, material subsistence, and elemental equality.

1. Role of Forensic Psychologists

As discussed, ethical forensic practice must be understood in the context of international human rights law and international ethical codes of practice. In addition, a TJ approach requires forensic psychologists to understand the law and attempt to apply it to therapeutic effect. What does *therapeutic* mean in the context of corrections? To date, TJ has not clearly defined the concept (see Kress, 1999) and it is unclear whether social scientists, legal actors, legislators (or indeed defendants/offenders) ought to define the concept (Roderick & Krumholz, 2006; Slobogin, 1999b). Despite this problem, Birgden (2008) has argued that a TJ approach in corrections requires a balance between community rights and offender rights in order to manage offender risk *for the community* and meet offender needs *for the offender*, weighing justice principles and therapeutic principles to enhance community protection. In this way, the

[8] See also Birgden, 2009, p. 43: " Therapeutic jurisprudence should describe itself as a philosophy and therefore take a normative stance, based on a human rights perspective."

[9] On the "good lives" model from which these concepts are derived, see Birgden, 2002.

offender can be managed as both a rights-violator and a rights-holder (Ward & Birgden, 2007).

Psychologists are to demonstrate respect for individuals by acknowledging their legal rights and moral rights, their dignity, and right to participate in decisions affecting their lives (see Australian Psychological Society, 2007). However, very little literature has considered the intersection between forensic psychology and human rights (see Ward & Birgden, 2007; Perlin, 2005b, 2006; Perlin & Dlugacz, 2007; Day & Casey, 2009). Despite the rapid development of forensic psychology, Ward and Birgden (2009) have noted that there is a lack of theoretical and research attention paid to moral, social, and legal rights in prisoners (but see Ward & Salmon, 2009). Such concerns are particularly applicable to prisoners with a mental illness.

The United Nations Standard Minimum Rules for the Treatment of Prisoners (1957) require prison staff to display integrity, humanity, competence, and personal suitability for the work. Forensic psychologists are also required to adhere to codes of professional conduct. Codes are a public commitment by a professional group to a particular set of standards and rules and the highest standards of ethical practice (Glaser, 2003). For example, the American Psychological Association ethical code determines that psychologists must recognize "fairness and justice," the Speciality Guidelines for Forensic Psychologists also cover a range of professional behaviors (Perlin, 2005b), and the Australian Psychological Society (2007) addresses three general principles—respect, propriety, and integrity in its Code of Ethics. In terms of legal consequences for breaching codes, it is rare for forensic psychologists to be censured.

By way of example, there have apparently been only two cases in the United States in which forensic psychologists had been brought before state licensing boards for poor professional conduct and one criminal case where professional standards were scrutinized (Perlin, 2005b). In Australia, only two states provide publicly accessible information regarding professional practice over a period of time. In South Australia, there were 24 cases between 1991 and 2007, but none were forensic psychologists (South Australian Psychological Board, 2007). In Victoria, there were 34 cases between 1999 and 2007, and two of these were forensic psychologists (Psychologists Registration Board of Victoria, 2007). One psychologist was reprimanded for professional misconduct, later deregistered for separate criminal charges, and in 2003 was reregistered with conditions. The other psychologist was deregistered for professional misconduct. An additional problem with existing codes is that such standards and rules are not based on a theory linking them to human rights. Ward and Birgden (2007) suggest that forensic psychologists as therapeutic agents (in therapeutic jurisprudence terms) should use the concept of human rights to structure and guide the assessment, treatment, and management of offenders (see Ward, Gannon & Birgden, 2007, as an example applied to sex offenders) and ground ethical principles for psychological practice (see Ward, Gannon & Vess, 2009, regarding the American Psychological Association).

If forensic psychologists do not recognize that the business of corrections is to promote and monitor respect for human rights and prevent, detect, and remedy human rights violations, systemic abuses of power will be inevitable (Zinger, 2006). Article 15 of the United Nations Body of Principles for the Protection of all Persons under Any Form of Detention or Imprisonment (1988) clearly states that no individual should be subjected to torture, or to cruel, inhuman, or degrading treatment or punishment. However, in recent years, there has been a dramatic increase in the attention paid to the issue of the standards of behavior that govern the practice of forensic psychologists (and forensic psychiatrists). This new attention flows mostly from revelations of the sanction of torture at prison camps in Guantanamo Bay and Abu Ghraib (see Pope & Gutheil, 2009). These human rights violations have led to the question of whether this ongoing (and fierce) debate will be limited to the extraordinarily important (but clearly, relatively narrow) question of the relationship between forensic psychology and torture as a function of international human rights law, or whether it will it be expanded to a broader inquiry that considers the relationship between international human rights law and all professional practice in which forensic psychologists engage (Perlin & Dlugacz, 2007). I believe that the latter should occur, particularly in relation to freedom and well-being.

In an earlier work, Professor Astrid Birgden and I sought to articulate a constellation of principles that, when combined, would link therapeutic jurisprudence, ethical forensic practice, and international human rights law (see Birgden & Perlin, 2009, pp. 59–88, listing principles of respect for dignity, competent caring for individuals' well-being, integrity of mental health professionals participating in forensic systems, and demonstrating professional and scientific responsibilities to the larger community). In my earlier discussion of the universal factors of mental disability law, I concluded that "Depressingly, persons in the forensic system receive—if this even seems possible—less humane services than do civil patients" (see supra chapter 5, p. 100). I believe that a turn toward the TJ-focused principles suggested in these articles that I coauthored with Professor Birgden (as well as her own and those that she has coauthored with Tony Ward) would offer some measure of relief from these onerous conditions.

C. Conclusion

Institutionalized individuals, particularly prisoners and detainees with mental illness, are confined in prison and forensic facilities that regularly and grossly violate international human rights standards (Perlin, 2002, 2006, 2007; Perlin et al., 2006; Perlin & Dlugacz, 2007, 2009). Forensic psychology has been strangely—and problematically—silent about these abuses and their impact on the mental health and well-being of those so institutionalized (Perlin, 2006).

Therapeutic jurisprudence offers a potentially redemptive solution to this state of affairs. Its principles can, and should, be taken seriously to address the human rights problems that I discuss in this book. Therapeutic jurisprudence can suggest therapeutic laws, procedures, and roles that maximize the core values of freedom and well-being (and the related objects) for prisoners and detainees with a mental illness. Therapeutic jurisprudence offers an intersection between forensic psychology and human rights with its normative, humanistic, and interdisciplinary approach. Conversely, the normative base of therapeutic jurisprudence can be strengthened by the application of human rights principles regarding moral, social, and legal rights and when values conflict, therapeutic jurisprudence ought to always support well-being and only accept curtailed freedom as the least restrictive alternative. As duty-bearers, forensic psychologists have a responsibility to actively address the panoply of legal rights discussed in this chapter and to expand their attention to moral and social rights.

III. Therapeutic Jurisprudence and International Human Rights Law

Very little literature has considered the intersection between therapeutic jurisprudence and human rights (see Ferencz & McGuire, 2000; Ward & Birgden, 2007; Winick, 2002; Birgden & Perlin, 2009). As discussed above, therapeutic jurisprudence originated from consideration of mental health law. Winick describes the progress of mental health law from the medical model (with lack of treatment and human rights abuses in institutions) to a legal rights–based model (with improved but vague civil commitment and due process standards) to a therapeutic jurisprudence model (to balance legal and therapeutic needs of civilly committed patients). He identifies the convergence between therapeutic jurisprudence and human rights values in civil commitment procedures such as liberty, due process, the right to treatment and to refuse treatment, and the exercise of decision making.[10] In this analysis, he concluded that:

> The remedy for the abuses in the mental health system of Hungary and other Eastern European nations is a healthy dose of international human rights law and therapeutic jurisprudence. As that region moves from a medical, to a legal, to a therapeutic jurisprudence model of civil commitment, we can expect to see reforms in mental health law and practice that will both protect individual liberty and promote improved mental health and psychological well-being. (Winick, 2002, p. 572)

[10] See Tait, 2003, p. 92, calling for a careful examination of the "emotional and symbolic aspects" of civil commitment hearing procedures via a therapeutic jurisprudence perspective.

In an analysis of a British policy allowing for informal detention in a civil commitment context, Professor Kristy Keywood concludes that both a human rights–based analysis and a TJ perspective highlights the process "by which vulnerable people are rendered yet more vulnerable" through this mechanism (2005, p. 115, discussing decision in *R. v. Bournewood*, 1999[11]; see also, Kinderman & Tai, 2008, discussing the relationship between international human rights and assisted outpatient commitment from a TJ perspective).

There have been significant TJ developments in many aspects of international law. Michael King catalogs these, making reference to, inter alia,

- Allan and Allan's study (2000) of the therapeutic aspects of South Africa's Truth and Reconciliation Commission,
- Cooper's consideration (1999) of the implications of therapeutic jurisprudence for the human right of self-determination in international law,
- King and Guthrie's suggestion (2008) that the Northern Territory Emergency Response legislation in Australia is antitherapeutic, hindering the legislation's objective of the well-being of the relevant Northern Territory communities,
- Olowu's evaluation (2010) of TJ as a means of humanizing criminal justice in Africa,
- Nicholson's examination (2008) of the antitherapeutic effects of child labor laws in South Africa, and
- Munir's study (2007) of therapeutic jurisprudence in relation to juvenile justice in Pakistan (King, 2008, p. 1112).

But only Winick's article (2002) has, as of yet, made the explicit connection between international *human rights law* and TJ.[12]

I believe that, if we consider the major focal points of this book, this connection jumps out. The use of state-sanctioned psychiatry to suppress political dissent (see supra chapter 4, and see especially, Munro, 2000) violates dignity and suppresses the voice of those institutionalized (Ronner, 2002, 2010), and also delegitimatizes the process involved, making that process antitherapeutic not solely for those institutionalized because of political actions but also for all others whose commitments are based on the same laws (see generally, Lind & Tyler, 1988). Professor Christopher Slobogin phrases it this way:

> The procedural justice literature has clearly established that a procedure that gives participants a full opportunity to present their version of the facts enhances perceptions of fairness, satisfaction

[11] For a careful analysis of the *Bournewood* case in the context of the impact of mental health laws on those "compliant" with treatment, see McSherry, 2009.

[12] Inexplicably, to my mind, there has been virtually no discussion of the Winick article in the law review or behavioral literature other than by me and by Professor Birgden.

with outcomes, and respect for the process. Conversely, a procedure that does not do so is more likely to create antipathy toward the system among those it has frustrated. (1999a, p. 117)

Writing with two coauthors some 15 years ago about patients rights and TJ, I concluded that "A reexamination of involuntary civil commitment, right to treatment, and right-to-refuse-treatment law from a therapeutic jurisprudence perspective [makes it] clear that therapeutic jurisprudence is compatible with an expanded rights-based perspective in all three areas" of the law (Perlin, Gould & Dorfman, 1995, p. 118).[13] A consideration of the universal factors discussed earlier (see supra chapter 5) reveals that this same conclusion holds true for each of those areas of the law and social policy.

First, as stated flatly by Judge Juan Ramirez and Professor Amy Ronner, "the right to counsel is . . . the core of therapeutic jurisprudence" (2004, p. 119; see, e.g., Winick & Wren, 2002, articulating a TJ basis for the right to counsel in juvenile cases). If there is no mental health law—much less no mental health lawyers—it strains credulity to argue that such a practice might comport with TJ principles. As I have argued many times, TJ is the perfect mechanism "to expose [the law's] pretextuality" (e.g., Perlin, 2002/2003, p. 544), and it is equally appropriate in cases when there is no law to expose.[14]

Second, if there is no law at all, the mental health system cannot comport with TJ principles. This should be self-evident, but requires some mention. By analogy, David Wexler has noted, in writing about the contingency structures of criminal commitment, how the absence of articulated legal standards is both bad psychology and bad law (1977).[15] If there is a prima facie duty to obey law (as reflected in the writings of social contract theorists such as Hobbes and Locke or utilitarian theorists such as Bentham and Mill; see Ostas, 2010), the *absence* of law must inevitably cause social and cognitive dissonance, and thus detrimental to mental health and antitherapeutic. (Winick, 2010).

---

[13] See also, e.g., Fischer, 2006, p. 158:

> One of the most notable cases demonstrating the therapeutic jurisprudence perspective is *Lessard v. Schmidt,* the United States case that established that "a finding of 'dangerousness' to self or others is necessary in order to deprive an individual of his or her freedom" for treatment of a mental illness.

[14] On the relationship between TJ and dignity in the context of the involuntary civil commitment appeals process, see Frueh, 2008. On a TJ perspective of how mental health proceedings have the potential to reinforce consumers' sense of dignity, see Diesfeld & McKenna, 2007. On the relationship between TJ and the adequacy of counsel in the civil commitment process, see *In re Mental Health of K.G.F.*, 2001.

[15] Compare Hinshaw, 2005, p. 338, n. 49, citing Slobogin, p. 210, for the proposition that TJ may lead to situations in which too much discretion is placed in individuals, potentially leading to antitherapeutic outcomes.

Third, there can be no question that the institutional conditions discussed in chapter 5 are utterly antitherapeutic.[16] When my coauthors and I discussed how the court's decision in *Wyatt v. Stickney* (1971, 1972) was totally consonant with therapeutic ends, we framed that conclusion in the context of the conditions that had been exposed in the Alabama hospital that was at the center of the *Wyatt* case:

> A resident was scalded to death by hydrant water, . . . a resident was restrained in a strait jacket for nine years in order to prevent hand and finger sucking, . . . and a resident died from the insertion by another resident of a running water hose into his rectum. (Perlin, Gould & Dorfman, 1995, p. 100, quoting, *Wyatt*, 1972, p. 394, n. 13).[17]

The conditions I discuss in hospitals in Nicaragua, Bulgaria, Kyrgyzstan, and other nations (see supra chapter 5; and see Winick, 2002) glumly and tragically reflect conditions similar to those in *Wyatt* and in other "first generation" right-to-treatment/institutional conditions cases in the United States (see id., p. 99, discussing *New York State Ass'n for Retarded Children v. Rockefeller*, 1973 [Willowbrook case]). Writing earlier about the "universal factors" that are the centerpiece of chapter 5, I made this exact connection: "[These] conditions . . . eerily reflected the conditions at Willowbrook State School in New York City when they were exposed to a stunned nation some thirty years ago" (Perlin, 2007, p. 347, quoting, in part, Perlin, 2002, pp. 424–425). Not unimportantly, the court's final order in that case was "overtly premised on therapeutic ends" (Perlin, Gould & Dorfman, 1995, p. 100).[18]

Fourth, if there is no objectively fair means of assessing the need for a person to be hospitalized and/or no procedural or substantive standards for determining the need for hospitalization, such a system is antitherapeutic per se (see Winick, 1999, 2005). By way of example, the literature demonstrates that patients' negative perceptions of the civil commitment process "can potentially hinder their progress under traditional mental-health therapies

---

[16] See e.g., Policy Brief, 2008, p. 2.

> The laws [of Ghana, Uganda and Zambia] fail to promote the dignity, respect, autonomy and nondiscrimination of people with mental disabilities or to incorporate safeguards against abuses related to involuntary admission and treatment. Critical issues related to free and informed consent are overlooked and essential safeguards to prevent abuse of seclusion and restraints special treatments or clinical and experimental research are lacking.

[17] On the relationship between *Wyatt*, international human rights and therapeutic jurisprudence, see Perlin, 2011a.

[18] On the role of the judiciary in promoting democratic ends consonant with TJ values, see Twinomugisha, 2009.

and treatment" (Frueh, 2008, pp. 308–309, citing to, inter alia, Tyler & Huo, 2002; Winick, 1997).[19]

In his book-length treatment of the relationship between civil commitment and therapeutic jurisprudence, Professor Bruce Winick characterized the traditional commitment process as a "phony ritual [, producing] distrust on the part of the patient that undermines the presumed benefits of hospitalization" (Winick, 2005, p. 6, citing Perlin, 2000). Interestingly, in the same book, Winick argues, based on a TJ model, for the incorporation of international human rights principles into the commitment process, concluding that, in the eastern European context, such a model "can do much to convert the mental health system . . . into a more humane and therapeutic one that can provide help to those suffering from mental illness without in the process harming them" (Winick, 2005, p. 324).

Fifth, the examples that I offer in chapter 5[20] demonstrate how badly the current state of community treatment fails when assessed by the standards of therapeutic jurisprudence.[21] It should be evident that a failure to provide community services—especially to individuals that the institution concedes need not be in the hospital and are not benefiting from hospitalization—is antitherapeutic per se. Explicitly, the concept of TJ demands "greater access to community services" (Freeman, 2010, p. 255). Writing about the significance of the U.S. Supreme Court's decision in *Olmstead v. L.C.* (1999), I said this:

> We have known—for decades—that community treatment "works" better, that there is less improper use of antipsychotic medication in community settings, that community patients are less stigmatized, and stand a better chance of authentic reintegration into all aspects of social, economic and personal life. (Perlin, 2000, p. 1051)[22]

---

[19] For a TJ perspective on the use of mental health review tribunals, see Freckelton, 2003; Diesfeld & McKenna, 2006.

[20] See, e.g., Moncada, 1994, p. 617: Hospital authorities in Uruguay told researchers that "between one third and two thirds of the total inpatient population need not be committed but are held because they have nowhere else to go."

[21] Although she does not explicitly refer to therapeutic jurisprudence in her article, Professor Anna Lawson's analysis of how adhering to the principle of reasonable accommodation "has the potential to play a powerful role in ensuring that people with psychosocial impairments and conditions are genuinely included in mainstream society and permitted to participate fully in the life of their communities" (2008, p. 80) fits squarely within the best goals and aspirations of TJ scholarship.

[22] See also, Spaulding et al., 2000, p. 153: "The recent U.S. Supreme Court decision in *Olmstead*... provides a valuable precedent for future advocacy applications of TJ." On how pre-*Olmstead* decisions—refusing to find a constitutional right to community services—were "profoundly anti-therapeutic," see Perlin, 2000, p. 1050.

Sixth, it is crystal clear that the state of forensic facilities around the world are textbook examples of antitherapeutic conditions.[23] Astrid Birgden argues forcefully that "applying therapeutic jurisprudence can assist forensic psychologists in actively addressing human rights in general, as well as prisoners and detainees with mental disabilities in particular" (2009, p. 56; see also, Birgden & Perlin, 2008, 2009). Similarly, Ida Dickie notes how a TJ emphasis on procedural fairness and respect for autonomy can help all stakeholders in the criminal justice system (Waldman, 2008, discussing Dickie, 2008). The sorts of "shock-the-conscience" conditions in forensic facilities around the world—exposed by those whom I rely on and quote in chapter 5—scream out for an in-depth TJ analysis, to demonstrate their destructiveness and their negative impact on the mental health of those unlucky enough to be housed in such facilities.

The Convention on the Rights of Persons with Disabilities (CRPD) (see supra chapter 7) is a document that resonates with TJ values. It reflects the three principles articulated by Professor Ronner—voice, validation, and voluntariness—and "look[s] at law as it actually impacts people's lives" (Winick, 2009, p. 535). Each section of the CRPD empowers persons with mental disabilities, and one of the major aims of TJ is explicitly the empowerment of those whose lives are regulated by the legal system (see, e.g., King, 2008; Baker, 2008; Barton, 1999; Freeman, 2010; Perlmutter, 2005).[24] I believe that the time is right for scholars to engage in a close and careful reading of the TJ literature, and then apply their findings to questions related to the implementation of this Convention.[25]

Of course, the CRPD does not exist in a vacuum. As I argued earlier (see supra chapter 8), the lynchpin for effective and meaningful CRPD enforcement is the presence of dedicated, advocacy-focused counsel available to represent persons with CRPD complaints or grievances. And here, again, the picture is clear: "The failure to assign adequate counsel bespeaks sanism and pretextuality [see supra chapter 2] and a failure to consider the implications of therapeutic jurisprudence" (Perlin, 2005, p. 750; see also, Perlin & Dorfman, 1996). In reinforcing their position that therapeutic goals not trump other "important goals," Winick and Wexler emphasize that "the due process right to effective counsel is one such goal" (2002, p. 484).[26]

---

[23] On the value of using TJ to analyze forensic mental health systems in the United States, see Perlin, 1994. I discuss this issue in more depth earlier in this chapter.

[24] See also, e.g., Prior, 2003, considering, from an international human rights perspective, the significance of a mental illness label in parental removal cases.

[25] For a recent consideration of how the promotion of mediation and alternative conflict resolution through the CRPD can promote therapeutic jurisprudence values, see Petersen, 2010.

[26] On how adherence to TJ goals can make counsel more effective in individual cases, see Perlmutter, 2005. On the relationship between TJ and the representation scheme in commitment cases in Tasmania (Australia), see Rigby, 2006.

In an earlier analysis of the quality of counsel in death penalty cases, I reasoned that any system offering inadequate counsel would lead to a failure to ensure that mental disability evidence is adequately considered and contextualized by death penalty decision-makers, and that such a system "fails miserably from a therapeutic jurisprudence perspective" (Perlin, 1996, p. 235; see also, Dlugacz, 2008/2009; Talley, 2008/2009). Certainly, nations that provide *no* counsel for persons facing civil commitment, institutionalized, or seeking release and/or aftercare treatment fail just as miserably. Again consider the conclusion of Judge Ramirez and Professor Ronner: "the right to counsel is also the core of therapeutic jurisprudence" (Ramirez & Ronner, 2004, p. 119). Without such counsel, the entire mental disability law process is nothing more than a "pretextual charade" (Perlin, 1994, p. 381). Again, scholars need to carefully consider the TJ implications of this "charade" from an international human rights law perspective.[27]

Finally, consider the plight of individuals with mental disabilities in Asia, currently unable to take their grievances to an interregional court or commission (see supra chapter 8). Given the lack of counsel available, the promise of the CRPD may be little more than an empty shell for individuals from this region. In arguing why a Disability Rights Tribunal was needed for Asia and the Pacific, I earlier said that without such a Tribunal, "persons with mental disabilities will continue to suffer severe violations of their human rights by the States as there is no way to feasibly or realistically enforce these rights nor any way for persons with mental disabilities to meaningfully address these violations" (supra, p. 200). The continued suffering of these severe violations is a complete repudiation of the spirit and the substance of therapeutic jurisprudence.

IV. Conclusion

Fifteen years ago, two coauthors and I concluded our investigation of the state of domestic mental disability law from a TJ perspective with these words:

> The legal research that we have conducted for this article has confirmed our intuitive feelings: that therapeutic jurisprudence analyses largely support a rights-based perspective in mental disability law; that therapeutic jurisprudence can be an effective tool for ferreting out the law's sanist and pretextual bases; that it is not oxymoronic to characterize a constitutionally grounded jurisprudence as "therapeutic"; and that, finally, as the pendulum continues to swing (and as public ire grows over the perceived

[27] See Perlin, 2005, p. 750 (discussing right to refuse treatment cases in the United States): "The failure to assign adequate counsel bespeaks sanism and pretextuality, and a failure to consider the implications of therapeutic jurisprudence."

> rights-based excesses of mental disability law), therapeutic jurisprudence may indeed offer a path to redemption for a constitutionally based mental disability law jurisprudence. (Perlin, Gould & Dorfman, 1995, p. 119)

I submit that these same arguments are equally persuasive today in an international human rights law context.

Although therapeutic jurisprudence has grown exponentially in the past 20 years, there has been remarkably little written about it in the international human rights context, and even less in the international human rights context as it relates to mental disability law. A preliminary exploration of this relationship reveals significant and robust connections between TJ principles and international human rights principles as they relate to mental disability law–specific questions. My hope is that this chapter will lead TJ scholars (and international human rights law scholars) to consider these connections seriously in the future.

11

Conclusion

I began practicing law in 1971. Soon thereafter, I began representing persons with mental disabilities. By 1974, I was practicing mental disability law full-time. I started teaching in 1984. By 1992, I was regularly teaching four mental disability law courses. Yet, in none of my years of legal practice, and in none of the courses that I was teaching as of that time were questions of international human rights law discussed. It was simply not a question for the courts or for academics teaching mental disability law.

In 1993, Eric Rosenthal and Leonard Rubenstein wrote an article, "International Human Rights Advocacy under the 'Principles for the Protection of Persons with Mental Illness.'" This was the first publication of a theoretical article that explored the relationship between international human rights law and mental disability law (see supra chapter 1). There was, at this time, a robust case law in this area of law in the United States as well as a number of important cases decided by the European Court on Human Rights (see supra chapter 3). The publication by the United Nations of the MI Principles—which spurred the Rosenthal and Rubenstein article—was the first detailed international statement of the rights of persons with mental illness, and was the first acknowledgment on the part of the United Nations that this most marginalized population was entitled to the basic human rights articulated in a series of UN documents dating to 1948 (see supra chapter 2A).

Over the past 17 years, since Rosenthal and Rubenstein published their article, developments have exploded and continue to explode. There is now a coherent and sophisticated corpus of scholarship about all of the issues discussed in this book. Courses in this academic discipline are offered in the United States and elsewhere. Case law has developed in all regional courts and commissions, and in European constitutional courts, and continues to proliferate in the United States and the United Kingdom (see supra chapter 3). And the ratification of the Convention on the Rights of Persons with Disabilities (CRPD) is the single most important development yet in this area of law and policy (see supra chapter 7).

This acceleration of developments—and proliferation of case law, scholarship, and "hard" international law—does not, by any means, signify a positive resolution of all the topics discussed in this work. Institutional life is still abjectly miserable in most areas of the world, and persons locked up in psychiatric hospitals (as well as individuals with mental disabilities in jails and prisons, see Perlin & Dlugacz, 2009; see supra chapter 6, "Corrections Law") are regularly denied the basic elements of humanity, dignity, and decency (see Gostin, 2008[1]; see supra chapter 5). Few who are not involved in this area on a regular or organized basis seem to care.[2] Many nations still have no mental disability law; others pay only lip service to law-on-the-books (see supra chapter 5). Counsel and advocacy services are rarely available to persons languishing in, or institutionalized in, large, impersonal, and dangerous institutions.[3] When lawyers *are* provided, they are often roleless, focusless, and disinterested (see supra chapter 8). There is no question that there is a direct and causal relationship between this abject record on the part of assigned counsel and the pervasiveness of sanism (see Perlin, 2003; see supra chapter 2).[4] Also, the use of state-sanctioned psychiatry as a tool for the suppression of political dissent is by no means a dead issue (see supra chapter 4).

This shameful state of affairs is mostly not on the reform agenda of the culpable governments, until such time that it threatens to interfere with opportunities for external political or economic advantage, such as accession to the European Union (see supra chapter 5). The stigma—or sanism—that has always been the hallmark of society's views about mental disability and persons with mental disability persists, and the label of "patient" or "ex-patient" continues to be a "scarlet letter" in most parts of the world (see supra chapter 2). When persons with mental disabilities participate in the court process, dignity is often totally missing (see supra chapter 2).

---

1 "There has evolved a vicious cycle of neglect, abandonment, indignity, cruel and inhuman treatment, and punishment of persons with mental illness." Id., p. 906.

2 On the lack of interest on the part of "global" NGOs in these questions, see supra chapter 1.

3 See Lippmann & Goldberg, 1973, p. 17, quoted in Perlin, 1991, p. 100, n. 215, characterizing the Pennhurst State School and Hospital (in suburban Philadelphia, Pennsylvania), as "Dachau, without ovens."

4 See also, Dhir, 2008, p. 108 (on patient's counsel's "sanist predilections").

But, as I have sought to demonstrate in this book, there *are* beacons of light and hope. Among the most significant are these:

- (again), the ratification of the CRPD and the greater acceptance of a social model of disability (see supra chapters 1 & 7);[5]
- the emergence of authentic grassroots advocacy movements;
- a comprehension on the part of individual judges and courts that the issues before them "matter"—that they involve "real people" and that enforcement of international human rights in cases dealing with this population is as important as the enforcement of human rights in cases that revolve around issues of gender, age, sexual orientation, or ethnic minority status;[6]
- burgeoning case law in the United States and Europe, and some case law in the Inter-American and African regional court/commission systems;[7]
- the first steps taken in Asia to create a tribunal that will give persons with mental disabilities (and those with other disabilities) similar access to a regional adjudicatory body to which they can bring their complaints when discriminated against because of disability.

These are important first steps, but, globally, progress still remains modest.

Several years ago, speaking to the British Institute of Human Rights, Baroness Hale of the House of Lords characterized the European Convention on Human Rights in this manner: "We need to be able to use it to promote respect for the inherent dignity of all human beings but especially those who are most vulnerable to having that dignity ignored" (Lawson, 2006, p. 491).

This vision is one that can and should be adopted by courts and commissions that will soon be adjudicating cases brought under the CRPD. Earlier (see supra chapter 7), I discussed extensively the case of *In the Matter of Mark C.H.* (2010), a New York State court guardianship case in which Surrogate Judge Kristen Booth Glen applied the CRPD's principles to support her conclusion that guardianship appointment be subject to periodic reporting and review. Just as the Montana Supreme Court case of *In re Mental Health of K.G.F* (2001; see supra chapter 2), can and should serve—globally—as a template for all questions involving adequacy of counsel, so can *Mark C.H.*

---

5 See Lawson, 2006, p. 462 ("The disability movement . . . calls for the dismantling of disabling social obstacles and for the development of laws and policies which foster principles of inclusion and participation").

6 See Twinomugisha, 2009 (on the importance of judicial review in human rights enforcement).

7 See Prior, 2007, p. 556 (case law in nations such as Belgium, Norway, the UK, and the Netherlands have "ensure[d] an international debate for strong legal protection for this group of disempowered individuals").

serve—globally—as a template for all questions involving the right to self-determination.

But these two cases are hardly a trend. Writing two years ago about the role of dignity in international human rights adjudication, Christopher McCrudden ruefully acknowledged that "the use of the concept of human dignity has not given rise to a detailed universal interpretation, nor even particularly coherent national interpretations" (2008, p. 722). Five years ago, I conceded that the statutory presumption of capacity in right to refuse treatment cases was often nothing more than "an illusory safeguard" (Perlin, 2005, p. 747). Two years ago, Professor Larry Gostin charged that "Governments and civil society, *in all parts of the world*, have treated persons with mental illness horribly in old and new institutions," continuing that "countless promises have been made to right the wrongs, but these promises were dishonoured in practice" (2008, p. 912; emphasis added). The question is on the table: to what extent will the CRPD be used as a vigorous advocacy tool to remediate these findings?

"International human rights reality still routinely lags behind human rights aspirations" (Stacy, 2009, p. 6). The gap between aspiration and reality is particularly pronounced in Asia (see supra chapter 9). I devoted the longest chapter in this book to Asia and the visions of a Disability Rights Tribunal for Asia and the Pacific to serve as an instrument for the considerations of complaints brought by and on behalf of persons with disabilities. I did this because I believe that the "universality" of human rights—articulated formally more than 60 years ago in the Universal Declaration of Human Rights, but derived from Locke and Rousseau, and other sources predating the Enlightenment (see Butler, 2009; see supra chapter 2)—can only come to fruition for persons with disabilities if such a Tribunal is, finally, created (see Perlin & Ikehara, 2010). Until such time, it is futile to expect that there will be any meaningful progress in eradicating sanism or upholding the dignity of persons with disabilities in the nations in this region.

My concluding substantive chapter (see supra chapter 10) focused on therapeutic jurisprudence (TJ) both as a school of legal thought/scholarship and as a strategy for uprooting sanism and pretextuality, by illuminating the importance of voice, validation, and voluntariness (see Ronner, 2002, 2008) in the court process. In other books (Perlin, 1994, 2000), I have chosen to conclude the same way, because of my belief that TJ "has the far-reaching potential to allow us—finally—to come to grips with the pernicious power of sanism and pretextuality and to offer us an opportunity to make coherent what has been incoherent—and to expose what has been hidden—for far too long" (id., p. 303). I similarly believe, after representing, writing about, and teaching about persons with mental disabilities for nearly 40 years, that TJ offers the best possible means of redemption and remediation of the issues under discussion in this volume.

This book has covered multiple substantive areas of law and social policy, ranging from "traditional" mental disability law topics (commitment, institutional rights, deinstitutionalization) (see supra chapters 3 & 5); to counsel assignment procedures (see supra chapter 8); and pedagogy, expert evidence, psychotherapeutic privilege, and corrections law (see supra chapter 6). The CRPD articulates broad, enforceable statements of international human rights law (see supra chapter 7)—both positive and negative (see supra chapter 2)—that, eventually, can demarginalize this most marginalized population and make the invisible visible, eradicate sanism and bring a serious measure of dignity to the way that the legal system deals with such individuals.[8]

In their thorough and thoughtful analysis of the treatment of mental disability issues under the European Convention on Human Rights, Peter Bartlett and his colleagues lay down the gauntlet: the challenge of the next 25 years will be "to breathe life into Convention provisions as they apply to [persons with mental disabilities] and to press for full implementation of the standards that are won through litigation and political advances" (Bartlett, Lewis & Thorold, 2007, p. 28). They continue by stressing that the issues are one of "basic human dignity" (id.). I have written this book in an effort to shed light on these issues and to urge policymakers to take them seriously.

My first Article about the relationship between international human rights and mental disability law drew on Bob Dylan's song "Chimes of Freedom" (see supra chapter 1) in its title. (Perlin, 2002). There, I noted that the first verse of the song concludes:

> Flashing for the warriors whose strength is not to fight,
> Flashing for the refugees on the unarmed road of flight,
> An' for each an' ev'ry underdog soldier in the night,
> An' we gazed upon the chimes of freedom flashing.

I then concluded that article: "For the first time, I truly believe I have the capacity to 'gaze upon the chimes of freedom flashing'" (id., p. 433). I wrote that article almost nine years ago. Since then, the ratification of the CRPD, the proliferation of new case law, the ever-expanding literature, and the attention finally being paid by human rights organizations around the world all tell me that, perhaps, someday soon, I will be able to do this.

---

[8] It should go without saying that community human rights education is vital in efforts to eradicate this stigma. See Kinley, 2007.

References

Preface

Perlin, M.L. (2002). Symposium: International human rights law and the institutional treatment of persons with mental disabilities: The case of Hungary. *New York Law School Journal of International and Comparative Law, 21*, 361–386.

Chapter 1

Alfredsson, G. (2009). Minority rights, norms, and institutions. In *New Institutions for Human Rights Protection*, 175–206 (Boyle, K., ed.). London, UK: Oxford University Press.

Andersen-Watts, R. (2008). Recognizing our dangerous gifts: Applying the social model to individuals with mental illness. *Michigan State University Journal of Medicine and Law, 12*, 141–162.

Arboleda-Florez, J. & Weisstub, D.N. (2008). Mental health rights: The relationship between constitution and bioethics. In *Autonomy and Human Rights in Health Care: An International Perspective*, 309–327 (Weisstub, D.N. & Diaz Pintos, G., eds.). Dordrecht, The Netherlands: Springer.

Asplund, K.D. (2009). Resistance to human rights in Indonesia: Asian values and beyond. *Asia-Pacific Journal on Human Rights and the Law, 10*, 27–47.

Besner, E.A. (1995). Employment legislation for disabled individuals: What can France learn from the Americans with Disabilities Act? *Comparative Labor Law Journal, 16*, 399–419.

Birgden, A. & Perlin, M.L. (2008). "Tolling for the luckless, the abandoned and forsaked": Community safety, therapeutic jurisprudence and international human rights law as applied to prisoners and detainees. *Legal and Criminological Psychology, 13,* 231–243.

Birgden, A. & Perlin, M.L. (2009). "Where the home in the valley meets the damp dirty prison": The impact of international human rights law on domestic jail and prison law. *Aggression and Violent Behavior, 14,* 256–263.

Bliss, J. (2002). Symposium: International Human Rights Law and the Institutional Treatment of Persons with Mental Disabilities: The Case of Hungary. *New York Law School Journal of International and Comparative Law,* 21, 361–387.

Boyadjiev, B. & Onchev, G. (2007). Legal and cultural aspects of involuntary psychiatric treatment regulation in post-totalitarian milieu: The Bulgarian perspective. *European Journal of Psychiatry, 21,* 179–188.

Butcher, A.P. (2000). The relative irrelevance of human rights for the care and protection of the mentally ill. *Australian Journal of Political Science, 35,* 85–97.

Cantor, J.D. (2009). Defining disabled: Exporting the ADA to Europe and the social model of disability. *Connecticut Journal of International Law, 24,* 399–434.

Cassel, D. (2001). Does international human rights law make a difference? *Chicago Journal of International Law, 2,* 121–136.

Chaffin, S. (2005). Challenging the United States position on a United Nations Convention on disability. *Temple Political & Civil Rights Law Review, 15,* 121–145.

Cheah, P. (1997). Posit(ion)ing human rights in the current global conjecture. *Public Culture, 9,* 233–266.

City of Cleburne v. Cleburne Living Center, 573 U.S. 432 (1985).

Convention on the Rights of Persons with Disabilities. *UN Enable.* Retrieved September 15, 2010, from http://www.un.org/disabilities/default.asp?id=150.

Cooper, J. & Whittle, R. (1998). Enforcing the rights and freedoms of disabled people: The role of transnational law (Part I). *Mountbatten Journal of Legal Studies, 2,* 1–37.

Daes Report. (1983). Principles, Guidelines, and Guarantees for the Protection of Persons Detained on Ground of Mental Ill-Health Suffering from Mental Disorder, U.N. Doc. E/CN. 4/Sub. 2/1983/17 (report by Erica-Irene Daes).

De Alwis, R.d.S. (2009). Mining the intersections: Advancing the rights of women and children with disabilities within an interrelated web of human rights. *Pacific Rim Law and Policy Journal, 18,* 293–315.

Degener, T. (2000). International disability law—a new legal subject on the rise: The interregional experts' meeting in Hong Kong, December 13–17, 1999. *Berkeley Journal of International Law, 18,* 180–195.

DeSoto, H. (1989). *The Other Path: The Economic Answer to Terrorism.* New York City: Basic Books.

Despouy Report. (1991). United Nations, Economic and Social Council, Commission on Human Rights, Sub-Commission on Prevention of Discrimination and Protection of Minorities: Human Rights and Disability, U.N. Doc. E/CN. 4/Sub. 2/1991/31 (report by Leandro Despouy).

Dhir, A.A. (2008). Relationships of force: Reflections on law, psychiatry, and human rights. *Windsor Review of Legal and Social Issues, 25,* 103–112.

Dhoest v. Belgium, 12 Eur. Ct. H.R. 135 (1987).

Dimopoulos, A. (2010). *Issues in Human Rights Protection of Intellectually Disabled Persons.* Surrey, England: Ashgate Press.

Diniz, D., Barboso, L. & does Santos, W.R. (2010). Disability, human rights, and justice. *SUR International Journal on Human Rights, 6,* 61–72.
Dole, B. (1994). Promises to people with disabilities?—Commentary on Blanck. *Iowa Law Review, 79,* 925–934.
Dylan, B. (1964). Chimes of freedom. Accessible at http://www.bobdylan.com/#/songs/chimes-of-freedom.
Eckstein, S., ed. (2001). *Power and Popular Protests: Latin American Social Movements.* Berkeley: University of California Press.
Fennell, P. (2008). Human rights, bioethics, and mental disorder. *Medicine and Law, 27,* 95–107.
Fidler, D.P. (2010). Asia's participation in global health diplomacy and global health governance. *Asian Journal of WTO & International Health Law and Policy, 5,* 269–300.
Fischer, J. (2005). A comparative look at the right to refuse treatment for involuntarily hospitalized persons with a mental illness. *Hastings International and Comparative Law Review, 29,* 153–186.
Follesdal, A. (2009). Why the European Court of Human Rights might be democratically legitimate—A modest defense. *Nordisk Tiddskrift for Menneskerettigheter, 27,* 289–303.
GA Resolution. 123, U.N. GAOR, 31st Session (1976).
GA Resolution. 52, U.N. GAOR, 37th Session (1982a).
GA Resolution. 53, U.N. GAOR, 37th Session (1982b).
GA Resolution. 119, U.N. GAOR, 46th Sess., Supp. No. 49, Annex at 189, U.N. Doc. A/46/49 (1991).
GA Resolution. 56/168 (2001).
GA Resolution. A/61/106 (2006a).
GA Resolution. A/61/611 (2006b) (UN Convention).
Gable, L. (2007). The proliferation of human rights in global health governance. *Journal of Law, Medicine and Ethics, 35,* 534–544.
Gable, L. (2009). Mental health as a human right. In *Realizing the Right to Health: Swiss Human Rights Book,* vol. 3, 249–261 (Clapham, A. et al., eds.). Zurich, Switzerland: Ruffer & Rub Publishers.
Gable, L. & Gostin, L.O. (2008). Global mental health: Changing norms, constant rights. *Georgetown Journal of International Affairs, 9,* 83–92.
Gable, L. & Gostin, L.O. (2009). Mental health as a human right. In *Realizing the Right to Health: Swiss Human Rights Book,* vol. 3, 249–261 (Clapham, A. et al., eds.). Zurich, Switzerland: Rüffer & Rub.
Galeano, E. (1997). *Open Veins of Latin America: Five Centuries of the Pillage of a Continent.* New York City: Monthly Review Press.
Gendreau, C. (1997). The rights of psychiatric patients in the light of the principles announced by the United Nations: A recognition of the right to consent to treatment? *International Journal of Law & Psychiatry, 20,* 259–278.
Gombos, G. et al. (2002). Hungary: The social care home report. *New York Law School Journal of International and Comparative Law,* 21, 361–386.
Gostin, L.O. (2000). Human rights of persons with mental disabilities: The European Convention of Human Rights. *International Journal of Law and Psychology, 23,* 125–159.
Gunn, P.C. (2009). Health care refugees. *Loyola University Chicago International Law Review, 6,* 339–365.

Halliday, T.C. & Oshinsky, P. (2006). Globalization of law. *Annual Review of Sociology, 32,* 447–470.

Harding, T.W. (1989). The application of the European Convention of Human Rights to the field of psychiatry. *International Journal of Law and Psychology, 12,* 245–262.

Harding, T.W. (2000). Human rights law in the field of mental health: A critical review. *Acta Psychiatrica Scandinavica, 101,* 24–30.

Helfer, L.R. (2002). Overlegalizing human rights: International relations theory and the Commonwealth Caribbean backlash against human rights regimes. *Columbia Law Review, 102,* 1832–1911.

Hendriks, A. & Degener, T. (1994). The evolution of a European perspective on disability legislation. *European Journal of Health Law, 1,* 343–365.

Henkin, L. (1981). *The International Bill of Rights: The Covenant on Civil and Political Rights.* New York: Columbia University Press.

Henkin, L. (1989). The universality of the concept of human rights. *Annals of the American Academy of Political and Social Science, 506,* 10–16.

Heyer, K. (2000). From special needs to equal rights: Disability law in Japan. *Asian-Pacific Law & Policy Journal, 1,* 7–21.

Herczegfalvy v. *Austria,* 15 Eur. Ct. H.R. 437 (1993).

Hewitt, D. (2001). Do human rights impact on mental health law? *New Law Journal, 151,* 1278–1287.

Honig, J. & Fendell, S. (2000). Meeting the needs of female trauma survivors: The effectiveness of the Massachusetts mental health managed care system. *Berkeley Women's Law Journal, 15,* 161–228.

Howard-Hassmann, R.E. (2005). The second great transformation: Human rights leapfrogging in the era of globalization. *Human Rights Quarterly, 27,* 1–40.

In the Matter of Victor Rosario Congo, Report No. 63/99 Case 11.427 (April 13, 1999).

Iwata, Y. (1993). The mental health consumers' self-help movement in Japan. *New Directions in Mental Health Services, 60,* 77–87.

Jones, M. & Marks, L.A.B. (1999). Law and the social construction of disability. In *Disability, Divers-Ability and Legal Change,* 1–24. The Hague: Martinus Nijhoff.

Kaiser, H.A. (2009). Canadian mental health law: The slow process of redirecting the ship of state. *Health Law Journal, 17,* 139–194.

Kampf, A. (2008). The Disabilities Convention and its consequence for mental health laws in Australia. *Law in Context, 26,* 10–36.

Kanev, K. (2002). State, human rights, and mental health in Bulgaria. *New York Law School Journal of International and Comparative Law, 21,* 435–468.

Kanter, A.S. (2003). The globalization of disability rights law. *Syracuse Journal of International Law and Commerce, 30,* 241–269.

Katner, D. (2006). The mental health paradigm and the MacArthur study: Emerging issues challenging the competence of juveniles in delinquency systems. *American Journal of Law and Medicine, 32,* 503–583.

Kayess, R. & French, P. (2008). Out of darkness into light? Introducing the Convention on the Rights of Persons with Disabilities. *Human Rights Law Review, 8,* 1–34.

Kumar, C.R. (2003). Moving beyond constitutionalization and judicial protection of human rights—Building on the Hong Kong experience of civil society empowerment. *Loyola of Los Angeles International and Comparative Law Review, 26,* 281–314.
Law, D.S. (2008). Globalization and the future of constitutional rights. *Northwestern University Law Review, 102,* 1277–1349.
Lawson, A. (2006). Disability, degradation, and dignity: The role of Article 3 of the European Convention on Human Rights. *Northern Ireland Legal Q, 56,* 462–491.
Lee, S.S-J. (2009). Social networking in the age of personal genomics. *Saint Louis University Journal of Health Law & Policy, 3,* 41–59.
Lee, Y. (2009). Expanding human rights to persons with disabilities: Laying the groundwork for a twenty-first century movement. *Pacific Rim Law and Policy Journal, 18,* 283–292.
Lessard v. Schmidt, 349 F.Supp. 1078 (E.D. Wis. 1972).
Lewis, O. (2002). Protecting the rights of people with mental disabilities: The European Convention on Human Rights. *European Journal of Health Law, 9,* 293–320.
Lord, J. (2004). NGO participation in human rights law and process: Latest developments in the effort to develop an international treaty on the rights of persons with disabilities. *ILSA Journal of International & Comparative Law, 10,* 311–318.
Lord, J.E. & Brown, R. (2010). The role of reasonable accommodation in securing substantive equality for persons with disabilities: The UN Convention on the Rights of Persons with Disabilities. Accessible at http://papers.ssrn.com/sol3/papers.cfm?abstract_id=1618903
MacKay, D. (2007). The United Nations Convention on the Rights of Persons with Disabilities. *Syracuse Journal of International Law and Commerce, 34,* 323–331.
Margulies, P. (1992). The cognitive politics of professional conflict: Law reform, mental health treatment technology, and citizen governance. *Harvard Journal of Law and Technology, 5,* 25–64.
Marsh, C. & Payne, C.P. (2007). The globalization of human rights and the socialization of human rights norms. *Brigham Young University Law Review,* 665–687.
Megret, F. (2008a). The Disabilities Convention: Human rights of persons with disabilities or disability rights? *Human Rights Quarterly, 30,* 494–516.
Megret, F. (2008b). The Disabilities Convention: Toward a holistic concept of rights. *International Journal of Human Rights, 12,* 261–278.
Meier, B.M. (2007). Advancing health rights in a globalized world: Responding to globalization through a collective human right to public health. *Journal of Law, Medicine and Ethics, 35,* 545–553.
Melish, T. (2007, Winter). The UN Disability Convention: Historic process, strong prospects, and why the U.S. should ratify. *Human Rights Brief, 14,* 37–45.
Mental Disability Rights International (1995). *Human Rights and Mental Health Uruguay.* (MDRI Uruguay Report.)
Mental Disability Rights International (1997). *Human Rights and Mental Health Hungary.* (MDRI Hungary Report.)
Mental Disability Rights International (1999). *Children in Russia's Institutions: Human Rights and Opportunities for Reform.*

Mental Disability Rights International (2000). *Human Rights and Mental Health Mexico.* (MDRI Mexico Report.)

Mental Disability Rights International (2007a). *Ruined Lives: Segregation from Society in Argentina's Psychiatric Asylums.* (MDRI Argentina Report.)

Mental Disability Rights International (2007b). *Torment Not Treatment: Serbia's Segregation and Abuse of Children and Adults with Disabilities.* (MDRI Serbia Report.)

Moncada, A.C. (1994). Involuntary commitment and the use of seclusion and restraint in Uruguay: A comparison with the United Nations Principles for the Protection of Persons with Mental Illness. *University of Miami Inter-American Law Review, 25,* 589–620.

Mor, S. (2006). Between charity, welfare and warfare: A disability legal studies analysis of privilege and neglect in Israeli disability policy. *Yale Journal of Law and the Humanities, 18,* 63–137.

Nixon, S.A. & Forman, L. (2008). Exploring synergies between human rights and public health ethics: A whole greater than the sum of its parts. *BMC International Health and Human Rights, 8,* 2. Accessible at http://www.biomedcentral.com/content/pdf/1472–698X-8–2.pdf

Oberdörster, U. (2008). Why ratify? Lessons from treaty ratification campaigns. *Vanderbilt Law Review, 61,* 681–712.

O'Connor v. Donaldson, 422 U.S. 563 (1975).

Pan American Health Organization (2010). *Human Rights and Health: Persons with Mental Disabilities.* Accessible at http://www.paho.org/english/dd/pub/10069_Mental.pdf ("PAHO Position Paper").

Pearson, M. (2004). Representing the mentally ill: The critical role of advocacy under the *Mental Health Act 1986* (Vic). *Alternative Law Journal, 29,* 174–177, 196.

Perlin, M.L. (1993). Pretexts and mental disability law: The case of competency. University of Miami Law Review, *47,* 625–688.

Perlin, M.L. (1993–1994). The ADA and persons with mental disabilities: Can sanist attitudes be undone? *Journal of Law and Health, 8,* 15–45.

Perlin, M.L. (1997a). "Make promises by the hour": Sex, drugs, the ADA, and psychiatric hospitalization. *DePaul Law Review, 46,* 947–985.

Perlin, M.L. (1997b). "The borderline which separated you from me": The insanity defense, the authoritarian spirit, the fear of faking, and the culture of punishment. *Iowa Law Review, 82,* 1375–1426.

Perlin, M.L. (1998). *Mental Disability Law: Civil and Criminal* (2nd ed., Vol. 1). Newark, NJ: Lexis-Nexis.

Perlin, M.L. (1999a)."Half-wracked prejudice leaped forth": Sanism, pretextuality, and why and how mental disability law developed as it did. *Journal of Contemporary Legal Issues, 10,* 3–36.

Perlin, M.L. (1999b). *Mental Disability Law: Civil and Criminal* (2nd ed., Vol. 2). Newark, NJ: Lexis-Nexis.

Perlin, M.L. (2000a). *Mental Disability Law: Civil and Criminal* (2nd ed., Vol. 3). Newark, NJ: Lexis-Nexis Publ.

Perlin, M.L. (2000b). *The Hidden Prejudice: Mental Disability on Trial.* Washington, DC: American Psychological Association Press.

Perlin, M.L. (2001–2002). "What's good is bad, what's bad is good, you'll find out when you reach the top, you're on the bottom": Are the Americans with

Disabilities Act (and *Olmstead v. L.C.*) anything more than "idiot wind"? *University of Michigan Journal of Law Reform, 35,* 235–261.
Perlin, M.L. (2002a). "Chimes of freedom": International human rights and institutional mental disability law. *New York Law School Journal of International and Comparative Law, 21,* 423–433.
Perlin, M.L. (2002b). *Mental Disability Law: Civil and Criminal* (2nd ed., Vol. 4). Newark, NJ: Lexis-Nexis.
Perlin, M.L. (2002c). Symposium: International human rights law and the institutional treatment of persons with mental disabilities: The case of Hungary. *New York Law School Journal of International and Comparative Law, 21,* 361–386.
Perlin, M.L. (2002–2003). "Things have changed": Looking at non-institutional mental disability law through the sanism filter. *New York Law School Law Review, 46,* 535–545.
Perlin, M.L. (2003a). "Life is in mirrors, death disappears": Giving life to Atkins. *New Mexico Law Review, 33,* 315–348.
Perlin, M.L. (2003b). Therapeutic jurisprudence and outpatient commitment: Kendra's law as case study. Psychology, *Public Policy, and Law, 9,* 183–208.
Perlin, M.L. (2003c). "You have discussed lepers and crooks": Sanism in clinical teaching. *Clinical Law Review, 9,* 683–729.
Perlin, M.L. (2006a). International human rights and comparative mental disability law: The role of institutional psychiatry in the suppression of political dissent. *Israel Law Review, 39,* 69–97.
Perlin, M.L. (2006b)."You got no secrets to conceal": Considering the application of the *Tarasoff* doctrine abroad. *University of Cincinnati Law Review, 75,* 611–629.
Perlin, M.L. (2007a). An internet-based mental disability law program: Implications for social change in nations with developing economies. *Fordham International Law Journal, 40,* 435–454.
Perlin, M.L. (2007b). International human rights law and comparative mental disability law: The universal factors. *Syracuse Journal of International Law and Commerce, 34,* 333–358.
Perlin, M.L. (2008a). "Everybody is making love/or else expecting rain": Considering the sexual autonomy rights of persons institutionalized because of mental disability in forensic hospitals and in Asia. *Washington Law Review, 83,* 481–512.
Perlin, M.L. (2008b)."I might need a good lawyer, could be your funeral, my trial": Global clinical legal education and the right to counsel in civil commitment cases. *Washington University Journal of Law & Policy, 28,* 241–264.
Perlin, M.L. (2008c). "Through the wild cathedral evening": Barriers, attitudes, participatory democracy, Professor tenBroek, and the rights of persons with mental disabilities. *Texas Journal on Civil Liberties & Civil Rights, 13,* 413–419.
Perlin, M.L. (2008d, March). "When the winds of changes shift": International teaching for social change, or, Why doing what we do keeps us "forever young." Paper presented at Society of American Law Teachers conference, University of California Berkeley Law School.
Perlin, M.L. (2009a). "A change is gonna come": The implications of the United Nations Convention on the Rights of Persons with Disabilities for the

domestic practice of constitutional mental disability law. *Northern Illinois University Law Review, 29,* 483–498.

Perlin, M.L. (2009b). "His brain has been mismanaged with great skill": How will jurors respond to neuroimaging testimony in insanity defense cases? *Akron Law Review, 42,* 885–916.

Perlin, M.L. et al. (2006). *International Human Rights and Comparative Mental Disability Law: Cases and Materials.* Durham, NC: Carolina Academic Press.

Perlin, M.L., Birgden, A. & Gledhill, K. (2009). "The witness who saw, /he left little doubt": A comparative consideration of expert testimony in mental disability law cases. *Journal of Investigative Psychology & Offender Profiling, 6,* 59–88.

Perlin, M.L. & Dlugacz, H.A. (2009). "It's doom alone that counts": Can international human rights law be an effective source of rights in correctional conditions litigation? *Behavioral Sciences & Law, 27,* 675–694.

Perlin, M.L. & Szeli, E. (2010). Mental health law and human rights: Evolution, challenges, and the promise of the new Convention. In *United Nations Convention on the Rights of Persons with Disabilities: Multidisciplinary Perspectives,* 241–255 (Kumpuvuori, J. & Scheninen. M., eds.). Helsinki, Finland: The Center for Human Rights of Persons with Disabilities in Finland (VIKE).

Perlin, M.L. & Szeli, E. (2011). Mental health law and human rights: Evolution and contemporary challenges. In *Mental Health and Human Rights* (Dudley, M.E., ed.). Oxford, UK: Oxford University Press. (in press)

Perlin, M.L., Gould, K.K. & Dorfman, D.A. (1995). Therapeutic jurisprudence and the civil rights of institutionalized mentally disabled persons: Hopeless oxymoron or path to redemption? *Psychology, Public Policy and Law, 1,* 80–119.

Popkin, M. (2000). *Peace without Justice: Obstacles to Building the Rule of Law in El Salvador.* University Park: Pennsylvania State University Press.

Purohit & Moore v. The Gambia, Comm. No. 241/2001, 16th activity report of the Afr. C.H.P.R. (2002–2003).

Quinn, G. (2009). The United Nations Convention on the Rights of Persons with Disabilities: Toward a new international politics of disability. *Texas Journal on Civil Liberties & Civil Rights, 15,* 33–50.

Ramcharan, B.G. (1991). Strategies for the international protection of human rights in the 1990s. *Human Rights Quarterly, 13,* 155–169.

Ronner, A. (2008). The learned-helpless lawyer: Clinical legal education and therapeutic jurisprudence as antidotes to Bartleby syndrome. *Touro Law Review, 24,* 601–664.

Rosenthal, E. & Rubenstein, L.S. (1993). International human rights advocacy under the "principles for the protection of persons with mental illness. *International Journal of Law & Psychiatry, 16,* 257–300.

Rosenthal, E. & Sundram, C.J. (2002). International human rights in mental health legislation. *New York Law School Journal of International and Comparative Law, 21,* 469–536.

Ruger, J.P. (2008). Normative foundations of global health law. *Georgetown Law Journal, 96,* 423–443.

Shelton, D. (2002). Protecting human rights in a globalized world. *Boston College International and Comparative Law Review, 25,* 273–322.

Shelton, R. (1997). *No Direction Home: The Life and Music of Bob Dylan.* Cambridge, MA: Da Capo Press.

Skohly, S.I. (2009). Global responsibility for human rights. *Oxford Journal of Legal Studies, 29,* 827–847.

Slaughter, A-M. (2000). Judicial globalization. *Virginia Journal of International Law, 40,* 1103–1124.

Stacy, H.M. (2009). *Human Rights for the 21st Century: Sovereignty, Civil Society, Culture.* Stanford, CA: Stanford University Press.

Stefan, S. (2001). *Unequal Rights: Discrimination against People with Mental Disabilities and the Americans with Disabilities Act.* Washington, DC: American Psychological Association Press.

Stefan, S. (2003). "Discredited" and "discreditable": The search for political identity by people with psychiatric diagnoses. *William and Mary Law Review, 44,* 1341–1380.

Stein, M.A. & Stein, P.J.S. (2007). Beyond disability civil rights. *Hastings Law Review, 58,* 1203–1240.

Symposium, The application of international human rights law to institutional mental disability law. *New York Law School Journal of International and Comparative Law, 21,* 387–397.

"Taking Issue." (1997). Taking issue with taking issue: Psychiatric survivors' reconsidered. *Psychiatric Services, 48,* 601–605.

Taylor, A.L. (1999). Globalization and biotechnology: UNESCO and an international strategy to advance human rights and public health. *American Journal of Law and Medicine, 25,* 479–541.

Thornburgh, D. (2008). Globalizing a response to disability discrimination. *Washington Law Review, 83,* 439–448.

Waddington, L. (2001). Evolving disability policies: From social-welfare to human rights: An international trend from a European perspective. *Netherlands Quarterly of Human Rights, 19,* 141–165.

Waddington, L. (2008). When is it reasonable for Europeans to be confused: Understanding when a disability accommodation is "reasonable" from a comparative perspective. *Comparative Labor Law and Policy Journal, 29,* 317–340.

Waterstone, M. (2004). Civil rights and the administration of elections—Toward secret ballots and polling place access. *The Journal of Gender, Race & Justice, 8,* 101–152.

Weissbrodt, D. et al. (2009). *International Human Rights: Law, Policy, and Process.* Newark, NJ: Lexis/Nexis.

Wexler, D.B. & Winick, B.J., eds. (1996). *Law in a Therapeutic Key: Recent Developments in Therapeutic Jurisprudence.* Durham, NC: Carolina Academic Press.

Winick, B.J. (2002). Therapeutic jurisprudence and the treatment of people with mental illness in Eastern Europe: Construing international human rights law. *New York Law School Journal of International & Comparative Law, 21,* 537–572.

Winterwerp v. the Netherlands, 33 Eur. Ct. H.R. (ser. A), reported at 2 E.H.R.R. 387 (1979).

WNUSP position paper (2010). http://www.wnusp.org/human-rights-position-paper.htm.

Wyatt v. Aderholt, 503 F. 2d 1305 (5th Cir. 1974).
Wyatt v. Stickney, 325 F.Supp. 781 (M.D. Ala. 1971), aff'd *sub. nom. Wyatt v. Aderholt*, 503 F. 2d 1305 (5th Cir. 1974).

Chapter 2

Chapter 2A

Allo, A.K. (2009). Derogations or limitations? Rethinking the African human rights system of derogation in light of the European system. *Ethiopian Journal of Legal Education, 2,* 21–52.
Alvarez, J. (2003). The new dispute settlers: (Half) truths and consequences. *Texas International Law Journal, 38,* 405–444.
Anderson, A. (2009). On dignity and whether the Universal Declaration of Human Rights remains a place of refuge after 60 years. *American University International Law Review, 25,* 115–143.
Anghie, A. & Chimni, B.S. (2003). Third World approaches to international law and individual responsibility in internal conflicts. *Chinese Journal of International Law, 2,* 77–102.
Barelli, M. (2009). The role of soft law in the international legal system: The case of the United Nations Declaration on the Rights of Indigenous Peoples. International and Comparative Law Quarterly, *58,* 957–983.
Baxi, U. (2009). Voices of suffering and the future of human rights. In *Human Rights, Southern Voices,* 162–204 (Twining, W., ed.). Cambridge, UK: Cambridge University Press.
Beck, G. (2008). Legitimation crisis, reifying human rights and the norm-creating power of the factual: Reply to "Reifying law: Let them be lions." *Penn State International Law Review, 26,* 565–605.
Bederman, D.J. (2001). Constructivism, positivism, and empiricism in international law. *Georgetown Law Journal, 89,* 469–499.
Benko, D. & Benowitz, B. (2001, #1). The application of universal human rights law to people with mental disabilities. *Human Rights Brief, 9,* 9–12.
Binder, G. (1999). Cultural relativism and cultural imperialism in human rights law. *Buffalo Human Rights Law Review, 5,* 211–221.
Butler, G. (2009). The essence of human rights: A religious critique. *University of Richmond Law Review, 43,* 1255–1317.
Cantor, J.D. (2005). Of pills and needles: Involuntarily medicating the psychotic inmate when execution looms. *Indiana Health Law Review, 2,* 119–170.
Cardenas, S. (2007). *Conflict and Compliance: State Responses to International Human Rights Pressure.* Philadelphia: University of Pennsylvania Press.
Cheng, T-H. (2008). The Universal Declaration of Human Rights at sixty: Is it still right for the United States? *Cornell International Law Journal, 41,* 251–304.
Chinkin, C. (2000). Normative development in the international legal system. In *Commitment and Compliance: The Role of Non-Binding Norms in the International Legal System,* 21–42 (Shelton, D., ed.). Oxford, UK: Oxford University Press.
Collins, H. (2003). *Employment Law.* Oxford, UK: Clarendon Law Series, Oxford University Press.

Courtis, C. (2002–2003). Disability rights in Latin America and international cooperation. *Southwestern Journal of Law and Trade in the Americas, 9,* 109–130.

Davis, M.C. (1998). Constitutionalism and political culture: The debate over human rights and Asian values. *Harvard Human Rights Journal, 11,* 109–147.

De Albuquerque, C. (2010). Chronicle of an announced birth: The coming into life of the optional protocol to the International Covenant on Economic, Social and Cultural Rights—The missing piece of the International Bill of Human Rights. *Human Rights Quarterly, 32,* 144–178.

Di Robilant, A. (2006). Genealogies of soft law. *American Journal of Comparative Law, 54,* 499–554.

Dillard, C. (2009). Prospective parents and the children's rights convention. *American University International Law Review, 25,* 485–529.

Engle, K. (2000). Culture and human rights: The Asian values debate in context. *New York University Journal of International Law and Politics, 32,* 291–333.

Fellmeth, A.X. (2008). State regulation of sexuality in international human rights law and theory. *William and Mary Law Review, 50,* 797–935.

Fellmeth, A.X. (2009). Nondiscrimination as a universal human right. *Yale Journal of International Law, 34,* 588–595.

Fennell, P. (2008). Human rights, bioethics, and mental disorder. *Medicine and Law, 27,* 95–107.

Fitzpatrick, J. (1994). *Human Rights in Crisis: The International System for Protecting Rights during States of Emergency.* Philadelphia: University of Pennsylvania Press.

Fletcher, A. & O'Brien, N. (2006). Disability Rights Commission: From civil rights to social rights. *Journal of Law and Society, 35,* 520–550.

GA Resolution. 119, U.N. GAOR, 46th Sess., 3d Comm., 75th plen. mtg., reprinted in [1991] 45 U.N.Y.B. 620, U.N. Sales No. E. 92. I. 1 ("MI Principles") (1991).

Gable, L. & Gostin, L.O. (2009). Mental health as a human right. In *Realizing the Right to Health: Swiss Human Rights Book,* vol. 3, 249–261 (Clapham, A. et al., eds.). Zurich: Rüffer & Rub.

Gardbaum, S. (2008). Human rights as international constitutional rights. *European Journal of International Law, 19,* 749–678.

Gathii, J.T. (2009). Defining the relationship between human rights and corruption. *University of Pennsylvania Journal of International Law, 31,* 125–202.

Ghai, Y. (2009). Understanding human rights in Asia. In *Human Rights, Southern Voices,* 120–150 (Twining, W., ed.). Cambridge, UK: Cambridge University Press.

Glendon, M.A. (2001). *A World Made New.* New York City: Random House.

Goodman, R. & Jinks, D. (2003). Measuring the effects of human rights treaties. *European Journal of International Law, 14,* 171–183.

Goodman, R. & Jinks, D. (2004a). How to influence states: Socialization and international human rights law. *Duke Law Journal, 54,* 621–704.

Goodman, R. & Jinks, D. (2004b). International law and state socialization: Conceptual, empirical, and normative challenges. *Duke Law Journal, 54,* 983–998.

Guzman, A.T. & Meyer, T.L. (2009). International common law: The soft law of international tribunals. *Chicago Journal of International Law, 9*, 515–535.
Hafner-Burton, E.M. & Tsutsui, K. (2005). Human rights in a globalizing world: The paradox of empty promises. *American Journal of Sociology, 110*, 1373–1411.
Hafner-Burton, E.M., Tsutsui, K. & Meyer, J.W. (2008). International human rights law and the politics of legitimation: Repressive states and human rights treaties. *International Sociology, 23*, 115–141.
Henkin, L. (1979). *How Nations Behave.* New York: Columbia University Press.
Henkin, L. (1984). International human rights and rights in the United States. In *Human Rights in International Law: Legal and Policy Issues* (Meron, T., ed.). Oxford, UK: Clarendon Press.
Higgins, R. (1976–1977). Derogations under human rights treaties. *British Yearbook of International Law 48*, 281–320.
Higgins, R. (1994). *Problems and Process: International Law and How We Use It.* Gloucestershire, UK: Clarendon Press.
Hui, P.T.C. (2002). Birth control in China: Cultural, gender, socio-economic and legislative perspectives in light of CEDAW standards. *Hong Kong Law Journal, 32*, 187–205.
In the Matter of Victor Rosario Congo, Report No. 63/99 Case 11.427 (April 13, 1999).
Ishay, M. (2004). *History of Human Rights.* Berkeley: University of California Press.
Janis, M.W. (2008). *International Law*, 5th ed. New York: Aspen Publishers.
Johnstone, I. (2008). Law-making through the operational activities of international organizations. *George Washington International Law Review, 40*, 87–122.
Kahn, S.L. (1984). The right to adequate treatment versus the right to refuse antipsychotic drug treatment: A solution to the dilemma of the involuntarily committed psychiatric patient. *Emory Law Journal, 33*, 441–485.
Kalb, J. (2010). Dynamic federalism in human rights treaty implementation. *Tulane Law Review, 84*, 1025–1066.
Kamminga, M.T. (2009). Final report on the impact of international human rights law on general international law. In *The Impact of Human Rights Law on General International Law* (Kamminga, N.Y. & Schein, M., eds.). London, UK: Oxford University Press.
Kelley, C.R. (2004). Realist theory and real constraints. *Virginia Journal of International Law, 44*, 545–636.
Kelly, J.P. (2000). The twilight of customary international law. *Virginia Journal of International Law, 40*, 450–543.
Kinley, D. (2007). Human rights fundamentalisms. *Sydney Law Review, 29*, 545–575.
Klein, R. (2001). Cultural relativism, economic development and international human rights in the Asian context. *Touro International Law Review, 9*, 1–69.
Koenig, M. (2008). International human rights and the construction of collective identities. *International Sociology, 23*, 95–114.
Lawson, A. (2007). The United Nations Convention on the Rights of Persons with Disabilities: New era or false dawn? *Syracuse Journal of International Law and Commerce, 34*, 563–619.

Lee, M.Y.K. (2008). Universal human dignity: Some reflections in the Asian context. *Asian J. Compar. Law, 3,* 1–33.
Luard, E. (1967). The origins of human rights. In *The International Protection of Human Rights* (E. Luard, ed.). Santa Barbara, CA: Praeger.
Mandhane, R. (2004). The use of human rights discourse to secure women's interests: Critical analysis of the implications. *Michigan Journal of Gender and the Law, 10,* 275–326.
Marks, S.P. (2009). The past and future of the separation of human rights into categories. *Maryland International Law Journal, 24,* 209–243.
Melish, T. (2009). Introductory note to the Optional Protocol to the International Covenant on Economic, Social, and Cultural Rights. *International Legal Materials, 48,* 256–259.
Merry, S.E. (2006). Transnational human rights and local activism: Mapping the middle. *American Anthropologist, 108,* 38–51.
Meyer, T. (2009). Soft law as delegation. *Fordham International Law Journal, 32,* 888–942.
Mutua, M.W. (1996). The ideology of human rights. *Virginia Journal of International Law, 36,* 589–657.
Neumayer, E. (2010). Do governments mean business when they derogate? Human rights violations during declared states of emergency. Available at http://papers.ssrn.com/sol3/papers.cfm?abstract_id=1654001.
O'Shea, A. (2001). A critical reflection on the proposed African Court on Human and Peoples' Rights. *African Human Rights Journal, 2,* 285–298.
Paul, J. (2000). Cultural resistance to global governance. *Michigan Journal of International Law, 27,* 1–53.
Peerenboom, R. (2003). Beyond universalism and relativism: The evolving debates about "values in Asia." *Indiana International & Comparative Law Review, 14,* 1–85.
Perlin, M.L. (2007). An internet-based mental disability law program: Implications for social change in nations with developing economies. *Fordham International Law Journal, 30,* 435–454.
Perlin, M.L. (2008). "I might need a good lawyer, could be your funeral, my trial": Global clinical legal education and the right to counsel in civil commitment cases. *Washington University Journal of Law and Policy, 28,* 241–264.
Perlin, M.L. & Dlugacz, H.A. (2008). *Mental Health Issues in Jails and Prisons: Cases and Materials.* Durham, NC: Carolina Academic Press.
Perlin, M.L., et al. (2006). *International Human Rights and Comparative Mental Disability Law.* Durham, NC: Carolina Academic Press.
Pillay, N. (2008). Are human rights universal? *U.N. Chronicle* (No. 2/3), 4–8.
Posner, E.A. (2008). Human welfare, not human rights. *Columbia Law Review, 108,* 1758–1800.
Preis, A.S. (1995). Human rights as cultural practice: An anthropological critique. *Human Rights Quarterly, 18,* 286–315.
Rao, A. (1995). The politics of gender and culture in international human rights discourse. In *Women's Rights Human Rights: International Feminist Perspectives,* 167–175 (Peters, J. & Wolper, A., eds.). New York: Routledge.
Ramcharan, B.G. (2009). The national responsibility to protect human rights. *Hong Kong Law Journal, 39,* 361–399.

Rehman, J. (2003). *International Human Rights Law: A Practical Approach.* New York: Longman.

Risse, T. & Ropp, S.C. (1999). International human rights norms and domestic change: Conclusions. In *The Power of Human Rights: International Norms and Domestic Change,* 234–278 (Risse T, Ropp, S.C. & Sikkink, K., eds.). New York: Cambridge University Press.

Risse, T. & Sikkink, K. (1999). The socialization of international human rights norms into domestic practices: Introduction. In *The Power of Human Rights: International Norms and Domestic Change,* 1–38 (Risse T., Ropp, S.C. & Sikkink, K., eds.). New York: Cambridge University Press.

Robbins, M. (2005). Powerful states, customary law, and the erosion of human rights through regional enforcement. *California Western International Law Journal, 35,* 275–302.

Rosenthal, E. & Sundram, C.J. (2002). International human rights in mental health legislation. *New York Law School Journal of International and Comparative Law, 21,* 469–536.

Satterthwaite, M. (2005). Crossing borders, claiming rights: Using human rights law to empower women migrant workers. *Yale Human Rights & Development Law Journal, 8,* 1–66.

Scharf, M.P. (2009). International law in crisis: A qualitative empirical contribution to the compliance debate. *Cardozo Law Review, 31,* 45–97.

Shany, Y. (2005). Toward a general margin of appreciation doctrine in international law. *European Journal of International Law, 16,* 907–940.

Simmons, B. (2009a). Civil rights in international law: Compliance with aspects of the "International Bill of Rights." *Indiana Journal of Global Legal Studies, 16,* 437–481.

Simmons, B. (2009b). Should states ratify?—Process and consequences of the optional protocol to the ICESCR. *Norwegian Journal of Human Rights, 27,* 64–81.

Singh, R. (1999, #1). Is there a role for the "margin of appreciation" doctrine in national law after the Human Rights Act? *European Human Rights Law Review, 4,* 15–22.

Stefan, S. (2003). "Discredited" and "discreditable": The search for political identity by people with psychiatric diagnoses. *William and Mary Law Review, 44,* 1341–1380.

Steiner, H.J. & Alston, P. (2000). Comment on the universalist-relativist debate. In *International Human Rights in Context,* 366–368. New York: Oxford University Press.

Tay, S.S.C. (1996). Human rights, culture and the Singapore example. *McGill Law Journal, 41,* 743–780.

Tay, S.S.C. (1999). South East Asian fires: The challenge to international law and sustainable development. *Georgetown International Environmental Law Review, 11,* 241–300.

Stark, B. (2009). Reproductive rights and the reproduction of gender. In *Gender Equality: Dimensions of Women's Equal Citizenship,* 345–346. New York: Cambridge University Press.

Varayudej, S. (2006). Right to democracy in international law: Its implications for Asia. *Annual Survey of International & Comparative Law, 12,* 1–17.

Wang, Y.S. (2009). The triumph of Confucianism: How a subjugated legal system is failing a generation of Chinese women and girls. *Cardozo Journal of Law and Gender, 15,* 691–719.
Weissbrodt, D. (1989). An introduction to the sources of international law. *ALI-ABA Course of Study Materials, International Human Rights C* 399, 3–6. (Philadelphia, PA: American Law Institute-American Bar Association.
Wilansky, D.P. (2006). Civil rights: Prisoners' right to treatment information under *Pabon v. Wright. Journal of Law, Medicine & Ethics, 34,* 831–832.
Wilson, J.C. (2008). Russia's cultural aversion to the rule of law. *Columbia Journal of Eastern European Law, 2,* 195–232.
Woods, A.K. (2010). A behavioral approach to human rights. *Harvard International Law Journal, 51,* 51–112.
Yourow, H.C. (1987). The margin of appreciation doctrine in the dynamics of European human rights jurisprudence. *Connecticut Journal of International Law, 3,* 111–159.

Chapter 2B

Arboleda-Florez, J. & Weisstub. D.N. (2008). Mental health rights: The relationship between constitution and bioethics. In *Autonomy and Human Rights in Health Care: An International Perspective,* 309–327 (Weisstub, D.N. & Diaz Pintos, G., eds.). Dordrecht, The Netherlands: Springer.
Asplund, K.D. (2009). Resistance to human rights in Indonesia: Asian values and beyond. *Asia-Pacific Journal on Human Rights and the Law, 10,* 27–47.
Ay, P., Save, D. & Fidanoglu, O. (2005). Does stigma concerning mental disorders differ through medical education? A survey among medical students in Turkey. *Social Psychiatry and Psychiatric Epidemiology, 41,* 63–67.
Birnbaum, M. (1974). The right to treatment: Some comments on its development. In *Medical, Moral and Legal Issues in Health Care,* 97–141 (F. Ayd, ed.). Baltimore: Williams & Wilkins Company.
Boyadjiev, B. & Onchev, G. (2007). Legal and cultural aspects of involuntary psychiatric treatment regulation in post-totalitarian milieu: The Bulgarian perspective. *European Journal of Psychiatry, 21,* 179–188.
Canvin, K., Barlett, A. & Pinfold, V. (2002). A "bittersweet pill to swallow": Learning from mental health service users' responses to compulsory community care in England. *Health and Social Care in the Community, 19,* 361–369.
Chanpattana, W. (2010). Asia's mental health crisis in the 21st century. *Journal of ECT, 26,* 2–4.
Crisp, A.H. et al. (2000). Stigmatisation of people with mental illnesses. *British Journal of Psychiatry, 177,* 4–7.
De Girolamo, G. (1996). WHO studies on schizophrenia: An overview of the results and their implications for the understanding of the disorder. In *Psychosocial Approaches to Deeply Disturbed Persons,* 213–231 (Breggin, P.R. & Stern, E.M., eds.). London: Haworth Press.
Dheost v. Belgium, 12 Eur. Ct. H.R. 135 (1987).
Diniz, D., Barboso, L. & does Santos, W.R. (2010, #11). Disability, human rights, and justice. *SUR International Journal on Human Rights, 6,* 61–72.

Fischer, J. (2005). A comparative look at the right to refuse treatment for involuntarily hospitalized persons with a mental illness. *Hastings International and Comparative Law Review, 29,* 153–186.

Fung, K.M.T. et al. (2007). Measuring self-stigma of mental illness in China and its implications for recovery. *International Journal of Social Psychiatry, 53,* 408–418.

Gibbs, A. et al. (2005). How patients in New Zealand view community treatment orders. *Journal of Mental Health, 14,* 357–368.

Gostin, L. (1987). Human rights in mental health: A proposal for five international standards based upon the Japanese experience. *International Journal of Law and Psychiatry, 10,* 353–366.

Hayward, P. & Bright, J.A. (1997). Stigma and mental illness: A review and critique. *Journal of Mental Health, 6,* 345–354.

Herczegfalvy v. Austria, 15 Eur. Ct. H.R. 437 (1993).

Hewitt, D. (2001). Do human rights impact on mental health law? *New Law Journal, 151,* 1278–1287.

Heyer, K. (2000). From special needs to equal rights: Japanese disability law. *Asian-Pacific Law and Policy Journal, 1,* 7–21.

Honig, J. & Fendell, S. (2000). Meeting the needs of female trauma survivors: The effectiveness of the Massachusetts mental health managed care system. *Berkeley Women's Law Journal, 15,* 161–228.

Katner, D. (2006). The mental health paradigm and the MacArthur study: Emerging issues challenging the competence of juveniles in delinquency systems. *American Journal of Law & Medicine, 32,* 503–584.

Kayess R. & French, P. (2008). Out of darkness into light? Introducing the Convention on the Rights of Persons with Disabilities, *Human Rights Law Review, 8,* 1–34.

Kung, W.W. (2003). The illness, stigma, culture, or immigration? Burdens on Chinese American caregivers of patients with schizophrenia. *Families in Society: The Journal of Contemporary Human Services, 84,* 547–557.

Lawson, A. (2008). People with psychosocial impairments or conditions, reasonable accommodation and the Convention on the Rights of Persons with Disabilities. *Law in Context, 26,* 62–84.

Lindblom, L. (2006, #4). The genocide caused more disability than the war in Rwanda. Human Rights Africa, 9–15.

Margulies, P. (1992). The cognitive politics of professional conflict: Law reform, mental health treatment technology, and citizen governance. *Harvard Journal of Law & Technology, 5,* 25–63.

Melish, T. (2007). The UN Disability Convention: Historic process, strong prospects, and why the U.S. should ratify. *Human Rights Brief, 14,* 37–46.

Mugwanya, G.W. (1999). Realizing universal human rights norms through regional human rights mechanisms: Reinvigorating the African system. *Indiana International & Comparative Law Review, 10,* 35–50.

Neaman, J.S. (1975). *Suggestion of the Devil: The Origins of Madness.* Garden City, NY: Anchor Books.

Pearson, V. & Tsang, H.W.H. (2004). Duty, burden, and ambivalence: Families of forensic psychiatric patients in Hong Kong. *International Journal of Law and Psychiatry, 27,* 361–374.

Pearson, V. & Yiu, M-Y. (1993). Public attitudes towards mental health facilities: A study in Hong Kong. *Social Work and Social Sciences Review, 4,* 59–82.

Perlin, M.L. (1991). Morality and pretextuality, psychiatry and law: Of "ordinary common sense," heuristic reasoning, and cognitive dissonance. *Bulletin of the American Academy of Psychiatry & the Law, 19,* 131–150.

Perlin, M.L. (1992). On "sanism." *SMU Law Review, 46,* 373–407.

Perlin, M.L. (1993). Pretexts and mental disability law: The case of competency. *University of Miami Law Review, 47,* 625–688.

Perlin, M.L. (1993–1994a) Hospitalized patients and the right to sexual interaction: Beyond the last frontier? *New York University Review of Law & Social Change, 20,* 302.

Perlin, M.L. (1993–1994b). The ADA and persons with mental disabilities: Can sanist attitudes be undone? *Journal of Law and Health, 8,* 15–45.

Perlin, M.L. (1994). The sanist lives of jurors in death penalty cases: The puzzling role of mitigating mental disability evidence. *Notre Dame Journal of Law, Ethics & Public Policy, 8,* 239–279.

Perlin, M.L. (1996). "Dignity was the first to leave": *Godinez v. Moran. Colin Ferguson,* and the trial of mentally disabled criminal defendants. *Behavioral Sciences and the Law, 14,* 61–81.

Perlin, M.L. (1997a). "Make promises by the hour": Sex, drugs, the ADA, and psychiatric hospitalization. *DePaul Law Review, 46,* 947–985.

Perlin, M.L. (1997b). "The borderline which separated you from me": The insanity defense, the authoritarian spirit, the fear of faking, and the culture of punishment. *Iowa Law Review, 82,* 1375, 1426.

Perlin, M.L. (1999)."Half-wracked prejudice leaped forth": Sanism, pretextuality, and why and how mental disability law developed as it did. *Journal of Contemporary Legal Issues, 10,* 3–36.

Perlin, M.L. (2000). *The Hidden Prejudice: Mental Disability on Trial.* Washington, DC: American Psychological Association Press.

Perlin, M.L. (2002). "Chimes of freedom": International human rights and institutional mental disability law. *New York Law School Journal of International and Comparative Law, 21,* 423–433.

Perlin, M.L. (2002–2003). "Things have changed": Looking at non-institutional mental disability law through the sanism filter. *New York Law School Law Review, 46,* 535–545.

Perlin, M.L. (2003a). Therapeutic jurisprudence and outpatient commitment: Kendra's law as case study. Psychology, Public Policy, and Law, *9,* 183–208.

Perlin, M.L. (2003b). "You have discussed lepers and crooks": Sanism in clinical teaching. *Clinical Law Review, 9,* 683–729.

Perlin, M.L. (2004)."Everything's a little upside down, as a matter of fact the wheels have stopped": The fraudulence of the incompetency evaluation process. *Houston Journal of Health Law & Policy, 4,* 239–253.

Perlin, M.L. (2005). "And my best friend, my doctor/Won't even say what it is I've got": The role and significance of counsel in right to refuse treatment cases. *San Diego Law Review, 42,* 735–755.

Perlin, M.L. (2006). International human rights and comparative mental disability law: The role of institutional psychiatry in the suppression of political dissent. *Israel Law Review, 39,* 69–97.

Perlin, M.L. (2007). International human rights law and comparative mental disability law: The universal factors. *Syracuse Journal of International Law and Commerce, 34,* 333–358.

Perlin, M.L. (2008a). "Baby, look inside your mirror": The legal profession's willful and sanist blindness to lawyers with mental disabilities. *University of Pittsburgh Law Review, 69,* 589–607.

Perlin, M.L. (2008b)."I might need a good lawyer, could be your funeral, my trial": Global clinical legal education and the right to counsel in civil commitment cases. *Washington University Journal of Law & Policy, 28,* 241–264.

Perlin, M.L. (2008c). "Through the wild cathedral evening": Barriers, attitudes, participatory democracy, Professor tenBroek, and the rights of persons with mental disabilities. *Texas Journal on Civil Liberties & Civil Rights, 13,* 413–419.

Perlin, M.L. (2009a). "A change is gonna come": The implications of the United Nations Convention on the Rights of Persons with Disabilities for the domestic practice of constitutional mental disability law. *Northern Illinois University Law Review, 29,* 483–498.

Perlin, M.L. (2009b). "His brain has been mismanaged with great skill": How will jurors respond to neuroimaging testimony in insanity defense cases? *Akron Law Review, 42,* 885–916.

Perlin, M.L. & Dorfman, D.A. (1996) "Is it more than dodging lions and wastin' time"? Adequacy of counsel, questions of competence, and the judicial process in individual right to refuse treatment cases. *Psychology, Public Policy, and Law, 2,* 114–136.

Perlin, M.L. & Szeli, E. (2011). Mental health law and human rights: Evolution and contemporary challenges. In *Mental Health and Human Rights* (Dudley, M., ed.). Oxford, UK: Oxford University Press. (in press).

Perlin, M.L. et al. (2006). *International Human Rights and Comparative Mental Disability Law: Cases and Materials.* Durham, NC: Carolina Academic Press.

Phillips, M. & Xiong, W. (1995). Expressed emotion on mainland China: Chinese families with schizophrenic patients. *International Journal of Mental Health, 24,* 54–75.

Phillips, M. et al. (2002). Stigma and expressed emotion: A study of people with schizophrenia and their family members in China. *British Journal of Psychiatry, 181,* 488–493.

Powers, A. (2002). Justice denied? The adjudication of extradition applications. *Texas International Law Journal, 37,* 277–328.

Read, J. (2007). Why promoting biological ideology increases prejudice against people labeled "schizophrenic." *Australian Psychologist, 42,* 118–128.

Reilly, M. (1995). Human rights in the Japanese mental health system. In *Human Rights and Chinese Values: Legal, Philosophical, and Political Perspectives,* 141–183 (Davis, M.C., ed.). Hong Kong: Oxford University Press.

"Taking Issue" (1997). Taking issue with taking issue: "Psychiatric survivors" reconsidered. *Psychiatric Services, 48,* 601–605.

Takizawa, T. (1993). Patients and their families in Japanese mental health. *New Directions for Mental Health Services, 60,* 25–34.

Tsang, H.W.H. et al. (2007). A cross-cultural study of employers' concerns about hiring people with psychotic disorder: Implications for recovery. *Social Psychiatry and Psychiatric Epidemiology, 42,* 723–733.

Tuohimaki, C. et al. (2001). Psychiatric inpatients' views on self-determination. *International Journal of Law and Psychiatry, 24,* 61–69.

Verhaeghe, M., Bracke, P. & Bruynoogghe, K. (2008). Stigmatization and self-esteem of persons in recovery from mental illness: The role of peer support. *International Journal of Social Psychiatry, 54,* 206–218.
WHO European Ministerial Conference on Mental health (2005). Facing the challenges, building solutions. ("WHO Report").
Yip, K-S. (2005). Coping with public labeling of clients with mental illness in Hong Kong: A report of personal experiences. *International Journal of Psychosocial Rehabilitation, 9.* Available at http://www.psychosocial.com/IJPR_9/Coping_with_Public_Labeling_Hong_Kong.htm (last accessed, May 28, 2010).

Chapter 2C

Banks, R. (1999). More than law: Advocacy for disability rights. In *Disability, Divers-Ability and Legal Change,* 343–362. The Hague: Martinus Nijhoff.
Beaupert, F. (2009). Mental health tribunal processes and advocacy arrangements: "Little wins" are "no small feat." *Psychiatry, Psychology and Law, 16,* 90–107.
Birgden, A. & Perlin, M.L. (2008). "Tolling for the luckless, the abandoned and forsaked": Therapeutic jurisprudence and international human rights law as applied to prisoners and detainees by forensic psychologists. *Legal and Criminological Psychology, 13,* 231–243.
Birgden, A. & Perlin, M.L. (2009). "Where the home in the valley meets the damp dirty prison": A human rights perspective on therapeutic jurisprudence and the role of forensic psychologists in correctional settings. *Aggression and Violent Behavior, 14,* 256–263.
Chaffin, S. (2005). Challenging the United States position on a United Nations Convention on Disability. *Temple Political and Civil Rights Law Review, 15,* 121–145.
Chakalson, A. Human dignity as a constitutional value. In *The Concept of Human Dignity in Human Rights Discourse,* 133–144. (Kretzmer D. & Klein, E., eds.). The Hague: Kluwer Law International.
Connelly, U.B. (2009). Disability rights in Cambodia: Using the Convention on the Rights of People with Disabilities to expose human rights violations. *Pacific Rim Law and Policy Journal, 18,* 123–153.
Dhir, A. (2005). Human rights treaty drafting through the lens of mental disability: The proposed International Convention on Protection and Promotion of the Rights and Dignity of Persons with Disabilities. *Stanford Journal of International Law, 41,* 181–216.
Dhir, A.A. (2008). Relationships of force: Exploring the legal and social issues surrounding mental disability. *Windsor Review of Legal and Social Issues, 25,* 103–112.
Dicke, K. (2002). The founding function of human dignity in the Universal Declaration of Human Rights. In *The Concept of Human Dignity in Human Rights Discourse,* 111–120 (Kretzmer, D. & Klein, E., eds.). The Hague: Kluwer Law International.
Donnelly, M. (2008). From autonomy to dignity: Treatment for mental disorders and the focus for patient rights. *Law in Context, 26,* 37–61.
Fleming v. Reid (1991), 4 O.R. (3d) 74 (C.A.).
Funk, M. et al. (2005). Advocacy for mental health: Roles for consumer and family organizations and governments. *Health Promotion International, 21,* 70–75.

GA Resolution. 56/168, U.N. Doc. A/RES/56/168 (Dec. 19, 2001) (General Assembly Resolution).

Gostin, L. (2004, March–April). International human rights law and mental disability. *Hastings Center Report,* 11–12.

Helen L. v. DiDario, 46 F.3d 325 (3d Cir. 1995), cert. denied, 516 U.S. 813 (1995).

http://humiliationstudies.org/index.php (last accessed, May 27, 2010).

In re Mental Health of K.G.F., 29 P.3d 485 (Mont. 2001).

Indiana v. Edwards, 554 U.S. 164 (2008).

International Covenant on Civil and Political Rights. (1966a). Retrieved from http://www2.ohchr.org/English/law/ccpr.htm

International Covenant on Economic, Social and Cultural Rights. (1966b). Office of the United Nations High Commissioner for Human Rights. Retrieved September 27, 2010, from http://www2.ohchr.org/English/law/cescr.htm

Law, S.K. (1991). Comment, The American with Disabilities Act of 1990: Burden on business or dignity for the disabled? *Duquesne Law Review, 30,* 99–114.

Lawson, A. (2006). Disability, degradation, and dignity: The role of Article 3 of the European Convention on Human Rights. *Northern Ireland Legal Quarterly, 56,* 462–491.

Mahlman, M. (2010). The basic law at 60—Human dignity and the culture of republicanism. *German Law Journal, 11,* 9–31.

Maris, C. (2010). A not = A: Or, freaky justice. *Cardozo Law Review, 31,* 1133–1169.

Marquez v. Collins, 11 F. 3d 1241 (5th Cir. 1994).

McCrudden, C. (2008). Human dignity and judicial interpretation of human rights. *European Journal of International Law, 19,* 655–723.

Monsalve, V.B. & Roman, J.A. (2010, # 11). Tensions of human dignity: Conceptualization and application to international human rights law. *SUR International Journal on Human Rights, 6,* 39–60.

Perlin, M.L. (1992). Fatal assumption: A critical evaluation of the role of counsel in mental disability cases. *Law and Human Behavior, 16,* 61–81.

Perlin, M.L. (2001–2002). "What's good is bad, what's bad is good, you'll find out when you reach the top, you're on the bottom": Are the Americans with Disabilities Act (and *Olmstead v. L.C.*) anything more than "Idiot Wind"? *University of Michigan Journal of Law Reform, 35,* 235–261.

Perlin, M.L. (2008). "I might need a good lawyer, could be your funeral, my trial": Global clinical legal education and the right to counsel in civil commitment cases. *Washington University Journal of Law & Policy, 28,* 241–264.

Perlin, M.L. (2009). "A change is gonna come": The implications of the United Nations Convention on the Rights of Persons with Disabilities for the domestic practice of constitutional mental disability law. *Northern Illinois University Law Review, 29,* 483–498.

Perlin, M.L. & Dorfman, D.A. (1996). "Is it more than dodging lions and wastin' time"? Adequacy of counsel, questions of competence, and the judicial process in individual right to refuse treatment cases. *Psychology, Public Policy, and Law, 2,* 114–136.

Perlin, M.L. & Dlugacz, H.A. (2009). "It's doom alone that counts": Can international human rights law be an effective source of rights in correctional conditions litigation? *Behavioral Sciences and the Law, 27,* 675–694.

Perlin, M.L. & McClain, V. (2009). "Where souls are forgotten": Cultural competencies, forensic evaluations, and international human rights. *Psychology, Public Policy and Law, 15,* 257–277.
Quinn, G. & Degener, T. (2002). *Human Rights and Disability: The Current Use and Future Potential of United Nations Human Rights Instruments in the Context of Disability.* Blue Ridge Summit, PA: United Nations Publication.
Sailas, E. & Wahlbeck, K. (2005). Restraint and seclusion in psychiatric inpatient wards. *Current Opinion in Psychiatry, 18,* 555–559.
Schwartz, S.J. et al. (1983). Protecting the rights and enhancing the dignity of people with mental disabilities: Standards for effective legal advocacy. *Rutgers Law Journal, 14,* 541–594.
Statman, D. (2002). Humiliation, dignity and self-respect. In *The Concept of Human Dignity in Human Rights Discourse,* 209–222. (Kretzmer, D. & Klein, E., eds.). The Hague: Kluwer Law International.
Stein, M.A. (2007). Disability human rights. *California Law Review, 95,* 75–121.
Tyler, T.R. (1992). The psychological consequences of judicial procedures: Implications for civil commitment hearings. *SMU Law Review, 46,* 433–445.
U.N. Body of Principles for the Protection of all Persons under Any Form of Detention or Imprisonment. (1988, December). *The UN Refugee Agency.* Retrieved September 27, 2010, from http://www.unhchr.ch/html/menu3/b/h_comp36.htm
U.N. Convention on the Rights of Persons with Disabilities. (2006a). *United Nations Enable.* Retrieved September 27, 2010, from http://www.un.org/disabilities/convention/conventionfull
U.N. Universal Declaration of Human Rights. (1948, December 10). United Nations. Retrieved September 27, 2010, from http://www.un.org/en/documents/udhr/index.shtml
Viljoen, F. (2004). A human rights court for Africa, and Africans. *Brooklyn Journal of International Law, 30,* 1–66.
Ward, T. & Birgden, A. (2009). Accountability and dignity: Ethical issues in forensic and correctional practice. *Aggression and Violent Behavior, 14,* 227–231.
Zhang, E.G. (2007). Employment of people with disabilities: International standards and domestic legislation and practices in China? *Syracuse Journal of International Law and Commerce, 34,* 517–561.

Chapter 3

Abudu, N.G. et al. (2008). Human rights. *International Lawyer, 42,* 755–795.
Addington v. Texas, 441 U.S. 418 (1979).
Ahmad, T. & Butler, I.d.J. (2006). The European Union and human rights: An international law perspective. *European Journal of International Law, 17,* 771–801.
Ajibola, B. (1998). Individual human rights in the African context. In *Legal Visions of the 21st Century: Essays in Honour of Judge Christopher Weeramantry,* 125–144 (Anghie, A. & Sturgess, G., eds.). The Hague: Kluwer Law International.
Alem, A., Jacobsson, L. & Hanlon, C. (2008). Community-based mental health care in Africa: Mental health worker' views. *World Psychiatry, 7,* 54–57.

Allo, A.K. (2009). Derogations or limitations? Rethinking the African human rights system of derogation in light of the European system. *Ethiopian Journal of Legal Education, 2,* 21–52.

Amoah, P. (1992). The African Charter on Human and Peoples' Rights—An effective weapon for human rights? *Radic, 4,* 226–240.

Amos, M. (2007). The impact of the Human Rights Act of the United Kingdom on the United Kingdom's performance before the European Court of Human Rights. *Public Law,* WIN, 655–676.

Arold, N-L. (2007). The European Court of Human Rights as an example of convergence. *Nordic Journal of International Law, 76,* 305–322.

Baderin, M.A. (2005). Recent developments in the African Regional Human Rights system. *Human Rights Law Review, 5,* 117–149.

Bartlett, P., Lewis, O. & Thorold, O. (2007). *Mental Disability and the European Convention on Human Rights.* Leiden, The Netherlands: Martinus Nijhoff Publishers.

Basch, F. et al. (2010, June). The effectiveness of the Inter-American system of human rights protection: A quantitative approach to its functioning and compliance with its decisions. *SUR: International Journal on Human Rights, 7,* 9–35.

Bauer, A. et al. (2005). Regional psychiatric boards in Israel: Expectations and realities. *International Journal of Law and Psychiatry, 28,* 661–669.

Beaupert, F. (2009). Mental health tribunal processes and advocacy arrangements: "Little wins" are "no small feat." *Psychiatry, Psychology and Law, 16,* 90–107.

Behrend, U. (1999). *Alice Lakwena and the Holy Spirits: War in Northern Uganda 1985–1987.* Oxford, UK: James Currey Press.

Bindman, J., Maingay, S. & Szmukler, G. (2003). The Human Rights Act and mental health legislation. *British Journal of Psychiatry, 182,* 91–94.

Bondzie-Simpson, E. (1988). A critique of the African Charter in Human and People's Rights. *Howard Law Journal, 31,* 643–665.

Brunwasser, M. (2009, January 4). In eastern Europe, lives languish in mental facilities. *New York Times,* A7.

Buchanan, A. & Keohane, R.O. (2006). The legitimacy of global governance institutions. *Ethics and International Affairs, 20,* 405–437.

Cabot, A. et al. (2006, #1). Updates from the regional human rights systems. *Human Rights Brief, 14,* 44–46.

Cameron, I. (1999). The Swedish experience of the European Convention on Human Rights since incorporation. *International and Comparative Law Quarterly, 48,* 20–56.7.

Carney, T. (2003). Mental health law in postmodern society: Time for new paradigms? *Psychiatry, Psychology and Law, 10,* 12–32.

Carney, T. & Beaupert, F. (2008). Mental health tribunals: Rights drowning in un-"chartered" health waters? *Australian Journal of Human Rights, 13,* 181–208.

Carney, T., Beaupert, F., Perry, J. & Tait, D. (2008). Advocacy and participation in mental health cases: Realisable rights or pipe dream? *Law in Context, 26,* 125–147.

Carney, T., Tait, D. & Beaupert, F. (2008). Pushing the boundaries: Realising rights through mental health tribunal processes. *Sydney Law Review, 30,* 329–356.

Carver, R. (2010). A new answer to an old question: National Human Rights Institutions and the domestication of international law. *Human Rights Law Review, 10,* 1–32.

Cavallaro, J.L. (2002). Toward fair play: A decade of transformation and resistance in international human rights advocacy in Brazil. *Chicago Journal of International Law, 3,* 481–492.

Cavallaro, J.L. & Brewer, S.E. (2008a). Reevaluating regional human rights litigation in the twenty-first century: The case of the Inter-American Court. American Journal of International Law, *102,* 768–827.

Cavallaro, J.L. & Brewer, S.E. (2008b). The virtue of following: The role of inter-American litigation in campaigns for social justice. *SUR: International Journal on Human Rights, 5,* 85–97.

Cavallaro, J.L. & Schaffer, E. (2006). Rejoinder: Justice before justiciability: Inter-American litigation and social change. *New York University Journal of International Law and Politics,* 39, 345–383.

Christiansen, E.C. (2007). Adjudicating non-justiciable rights: Socio-economic rights and the South African constitutional court. *Columbia Human Rights Law Review, 38,* 321–386.

City of Cleburne v. Cleburne Living Center, 473, U.S. 432 (1985).

Curtice, M.J.R. & Sandford, J.J. (2009). Article 8 of the Human Rights Act 1998: A review of case law related to forensic psychiatry and prisoners in the United Kingdom. Journal of the American Academy of Psychiatry and Law, *37,* 232–238.

Dawson, J. (2008). Community treatment orders and human rights. *Law in Context, 26,* 148–159.

Dawson, J. & Kämpf, A. (2006). Incapacity principles in mental health laws in Europe. *Psychology, Public Policy, and Law, 12,* 310–331.

de Almeida, J.M.C. & Horvitz-Lennon, M. (2010). An overview of mental health care reforms in Latin America and the Caribbean. *Psychiatric Services, 61,* 218–221.

deBeco, G. (2007). National Human Rights Institutions in Europe. *Human Rights Law Review, 7,* 331–368.

Defeis, E.F. (2004). Equality and the European Union. *Georgia Journal of International and Comparative Law, 32,* 73–98.

Delaney, S. (2003). An optimally rights recognizing Mental Health Tribunal—What can be learnt from Australian jurisdictions? *Psychiatry, Psychology, and Law, 10,* 71–78.

Dhoest v. Belgium, 12 Eur. Ct. H.R. 135 (1987).

Dickson, B. (2003). The contribution of Human Rights Commissions to the protection of human rights. *Public Law,* 272–285.

Diefeld, K. & McKenna, B. (2006). The therapeutic intent of the New Zealand Mental Health Review Tribunal. *Psychiatry, Psychology and Law, 13,* 100–109.

Diefeld, K. & McKenna, B. (2007). The unintended impact of the therapeutic intentions of the New Zealand Mental Health Review tribunal: Therapeutic jurisprudence perspectives. *Journal of Legal Medicine, 14,* 566–574.

Dimopoulos, A. (2009). Intellectually disabled parents before the European Court of Human Rights and English courts. *European Human Rights Law Review, 1,* 70–83.

Dressing, H. & Salize, H.J. (2006). Forensic psychiatric assessment in European Union member states. *Acta Psychiatrica Scandinavica, 114,* 282–289.

E. v. Norway, 17 Eur. Ct. H.R. 30, P 63 (1990).

Fennell, P. (1999). The third way in mental health policy: Negative rights, positive rights, and the Convention. *Journal of Law in Society, 26,* 103–127.

Fennell, P. & Goldstein, R.L. (2006). The application of civil commitment law and practices to a case of delusional disorder: A cross-national comparison of legal approaches in the United States and the United Kingdom. Behavioral Sciences and the Law, *24,* 385–406.

Ferencz, N. & McGuire, J. (2000). Mental Health Review Tribunals in the U.K.: Applying a therapeutic jurisprudence perspective. *Court Review: The Journal of the American Judges Association, 37,* 48. Available at http://aja.ncsc.dni.us/courtrv/review.html.

Fistein, E.C. et al. (2009). A comparison of mental health legislation from diverse Commonwealth jurisdictions. *International Journal of Law and Psychiatry, 32,* 147–155.

Follesdal, A. (2009). The legitimacy of international human rights review: The case of the European Court of Human Rights. Journal of Social Philosophy, *40,* 595–607.

Gable, L. et al. (2005). Mental health and due process in the Americas: Protecting the human rights of persons involuntarily admitted to and detained in psychiatric institutions. *Pan American Journal of Public Health, 18,* 366–373.

Gaer, F.D. (1992). First fruits: Reporting by states under the African Charter on Human and Peoples' Rights. *Netherlands Quarterly of Human Rights, 10,* 29–42.

Gearty, C.A. & Sutherland, P.J. (1992). Insanity and the European Court of Human Rights. *Criminal Law Review,* 418–424.

Gledhill, K. (2007). Human rights instruments and mental health law: The English experience of the incorporation of the European Convention on Human Rights. *Syracuse Journal of International Law and Commerce, 34,* 359–403.

Gledhill, K. (2010). The model law fusing incapacity and mental health legislation—A comment on the forensic aspects of the proposal. *Journal of Mental Health Law, 20,* 42–54.

Godinez v. Moran, 509 U.S. 389 (1993).

Goldkamp, J. & Irons-Guynn, C. (2000). Emerging judicial strategies for the mentally ill in the criminal caseload: Mental health courts in Ft. Lauderdale, Seattle, San Bernardino, and Anchorage. *National Criminal Justice Reference Service.* Retrieved September 19, 2010, from http://www.ncjrs.gov/pdffiles1/bja/182504.pdf.

Goldman, R.K. (2009). History and action: The inter-American human rights system and the role of the Inter-American Commission on Human Rights. *Human Rights Quarterly, 31,* 856–887.

Gostin, L. (1982). Human rights, judicial review, and the mentally disordered offender. *Criminal Law Review,* 779–793.

Gostin, L. (2000). Human rights of persons with mental disabilities: The European Convention of Human Rights. *International Journal of Law and Psychiatry, 23,* 125–159.

Gostin, L. & Gable, L. (2004). The human rights of persons with mental disabilities: A global perspective on the application of human rights principles to mental health. *Maryland Law Review, 63,* 20–121.

Grossman, C. (2008). The inter-American system of human rights: Challenges for the future. *Indiana Law Journal, 83,* 1267–1282.

Gumedze, S. (2005). Human rights and the rule of law in Swaziland. *African Human Rights Law Journal, 5,* 266–286.

Hale, B. (2007). Justice and equality in mental health law: The European experience. *International Journal of Law and Psychiatry, 30,* 18–28.

Harding, T.W. (1989). The application of the European Convention of Human Rights to the field of psychiatry. *International Journal of Law and Psychiatry, 12,* 245–262.

Hayward, D., White, T. & Kauye, F. (2010. Review of the forensic psychiatry service at Zomba Mental Hospital and a comparison of forensic psychiatry services in Malawi and Scotland. *Medicine, Science, and the Law, 50,* 67–71.

Herczegfalvy v. Austria, 15 Eur. Ct. H.R. 437 (1993).

Helfer, L.R. & Slaughter, A-M. (1997). Toward a theory of effective supranational adjudication. *Yale Law Journal, 107,* 273–391.

Heller v. Doe, 509 U.S. 312 (1993).

Hewitt, D. (1998). Mental health law. In *Human Rights Act 1998: A Practitioner's Guide,* 311 (Baker, C., ed.). London: Sweet & Maxwell.

Hewitt, D. (2001). Do human rights impact on mental health law? *New Law Journal, 15,* 1278–1278.

Hillman, A.A. (2005). Protecting mental disability rights: A success story in the Inter-American human rights system. *Human Rights Brief, 12*(3), 25–28.

Hunt, M. (2005). State obligations following a judgment from the European Court of Human Rights. In *European Court of Human Rights: Remedies and Execution of Judgments,* 25–47. (Christou, T.A. & Raymond, J.P., eds.). London: British Institute of International and Comparative Law.

In the Matter of Victor Rosario Congo, Report No. 63/99 Case 11.427 (ECUADOR April 13, 1999).

Ingstad, B. & Whyte, S.R., eds. (1995). *Disability and Culture.* Berkeley: University of California Press.

Jackson v. Indiana, 406 U.S. 715 (1972).

Jones v. United States, 463 U.S. 354 (1983).

Jones, R. & Kingdon, D. (2005). Council of Europe recommendation on human rights and psychiatry: A major opportunity for mental health services (editorial). *European Psychiatry, 20,* 461–464.

Juma, D. (2007). Access to the African Court on Human and Peoples' Rights: A case of the poacher turned gamekeeper. Essex Human Rights Law Review, *4,* 1–21.

Kamminga, M.T. (1994). Is the European Convention on Human Rights sufficiently equipped to deal with gross and systematic violations? *Netherlands Quarterly of Human Rights, 2,* 153–164.

Kanev, K. (2002). State, human rights, and mental health in Bulgaria. *New York Law School Journal of International and Comparative Law,* 21, 435–467.

Kansas v. Hendricks, 521 U.S. 346 (1997).

Kanter, A.S. (2009). The United Nations Convention on the Rights of Persons with Disabilities and its implications for the rights of elderly people under international law. *Georgia State University Law Review, 25,* 527–573.

Keener, S.R. & Vasquez, J. (2009). A life worth living: Enforcement of the right to health through the right to life in the Inter-American Court of Human Rights. *Columbia Human Rights Law Review, 40,* 595–624.

Kelley, T.A. (2007). Exporting western law to the developing world: The troubling case of Niger. George Washington International Law Review, *39,* 321–366.

Keith, L.C. & Ogundele, A. (2007). Legal systems and constitutionalism in sub-Sahara Africa: An empirical examination of colonial influences on human rights. *Human Rights Quarterly, 29,* 1065–1097.

Khushalani, Y. (1983), Human rights in Africa and Asia. *Human Rights Law Journal, 4,* 403–442.

King-Hopkins, K.D. (2000). Inter-American commission on human rights: Is its bark worse than its bite in resolving human rights disputes? *Tulsa Law Journal, 35,* 421–443.

Kingdon, D. et al. (2004). Protecting the human rights of people with mental disorder: New recommendations emerging from the Council of Europe. *British Journal of Psychiatry, 185,* 277–279.

Kiss v. Hungary, Application no. 38832/06, Council of Europe: European Court of Human Rights, May 20, 2010. Available at: http://www.unhcr.org/refworld/docid/4bf665f58.html [accessed September 7, 2010].

Kludze, A.K.P. (2008). Constitutional rights and their relationship with international human rights in Ghana. *Israel Law Review, 41,* 677–702.

Konrad, N. (2001). Redevelopment of forensic-psychiatric institutions in former East Germany. *International Journal of Law and Psychiatry, 24,* 509–526.

Korkeila, J. et al. (2003). Establishing a set of mental health indicators for Europe. *Scandinavian Journal of Public Health, 31,* 451–459.

Kruger, A. (1980). *Mental Health Law in South Africa.* Durban, SA: Butterworth.

Kumar, C.R. (2006). National Human Rights Institutions and economic, social, and cultural rights Toward the institutionalization and developmentalization of human rights. *Human Rights Quarterly, 28,* 755–779.

Kutzner v. Germany, 35 E.H.R.R. 25 ECtHR (2002).

Lawson, A. (2006). Disability, degradation, and dignity: The role of Article 3 of the European Convention on Human Rights. *Northern Ireland Legal Quarterly, 56,* 462–491.

Lessard v. Schmidt, 349 F.Supp. 1078 (E.D. Wis. 1972).

Levitt, J.I. (2010). Africa: A maker of international law. In *Africa: Mapping New Boundaries in International Law* 1–10 (Levitt, J.I., ed.). Portland, OR: Hart Publishing.

Liddicoat, J. (2009). Human rights mechanisms in small Pacific states: Implications for dialogue about regional human rights mechanisms. *Victoria University of Wellington Law Review, 40,* 279–291.

Lord, J. (2004). NGO participation in human rights law and process: Latest developments in the effort to develop an international treaty on the rights of persons with disabilities. *ILSA Journal of International & Comparative Law, 10,* 311–318.

Lurigio, A. et al. (2001). Therapeutic jurisprudence in action: Specialized courts for the mentally ill. *Judicature, 84,* 184–189.

Lynch, P. (2006). Harmonising international human rights law and domestic law and policy: The establishment and role of the Human Rights Law Resource Centre. *Melbourne Journal of International Law, 7*, 225–244.

Mabett, D. (2005). The development of rights-based social policy in the European union: The example of disability rights. *Journal of Common Market Studies, 43*, 97–120.

Macken, C. (2006). Preventive detention and the right to personal liberty and security under Article 5 ECHR. *International Journal of Human Rights, 10*, 195–217.

Mbaya, E-R. (1996). The compatibility of regional human rights systems with international standards. In *Conditions for Civilized Politics: Political Regimes and Compliance with Human Rights*, 66–89 (Eide, A. & Hagtvet, B., eds.). Oslo: Scandinavian University Press.

Mbondenyi, M.K. (2008). Improving the substance and content of civil and political rights under the African human rights system. *Lesotho Law Journal, 17*, 37–103.

Medda-Windischer, R. (2001). The jurisprudence of the European Court of Human Rights. *European Yearbook of Minority Rights, 1*, 487–534.

Megyeri v. Germany, App. No. 13770/88, 15 Eur. H.R. Rep. 584 (1992).

Melish, T.J. (2006). Rethinking the "less as more" thesis: Supranational litigation of economic, social, and cultural rights in the Americas. *New York University Journal of International Law and Politics, 39*, 171–343.

Milner, A. (1966). *M'naghten* and the witch-doctor: Psychiatry and crime in Africa. *University of Pennsylvania Law Review, 114*, 1134–1169.

Mills v. Rogers, 457 U.S. 291 (1982).

Moyo, A. (2009). Defending human rights and the rule of law by the SADC Tribunal: *Campbell* and beyond. *African Human Rights Law Journal, 9*, 590–614.

Mubangizi, J.C. (2006). Some reflections on recent and current trends in the promotion and protection of human rights in Africa: the pains and the gains. *African Human Rights Law Journal, 6*, 146–165.

Mugwanya, G.W. (2003). Human rights in Africa: Enhancing human rights through the African regional human rights system. Ardsley, NY: Transnational Publishers.

Murungu, C.B. (2009). Judgment in the first case before the African Court on Human and Peoples' Rights: A missed opportunity or mockery of international law in Africa? Available at http://papers.ssrn.com/sol3/papers.cfm?abstract_id=1526539 (last accessed May 26, 2010).

Mutua, M.W. (1995). The Banjul Charter and the African cultural fingerprint: An evaluation of the language of duties. *Virginia Journal of International Law, 35*, 339–378.

Muzuji, J.D. (2009). International human rights law and foreign case law in interpreting constitutional rights: The Supreme Court of Uganda and the death penalty question. *African Human Rights Law Journal, 9*, 576–589.

Nedopil, N. (2009). The role of forensic psychiatry in mental health systems in Europe. *Criminal Behaviour and Mental Health, 19*, 224–234.

Njenga, F. (2006). Forensic psychiatry: The African experience. *World Psychiatry, 5*, 97.

Niveau, G. & Matori, J. (2006). Psychiatric commitment: Over 50 years of case law from the European Court of Human Rights. *European Psychiatry, 21*, 427–435.

Nmehielle, V.O. (2003). The African Union and African renaissance: A new era for human rights protection in Africa? *Singapore Journal of International and Comparative Law, 2*, 412–446.

Nolan, A. (2009). Addressing economic and social rights violations by non-state actors through the role of the state: A comparison of regional approaches to the "obligation to protect." *Human Rights Law Review, 9*, 225–255.

Nowicka v. Poland, App. No. 30218/96, paras. 64–65 (Dec. 3, 2002) (Court report). Available at http://hudoc/echr.coe.int

O'Brien, T.A. et al. (1995). A one year analysis of appeals made to mental health review tribunals in New Zealand. *Australian and New Zealand Journal of Psychiatry, 29*, 661–665.

O'Connor v. Donaldson, 422 U.S. 563 (1975).

Okasha, A. (2003). Mental health services in the Arab world *Arab Studies Quarterly, 25*, 39–52.

Olmstead v. L.C., 527 U.S. 581 (1999).

Orakhelashvili, A. (2003). Restrictive interpretation of human rights treaties in the recent jurisprudence of the European Court of Human Rights. *European Journal of International Law, 14*, 529–568.

Osaka, H. (1997). Government human rights work: National Human Rights Institutions. In *Human Rights in Asian Cultures Continuity and Change*, 323–374. Osaka, Japan: Hurights.

Pan American Health Organization (2008). *PAHO and the Reformulation of Mental Health in the Americas.* http://www.paho.org/English/DD/PIN/mentalhealth_004.htm. (PAHO).

Palmer, E. (2009). Protecting socio-economic rights through the European Convention on Human Rights: Trends and developments in the European Court of Human Rights. *Erasmus Law Review, 2*, 397–425.

Parham v. J.R., 442 U.S. 584 (1979).

Pasqualucci, J.M. (2002). Advisory practice of the Inter-American Court of Human Rights: Contributing to the evolution of international human rights law. *Stanford Journal of International Law, 38*, 241–288.

Pasqualucci, J.M. (2008). The right to a dignified life (vida digna): The integration of economic and social rights with civil and political rights in the inter-American human rights system. *Hastings International and Comparative Law Review, 31*, 1–32.

Perkins, E. (2003). A new tribunal? *Psychiatry, Psychology, and Law, 10*, 113–121.

Perlin, M.L. (1998). *Mental Disability Law: Civil and Criminal* (2nd ed., Vol. 1). Newark, NJ: Lexis-Nexis.

Perlin, M.L. (1999). *Mental Disability Law: Civil and Criminal* (2nd ed.). (Vol. 2). (Newark, NJ: Lexis-Nexis Publ.).

Perlin, M.L. (2000). *Mental Disability Law: Civil and Criminal* (2nd ed.). (Vol. 3). (Newark, NJ: Lexis-Nexis Publ.).

Perlin, M.L. (2002). *Mental Disability Law: Civil and Criminal* (2nd ed.). (Vol. 4). (Newark, NJ: Lexis-Nexis Publ.).

Perlin, M.L. (2003). Therapeutic jurisprudence and outpatient commitment law: Kendra's Law as case study. *Psychology, Public Policy & Law, 9*, 183–208.

Perlin, M.L. (2007). An internet-based mental disability law program: Implications for social change in nations with developing economies. *Fordham International Law Journal, 30,* 435–454.

Perlin, M.L. (2009). Beyond Article 12: Implications of the Convention on the Rights of Persons with Disabilities for the advocacy movement in the US and abroad (with special attention to Asia). Paper presented at the annual convention of the National Association of Rights, Protection and Advocacy (Phoenix, AZ).

Perlin, M.L. (2011). "Abandoned love": The impact of *Wyatt v. Stickney* on the intersection between international human rights and domestic mental disability law. *Law and Psychology* (in press).

Perlin, M.L. & Dorfman, D.A. (1996). Is it more than "dodging lions and wastin' time"? Adequacy of counsel, questions of competence, and the judicial process in individual right to refuse treatment cases. *Psychology, Public Policy and Law, 2,* 114–136.

Perlin, M.L., Birgden, A. & Gledhill, K. (2009). "The witness who saw/He left little doubt": A comparative consideration of expert testimony in mental disability law cases in common and civil law systems. *Journal of Investigative Psychology and Offender Profiling, 6,* 59–88.

Petrila, J. et al. (2001). Preliminary observations from an evaluation of the Broward Country Mental Health Court, *Court Review, 37,* 14–22.

Poythress, N.J. et al. (2002). Perceived coercion and procedural justice in the Broward Mental Health Court. *International Journal of Law and Psychiatry, 25,* 517–533.

Prempeh, H.K. (2006). *Marbury* in Africa: Judicial review and the challenge of constitutionalism in contemporary Africa. *Tulane Law Review, 80,* 1–84.

Prempeh, H.K. (2007). Africa's "constitutionalism revival": False start or new dawn? *International Journal of Constitutional Law, 5,* 1–38.

Prior, P.M. (2007). Mentally disordered offenders and the European Court of Human Rights. *International Journal of Law and Psychiatry, 30,* 546–557.

Purohit and Moore v. The Gambia, African Commission on Human and Peoples' Rights, Comm. No. 241/2001 (2003).

Quinn, G. (1992). Civil commitment and the right to treatment under the European Convention on Human Rights. *Harvard Human Rights Journal, 5,* 1–49.

Rakevich v. Russia, ECHR Application 58973/00, at para. 44 (2004).

Rees, N. (2003). International human rights obligations and mental health review tribunals. *Psychiatry, Psychology, and Law, 10,* 33–43.

Reif, C.L. (2000). Building democratic institutions: The role of National Human Rights Institutions in good governance and human rights protection. *Harvard Human Rights Journal, 13,* 1–69.

Rennie v. Klein, 653 F.2d 836 (3d Cir. 1981).

Richardson, G. (2005). The European convention and mental health law in England and Wales: Moving beyond process? *International Journal of Law and Psychiatry, 28,* 127–139.

Riggins v. Nevada, 504 U.S. 127 (1992).

Rivers v. Katz, 67 N.Y.2d 485, 504 N.Y.S.2d 74 (1986).

Robbins, M. (2005). Powerful states, customary law, and the erosion of human rights through regional enforcement. *California Western International Law Journal, 35,* 275–302.

Rogers v. Okin, 634 F.2d 650 (1st Cir. 1980).

Salize, H.J. & Dressing, H. (2004). Epidemiology of involuntary placement of mentally ill people across the European Union. *British Journal of Psychiatry, 184,* 163–168.

Salize, H.J. & Dressing, H. (2005). Admission of mentally disordered offenders to specialized forensic care in fifteen European Union member states. *Social Psychiatry and Psychiatric Epidemiology, 42,* 336–342.

Salize, H.J., Lepping, P. & Dressing, H. (2005). How harmonized are we? Forensic mental health legislation and service provision in the European Union. *Criminal Behaviour and Mental Health, 15,* 191–195.

Sarkar, S.P. & Adshead, G. (2005). Black robes and white coats: Who will win the new mental health tribunals? *British Journal of Psychiatry, 186,* 94–96.

Schoenberger, A. (2006). The not so great writ: The European Court of Human Rights finds habeas corpus an inadequate remedy: Should American courts reexamine the writ? *Catholic University Law Review, 56,* 47–66.

Sharma, S. (2003). Human rights of mental patients in India: A global perspective. *Current Opinion in Psychiatry, 16,* 547–551.

Sinha, M.K. (2004). Establishment of the African Court of Human Rights: A reality? *Indian Journal of International Law, 44,* 160–166.

Stacy, H.M. (2009). *Human Rights for the 21st Century: Sovereignty, Civil Society, Culture.* Stanford, CA: Stanford University Press.

Stanev v. Bulgaria (ECHR application no. 36760/06). Accessible at http://mdac.info/en/social-care-institution-case-sent-grand-chamber-eu.

Szmukler, G., Daw, R. & Dawson, J. (2010). A model law fusing incapacity and mental health legislation. *Journal of Mental Health Law, 20,* 11–24.

Tait, D. (2003). The ritual environment of the mental health tribunal hearing: Inquiries and reflections. *Psychiatry, Psychology, and Law, 10,* 91–96.

Taiwo, E.A. (2009). Enforcement of fundamental rights and the standing rules under the Nigerian Constitution: A need for a more liberal provision. *African Human Rights Law Journal, 9,* 546–576.

Thorold, O. (1996). The implications of the European Convention on Human Rights for United Kingdom mental health legislation. *European Human Rights Law Review, 6,* 619–636.

Twinomugisha, B.K. (2009). The role of the judiciary in the promotion of democracy in Uganda. *African Human Rights Journal, 9,* 1–22.

Udombana, N.J. (2000). Toward the African Court on Human and Peoples' Rights: Better late than never. *Yale Human Rights and Development Law Journal, 3,* 45–111.

Ugochukwu, B. (2010). "Africanizing" human rights: Nigeria and Kenya Constitutions in context. Accessible at http://papers.ssrn.com/sol3/papers.cfm?abstract_id=1691004.

Van der Leer v. Netherlands, App. No. 11509/85, 12 Eur. H.R. Rep. 567 (1990).

Varbanov v. Bulgaria, Eur. Ct. H.R. 31365/96, § 43–53 (2000).

Vess, J. (2005). Preventive detention versus civil commitment: Alternative policies for public protection in New Zealand and California. *Psychiatry, Psychology, and Law, 12,* 357–366.

Viljoen, F. & Louw, L. (2007). State compliance with the recommendations of the African Commission on Human and Peoples' Rights. *American Journal of International Law, 101,* 1–34.
Vitek v. Jones, 445 U.S. 480 (1980).
Wachenfeld, M.G. (1991). The human rights of the mentally ill in Europe. *Nordic Journal of International Law, 60,* 109–165.
Walker, A. (2009, April 29). Locking up Nigeria's "civil lunatics." *BBC News: Africa.*
Weston, B.H., Lukes, R.A. & Hnatt, K.M. (1987). Regional human rights regimes: A comparison and appraisal. *Vanderbilt Journal of Transnational Law, 20,* 585–637.
Wicks, E. (2001). The right to refuse treatment under the European Convention of Human Rights. *Medical Law Review, 9,* 17–40.
Wildhaber, L. (2007). The European Convention on Human Rights and international law. *International and Comparative Law Quarterly, 56,* 217–231.
Winick, B.J. (2002). Therapeutic jurisprudence and the treatment of people with mental illness in Eastern Europe: Construing international human rights law. *New York Law School Journal of International and Comparative Law, 21,* 537–572.
Winick, B. (2003). Outpatient commitment: A therapeutic jurisprudence analysis. *Psychology, Public Policy and Law, 9,* 107–141.
Wright, R. (2006). Finding an impetus for institutional change at the African Court on Human and Peoples' Rights. *Berkeley Journal of International Law, 24,* 463–498.
Weller, P. (2009). Human rights and social justice: The Convention on the Rights of Persons with Disabilities and the quiet revolution in international law. *Public Space: The Journal of Law and Social Justice, 4,* 74–91.
Williams, V. (2006). The challenge for Australian jurisdictions to guarantee free qualified representation before mental health tribunals and boards of review: Learning from the Tasmanian experience? (unpublished manuscript, on file with author).
Wilner, G.M. (1995/1996). Reflections on regional human rights law. *Georgia Journal of International and Comparative Law, 25,* 407–426.
Washington v. Harper (1990). 494 U.S. 210.
Winterwerp v. Netherlands, 2 EHRR 387 (1979).
Wyatt v. Aderholt, 503 F.2d 1305 (5th Cir. 1974).
Wyatt v. Stickney, 325 F.Supp. 781 (M.D. Ala. 1971).
X v. UK, 46 Eur. Ct. H.R. (ser. A) (1981). Reprinted in *Eur. Hum. Rts. Rev., 4,* 188 (1981).
Ximenes-Lopes v. Brazil (2006 Inter-Am. Ct. H.R. (ser. C) No. 149 (July 4, 2006).
Youngberg v. Romeo, 457 U.S. 307 (1982).
Zinermon v. Burch, 494 U.S. 113 (1990).
Zuckerberg, J. (2007). International human rights for mentally ill persons: The Ontario experience, *International Journal of Law and Psychiatry, 30,* 512–529.

Chapter 4

Addington v. Texas, 441 U.S. 418 (1979).
Alexander, G. (1993). Big mother: The state's use of mental health experts in dependency cases. *Pacific Law Journal, 24,* 1465–1496.

Alexander, G. (1997). International human rights protection against political abuses. *Santa Clara Law Review, 37,* 387–426.

Alvarez, J. (2003). The new dispute settlers: (Half) truths and consequences. *Texas International Law Journal, 38,* 405–421.

Americans with Disabilities Act, 42 U.S.C. §§ 12101 et seq. (1990).

Amnesty International press release, Bulgaria: Disabled Women Condemned to "Slow Death." (2001). AI-Index: EUR 15/002/2001.

Amnesty International, Romania, Memorandum to the Government Concerning Inpatient Psychiatric Treatment (2004). available at http://www.web.amnesty.org/library/print/engeur390032004.

Appelbaum, P.S. (2001). Law and psychiatry: Abuses of law and psychiatry in China. *Psychiatric Services, 52,* 1297–1298.

Baker, J.D. (1987). Nonimputability in Soviet criminal law: The Soviet approach to the insanity plea. *Law & Psychology Review, 11,* 55–102.

Bliss, J. (2002). Symposium: International human rights law and the institutional treatment of persons with mental disabilities: The case of Hungary. *New York Law School Journal of International and Comparative Law,* 21, 361–387.

Bloch, S. & Reddaway, P. (1977). *Psychiatric Terror: How Soviet Psychiatry Is Used to Suppress Dissent.* New York City: Basic Books.

Bloch, S. & Reddaway, P. (1984). *Soviet Psychiatric Abuse: The Shadow over World Psychiatry.* Boulder, CO: Westview Press.

Bloch, S. & Reddaway, P. (1985). Psychiatrists and dissenters in the Soviet Union. In *The Breaking of Bodies and Minds: Torture, Psychiatric Abuse, and the Health Professions,* 147–158 (Stover, E. & Nightingale, E. O., eds.). New York: W.H. Freeman & Co.

Bloche, M.G. (2001). Caretakers and collaborators. *Cambridge Quarterly of Healthcare Ethics, 10,* 275–284.

Bonnie, R. (1990). Soviet psychiatry and human rights: Reflections on the report of the U.S. delegation. *Law, Medicine, and Health Care, 18,* 123–131.

Bonnie, R.J. (1994). Law of the Russian Federation on psychiatric care and guarantees of citizens' rights in its provision. *Journal of Russian and East European Psychiatry, 27,* 69–96.

Bonnie R. (2002). Political abuse of psychiatry in the Soviet Union and in China: Complexities and controversies, *Journal of the American Academy of Psychiatry & Law, 30,* 136–144.

Bonnie, R.J. & Polubinskaya, S.V. (1999). Unraveling Soviet psychiatry. *Journal of Contemporary Legal Issues, 10,* 279–298.

Boyadjiev, B. & Onchev, G. (2007). Legal and cultural aspects of involuntary psychiatric treatment regulation in post-totalitarian milieu: The Bulgarian perspective. *European Journal of Psychiatry, 21,* 179–188.

Chaney, C. (2005). The despotic State Department in refugee law: Creating legal fictions to support Falun Gong asylum claims. *Asian Pacific Law and Policy Journal, 6,* 130–173.

Chen, J. (2009). Modernisation, westernisation, and globalization: Legal transplant in China. In *One Country, Two Systems, Three Legal Orders,* 91–113 (Olivera, J.C. & Cardinal, P., eds.). Berlin: Springer-Verlag.

Children in Russia's Institutions: Human Rights and Opportunities for Reform. (1999). Mental Disability Rights International. Retrieved September 30, 2010, from http://www.mdri.org/mdri-reports-publications.html.

Chu, T. (2005, July). *Justice against Crime of Genocide.* Paper presented at the International Academy of Law and Mental Health, Paris.

City of Cleburne v. Cleburne Living Center, 573 U.S. 432 (1985).

Congo v. Ecuador, Case 11.427, Inter-Am. C.H.R., OEA/Ser. L/V/II. 95 Doc. 7 revat 475, para. 111 (1998).

Courtis, C. (2002–2003). Disability rights in Latin America and international cooperation. *Southwestern Journal of Law and Trade in the Americas, 9*, 109–129.

Dangerous minds: Political psychiatry in China today and its origins in the Mao era. *Human Rights Watch.* Retrieved September 24, 2010, from http://hrw.org/reports/2002/china02.

Degener, T. (2000). International disability law—A new legal subject on the rise: The interregional experts' meeting in Hong Kong, December 13–17, 1999. *Berkeley Journal of International Law, 18*, 180–195.

Degener, T. & Quinn, G. (2002). A survey of international, comparative and regional disability law reform. In *Disability Rights Law & Policy: International Perspectives*, 3–129 (Breslin, M.L. & Yee, S., eds.). Leiden, The Netherlands: Hotei Publishing.

Dhir, A.A. (2008). Relationships of force: Exploring the legal and social issues surrounding mental disability. *Windsor Review of Legal and Social Issues, 25*, 103–112.

ECHR. (1998). Convention for the Protection of Human Rights and Fundamental Freedoms, as amended by Protocol No. 11, Nov. 1, 1998. Retrieved October 11, 2010, from http://www.echr.coe.int/NR/rdonlyres/D5CC24A7DC13–4318-B457–5C9014916D7A/0/EnglishAnglais.pdf

ECHR. (1998). European Convention for the Protection of Human Rights and Fundamental Freedoms, (ETS No. 5), 213 U.N.T.S 222, signed at Rome, Nov. 4, 1950, entered into force Sept. 3, 1953, as amended by Protocol No. 11, entered into force Nov. 1, 1998.

European Union Calls on Turkey to Improve Rights of People with Mental Disabilities. (2006). Reprinted at http://www.disabilityworld.org/12–01_06/mdriturkey.shtml (last visited September 25, 2010).

Finn, P. (2006, September 30). In Russia, psychiatry is again a tool against dissent. *The Washington Post.* Retrieved September 24, 2010, from http://www.washingtonpost.com/wp-dyn/content/article/2006/09/29/AR2006092901592_pf.html.

Foucault, M. (1965). *Madness and Civilization: A History of Insanity in the Age of Reason* (Howard, R., trans.). London, UK: Tavistock Publications.

GA Resolution. (Dec. 14, 1978). 33/53, U.N. *GAOR*, 33d Sess., U.N. Doc. A/33/475.

Galli, V. & Lu, S.Y. (2004). Mental health policy in China; The persecution of the Falun Gong. In *Mental Health: Global Policies and Human Rights*, 149–165 (Morrall, P. & Hazelton, M., eds.). London, UK: Whurr Publishers.

Geisinger, A. & Stein. M.A. (2008). Rational choice, reputation, and human rights treaties. *Michigan Law Review, 106*, 1129–1142.

Gostin, L.O. & Gable, L. (2004). The human rights of persons with mental disabilities: A global perspective on the application of human rights principles to mental health. *Maryland Law Review, 63*, 20–121.

Hickling, F.W. (2002). The political misuse of psychiatry: An African-Caribbean perspective. *Journal of the American Academy of Psychiatry and Law, 30,* 112–119.
Human Rights & Mental Health: Mexico. (2000). Mental Disability Rights International. Retrieved September 30, 2010, from http://www.mdri.org/mdri-reports-publications.html.
Human Rights & Mental Health: Hungary. (1997). Mental Disability Rights International. Retrieved September 30, 2010, from http://www.mdri.org/mdri-reports-publications.html.
Human Rights & Mental Health: Uruguay. (1995). Mental Disability Rights International. Retrieved September 30, 2010, from http://www.mdri.org/mdri-reports-publications.html.
Jones, D.K. (2004). The neglected role of international altruistic investment in the Chinese transition economy. *George Washington International Law Review, 36,* 71–146.
Kahn, J. (2006, March 17). Sane Chinese put in asylum, doctors find. *New York Times.* Retrieved September 24, 2010, from http://www.nytimes.com.
Kanev, K. (2002). State, human rights, and mental health in Bulgaria. *New York Law School Journal of International and Comparative Law, 21,* 435–467.
Kanter, A.S. (2003). The globalization of disability rights law. *Syracuse Journal of International Law and Commerce, 30,* 241–269.
Kelley, T.A. (2007). Exporting western law to the developing world: The troubling case of Niger. *George Washington International Law Review, 39,* 321–366.
Kumar, C.J. (2003). Moving beyond constitutionalization and judicial protection of human rights—Building on the Hong Kong experience of civil society empowerment. *Loyola of Los Angeles International & Comparative Law Review, 26,* 281–314.
LaFreniere, S. (2010, November 10). Life in shadows for mentally ill in China. *New York Times.*
Lee, S. & Kleinman, A. (2002). Psychiatry in its political and professional contexts: A response to Robin Munro. *Journal of the American Academy of Psychiatry and Law, 30,* 120–125.
Lewis, O. (personal communication, February 28, 2006).
Leavy, M.J. (2004). Discrediting human rights abuse as an "act of state": A case study on the repression of the Falun Gong in China and commentary on international human rights law in U.S. courts. *Rutgers Law Journal, 35,* 749–823.
Loue, S. (2002). The involuntary civil commitment of mentally ill persons in the United States and Romania: A comparative analysis. *Journal of Legal Medicine, 23,* 211–250.
Lu, S.Y. & Galli, V.B. (2002). Psychiatric abuse of Falun Gong practitioners in China. *Journal of the American Academy of Psychiatry and Law, 30,* 126–130.
McMurrow, J.A. (2010). Professional responsibility in an uncertain profession: Legal ethics in China. *Akron Law Journal, 43,* 1081–1105.
Memorandum to the Government Concerning Inpatient Psychiatric Treatment (2004). *Amnesty International.* Retrieved September 23, 2010, from http://www.web.amnesty.org/library/print/engeur390032004
Mental Disability Rights International (2005). *Behind Closed Doors: Human Rights Abuses in the Psychiatric Facilities, Orphanages and Rehabilitation Centers of Turkey.* Retrieved October 11, 2010, from www.mdri.org/projects/turkey

Minkowitz, T. (2007). The United Nations Convention on the Rights of Persons with Disabilities and the right to be free from nonconsensual psychiatric interventions. *Syracuse Journal of International Law and Commerce, 34,* 405–427.

Moncada, A.C. (1994). Involuntary commitment and the use of seclusion and restraint in Uruguay: A comparison with the United Nations Principles for the Protection of Persons with Mental Illness. *University of Miami Inter-American Law Review, 25,* 589–620.

Morris, G. & Meloy, J.R. (1993). Out of mind? Out of sight: The uncivil commitment of permanently incompetent criminal defendants. *University of California Davis Law Review, 27,* 1–78.

Munro, R. (2000). Judicial psychiatry in China and its political abuse. *Columbia Journal of Asian Law, 14,* 1–128.

Munro, R. (2002). Political psychiatry in post-Mao China and its origins in the cultural revolution. *Journal of the American Academy of Psychiatry and Law, 30,* 97–106.

Neumann, J. (1991). Psychiatry in eastern Europe today: Mental health status, policies, and practices. *American Journal of Psychiatry, 148,* 1386–1389.

Ochberg, F.M. & Gunn, J. (1980). The psychiatrist and the policeman. *Psychiatric Annals, 10,* 35.

O'Connor v. Donaldson, 422 U.S. 563 (1975).

Perlin, M.L. (1998a). *Mental Disability Law: Civil and Criminal* (2nd ed., Vol. 1). Newark, NJ: Lexis-Nexis.

Perlin, M.L. (1998b). "Where the winds hit heavy on the borderline:" Mental disability law, theory and practice, us and them. *Loyola of Los Angeles Law Review, 31,* 775–793.

Perlin, M.L. (1999)."Half-wracked prejudice leaped forth": Sanism, pretextuality, and why and how mental disability law developed as it did. *Journal of Contemporary Legal Issues, 10,* 3–36.

Perlin, M.L. (2000a). "For the misdemeanor outlaw": The impact of the ADA on the institutionalization of criminal defendants with mental disabilities. *Alabama Law Review, 52,* 193–239.

Perlin, M.L. (2000b). "I ain't gonna work on Maggie's Farm no more": Institutional segregation, community treatment, the ADA, and the promise of Olmstead v. L.C. *Thomas M. Cooley Law Review, 17,* 53–90.

Perlin, M.L. (2000c). *The Hidden Prejudice: Mental Disability on Trial.* Washington, DC: American Psychological Press.

Perlin, M.L. (2000d). *Mental Disability Law: Civil and Criminal* (2nd ed., Vol. 2). Newark, NJ: Lexis-Nexis.

Perlin, M.L. (2000e). "Their promises of paradise:" Will *Olmstead v. L.C.* resuscitate the constitutional least restrictive alternative principle in mental disability law? *Houston Law Review, 37,* 999–1053.

Perlin, M.L. (2001–2002). "What's good is bad, what's bad is good, you'll find out when you reach the top, you're on the bottom": Are the Americans with Disabilities Act (and *Olmstead v. L.C.*) anything more than "Idiot Wind,"? *University of Michigan Journal of Law Reform, 35,* 235–261.

Perlin, M.L. (2002). Chimes of freedom: International human rights and institutional mental disability law. *New York Law School Journal of International and Comparative Law,* 21, 423–433.

Perlin, M.L. (2002–2003). "Things have changed": Looking at non-institutional mental disability law through the sanism filter. *New York Law School Law Review, 46,* 535–545.

Perlin, M.L. (2003). "She breaks just like a little girl": Neonaticide, the insanity defense, and the irrelevance of "ordinary common sense." *William and Mary Journal of Women and the Law, 10,* 1–31.

Perlin, M.L., et al. (2006a). *International Human Rights and Comparative Mental Disability Law: Cases and Materials.* Durham, NC: Carolina Academic Press.

Perlin M.L. (2006b). *International Human Rights And Comparative Mental Disability Law: Documents Supplement.* Durham, NC: Carolina Academic Press.

Perlin M.L. (2006c). International human rights and comparative mental disability law: The role of institutional psychiatry in the suppression of political dissent. *Israel Law Review, 39,* 69–97.

Perlin, M.L. (2007). International human rights and comparative mental disability law: The universal factors. *Syracuse Journal of International Law & Commerce, 34,* 333–357.

Perlin, M.L. (2008). "I might need a good lawyer, could be your funeral, my trial": Global clinical legal education and the right to counsel in civil commitment cases. *Washington University Journal of Law and Policy, 28,* 241–264.

Perlin, M.L. (2009). "A change is gonna come": The implications of the United Nations Convention on the Rights of Persons with Disabilities for the domestic practice of constitutional mental disability law. *Northern Illinois University Law Review, 29,* 483–498.

Physicians for Human Rights. (2006). *Dual Loyalty & Human Rights in Health Professional Practice: Proposed Guidelines and Institutional Mechanisms.* Retrieved September 24, 2010, from http://www. phrusa. org/healthrights/dl. html.

Principles for the Protection of Persons with Mental Illness and for the Improvement of Mental Health Care, G.A. Res. 119, U.N. GAOR, 46th Sess., Supp. No. 49, Annex, pp. 188–92, U.N. Doc. A/46/49 (1991). (MI Principles.)

Ramacharan, B.G. (1991). Strategies for the international protection of human rights in the 1990s. *Human Rights Quarterly, 13,* 155–169.

Robitscher, J. (1980). *The Powers of Psychiatry.* Chicago: Houghton Mifflin.

Rosenthal, E. et al. (2002). *Not on the Agenda: Human Rights of People with Mental Disabilities in Kosovo.* Mental Disability Rights International. Retrieved September 24, 2010, from http://www.mdri.org/mdri-reports-publications. html

Rosenthal, E. (2002). Symposium transcript: The application of international human rights law to institutional mental disability law. *New York Law School Journal of International and Comparative Law, 21,* 387–397.

Rosenthal, E. &. Rubenstein, L.S. (1993). International human rights advocacy under the Principles for the Protection of Persons with Mental Illness. *International Journal of Law & Psychiatry, 16,* 257–300.

RSFSR arts. 58–61 (Criminal Code). (1962). Reprinted in *The Soviet Codes of Law* 88–89 (Berman, H.J. &. Spindler, J.W., trans.; Simons, W.B., ed.). Cambridge, MA: Harvard University Press.

RSFSR arts. 410–413 (Code of Criminal Procedure). (1962). Reprinted In *The Soviet Codes of Law* 315–316 (Berman, H.J. &. Spindler, J.W., trans.; Simons, W.B., ed.). Cambridge, MA: Harvard University Press.

Russia's guardianship system challenged at the European Court of Human Rights. (2008). Mental Disability Advocacy Center. Retrieved September 30, 2010, from http://www.mdac.info/content/europes-highest-human-rights-court-holds-russia-violated-rights-man-mental-health-disabiliti.

Smith, C. (2005, September 28). Abuse of mentally ill is reported in Turkey. *New York Times.* Retrieved September 24, 2010, from http: //www.nytimes.com

Smith, T.C. & Ouszreuk, T.A. (1996). *No Asylum: State Psychiatric Repression in the Former USSR.* New York: New York University Press.

State v. Fields, 390 A. 2d 574 (N.J. 1978).

Stacy, H.M. (2009). *Human Rights for the 21st Century: Sovereignty, Civil Society, Culture.* Stanford, CA: Stanford University Press.

Vardanyan, A., Dorfman, D.A. & Awmiller, C. (2004). Mental Disability Advocacy Center, Mental Health Law of the Kyrgyz. Republic and Its Implementation, § 4.1.1 (2004), MDAC Report. *Eurasia Health.* Retrieved September 27, 2010, from http://www.eurasiahealth.org/health/resources/81502/

Winick, B. (2002). Therapeutic Jurisprudence and the Treatment of People with Mental Illness in Eastern Europe: Construing International Human Rights Law. *New York Law School Journal of International and Comparative Law, 21,* 537, 556–559.

Winterwerp v. The Netherlands, 33 Eur. Ct. H.R. (ser. A) (1979). http://www.mdac.info/news_reports/news_reports.htm (last visited September 25, 2010).

Van Voreb, R. (2002). Comparing Soviet and Chinese psychiatry. *Journal of the American Academy of Psychiatry and Law, 30,* 131–135.

Zhu, G. (2010). Prosecuting "evil cults": A critical examination of law regarding freedom of religious belief in mainland China. *Human Rights Quarterly, 32,* 471–501.

Chapter 5

Ahn, K-W. (2007). Korean legal system and the human rights of persons with mental disorders: Current state and challenges. *Journal of Korean Law, 7,* 1–23.

Ake v. Oklahoma, 470 U.S. 68 (1985).

Alem, A. (2000). Human rights and psychiatric care in Africa with particular reference to the Ethiopian situation. *Acta Psychiatrica Scandinavica, 101,* 93–96.

Alem, A., Jacobsson, L. & Hanlon, C. (2008). Community-based mental health care in Africa: Mental health workers' views. *World Psychiatry, 7,* 54–57.

Ales, E. (2003). Disability in Italy: The legal concept. *Comparative Labor Law and Policy Journal, 24,* 609–630.

Alhamed, A.M. (2006). Forensic psychiatry in Saudi Arabia: An overview. *American Journal of Forensic Psychiatry, 27,* 71–79.

Americans with Disabilities Act of 1990, 104 Stat. 328, 42 U.S.C. § 12101 (2007).

Amnesty International, Romania (2004). Memorandum to the government concerning inpatient psychiatric treatment. In Perlin, M.L. et al (2006). *International Human Rights and Comparative Mental Disability Law: Cases and Materials* 849–855. (Durham, NC: Carolina Academic Press) ("Romanian Memorandum".

Appelbaum, A. (1998). Present at the creation: Mental health law in Eastern Europe and the Soviet Union. *Psychiatric Services, 49,* 1299–1300.

Arikan, R. et al. (2007). Civil commitment in Turkey: Reflections on a bill drafted by psychiatrists. *International Journal of Law and Psychiatry, 30,* 29–35.

Aviram, U., Guy, D. & Sykes, I. (2007). Risk avoidance and missed opportunities in mental health reform: The case of Israel. *International Journal of Law and Psychiatry, 30,* 163–181.

Babu, P.S. (2004). Rights of the disabled. *Indian Journal of Human rights, 8,* 79–97.

Bagenstos, S.R. (2004). The future of disability law. *Yale Law Journal, 114,* 1–83.

Barak, P. & Gordon, H. (2002). Forensic psychiatry in Israel. *The Psychiatrist, 26,* 143–145.

Bartlett, P. (2010). Thinking about the rest of the world: Mental health and rights outside the "first world." In *Re-thinking Rights-Based Mental Health Law,* 397–418 (McSherry, B. & Weller, P., eds.). Oxford, UK: Hart Publishing.

Bauer, A. et al. (2005). Regional psychiatric boards in Israel: Expectations and realities. *International Journal of Law and Psychiatry, 28,* 661–669.

Bauer, A. et al. (2007). Trends in involuntary psychiatric hospitalization in Israel, 1991–2000. *International Journal of Law and Psychiatry, 30,* 60–70.

Bindman, J., Maingay, S. & Szmukler, G. (2003). The Human Rights Act and mental health legislation. *British Journal of Psychiatry, 182,* 91–94.

Birmontiene, T. (1996). Patient's rights legislation in Lithuania. *European Journal of Health Law, 3,* 85–94.

Bottomley, S. (1987). Mental health law reform and psychiatric deinstitutionalization: The issues in New South Wales. *International Journal of Law and Psychiatry, 10,* 369–382.

Boyd-Caine, T. & Chappell, D. (2005). The forensic patient population in New South Wales. *Current Issues in Criminal Justice, 17,* 5–29.

Browne, N. et al. (2006). Capital punishment and mental health issues: Global examples. *Saint Louis University Public Law Review, 25,* 383–407.

Burti, L. & Benson, P.R. (1996). Psychiatric reform in Italy: Developments since 1978. *International Journal of Law and Psychiatry, 19,* 373–390.

Byrnes, A. (2008). The Disability Discrimination Ordinance, the UN Convention on the Rights of Persons with Disabilities, and beyond: Achievements and challenges after ten years of Hong Kong anti-discrimination legislation. *Bepress Legal Repository.* Retrieved September 25, 2010, from http://law.bepress.com/unswwps/flrps08/art13

Chacón, J.M. (2010). A diversion of attention? Immigration courts and the adjudication of Fourth and Fifth Amendment rights. *Duke Law Journal, 59,* 1563–1633.

Chappell, D. (2004). Protecting the human rights of the mentally ill: Contemporary challenges for the Australian criminal justice system. *Psychiatry, Psychology, and Law, 11,* 13–22.

Clack, M. (2003). Caught between hope and despair: An analysis of the Japanese criminal justice system. *Denver Journal of International Law & Policy, 31,* 525–550.

Connelly, U.B. (2009). Disability rights in Cambodia: Using the Convention on the Rights of People with Disabilities to expose human rights violations. *Pacific Rim Law & Policy Journal, 18*, 123–153.

Constitutional Rights of the Mentally Ill, Hearing before the Senate Subcomm. on Constitutional Rights of the Judiciary, 87th Cong., 2d Sess. 40–42 (1961). Statement of Albert Deutsch.

Cremin, K. (2007). *General Hospital Psychiatric Units and Rehabilitation Centres in India: Do Law and Public Policy Present Barriers to Community-Based Mental Health Services?* Pune, India: Centre for Advocacy in Mental Health.

Daffern, M., Mayer, M.M. & Martin, M. (2003). A preliminary investigation into patterns of aggression in an Australian forensic psychiatric hospital. *Journal of Forensic Psychiatry & Psychology, 14*, 67–84.

Dawson, J. & Kämpf, A. (2006). Incapacity principles in mental health laws in Europe. *Psychology, Public Policy, and Law, 12*, 310–331.

de Almeida, J.N.C. & Horvitz-Lennon, M. (2010). An overview of mental health care reforms in Latin America and the Caribbean. *Psychiatric Services, 61*, 218–221.

Developmental Disabilities Bill of Rights Act, 42 U.S.C. § 6010 (1976).

Dhir, A. (2005). Human rights treaty drafting through the lens of mental disability: The proposed international convention on protection and promotion of the rights and dignity of persons with disabilities. *Stanford Journal of International Law, 41*, 181–216.

Dixon v. Weinberger, 405 F. Supp. 974 (D.D.C. 1975).

Dressing, H. & Salize, H.J. (2004). Compulsory admission of mentally ill patients in European Union member states. *Social Psychiatry and Psychiatric Epidemiology, 39*, 797–803.

Dressing, H. & Salize, H.J. (2006). Forensic psychiatric assessment in European Union member states. *Acta Psychiatrica Scandinavica, 114*, 282–289.

Edrmane, A. (2009). *Report on the Implementation of the World Health Organisation's Mental Health Declaration and Action Plan in Latvia.* Riga, Latvia: ZELDA Resource Center.

Erdmane, E. & Leimane-Veldmeijere, I. (2009, #4). Key developments in mental disability advocacy during January–September 2009. *ZELDA: Resource Center for People with Disability*, 1–5. ("Newsletter Zelda").

Estonian Soviet Socialist Republic Mental Health Act. (1997). *Psühhiaatrilise abi seadus [Mental Health Act] (Est.).* Retrieved September 25, 2010, http://www.legaltext.ee/text/en/X1050K3.htm

European Court of Human Rights hears first social care institution case. (2009, November 11). Mental Disability Advocacy Center. Retrieved September 25, 2010, from http://www.mdac.info/en/european-court-human-rights-hears-first-social-car

European Court of Human Rights upholds the right to vote of persons with disabilities. (2010, May 20). Mental Disability Advocacy Center. Retrieved September 25, 2010, from http://www.mdac.info/en/european-court-human-rights-upholds-right-vote-per

Fallberg, L.H. (2000). Patients rights in the Nordic countries. *European Journal of Health Law, 7*, 123–143.

Ferleger, D. (2010). The constitutional right to community services. *Georgia State University Law Review, 26,* 763–801.

Fischer, J. (2006). A comparative look at the right to refuse treatment for involuntarily hospitalized persons with a mental illness. *Hastings International and Comparative Law Review, 29,* 153–186.

Fisherow, S.H. (2005). Follow the leader? : Japan should abolish the execution of the mentally retarded in the wake of *Atkins v. Virginia. Pacific Rim Law & Policy Journal, 14,* 455–484.

Flynn, M. (2010). *Olmstead* plans revisited: Lessons learned from the U.N. Convention on the Rights of Persons with Disabilities. *Law and Inequality, 28,* 407–437.

Gable L. & Gostin, L.O. (2009). Mental health as a human right. In *Realizing the Right to Health: Swiss Human Rights Book* 249–261 (Vol. 3) (Clapham, A. et al., eds.). Zurich: Ruffer & Rub.

GA Resolution. 119. (1991). Principles for the Protection of Persons with Mental Illness and for the Improvement of Mental Health Care, G.A. Res. 119, princ. 9(1), U.N. GAOR, 46th Sess., Supp. No. 49, Annex, U.N. Doc. A/46/49 (Dec. 17, 1991).

Garpenby, P. (1993). From ideology to reality: Mental health care in Sweden. *European Journal of Public Health, 3,* 296–298.

Geist, F., Petermann, B. & Widhammer, V. (2003). Disability law in Germany. *Comparative Labor Law and Policy Journal, 24,* 563–608.

Getger, J.E. (2009). Untold truths: The exclusion of enforced sterilization from the Peruvian Truth Commission's final report. *Boston College Third World Law Journal, 29,* 1–34.

Global Initiative on Psychiatry. (2007). *Annual Report 2007.* Retrieved September 25, 2010, from http://www.gip-global.org/images/40/389.pdf

Goldman, H.H., Morrisey, J.P. & Bachrach, L.L. (1983). Deinstitutionalization in international perspective: Variations on a theme. *International Journal of Mental Health, 11,* 153–165.

Goldsmith, R. (2004, July 7). Czech man's week in a cage. *BBC News.* Retrieved September 25, 2010, from http://news.bbc.co.uk/2/hi/programmes/crossing_continents/3873123.stm

Gombos, G. (2002). Symposium: International Human Rights Law and the Institutional Treatment of Persons with Mental Disabilities: The Case of Hungary. *New York Law School Journal of International and Comparative Law, 21,* 361–387.

Gostin, L. (1987). Human rights in mental health: A proposal for five international standards based upon the Japanese experience. *International Journal of Law and Psychiatry, 10,* 353–366.

Gostin, L.O. (2008a). Meeting basic needs of the world's least healthy people: Towards a framework Convention on Global Health. *Georgetown Law Journal, 96,* 331–392.

Gostin, L.O. (2008b). "Old" and "new" institutions for persons with mental illness: Treatment, punishment, or preventive confinement? *Public Health, 122,* 906–913.

Guo, Z. (2010), Approaching visible justice: Procedural safeguards for mental examinations in China's capital cases. *Hastings International & Comparative Law Review, 33,* 21–54.

Hakkinen U. & Lehto, J. (2005). Reform, change, and continuity in Finnish health care. *Journal of Health Politics, Policy and Law, 30,* 79–96.

Helander, B. (1995). Disability as incurable illness: Health, process and personhood in Southern Somalia. In *Disability and Culture*, 73–93 (Ingstad, B. & Whyte, S.R., eds.). Berkeley: University of California Press.

Heyer, K.C. (2002). The ADA on the road: Disability rights in Germany. *Law and Social Inquiry, 27*, 723–760.

Hillman, A. (2005). Human rights and deinstitutionalization. *Pan American Journal of Public Health, 18*, 374–379.

Hollingsworth, E.J. (1992). Falling through the cracks: Care of the chronically mentally ill in the United States, Germany, and the United Kingdom. *Journal of Health Politics, Policy, and Law, 17*, 899–928.

Hugg, P.R. (2010). Accession aspirations degenerate: A new chapter for Turkey and the EU. *Washington University Global Studies Law Review, 9*, 225–281.

Hungary: Man Wins Historic Psychiatric Detention Case at European Court of Human Rights (2006). Accessible at http://www.dpi.org/lang-en/resources/topics_detail?page=735 ("Man Wins").

Jackson v. Indiana, 406 U.S. 715 (1972).

Jenkins, R. et al. (2010a). Mental health and the development agenda in sub-Saharan Africa. *Psychiatric Services, 61*, 229–234.

Jenkins, R. et al. (2010b). Rehabilitation and social inclusion of people with mental illness in Russia. *Psychiatric Services, 61*, 222–224.

K, Y, and *W v. Secretary for Justice*, H.K.C. 796 (2000).

Kala, A.K. (2008). Mental health legislation in developing countries with special reference to South Asia: Problems and solutions. *Global Social Policy, 8*, 308–311.

Kallert, T.W., Rymaszewska, J. & Torres-Gonzalez, F. (2007). Differences of legal regulations concerning involuntary psychiatric hospitalization in twelve European countries: implications for clinical practice. *International Journal of Forensic Mental Health, 6*, 197–207.

Kaltiala-Heino, R. & Fröjd, S. (2007). Severe mental disorder as a basic commitment criteria for minors. *International Journal of Law and Psychiatry, 30*, 81–94.

Kaltiala-Heino, R. & Välimäki, M. (2002). Involuntary commitment in health care: An analysis of the status and rights of involuntarily treated psychiatric patients in comparison with patients treated involuntarily under other acts. *European Journal of Health Law, 8*, 299–316.

Kaltiala-Heino, R. et al. (2000). Coercion and restrictions in psychiatric inpatient treatment. *European Psychiatry, 15*, 213–219.

Kammel, K.P. (2008). Rebuilding the mental health system in Iraq in the context of transitional justice. *DePaul Journal of Health Care Law, 11*, 369–403.

Kedar, N. (2007). Law, culture and civil codification in a mixed legal system. *Canadian Journal of Law and Society, 17*, 177–196.

Kelley, T.A. (2007). Exporting western law to the developing world: The troubling case of Niger. *George Washington International Law Review, 39*, 321–366.

Kjellin, L., Östman, O. & Östman, M. (2008). Compulsory psychiatric care in Sweden—Development 1979–2002 and area variation. *International Journal of Law and Psychiatry, 31*, 51–59.

Klapper, A. (1993). Finding a right in state constitutions for community treatment of the mentally ill. *University of Pennsylvania Law Review, 142*, 739–835.

Kokonnen, P. (1993). Coercion and legal protection in psychiatric care in Finland. *Medicine and Law, 12,* 113–124.

Korkeila, J.A. et al. (2002). Predicting use of coercive measures in Finland. *Nordic Journal of Psychiatry, 56,* 339–345.

Lang, R. & Murangira, A. (2009). Barriers to the inclusion of disabled people in disability policy-making in seven African countries. In *United Nations Convention on the Rights of Persons with Disabilities: Multidisciplinary Perspectives,* 159–184 (Kumpuvuori, K. & Schenin, M., eds.). Turku, Finland: The Center for Human Rights for Persons with Disabilities in Finland.

Laplante, L.J. & Holguin, M.R. (2006). The Peruvian Truth Commission's mental health reparations: Empowering survivors of political violence to impact public health policy. *Health and Human Rights, 9,* 137–163.

Lawson, A. (2008). People with psychosocial impairments or conditions, reasonable accommodation and the Convention on the Rights of Persons with Disabilities. *Law in Context, 26,* 62–84.

Legamaate, J. (1995). Involuntary admission to a psychiatric hospital: Recent European developments. *European Journal of Health Law, 2,* 15–32.

Levav, I., Restrepo, H. & de Macedo, C.G. (1994). The restructuring of psychiatric care in Latin America: A new policy for mental health services. *Journal of Public Health Policy, 15,* 71–85.

Lewis, O. (2002a). Mental disability law in central and eastern Europe: Paper, practice, promise. *Journal of Mental Health Law, 8,* 293–303.

Lewis, O. (2002b). Protecting the rights of people with mental disabilities: The European Convention on Human Rights. *European Journal of Health Law, 9,* 293.

Ley No. 202 (1995, August 23). Ley de Prevención, Rehabilitación y Equiparación de Oportunidades para las Personas con Discapacidad [Prevention, Rehabilitation and Equal Opportunities for Persons with Disabilities Act] ch. II, sec. 5 (Nicar.), Disability Rights Education and Defense Fund. Retrieved September 27, 2010, from http://www.dredf.org/international/nicar1.html

Lindqvist, P. (2007). Mental disorder, substance misuse and violent behaviour: The Swedish experience of caring for the triply troubled. *Criminal Behaviour and Mental Health, 17,* 242–249.

Lippmann, L. & Goldberg, I.I. (1973). *The Right to Education: Anatomy of the Pennsylvania Case and Its Implication for Exceptional Children.* New York: Columbia University Teachers College Press.

Lord, J.E. & Brown, R. (2010). The role of reasonable accommodation in securing substantive equality for persons with disabilities: The UN Convention on the Rights of Persons with Disabilities. *Social Science Research Network.* Retrieved September 25, 2010, from http://papers.ssrn.com/sol3/papers.cfm?abstract_id=1618903

Lord, J.E. & Stein, M.A. (2008). The domestic incorporation of human rights law and the United Nations Convention on the Rights of Persons with Disabilities. *Washington Law Review, 83,* 449–479.

Lottman, M. (1976). Paper victories and hard realities. In *Paper Victories and Hard Realities: the Implementation of the Legal and Constitutional Rights of the Mentally Disabled* (Bradley, V.J. & G. Clarke, J., eds.). Washington, DC: Health Policy Center, Georgetown University.

Lu, H. & Zhang, L. (2005). Death penalty in China: The law and the practice. *Journal of Criminal Justice, 33,* 367–376.

Lund, C. et al. (2010). Pathways to impatient mental health care among people with schizophrenia spectrum disorders in South Africa. *Psychiatric Services, 61,* 235–240.

Mahtani, A. (2003). The right of refugee clients to an appropriate and ethical psychological service. *International Journal of Human Rights, 7,* 40–57.

McSherry, B.M. (2008). Mental health and human rights: The role of the law in developing a right to enjoy the highest attainable standard of mental health in Australia. *Journal of Law and Medicine, 15,* 773–781.

Megret, F. (2008). The disabilities convention: Human rights of persons with disabilities or disability rights? *Human Rights Quarterly, 30,* 494–516.

Meier, B.M. (2010). Global health governance and the contentious politics of human rights: Mainstreaming the right to health for public health advancement. *Stanford Journal of International Law, 46,* 1–50.

Memorandum to the Government Concerning Inpatient Psychiatric Treatment (2004). *Amnesty International.* Retrieved September 23, 2010, from http://www.web.amnesty.org/library/print/engeur390032004

Menezes, S.B., Oyebode, F. & Haque, M.S. (2007). Mentally disordered offenders in Zimbabwe and in England and Wales: A socio-demographic study. *Medicine, Science & Law, 47,* 253–261.

Mental Disability Advocacy Center, Priority Areas. (2010). *Mental Disability Advocacy Center.* Retrieved September 30, 2010, from http://www.mdac.info/priority_areas/priority_areas.htm

MDRI. Mental Disability Rights International. (2010). *Projects: Mental Disability Rights.* Retrieved September 30, 2010, from http://www.mdri.org/projects

MDRI Argentina Report. (2007). *Ruined Lives: Segregation from Society in Argentina's Psychiatric Asylums.* Washington, DC: Mental Disability Rights International.

MDRI Mexico Report. (2000). Mental Disability Rights International. *Human Rights and Mental Health: Mexico.*

MDRI Paraguay Report (2007) *Neuro-Psychiatric Hospital of Paraguay: Settlement Reached,* http:// www.mdri.org/projects/americas/paraguay/settlementreached.htm (Paraguay Settlement).

MDRI Paraguay Report. (2010). Mental Disability Rights International. *Projects: Neuro-Psychiatric Hospital of Paraguay.* Retrieved September 30, 2010, from http://www.mdri.org/projects/americas/paraguay/documentsabuses.htm

MDRI Paraguay Report Update. (2010). *Our Work: Country Reports: Paraguay.* Retrieved September 30, 2010, from http://www.mdri.org/paraguay-impact_5.html

MDRI Preliminary Uruguay Report. (1994). Mental Disability Rights International. *Human Rights and Mental Health Uruguay Preliminary Report.*

MDRI Uruguay Report. (1995). Mental Disability Rights International. *Human Rights and Mental Health Uruguay.*

Moncada, A.C. (1994). Involuntary commitment and the use of seclusion and restraint in Uruguay: A comparison with the United Nations Principles for the Protection of Persons with Mental Illness. *University of Miami Inter-American Law Review, 25,* 589–620.

Morrison, D. (2006). The Judicial Committee of the Privy Council and the death penalty in the Commonwealth Caribbean: Studies in judicial activism. *Nova Law Review, 30,* 403–424.

Moses, M. (2007). Analysis of the Uganda Mental Treatment Act from a human rights and public health perspective. *Social Science Research Network.* Retrieved September 25, 2010, from http://papers.ssrn.com/sol3/papers.cfm?abstract_id=1006230.

Mossialos, E., Murthy, A. & McDaid, D. (2003). European Union enlargement: Will mental health be forgotten again ? *European Journal of Public Health, 13,* 2–3.

Mulder, C.L. et al. (2008). Changing patterns in emergency involuntary admissions in the Netherlands in the period 2000–2004. *International Journal of Law and Psychiatry, 31,* 331–336.

Müller-Isberner, R. et al. (2000). Forensic psychiatric assessment and treatment in Germany: Legal framework, recent developments, and current practice. *International Journal of Law and Psychiatry, 23,* 467–480.

Nakatani, Y. et al. (2010). New legislation for offenders with mental disorders in Japan. *International Journal of Law and Psychiatry, 33,* 7–12.

Nedopil, N. (2009). The role of forensic psychiatry in the mental health systems in Europe. *Criminal Behaviour and Mental Health, 19,* 224–234.

Nienaber, A. (2009). The African regional human rights system and HIV-related human experimentation: Implications of *Zimbabwe Human Rights NGO Forum v. Zimbabwe. African Human Rights Law Journal, 9,* 524–545.

Ninega, F.G. (2006). Forensic psychiatry: The African experience. *World Psychiatry, 5,* 97–97.

Nmehielle, V.O. (2003). The African Union and African renaissance: A new era for human rights protection in Africa? *Singapore Journal of International and Comparative Law, 2,* 412–446.

Nowak, A. (2009). The decline of the mandatory death penalty in common law Africa: Constitutional decline and comparative jurisprudence in Malawi and Uganda. *Loyola Journal of Public Interest Law, 11,* 19–85.

Nowak, M. (2006). What practices constitute torture? US and UN standards. *Human Rights Quarterly, 28,* 809–841.

Nyanguru, A.C. (2000). The rights of elderly male prisoners in Lesotho. *Lesotho Law Journal, 16,* 120–149.

Olmstead v. L.C., 527 U.S. 581 (1999).

Okasha, A. (2003). Mental health services in the Arab world *Arab Studies Quarterly, 25,* 39–52.

Pan American Health Organization (2008). PAHO and the Reformulation of Mental Health in the Americas. Accessible at http://www.paho.org/English/DD/PIN/mentalhealth_004.htm. (PAHO)

Pennhurst State Sch. & Hosp. v. Halderman, 451 U.S. 1 (1981).

Pennhurst State Sch. & Hosp. v. Halderman, 465 U.S. 89 (1984).

Perlin, M.L. (1991). Competency, deinstitutionalization, and homelessness: A story of marginalization. *Houston Law Review, 28,* 63–142.

Perlin, M.L. (1998). *Mental Disability Law: Civil and Criminal* (2nd ed., Vol. 1). New York: Lexis Law Publishing.

Perlin, M.L. (1999). *Mental Disability Law: Civil and Criminal* (2nd ed., Vol. 2). New York: Lexis Law Publishing.

Perlin, M.L. (2000). "Their promises of paradise:" Will *Olmstead v. L.C.* resuscitate the constitutional least restrictive alternative principle in mental disability law? *Houston Law Review, 37,* 999–1054.

Perlin, M.L. (2001–2002). "What's good is bad, what's bad is good, you'll find out when you reach the top, you're on the bottom:" Are the Americans with Disabilities Act (and *Olmstead v. L.C.*) anything more than "Idiot Wind"? *University of Michigan Journal of Law Reform, 35,* 235–261.

Perlin, M.L. (2002a). Chimes of freedom: International human rights and institutional mental disability law. *New York Law School Journal of International and Comparative Law, 21,* 423–434.

Perlin, M.L. (2002b). *Mental Disability Law: Civil and Criminal* (2nd ed., Vol. 3). New York: Lexis Law Publishing.

Perlin, M.L. (2002c). Symposium: International human rights law and the institutional treatment of persons with mental disabilities: The case of Hungary. *New York Law School Journal of International and Comparative Law, 21,* 361–386.

Perlin, M.L. (2007). International human rights law and comparative mental disability law: The universal factors. *Syracuse Journal of International Law and Commerce, 34,* 333–357.

Perlin, M.L. (2008). "I might need a good lawyer, could be your funeral, my trial": Global clinical legal education and the right to counsel in civil commitment cases. *Washington University Journal of Law and Policy, 28,* 241–264.

Perlin, M.L. (2009). "A change is gonna come": The implications of the United Nations Convention on the Rights of Persons with Disabilities for the domestic practice of constitutional mental disability law. *Northern Illinois University Law Review, 29,* 483–498.

Perlin, M.L., et al. (2006a). International Human Rights and Comparative Mental Disability Law: Cases and Materials. Durham, NC: Carolina Academic Press.

Perlin, M.L. & Dlugacz, H.A. (2008). *Mental Health Issues in Jails and Prisons: Cases and Materials.* Durham, NC: Carolina Academic Press.

Perlin, M.L. & Dlugacz, H.A. (2009). "It's doom alone that counts": Can international human rights law be an effective source of rights in correctional conditions litigation? *Behavioral Sciences & Law, 27,* 675–694.

Perlin, M.L., Gould, K.K. & Dorfman, D.A. (1995). Therapeutic jurisprudence and the civil rights of institutionalized mentally disabled persons: Hopeless oxymoron or path to redemption? *Psychology, Public Policy, and Law, 1,* 80–119.

Perlin, M.L. & Ikehara, Y. (2010). Promoting social change in East Asia: The movement to create a disability rights tribunal and the promise of international online, distance learning. Paper presented at the inaugural conference of the East Asia Law and Society Association, University of Hong Kong, February, 2010. Accessible at http://papers.ssrn.com/sol3/papers.cfm?abstract_id=1743741.

Perlin, M.L. & McClain, V. (2009). "Where souls are forgotten": Cultural competencies, forensic evaluations, and international human rights. *Psychology, Public Policy and Law, 15,* 257–277.

Petersen, C.J. (2006). From British colony to special administrative region of China: Embracing human rights in Hong Kong. In *Human Rights in Asia: A Comparative Legal Study of Twelve Asian Jurisdictions, France and the USA,*

224–264 (Peerenboom, R., Petersen, C.J. & Chen, A.H.Y., eds.). London, UK: Routledge.

Phillimore, J. & Goodson, L. (2008). Making a place in the global city: The relevance of indicators of integration. *Journal of Refugee Studies, 21,* 305–325.

Phillips, S.D. (2009). Civil society and disability rights in post-Soviet Ukraine: NGOs and prospects for change. *Indiana Journal of Global Legal Studies, 16,* 275–291.

Press Release, AI. (2001). Press Release, Amnesty International, Bulgaria: Disabled Woman Condemned to "Slow Death," AI Index: EUR 15/002/2001 (Oct. 11, 2001). *Amnesty International.* Retrieved September 25, 2010, from http://web.amnesty.org/library/index/engeur150022001

Press Release, Amnesty International, Bulgaria: Disabled Woman Condemned to 'Slow Death,' AI Index: EUR 15/002/2001 (Oct. 11, 2001). Accessible at http://web.amnesty.org/library/index/engeur150022001 ("Press Release, 2001").

Press Release, Mental Disability Advocacy Center, MDAC Calls for Cage Bed Ban in Czech Republic (Nov. 24, 2003). Accessible at http:// www.mdac.info/documents/Press_Release_CR_Senate_Cage_Bed.doc ("Press Release, 2003").

Press Release, Mental Disability Advocacy Center, Harry Potter Joins the Fight to End Czech "Cage Bed" Use (July 16, 2004). Accessible at http://www.mdac.info/documents/czech%20cage%CC20bed%CC20press%20release.pdf #search='cage%20bed%CC20%CC26%20CPT ("Press Release, 2004").

Press Release, AI. (2002a). Press Release, Amnesty International, Bulgaria: Arbitrary Detention and Ill-treatment of People with Mental Disabilities, AI Index: EUR 15/008/2002 (Oct. 10, 2002a). *Amnesty International.* Retrieved September 25, 2010, from http://web.amnesty.org/library/index/ENGEUR150082002

Press Release, AI. (2002b). Press Release, Amnesty International, Bulgaria: Far from the Eyes of Society—Systematic Discrimination against People with Mental Disabilities, AI Index: EUR 15/005/002 (Oct. 10, 2002b). *Amnesty International.* Retrieved September 25, 2010, from http://web.amnesty.org/library/index/ENGEUR150052002

Press Release, AI. (2004). Press Release, Amnesty International, Romania: "Protection of Basic Rights of People with Mental Disabilities Placed in Psychiatric Establishments—An Imperative for the Romanian State," AI Index: EUR 39/014/2004 (Nov. 5, 2004). *Amnesty International.* Retrieved September 25, 2010, from http://web.amnesty.org/library/index/ENGEUR390142004

Press Release, MDAC. (2003). Press Release, Mental Disability Advocacy Center, MDAC Calls for Cage Bed Ban in Czech Republic (Nov. 24, 2003). *Mental Disability Advocacy Center.* Retrieved September 25, 2010, http://www.mdac.info/documents/Press_Release_CR_Senate_Cage_Bed.doc

Press Release, MDAC. (2004). Press Release, Mental Disability Advocacy Center, Harry Potter Joins the Fight to End Czech "Cage Bed" Use (July 16, 2004). *Mental Disability Advocacy Center.* Retrieved September 25, 2010, http://www.mdac.info/documents/czech%20cage%CC20bed%CC20press%20release.pdf #search="cage%20bed%CC20%CC26%20CPT

Press Release, MDAC. (2006a). Press Release, Mental Disability Advocacy Center, Hungary: Man Wins Historic Psychiatric Detention Case at European Court of Human Rights (Oct. 3, 2006). *Mental Disability Advocacy Center.*

Retrieved September 25, 2010, from http://www.mdac.info/documents/PR_MDAC_20061003_eng.pdf
Press Release, MDAC (2006b). Press Release, Mental Disability Advocacy Center, MDAC Urges EU to Include Human Rights in Mental Health Strategy (June 3, 2006). *Mental Disability Advocacy Center.* Retrieved September 25, 2010, from http://www.mdac.info/documents/PR_MDAC_ urges_EU_20060603_ eng. pdf
Press Release, MDRI. (2008). Press Release, Mental Disability Rights International. MRDI Exposes Deaths and Abuses in Paraguyan Psychiatric Hospital and Demands Immediate Government Action. (2008). *Mental Disability Rights International.* Retrieved September 25, 2010, from http://www.mdri.org/paraguay-news-alert.html
Press Release, WHO. (2005). Press Release, Shaky Mental Health Rules Fuel Abuse of Patients' Rights: WHO (June 21, 2005).
Prior, P.M. (2003). Removing children from the care of adults with diagnosed mental illnesses—A clash of human rights? *European Journal of Social Work, 6,* 179–190.
Prior, P.M. (2007) Mentally disordered offenders and the European Court of Human Rights, *International Journal of Law and Psychiatry, 30,* 546–557.
Putkonen, H. & Vollm, B. (2007). Compulsory psychiatric detention and treatment in Finland. *Psychiatric Bulletin, 31,* 101–103.
Reddy, M.V. & Chandrasekhar, C.R. (1998). Prevalence of mental and behavioural disorders in India: A meta-analysis. *Indian Journal of Psychiatry, 40,* 149–157.
Reilly, R. (July 2010). Disabilities among refugees and conflict-affected populations. *Forced Migration Review, 35,* 8–10.
Roberts, H. (2002). Mental health care still poor in eastern Europe. *Lancet, 360,* 552.
Rochin v. California, 342 U.S. 165 (1952).
Rosenthal, E. et al. (1999). Implementing the right to community integration for children with disabilities in Russia: A human rights framework for international action. *Health and Human Rights, 4,* 83–113.
Rosenthal, E. & Rubenstein, L.S. (1993). International human rights advocacy under the "Principles for the Protection of Persons with Mental Illness." *International Journal of Law & Psychiatry, 16,* 257–300.
Rössler, W., Salize, H-J. & Riecher-Rössler (1996). Changing patterns of mental health care in Germany. *International Journal of Law and Psychiatry, 19,* 391–411.
Russell, J. (2008). Book Review, Peter Bartlett, Oliver Lewis and Oliver Thorold, Mental Disability and the European Convention on Human Rights. *Human Rights Review, 8,* 200–203.
Rymaszewska, J. & Dabrowski, S. (2005, July). Rules and regulations for involuntary placement or treatment of mentally ill persons—Results from a Structured survey instrument in 12 European countries, and results from a quality assurance project on involuntary placement/treatment in Poland. Address at the International Academy of Law and Mental Health Conference, Paris, France.
Sahlin, R. (2008). Legislating discrimination protection for persons with disabilities in Australia and Sweden: A comparative analysis. *Australian Journal of Human Rights, 13,* 209–232.

Sailas, E. & Wahlbeck, K. (2005). Restraint and seclusion on psychiatric inpatient wards. *Current Opinion in Psychiatry, 18,* 555–559.

Salize, H.J., Schanda, H. & Dressing, H. (2008). From the hospital into the community and back again—A trend toward re-institutionalisation in mental health care? *International Review of Psychiatry, 20,* 527–534.

Salzberger, E. (2008). Judicial activism in Israel. In *Judicial Activism in Common Law Supreme Courts,* 217–271 (Dickson, B., ed.). New York: Oxford University Press.

Shera, W. et al. (2002). Mental health system reform: A multi country comparison. In *Social Work Health and Mental Health: Practice, Research and Programs,* 547–575 (Jackson, A.C. & Segal, S.P., eds.). Binghamton: Haworth Press.

Sheriff, R.J.S. (2010). Improving human resource provision for mental health in Somaliland. *Psychiatric Services, 61,* 225–227.

Shivji, A. (2010, July). Disability in displacement. *Forced Migration Review, 35,* 4–6.

Smith, C. (2005, September 28). Abuse of mentally ill is reported in Turkey. *International Herald Tribune, 1.*

Smith, C. (2006, May 10). Romania's orphans face widespread abuse, group says. *New York Times,* A3.

Solomon, H. (1958). Presidential address: The American Psychiatric Association in relation to American psychiatry. *American Journal of Psychiatry, 115,* 1–9.

Stefansson, C.-G. & Hanson, L. (1995). Mental health care reform in Sweden, 1995. *Acta Psychiatrica Scandinavica,* 104 (Suppl. 410), 82–88.

Stoll, K. & Johnson, P. (2007). Determinants of the psychosocial adjustment of southern Sudanese men. *Journal of Refugee Studies, 20,* 621–640.

Sukegawa, Y. (1993). Community support system for mentally disabled people: Public health and mental health centers in Kanagawa Prefecture. *New Directions for Mental Health Services, 60,* 45–56.

Szmukler, G., & Holloway, F. (1998). Mental health legislation is now a harmful anachronism. *Psychiatric Bulletin, 22,* 662–665.

Téllez, C. et al. (2004). Impact of legal reform on the practice of forensic psychiatry in Chile. *Current Opinion in Psychiatry, 17,* 387–390.

Tittemore, B.D. (2004), The mandatory death penalty in the Commonwealth Caribbean and the Inter-American Human Rights System: An evolution in the development and implementation of international human rights protections. *William & Mary Bill of Rights Journal, 13,* 445–520.

Toib, J.A. (2006). Challenges for Israeli mental health law in the next decade. *Israel Journal of Psychiatry and Related Sciences, 3,* 198–208.

Trivedi, J.K., Narang, P. & Dhyani, M. (2007). Mental health legislation in South Asia with special reference to India: Shortcomings and solutions. *Mental Health Review Journal, 12,* 22–29.

Tuen, J.T-H. (1999). Effects of the economic crisis on the placement of people with disabilities in Singapore. [Electronic version]. *Asia and Pacific Journal on Disability, 2,* 1. Accessible at http://www.dinf.ne.jp/doc/english/asia/resource/z00ap/004/z00ap00409.html.

Turner, K.P. (2008). Raising the bars: A comparative look at treatment standards for mentally ill prisoners in the United States, United Kingdom, and Australia. *Cardozo Journal of International & Comparative Law, 16,* 409–456.

Twinomugisha, B.T. (2009). The role of the judiciary in the promotion of democracy in Uganda. *African Human Rights Journal, 9,* 1–22.

UN Convention (2010). *UN Enable*. Retrieved September 27, 2010, from http://www.un.org/disabilities/default.asp?id=150

UNICEF (2005). Children and Disability in Transition in CEE/CIS and the Baltic States. Florence, Italy: UNICEF.

UNICEF (2005). *Children and Disability in Transition in the Baltic States.* Florence, Italy: UNICEF.

Välimäki, M. et al. (2009). Patients' rights to complain in Finnish psychiatric care: An overview. *International Journal of Law and Psychiatry, 32,* 184–188.

Vardanyan, A., et al. (2004). Mental Disability Advocacy Center, Mental Health Law of the Kyrgyz. Republic and Its Implementation § 4.1.1. *Eurasia Health Knowledge Network.* Retrieved September 25, 2010, from http://www.eurasiahealth.org/attaches/81502/118-e.pdf

Wachenfeld, M. (1991). The Human Rights of the Mentally Ill in Europe. *Nordic Journal of International Law, 60,* 109–109.

Waddington, L. (2008). When is it reasonable for Europeans to be confused: Understanding when a disability accommodation is "reasonable" from a comparative perspective. *Comparative Labor Law & Policy Journal, 29,* 317–340.

Walker, N. (2006). EU constitutionalism in the state constitutional tradition. *Social Science Research Network.* Retrieved September 25, 2010, from http://papers.ssrn.com/sol3/papers.cfm?abstract_id=939780.

Wallsten, T. & Kjellin, L. (2004). Involuntarily and voluntarily admitted patients' experiences of psychiatric admission and treatment—A comparison before and after changed legislation in Sweden. *European Psychiatry, 19,* 464–468.

Warren, M.G. & Moon, R.R. (1994). Dixon: In the absence of political will, carry a big stick. *Law & Psychology Rev., 18,* 329–360.

Waterstone, M. (2004). Civil rights and the administration of elections—Toward secret ballots and polling place access. *Journal of Gender, Race & Justice, 8,* 101–152.

Weisstub, D.N. & Carney, T. (2006) Forensic mental health law reform in Japan: From criminal warehousing to broad-spectrum specialist services? *International Journal of Law & Psychiatry, 29,* 86–100.

WHO Policy Brief (2008). Developing effective mental health laws in Africa. Available at http://www.who.int/mental_health/policy/development/MHPB7.pdf. (Policy Brief).

WHO-AIMS (2009a). *Mental Health Systems in Selected Low- and Middle-Income Countries: A WHO-AIMS Cross-national Analysis.* Malta: World Health Organization.

WHO-AIMS (2009b). *Report on the Mental Health Systems in Central America and the Dominican Republic.* Panama: Pan American Health Organization.

Whyte, S.R. (1995). Constructing epilepsy: Images and contexts in East Africa. In Disability and Culture, 226–263 (Ingstad, B. & Whyte, S.R., eds.). Berkeley: University of California Press.

Winick, B.J. (2002). Therapeutic jurisprudence and the treatment of people with mental illness in Eastern Europe: Construing international human rights law. *New York Law School Journal of International & Comparative Law, 21,* 537–572.

Woods, P. (2005). Cause lawyers and judicial community in Israel: Legal change in a diffuse, normative community. In *The Worlds Cause Lawyers Make: Structure and Agency in Legal Practice*, 307–348 (Sarat, A. & Scheingold, S.A., eds.). Stanford, CA: Stanford University Press.

Wyatt v. Stickney, 344 F. Supp 373 (M.D. Ala. 1972).

Convention on the Rights of Persons with Disabilities (2008). *United Nations Enable*. Retrieved September 25, 2010, from http://un.org/disabilities/default.asp?id=259.

Yamin, A.E. (2003). Not just a tragedy: Access to medications as a right under international law. *Boston University International Law Journal, 21*, 325–371.

Yanaka, T. (1993). The village of the hermit crab. *New Directions for Mental Health Services, 60*, 57–65.

Chapter 6

Chapter 6A

Aizawa, H. (2006). Japanese legal education in transition. *Wisconsin International Law Journal, 24*, 131–151.

Ake v. Oklahoma, 470 U.S. 68 (1985).

American Psychological Association. (2002). Ethical principles of psychologists and code of conduct.Washington, DC: American Psychological Association.

An-Na'im, A.A. (2005). Globalization and jurisprudence: An Islamic law perspective. *Emory Law Journal, 54*, 25–51.

Ashley, K.D. (2001). What I told the Law and Computers Association of Japan about information technology in law school education. *University of Pittsburgh Law Review, 62*, 545–579.

Australian Psychological Society. (2007). *Code of ethics*. Melbourne, Australia: Australian Psychological Society.

Backer, L.C. (2002). Human rights and legal education in the western hemisphere: Legal parochialism and hollow universalism. *Penn State International Law Review, 21*, 115–155.

Barry, M.M. (2007). Clinical legal education in the law university: Goals and challenges. *International Journal of Clinical Legal Education, 9*, 51–64.

Barry, M.M., Geer, M., Klein, C.F. & Kumari, V. (2008). Justice education and the evaluation process: Crossing borders. *Washington University Journal of Law & Policy, 28*, 195–237.

Berg, P. (2003). Using distance learning to enhance cross-listed interdisciplinary law school courses. *Rutgers University Computer and Technology Law Journal, 29*, 33–52.

Blanck, P. et al. (2003). Technology for independence: A community-based resource center. *Behavioral Science and Law, 21*, 51–62.

Blanck, P. & Ritchie, H. (2003). The promise of the internet for disability: A study of on-line services and web-site accessibility at centers for independent living. *Behavioral Science and Law, 21*, 5–26.

Blanck, P. & Sandler, L. (2000). ADA title III and the internet: Technology and civil rights. *Mental and Physical Disability Law Reports, 24*, 855–858.

Blomquist, H. (2004). Legal education, profession and society transition: Reform of Lithuanian legal education. *Review of Central and East European Law, 29*, 35–95.

British Psychological Society. (2006). *Code of ethics and conduct*. Leicester, UK: The British Psychological Society.

Brooks, S.L. (2005). Practicing (and teaching) therapeutic jurisprudence: Importing social work principles and techniques into clinical legal education. *St. Thomas Law Review, 17,* 513–530.

Bruun, O. & Jacobson, M. (2006). Introduction. In *Human Rights and Asian Values: Contesting National Identities and Cultural Representation in Asia,* 1–20. London: RoutledgeCurzon.

Bryxová, V., Tomoszek, M. & Vlcková, V. (2006). Introducing legal clinics in Olomauc, Czech Republic. *International Journal of Clinical Legal Education, 9,* 149–156.

Caplow, S. (2006). Clinical legal education in Hong Kong: Time to move forward. *Hong Kong Law Journal, 36,* 229–258.

Carrillo, A.J. (2004). Bringing international law home: The innovative role of human rights clinics in the transnational legal process. *Columbia Human Rights Law Review, 35,* 527–587.

Chavkin, D.F. (2009). Experiential learning: A critical element of legal education in China. *Pacific McGeorge Global Business & Development Law Journal, 22,* 3–20.

Cheah, P. (1997). Posit(ion)ing human rights in the current global conjuncture. *Public Culture, 9,* 233–266.

Chesterman, S. (2008). The globalization of legal education. *Singapore Journal of Legal Studies.* 58–67.

Choate, A. (2000). *Legal aid in China* (Asia Foundation, Working Paper No. 12). Accessible at http://www.asiafoundation.org/pdf/wp12.pdf.

Cody, A. & Green, S. (2007). Clinical legal education and Indigenous legal education: What's the connection? *International Journal of Clinical Legal Education, 9,* 51–64.

Cooney, L.L. (2005). Heart and soul: A new rhythm for clinical externships. *St. Thomas Law Review, 17,* 407–428.

Cukor, P. & McKnight, L. (2001). Knowledge, networks, the internet, and development. *Fletcher Forum of World Affairs, 25,* 43–57.

Cummings, S.L. & Trubek, L.G. (2008). Globalizing public interest law. *UCLA Journal of International Law and Foreign Affairs, 13,* 1–53.

Del Duca, L.F. (2000). Symposium on emerging worldwide strategies in internationalizing legal education. *Dickinson Journal of International Law, 18,* 411–428.

Dowdle, M.D. (2000). Preserving indigenous paradigms in an age of globalization: Pragmatic strategies for the development of clinical legal aid in China. *Fordham International Law Journal, 24,* S56–S82.

Dunham, C. & Friedland, S.I. (2009). Portable learning for the 21st century law school: Designing a new pedagogy for the modern global context. *John Marshall Journal of Computer and Information Law, 26,* 371–393.

Erie, M.S. (2009). Legal education reform in China through U.S.-inspired transplants. *Journal of Legal Education, 59,* 60–96.

Evans, A. & Hyams, R. (2008). Independent evaluation of clinical legal education programs: Appropriate objectives and processes in an Australian setting. *Griffith Law Review, 17,* 52–86.

Feldman, E. (1993). Mirroring minds: Recruitment and promotion in Japan's law faculties. *American Journal of Comparative Law, 41,* 465–479.

Foote, D.H. (2006). Forces driving and shaping legal training reform in Japan. *Australian Journal of Asian Law, 7,* 215–240.

Fu, H. (2009). Access to justice and constitutionalism in China. In *Building Constitutionalism in China,* 163–177 (Balme, S. & Dowdle, M.W., eds.). New York: Palgrave Macmillan.

Fu, H. & Cullen, R. (2008). *Weiquan* (rights protection) lawyering in an authoritarian state: Toward critical lawyering. http://ssrn.com/abstract=1083925

Gibson, F. (2010). Access to justice for people with disabilities: The response of the clinic. Accessed at http://papers.ssrn.com/sol3/papers.cfm?abstract_id=1540581.

Giddings, J. (2008). Contemplating the future of clinical legal education. *Griffith Law Review, 17,* 1–26.

Gould, K.K. & Perlin, M.L. (2000). "Johnny's in the basement/Mixing up his medicine"; Therapeutic jurisprudence and clinical teaching. *Seattle University Law Review, 24,* 339–371.

Grondine, R.F. (2001). An international perspective on Japan's new legal education system. *Asian-Pacific Law & Policy Journal, 2,* 1–25.

Grosberg, L.M. (2001). Clinical education in Russia: "Da and nyet" *Clinical Law Review, 7,* 469–496.

Grossman, C. (2004). Global legal education and human rights. *Human Rights Brief, 11* (No. 3), 20–23.

Grossman, C. (2006). Integrating international law into the first-year curriculum. *Penn State International Law Review, 24,* 835–839.

Guo, Z. (2010), Approaching visible justice: Procedural safeguards for mental examinations in China's capital cases. *Hastings International & Comparative Law Review, 33,* 21–54.

Haicong, Z. (2009). Legal education in China: Present and future. *Oklahoma City University Law Review, 34,* 51–58.

Haley, J.O. (2010). Why study Japanese law? *American Journal of Comparative Law, 58,* 1–14.

Harding, T.W. (1989). Prevention of torture and inhuman or degrading treatment: Medical implications of a new European Convention. *The Lancet, 333,* 1191–1193.

Hasegawa, K. (2006). Legal education reform and the idea of law. *Wisconsin International Law Journal, 24,* 23–27.

Haynes, D.F. (2006). Client-centered human rights advocacy. *Clinical Law Review, 13,* 379–416.

Henkin, L.,Neuman, G.L., Orentlicher, D.F., Leebron, D.W. (1999). *Human Rights.* (New York City: Foundation Press).

Hovhannisan, L. (2006). *Clinical Legal Education and the Bologna Process.* Budapest, Hungary: Public Interest Law Initiative. http://www.hrea.org/index.php (last ccessed, September 3, 2009). http://www.law.cuny.edu/clinics/clinicalofferings/IWHRC/skills.html; http://www.law.columbia.edu/focusareas/clinics/humanrights

Hurwitz, D.R. (2003). Lawyering for justice and the inevitability of international human rights clinics. *Yale Journal of International Law, 28,* 505–549.

Ibusuku, M. & Nottage, L. (2002). IT and transformations in legal practice and education in Japan and Australia. *University of Technology, Sydney Law Review, 4,* 31–54.
Irish, C.A. (2007). Reflections on the evolution of law and legal education in China and Vietnam. *Wisconsin International Law Journal, 25,* 243–254.
Iya, P.F. (2005). Enhancing the teaching of human rights in African universities: What role for law school clinics? *International Journal of Clinical Legal Education, 7,* 20–28.
Jeong, Y-C. K. (2010). Korean legal education for the age of professionalism: Suggestions for more concerted curricula. *East Asia Law Review, 5,* 155–196.
Jessup. G. (2002). Symbiotic relations: Clinical methodology—fostering new paradigms in African legal education. *Clinical Law Review, 8,* 377–404.
Joy, P.A., Miyagawa, S., Suami, T. & Weisselbaerg, C.D. (2006). Building clinical legal education programs in a country without a tradition of graduate professional legal education: Japan educational reform as a case study. *Clinical Law Review, 13,* 417–458.
Joyce, A. & Winfrey, T. (2004). Taming the red dragon: A realistic assessment of the ABA's legal reform efforts in China. *Georgetown Journal of Legal Ethics, 17,* 887–202.
Juwana, H. (2006). Legal education reform in Indonesia. *Asian Journal of Comparative Law,* 1. Article 8.
Kawabata, Y. (2002). The reform of legal education and training in Japan: Problems and prospects. *South Texas Law Review, 43,* 419–434.
Klein, B. (2008). Two nations at different places: A comparative look at disability law in United States and Japanese higher education. *Connecticut Journal of International Law, 23,* 417–434.
Kong, Q. (2009). Practice in legal education: International experience and Chinese response. *Pacific McGeorge Global Business & Development Law Journal, 22,* 35–44.
Kumho Tire Co. v Carmichael (1999). 426 US 137.
Lahav, P. (2009). American moment[s]: When, how, and why did Israeli law faculties come to resemble elite U.S. law schools? *Theoretical Inquiries in Law, 10,* 653–697.
Landsberg, B.K. (2009). Strategies to increase the availability of skills education in China. *Pacific McGeorge Global Business & Development Law Journal, 22,* 45–54.
Lempert, D. (1999). A tale of two law schools: Direction of legal education reform in Russia and a mirror for seeing ourselves. *Journal of Eastern European Law, 6,* 299–347.
Leskovac, H. (1998). Distance learning in legal education: Implications of frame relay videoconferencing. *Albany Law Journal of Science and Technology, 8,* 305–334.
Liebman, B.L. (1999). Legal aid and public interest law in China. *Texas International Law Journal, 34,* 211–286.
Liebman, B.L. (2007). Lawyers, legal aid, and legitimacy in China. In *Raising the Bar: The Emerging Legal Profession in East Asia,* 311 (Alford, W.P., ed.). Cambridge, MA: Harvard University Press.
Ling, M. (2007). Clinical legal education and the reform of the higher legal education system in China. *Fordham International Law Journal, 30,* 421–433.

Liu, T.M. (2008). Transmission of public interest law: A Chinese case study. UCLA Journal of International Law and Foreign Affairs, *13*, 263–294.

Lo, W-H.L. & Snape, E. (2005). Lawyers in the People's Republic of China: A study of commitment and professionalization. *American Journal of Comparative Law, 53*, 433–454.

Lu, H. & Miethe, T.D. (2002). Legal representation and criminal processing in China. *British Journal of Criminology, 42*, 267–280.

Lubbers, J.S. (2010). Japan's legal education reforms from an American law professor's perspective. Accessible at http://papers.ssrn.com/sol3/papers.cfm?abstract_id=1552094.

Maisel, P. (2008). The role of U.S. law faculty in developing countries: Striving for effective cross-cultural collaboration. *Clinical Law Review, 14*, 465–505.

Maisel, P. & Jones, S. (2008). Implementing the social and economic promise of the constitution: The role of South African legal education. In *Law and Rights: Global Perspectives on Constitutionalism and Governance*, 243–257 (Andrews, P.E. & Bazilli, S., eds.). Lake Mary, FL: Vandeplas Publishing.

Manteaw, S.O., (2008). Legal education in Africa: What type of lawyer does Africa need? *McGeorge Law Review, 39*, 903–976.

Martin, C. (2010). Glimmers of hope: The evolution of equality rights doctrine in Japanese courts from a comparative perspective. *Duke Journal of Comparative and International Law, 20*, 167–245.

Maru, V. (2006). Between law and society: Paralegals and the provision of justice services in Sierra Leone and worldwide. *Yale Journal of International Law, 31*, 427–476.

Matasar, R.A. (1998). Private publics, public privates: An essay on convergence in higher education. *University of Florida Journal of Law & Public Policy, 10*, 5–26.

Matasar, R.A. (2002–2003). Legal education skills and values education: Debate about the continuum continues. *New York Law School Law Review, 46*, 395–428.

Matasar, R.A. & Shiels, R. (1995). Electronic law students: Repercussions on legal education. *Valparaiso Law Review, 29*, 909–933.

McMurrow, J.A. (2010). Professional responsibility in an uncertain profession: Legal ethics in China. *Akron Law Journal, 43*, 1081–1105.

Merisotis, J.P. & Phipps, R.A. (1999, May/June). What's the difference? Outcomes of distance vs. traditional classroom-based learning. *Change, 31*, 13–17.

Milstein, E.S. (2009). Experiential education and the rule of law: Teaching values through clinical education in China. *Pacific McGeorge Global Business & Development Law Journal, 22*, 55–62.

Mitchell, J.B. (2007). Using global law to teach domestic advocacy. *Thomas M. Cooley Journal* of *Practical and Clinical Law, 9*, 63–89

Miyazawa, S. (2001). The politics of judicial reform in Japan: The rule of law at last? *Asian-Pacific Law and Policy Journal, 2*, 89–121.

Mohamedbhai, G. (2002). Globalisation and its implications on universities in developing countries. Available at www.bi.ulaval.ca/Globalisation-Universities/pages/actes/MohamedbhaiGoolam2.pdf.

Neziroğlu, I. (2007). A comparative analysis of mental and psychological suffering as torture, inhuman or degrading treatment or punishment under international human rights treaty law. *Essex Human Rights Review, 4*, 1–16.

Note. (2006). Adopting and adapting: Clinical legal education and access to justice in China. *Harvard Law Review, 120,* 2134–2155.
Nottage, L. (2001). Reformist conservatism and failures of imagination in Japanese legal education. *Asian-Pacific Law & Policy Journal, 2,* 29–65.
Nottage, L. (2006). Build postgraduate law schools in Kyoto, and will they come—Sooner *and* later? *Australian Journal of Asian Law, 7,* 241–263.
Oke-Samuel, O. (2008). Clinical legal education in Nigeria: Developments and challenges. *Griffith Law Review, 17,* 140–149.
Olowu, D. (2010). Therapeutic jurisprudence: Transforming legal education and humanising criminal justice in Africa. *De Jure, 1,* 95–116.
Ordor, A.O. (2007). Constructing a clinical legal education approach for large multicultural classes: Insights from the Nigerian law school. *International Journal of Clinical Legal Education, 9,* 65–78.
Orne, M. T. (2002). On the social psychology of the psychological experiment: With particular reference to demand characteristics and their implications. *Prevention & Treatment, 5,* 1–11.
Owens, J. (2010). Utilizing elearning in third world countries. Available at ezinearticles.com/?Utilizing-Elearning-in-Third-World-Countries&id=3934970
Pachnowski, L.M. & Jurczyk, J.P. (2010). Perceptions on faculty on the effect of distance learning technology on faculty preparation time. Available at www.westga.edu/~distance/ojdla/fall63/pachnowski64.html
Perlin, M.L. (2003). "You have discussed lepers and crooks": Sanism in clinical teaching. *Clinical Law Review, 9,* 683–729.
Perlin, M.L. (2006). "Ain't no goin' back": Teaching mental disability law courses on line. *New York Law School Law Review, 51,* 991–1001.
Perlin, M.L. (2007). An internet-based mental disability law program: Implications for social change in nations with developing economies. *Fordham International Law Journal, 30,* 435–454.
Perlin, M.L. (2008). "I might need a good lawyer, could be your funeral, my trial": A global perspective on the right to counsel in civil commitment cases, and its implications for clinical legal education. *Washington University Journal of Law & Social Policy, 28,* 241–264.
Perlin, M.L. (2009). "A change is gonna come": The implications of the United Nations Convention on the Rights of Persons with Disabilities for the domestic practice of constitutional mental disability law. *Northern Illinois University Law Review, 29,* 483–498.
Perlin, M.L. (2010). "They keep it all hid": The ghettoization of mental disability law and its implications for legal education. *Saint Louis University Law Journal, 54,* 857–876.
Perlin, M.L. (2011). Online, distance legal education as an agent of social change. *Pacific McGeorge Global Business and Development Law Journal* (in press).
Perlin, M.L. & Ikehara, Y. (2010). Promoting social change in East Asia: The movement to create a disability rights tribunal and the promise of international online, distance learning. Paper presented at the inaugural conference of the East Asia Law and Society Association, University of Hong Kong, February, 2010. Accessible at http://papers.ssrn.com/sol3/papers.cfm?abstract_id=1743741.

Perlmutter, B.P. (2005). George's Story: Voice and transformation through the teaching and practice of therapeutic jurisprudence in a law school child advocacy clinic. *St. Thomas Law Review, 17,* 561–621.

Phan, P.N. (2005). Clinical legal education in China: In pursuit of a culture of law and a mission of social justice. *Yale Human Rights and Development Law Journal, 8,* 117–152.

Pottenger, J. (2004). The role of [clinical] legal education in legal reform in the People's Republic of China: Chicken, egg—or fox? *International Journal of Clinical Legal Education, 7,* 65–80.

Reimann, M. (2004). From the law of nations to transnational law: Why we need a new basic course for the international curriculum. *Penn State International Law Review, 22,* 397–415.

Rich, R. et al. (2002). Critical legal and policy issues for people with disabilities. *DePaul Journal of Health Care Law, 6,* 1–53.

Riles, A. & Uchida, T. (2009). Reforming knowledge? A socio-legal critique of the legal education reforms in Japan. *Drexel Law Review, 1,* 3–51.

Ronner, A. (2008). The learned-helpless lawyer: Clinical legal education and therapeutic jurisprudence as antidotes to Bartleby Syndrome. *Touro Law Review, 13,* 601–696.

Saegusa, M. (2009). Why the Japanese law school was established: Co-optation as a defensive tactic in the face of global pressures. *Law & Social Inquiry, 34,* 365–398.

Sandberg, H. (2009). Legal colonialism—Americanization of legal education in Israel. Available at http://ssrn.com/abstracts=1443723.

Satsumi Y., & Oda, S. (1995). Mentally ill offenders referred for psychiatric examination in Japan: Descriptive statistics of a university unit of forensic assessment. *International Journal of Law and Psychiatry, 18(3),* 323–331.

Schmetzke, A. (2003). Online Distance education—"Anytime, anywhere" but not for everyone. *Information Technology and Disabilities E-Journal.* Retrieved September 24, 2010, from http://people.rit.edu/easi/itd/itdv07n2/axel.htm.

Schnasi, L.D. (2003). Globalizing: Clinical legal education: Successful under-developed country experiences. *Thomas M. Cooley Journal of Practical and Clinical Law, 6,* 129–214,

Skrodzka, M., Chia, J. & Bruce-Jones, E. (2008). The next step forward: The development of clinical legal education in Poland through a clinical pilot program in Bialystock. *Columbia Journal of European Law, 2,* 56–93.

Spiro, P.J. (2000). Globalization, international law, and the academy. *New York University Journal of International Law and Politics, 32,* 567–590.

Stuckey, R.T. (2002). Preparing students to practice law: A global problem in need of global solutions. *South Texas Law Review, 43,* 649–681.

Stuckey, R.T. (2005). Compilation of clinical law teachers with international teaching or consulting experience. Accessible at http://law.sc.edu/clinic/does/internationalsurvey.pdf.

Tan, C.H. et al. (2006). Legal education in Asia. *Asian Journal of Comparative Law, 1,* 1–22.

Tong, A. (2009). China's constitutional research and teaching: A state of the art. In *Building Constitutionalism in China,* 99–110. (Balme, S. & Dowdle, M.W., eds.). New York: Palgrave Macmillan.

Uphoff, R.J. (1999). Why in-house live client clinics won't work in Romania: Confessions of a clinician educator. *Clinical Law Review, 6,* 315–346.
Wilson, M.J. (2009). U.S. legal education methods and ideals: Application to the Japanese and Korean systems. Available at http://papers.ssrn.com/sol3/papers.cfm?abstract_id=1492166.
Wilson, R.J. (2004). Training for justice: The global reach of clinical legal education. *Penn State International Law Review, 22,* 421–431.
Woo, M.Y.K., Day. C. & Hugenberger, J. (2007). Migrant access to civil justice in Beijing. *Loyola University Chicago International Law Review, 4,* 167–209.
Wortham, L. (2006). Aiding clinical education abroad: What can be gained and the learning curve on how to do so effectively. Clinical Law Review, *12,* 615–685.
Xu, J. (2005). Justice and the need for legal aid NGOs in China. *China Rights Forum, 3,* 71–73.
Yeh, J.I. (2008). Promoting human rights in China through education: An empirical impact evaluation of the Swedish approach from a student perspective. *Asian-Pacific Law & Policy Journal, 10,* 114–167.
Zhengzhi, W., Tran, D., Fenglei, X. & Burris, Sc. (2004). Health law teaching and research in Chinese law schools: Results of a pre-SARS survey. *Temple International & Comparative Law Journal, 18,* 77–88.
Zhou, S. (2009). The reform strategy of legal education in China. *Pacific McGeorge Global Business & Development Law Journal, 22,* 69–74.
Zhu, S.L. (2009). An institutional inquiry into legal skills education in China. *Pacific McGeorge Global Business & Development Law Journal, 22,* 75–91.

Chapter 6B

Anderson, J.C., Lowe, D.J. & Reckers, P.M.J. (1993). Evaluation of auditor decisions: Hindsight bias effects and the expectation gap. *Journal of Economic Psychology, 14,* 711–737.
Andrews, D.A., Bonta, J. & Hoge, R.D. (1990). Classification for effective rehabilitation: Rediscovering psychology. *Criminal Justice and Behaviour, 17,* 19–52.
Appelbaum, P.S. (1987). In the wake of Ake: The ethics of expert testimony in an advocate's world. *Bulletin of the American Academy of Psychiatry and Law, 15,* 15–25.
Arenas, J. & Romey, C.M. (1999). Professional judgement standard and losing games for psychology, experts and the courts. *Revista Juridica Universidad de Puerto Rico, 68,* 159–208.
Arkes, H.R., Wortmann, R.L., Saville, P.D. & Harkness, A.R. (1981). Hindsight bias among physicians weighing the likelihood of diagnoses. *Journal of Applied Psychology, 66,* 252–254.
Arkes, H.R., Faust, D., Guilmette, T.J. & Hart, K. (1988). Eliminating the hindsight bias. *Journal of Applied Psychology, 73,* 305–307.
Barnes, W. (2005). Contemplating a civil law paradigm for a future international commercial code, *Louisiana Law Review, 65,* 677–774.
Beckham, J., Annis, L.V. & Gustafson, D.J. (1997). Decision-making and examiner bias in forensic expert recommendations for not guilty by reason of insanity. *Law & Human Behavior, 13,* 79–87.

Bernstein, D.E. (2008). Expert witnesses, adversarial bias, and the (partial) failure of the *Daubert* revolution. *Iowa Law Review, 93,* 451–489.

Bersoff, D.N. (1992). Judicial deference to nonlegal decisionmakers: Imposing simplistic solutions on problems of cognitive complexity in mental disability law*SMU Law Review, 46,* 329–372.

Bone, R.G. (2007). Who decides? A critical look at procedural discretion. *Cardozo Law Review, 28,* 1961–2023.

Browne, M.N., Williamson, C.L. & Barkacs, L.L. (2002). The perspectival nature of expert testimony in the United States, England, Korea, and France. *Connecticut Journal of International Law, 18,* 55–102.

Champine, P. (2006). Expertise and instinct in the assessment of testamentary capacity. *Villanova Law Review, 51,* 25–93.

Chapman, L.J. & Chapman, J.P. (1969). Illusory correlation as an obstacle to the use of valid psychodiagnostic signs. *Journal of Applied Psychology, 74,* 271–280.

Corso, P. (1993). Italy. In *Criminal Procedure Systems in the European Community,* 223–260 (Van Den Wyngaert, C., Gane, H., Kühne, H. & McAuleys, F., eds.). London: Butterworths.

Cound, J., Friedenthal, J., Miller, A. & Sexton, J. (2001) *Civil Procedure: Cases and Materials* (8th ed.). St. Paul, MN: West Publishing.

Deason, E.E. (1998). Court-appointed expert witnesses: Scientific positivism meets bias and deference. *Oregon Law Review, 77,* 59–156.

Dhir, A.A. (2005). Human rights treaty drafting through the lens of mental disability: The proposed International Convention on Protection and Promotion of the Eights and Dignity of Persons with Disabilities. *Stanford Journal of International Law, 41,* 181–216.

Dickey, I. (2008). Ethical dilemmas, forensic psychology, and therapeutic jurisprudence. *Thomas Jefferson Law Review, 30,* 455–461.

Dvoskin, J.A. & Guy, S.L. (2008). On being an expert witness: It's not about you. *Psychiatry, Psychology, and Law, 15,* 202–212.

Faust, D. (1993). Use and then prove, or prove and then use? Some thoughts on the ethics of mental health professionals' courtroom involvement. *Ethics & Behavior, 3,* 359–380.

Fellner, J. (2006). A conundrum for corrections, a tragedy for prisoners: Prisons as facilities for the mentally ill. *Washington University Journal of Law and Policy, 22,* 135–144.

Fon, V. & Parisi, F. (2006). Judicial precedents in civil law systems: A dynamic analysis. *International Review of Law and Economics, 26,* 519–535.

Greve, V. (1993). Criminal procedure in Denmark. In *Criminal Procedure Systems in the European Community,* 51–72 (Van Den Wyngaert, C., Gane, H., Kühne, H. & McAuleys, F., eds.). London: Butterworths.

Guthrie C., Rachlinski, J.J. & Wistrich, A.J. (2001). Inside the judicial mind. *Cornell Law Review, 86,* 777–830.

Haroun, A. & Morris, G. (1999). Weaving a tangled web: The deceptions of psychiatrists. *Journal of Contemporary Legal Issues, 10,* 227–246.

Haas, L.J. (1993). Competence and quality in the performance of forensic psychologists. *Ethics and Behavior, 3,* 251–266.

Hans, V. (2007). Judges, juries, and scientific evidence. *Journal of Law and Policy, 16,* 19–46.

Hanson, R.K. (1998). What do we know about sex offender risk assessment? *Psychology, Public Policy, and Law, 4,* 50–72.

International Union of Psychological Science. (2008). *Universal Declaration of Ethical Principles for Psychologists.* Retrieved October 1, 2010, from www.am.org/iupsys/ethics/univdecl2008.html

Jolls, C., Sunstein, C.R. & Thaler, R. (1998). A behavioral approach to law and economics. *Stanford Law Review, 50,* 1471–1550.

Kayess, R. & French, P. (2008). Out of darkness into light? Introducing the Convention on the Rights of Persons with Disabilities. *Human Rights Law Review, 8,* 1–34.

Kruglanski, A.W. & Ajzen, I. (1983). Bias and error in human judgment. *European Journal of Social Psychology, 13,* 1–44.

Kühne, H. (1993). Germany. In *Criminal Procedure Systems in the European Community,* 137–162 (Van Den Wyngaert, C., Gane, H., Kühne, H. & McAuleys, F., eds.). London: Butterworths.

La Fond, J.Q. & Durham, M.L. (1992). *Back to the Asylum: The Future of Mental Health Law and Policy in the United States.* New York City: Oxford University Press.

Lambie, I. (2001). Assessing competency in psychiatric contexts. *Journal of the American Academy of Psychiatry and Law, 29,* 31–52.

Lee, E.I. (1997). Expert evidence in the republic of Korea and under the US federal rules of evidence: A comparative study. *Loyola International and Comparative Law Review, 19,* 585–632.

Legrand, P. & Machado, A. (1998). Are civilians educable? *Legal Studies, 18,* 216–230.

Lord, J.E. & Stein, M.A. (2009). Social rights and the relational value of the rights to participate in sport, recreation, and play. *Boston University International Law Journal, 27,* 249–281.

Marcus, E.H. (1985). Unbiased medical testimony: Reality or myth? *American Journal of Forensic Psychiatry, 6,* 3–5.

McGuire, J. (1997). Ethical dilemmas in forensic clinical psychology. *Legal and Criminological Psychology, 2,* 177–192.

McNeil, B.J., Pauker, S.G., Sox, H.C. & Tversky, A. (1982). On the elicitation of preferences for alternative therapies. *New England Journal of Medicine, 306,* 1259–1262.

Meadow, W. & Sunstein, C.R. (2001). Statistics, not experts. *Duke Law Journal, 51,* 629–646.

Melish, T.J. (2007). The UN Disability Convention: Historic process, strong prospects, and why the US should ratify. *Human Rights Brief, 14,* 37–46.

Merlino, M.L., Murray, C.I. & Richardson, J.T. (2008). Judicial gatekeeping and the social construction of the admissibility of expert testimony. *Behavioral Sciences and the Law, 26,* 187–206.

Mnookin, J.L. (2007). Idealizing science and demonizing experts: An intellectual history of expert evidence. *Villanova Law Review, 52,* 763–801.

Mnookin, J.L. (2008). Expert evidence, partisanship and epistemic competence. *Brooklyn Law Review, 73,* 1009–1033.

Morse, S. (1982). Failed expectations and criminal responsibility: Experts and the unconscious. *Virginia Law Review, 68,* 971–1084.

Mossman, D. & Kapp, M.B. (1998). "Courtroom whores"?—Or, Why do attorneys call us? Findings from a survey on attorneys' use of mental health experts. *Journal of the American Academy of Psychiatry and Law, 26,* 27–36.

Mylonopoulos, C (1993). Greece. In *Criminal Procedure Systems in the European Community,* 163–184 (Van Den Wyngaert, C., Gane, H., Kühne, H. & McAuleys, F., eds.). London: Butterworths.

New Jersey Evidence Rule 104. Retrieved September 15, 2010, from http://www.njlawnet.com/njevidence.

Otto, R. (1989). Bias and expert testimony of mental health professionals in adversarial proceedings: A preliminary investigation. *Behavioral Sciences and the Law, 7,* 267–273.

Perlin, M.L. (1990). Are courts competent to decide competency questions? Stopping the facade from *United States v. Charters. University of Kansas Law Review, 38,* 957–1001.

Perlin, M.L. (1993). Pretexts and mental disability law: The case of competency. *University of Miami Law Review, 47,* 635–687.

Perlin, M.L. (1997). "The borderline which separated you from me": The insanity defence, the authoritarian spirit, the fear of faking, and the culture of punishment. *Iowa Law Review, 82,* 1375–1426.

Perlin, M.L. (2000a). A law of healing. *University of Cincinnati Law Review, 68,* 407–434.

Perlin, M.L. (2000b). *The Hidden Prejudice: Mental Disability On Trial.* Washington, DC: American Psychological Press.

Perlin, M.L. (2007). International human rights law and comparative mental disability law: The universal factors. *Syracuse Journal of International Law and Commerce, 34,* 333–357.

Perlin, M.L. (2008a). "Baby, look inside your mirror": The legal profession's willful and sanist blindness to lawyers with mental disabilities. *University of Pittsburgh Law Review, 69,* 589–607.

Perlin, M.L. (2008b). "They're an illusion to me now": Forensic ethics, sanism and pretextuality. In *Psychology, Crime and Law: Bridging the Gap,* 239–253 (Canter, D. & Zukauskiene, R., eds.). Hampshire, UK: Ashgate.

Perlin, M.L., Birgden, A. & Gledhill, K. (2009). "The witness who saw/He left little doubt": A comparative consideration of expert testimony in mental disability law cases. *Journal of Investigative Psychology and Offender Profiling, 6,* 59–88.

Perlin, M.L., et al. (2006). International human rights and comparative mental disability law: Cases and Materials. Durham, NC: Carolina Academic Press.

Plous, S. (1993). *The Psychology of Judgment and Decision-making.* New York: McGraw-Hill.

Pradel, J. (1993). France. In *Criminal Procedure Systems in the European Community,* 105–125. (Van Den Wyngaert, C., Gane, H., Kühne, H. & McAuleys, F., eds.). London: Butterworths.

Prentice, R.A. (2000). The SEC and MDP: Implications of the self-serving bias for independent auditing. *Ohio State Law Journal, 61,* 1597–1670.

Rachlinski, J.J. (2003). The uncertain psychological case for paternalism. *Northwestern University Law Review, 97,* 1165–1225.

Rachlinski, J.J., Guthrie, C. & Wistrich, A.J. (2006). Inside the bankruptcy judge's mind. *Boston University Law Review, 86,* 1227–1265.

Redding R.E., Floyd, M.Y. & Hawk, G.L. (2001). What judges and lawyers think about the testimony of mental health experts: A survey of the courts and bar. *Behavioral Sciences and the Law, 19,* 583–594.

Risinger, D.M. (2000). Navigating expert reliability: Are criminal standards of certainty being left on the dock? *Albany Law Review, 64,* 99–153.

Rowe, T.D., Sherry, S. & Tidmarsh, J. (2008). *Civil Procedure* (2d ed.). St. Paul, MN: Foundation Press.

Sanders, J., Diamond, S.S. & Vidmar, N. (2002). Legal perceptions of science and expert knowledge. *Psychology, Public Policy, and the Law, 8,* 139–153.

Schauer, F. (2006). Do cases make bad law? *University of Chicago Law Review, 73,* 883–918.

Schmidt, P. (2003). A review of China's new Civil Evidence Law. *Pacific Rim Law & Social Policy Journal 12,* 291–313.

Shuman, D.W. & Sales, B.D. (1998). The admissibility of expert testimony based upon clinical judgment and scientific research. *Psychology, Public Policy, and the Law, 4,* 1226–1252.

Simon, R.J. & Ahn-Redding, H. (2006). *The Insanity Defense, The World Over.* Portland. OR: Lexington Books.

Slobogin, C. (1985). The guilty but mentally ill verdict: An idea whose time should not have come. *George Washington Law Review, 53,* 494–527.

Slobogin, C. (2003). Pragmatic forensic psychology: A means of "scientizing" expert testimony from mental health professionals? *Psychology, Public Policy, and Law, 9,* 275–300.

Stein, M.A. & Stein, P.J.S. (2007). Beyond disability civil rights. *Hastings Law Journal, 58,* 1202–1240.

Stein, M.A. & Lord, J.E. (2008). Jacobus tenBroek, participatory justice, and the UN Convention on the Rights of Persons with Disabilities. *Texas Journal on Civil Liberties & Civil Rights, 13,* 167–185.

Taylor, R.F. (1996). A comparative study of expert testimony in France and the United States: Philosophical underpinnings, history, practice, and procedure. *Texas International Law Journal, 31,* 181–213.

Tikkanen, T. (2004). The European Diploma in Psychology (EuroPsy) and the future of the profession in Europe. *European Federation of Psychologists Associations,* 1–7. Retrieved September 15, 2010, from www.psychology-bg.org/rules/Status_o_profession_2003.pdf

Timmerbeil, S.G. (2003). The role of expert witnesses in German and US civil litigation. *Annual Survey of International and Comparative Law, 9,* 163–187.

Tversky, A. & Kahneman, D. (1993). Judgment under uncertainty: Heuristics and biases. In *Rationality in Action: Contemporary Approaches,* 171–188 (Moser, P.K., ed.). New York: Cambridge University Press.

United Nations. (2006). *Convention on the Rights of Persons with Disabilities.* Retrieved October 10, 2007, from http://www.un.org/disabilities/default.asp?navid = 12&pid = 150

Weinstein, H. et al. (2001). *Protecting the Mentally Disabled,* Carnegie Council (May 6, 2001), available at http:// www.cceia.org/resources/publications/dialogue/2_06/online_exclusive/654.html.

Chapter 6C

Alter, K.J. (2001). *Establishing the Supremacy of European Law: The Making of an International Rule of Law in Europe.* Oxford, UK: Oxford University Press.

Banakas, S. (2002), European tort law: Is it possible? *European Review of Private Law, 10,* 363–375.

Barrett v. London Borough of Enfield, (1999) P.I.Q.R. P272 (H.L.).

Cantu, D.A. (1998). When should federal courts require psychotherapists to testify about their patients? An interpretation of *Jaffee v Redmond. University of Chicago Legal Forum,* 375–394.

Curtice, M.J.R. & Sandford, J.J. (2009). Article 8 of the Human Rights Act 1998: A review of case law related to forensic psychiatry and prisoners in the United Kingdom. *Journal of the American Academy of Psychiatry and Law, 37,* 232–238.

D v. East Berkshire Community Health NHS Trust. [2005]. 2 A.C. 373 (H.L.).

Davies, A.C.L. (2001). The European Convention and negligence actions: *Osman* "reviewed." *Law Quarterly Review, 117,* 521–524.

Dubey, J. (1974). Confidentiality as a requirement of the therapist: Technical necessities for absolute privilege in psychotherapy. *American Journal of Psychiatry, 131,* 1093–1096.

English, R. (2001). Forensic immunity post-*Osman. Modern Law Review, 64,* 300–308.

European Tort Law. (2001). Oxford, UK: Oxford University Press.

Feldman, E.A. (2009). Law, society and medical malpractice litigation in Japan. *Washington University Global Studies Law Review, 8,* 257–284.

Flynn, M. (2010). *Olmstead* plans revisited: Lessons learned from the U.N. Convention on the Rights of Persons with Disabilities. *Law and Inequality, 28,* 407–437.

Fulero, S. (1988). *Tarasoff* 10 years later. *Professional Psychology: Research and Practice, 19,* 184–190.

Gavaghan, C. (2005). A *Tarasoff* for Europe? A European Human Rights perspective on the duty to protect. Abstracts of the XXIXth International Congress on Law and Mental Health, presentation 54.3, p. 162.

Gavaghan, C. (2007). A *Tarasoff* for Europe? A European Human Rights perspective on the duty to protect. *International Journal of Law and Psychiatry, 30,* 255–267.

Gearty, C. (2001). Unraveling *Osman. Modern Law Review, 64,* 159–190.

George, J.E. et al. (1983). The therapist's duty to protect third parties: A guide for the perplexed. *Rutgers Law Journal, 14,* 637–652.

Givelber, D.J. et al. (1985). The *Tarasoff* controversy: A summary of findings from an empirical study of legal, ethical, and clinical issues. In *The Potentially Violent Patient and the* Tarasoff *Decision in Psychiatric Practice,* 35ff. (Beck, J., ed.). Washington, DC: American Psychiatric Association.

Havers, P. (2001). The impact of the European Convention on Human Rights on medical law. *Medico Legal Journal, 70,* 57–70.

Hickman, T.R. (2002). Tort law and human rights. *King's College Law Journal, 13,* 253–261.

Hill, M. (2005). The permissible scope of legal limitations on the freedom of religion or belief in the United Kingdom. *Emory International Law Review, 19,* 1129–1186.

Hoffmann, L. (1999). Human rights and the House of Lords. *Modern Law Review, 62,* 159–166.

Human Rights Act (1998). U.K. *Legislation.gov.uk.* Retrieved September 15, 2010, from http://www.legislation.gov.uk/ukpga/1998/42/contents.

Jackson, J.H. (1992). Status of treaties in domestic legal systems: A policy analysis. *American Journal of International Law, 86,* 310–340.

Johnston, C. & Kaye, J. (2004). Does the UK biobank have a legal obligation to feedback individual findings to participants? *Medical Law Review, 12,* 239–267.

Kanter, A.S. (2003). The globalization of disability rights law. *Syracuse Journal of International Law and Commerce, 30,* 241–269.

Kwiecien, R. (2005). The primacy of European Union law over national law under the constitutional treaty. *German Law Journal, 6,* 1479–1496.

Li Suk Han Hana v. Sun Tien Lun Catherine, [2005] H.K.C. 758.

Lidbetter, A. & George, J. (2001). Negligent public authorities and convention rights—The legacy of *Osman. European Human Rights Law Review,* 599–615.

Masterman, R. (2005). Taking the Strasbourg jurisprudence into account: Developing a municipal law of "human rights" under the human rights act. *International and Comparative Law Quarterly, 54,* 907–931.

Mullender, R. (2003). Tort, human rights, and common law culture. *Oxford Journal of Legal Studies, 23,* 301–318.

Mullis, A. (2000). *Barrett v. Enfield London Borough Council:* A compensation-seeker's charter? *Child and Family Law Quarterly, 12,* 185–196.

Osman v. United Kingdom, 29 Eur. Ct. H.R. 245 (1998).

Palmer v. Tees Health Authority, [2000] P.I.Q.R. 1 (A.C.).

Perlin, M.L. (1992). *Tarasoff* and the dilemma of the dangerous patient: New directions for the 1990's. *Law and Psychology Review, 16,* 29–62.

Perlin, M.L. (2002). *Mental Disability Law: Civil and Criminal* (2d ed. Vol. 3). Newark, NJ: Lexis-Nexis Publ.)

Perlin, M.L. (2006). "You got no secrets to conceal": Considering the application of the *Tarasoff* doctrine abroad. *University of Cincinnati Law Review, 75,* 611–629.

R. v. Sec'y of State for Transp., ex parte Factortame Ltd. (No. 2), [1991] 1 AC 603 (H.L.).

Ross v. Fryer, [2003] NZFLR 666 (NZ Fam. Ct.).

Sharda v. Dharmpal, 2 LRI 173 (Ind. Sup. Ct. 2003).

Slynn, G.L. (2005). The development of human rights in the United Kingdom. *Fordham International Law Journal, 28,* 477–499.

Sullivan v. Moody, (2001) 207 CLR 562 (Austl.).

Tarasoff v. Regents of the Univ. of Cal., 551 P. 2d 334 (Cal. 1976).

Templeman, L. (1991). Treaty-making and the British Parliament. *Chicago-Kent Law Review, 67,* 459–471.

Tyrer v. United Kingdom, 2 Eur. Ct. H.R. 1 (1979–1980).

van Dijk, P. & van Hoof, G.J.H. (1990). *Theory and Practice of the European Convention on Human Rights* (2d ed.). Deventer, The Netherlands: Kluwer Law and Taxation Publishers.

van Gerven, W. (2002). The emergence of a common European law in the area of tort law: The EU contribution. In *Tort Liability of Public Authorities in*

Comparative Perspective, 125–136 (Fairgrieve, D., Andenas, M. & Bell, J., eds.). London: British Institute of International and Comparative Law.
W. v . Egdell, [1990] Ch. 359 (C.A.).
Wildhaber, L. (2007). The European Convention on Human Rights and international law. *International and Comparative Law Quarterly, 56*, 217–231.
Wise, T.P. (1978). Where the public peril begins: A survey of psychotherapists to determine the effects of *Tarasoff. Stanford Law Review, 31*, 165–190.
Wright, J. (2001). *Tort Law and Human Rights.* Oxford, UK: Hart Publishing.
Z. v. United Kingdom, 34 Eur. Ct. H.R. 3 (2002).

Chapter 6D

Abramowitz, M.Z. (2005). Prisons and the human rights of persons with mental disorders. *Current Opinions in Psychiatry, 18*, 525–529.
Adoption of Peggy, 767 N.E. 2d 29 (Mass. 2002).
Alexander, J.F. (2009). The International Criminal Court and the prevention of atrocities: Predicting the Court's impact. *Villanova Law Review, 54*, 1–55.
Almeida v. Correa, 465 P. 2d 564 (Hawai'i 1970).
American Friends Service. (2003). *Correlation of Prisoners' Issues and Conditions to International Covenants and Treaties: An AFSC Resource Guide.* Available at http://www.massdecarcerate.org/download/CJIssue_treaty_correlation200306.pdf
Birgden, A. & Perlin, M.L. (2008). "Tolling for the luckless, the abandoned and forsaked": Community safety, therapeutic jurisprudence and international human rights law as applied to prisoners and detainees. *Legal and Criminological Psychology, 13*, 231–243.
Birgden, A. & Perlin, M.L. (2009). "Where the home in the valley meets the damp dirty prison": A human rights perspective on therapeutic jurisprudence and the role of forensic psychologists in correctional settings. *Aggression & Violent Behavior, 14*, 256–263.
Bott v. DeLand, 922 P. 2d 732 (Utah 1996), overruled on other grounds in *Spackman ex rel. Spackman v. Bd. of Educ.*, 16 P. 3d 2000 (Utah 2000).
Bronstein, A. & Gainsborough, J. (2004). Using international human rights law and standards for U.S. prison reform. *Pace Law Review, 24*, 811–824.
Convention on the Rights of Persons with Disabilities. (2006). *UN Enable.* Retrieved September 15, 2010, from http://www.un.org/disabilities/default.asp?id=150
Curtice, M.J.R. & Sandford, J.J. (2009). Article 8 of the Human Rights Act 1998: A review of case law related to forensic psychiatry and prisoners in the United Kingdom. Journal of the American Academy of Psychiatry and Law, *37*, 232–238.
Dhir, A.A. (2005). Human rights treaty drafting through the lens of mental disability: The proposed international Convention on Protection and Promotion of the Rights and Dignity of Persons with Disabilities. *Stanford Journal of International Law, 41*, 181–216.
Elger, B.S. (2008). Towards equivalent health care of prisoners: European soft law and public health policy in Geneva. *Journal of Public Health Law Policy, 29*, 192–206.

Enforcing Human Rights: The U.N. Machinery. (1993). *United Nations Chronicle.* Retrieved October 11, 2010, from http://findarticles.com/p/articles/mi_m1309/is_n1_v30/ai_13830665/pg_4/?tag=content;col1

Farmer, P. (2003). *Pathologies of Power: Health, Human Rights, and the New War on the Poor.* Berkeley: University of California Press.

Fellner, J. (2006a). A conundrum for corrections, a tragedy for prisoners: Prisons as facilities for the mentally ill. *Washington University Journal of Law and Policy, 22,* 135–144.

Fellner, J. (2006b). A corrections quandary: Mental illness and prison rules. *Harvard Civil Rights-Civil Liberties Law Review, 41,* 391–412.

Flores v. Southern Peru Copper Corp., 414 F. 3d 233 (2d Cir. 2003).

Forest Grove School District v. T.A., 129 S. Ct. 2484 (2009).

GA Resolution. 56/168 (2001).

GA Resolution. A/61/106 (2006).

Gainsborough, J. (2008). Women in prison: International problems and human rights-based approaches to reform. *William & Mary Journal of Women and the Law, 14,* 271–304.

Geer, M.A. (2000). Human rights and wrongs in our own backyard: Incorporating international human rights protections under domestic civil rights law—A case study of women in United States prisons. Harvard Human Rights Journal, *13,* 71–133.

Graham v. Florida, 130 S.Ct. 2011 (2010).

Haney, C. (2003). Mental health issues in long-term solitary and "supermax" confinement. *Crime and Delinquency, 49,* 124–156.

Helfer, L. (2005). Exiting treaties. *Virginia Law Review, 91,* 1579–1648.

Henkin, L. (1997). International human rights standards in national law: The jurisprudence of the United States. In *Enforcing International Human Rights in Domestic Courts,* 189–205 (Conforti, B. & Francioni, F., eds.). The Hague: Kluwer Law International.

Hresko, T. (2006). In the cellars of the hollow men: Use of solitary confinement in U.S. prisons and its implications under international laws against torture, *Pace International Law Review, 18,* 1–27.

http://www.unhchr.ch/huridocda/huridoca.nsf/(Symbol)/A.CONF.157.23.En

International Covenant on Civil and Political Rights (1966). *Office of the United Nations High Commissioner for Human Rights.* Retrieved September 27, 2010, from http://www2.ohchr.org/English/law/cescr.htm

International Covenant on Economic, Social, and Cultural Rights. (1966). *Office of the United Nations High Commissioner for Human Rights.* Retrieved September 27, 2010, from http://www2.ohchr.org/English/law/cescr.htm

James, A. (2008). Children, the UNCRC, and family law in England and Wales. *Family Court Review, 46,* 53–62.

Jubilut, L.L. (2007). Death penalty and mental illness: The challenge of reconciling human rights, criminal law, and psychiatric standards. *Seattle Journal for Social Justice, 6,* 353–380.

Kayess, R. & French, P. (2008). Out of darkness into light? Introducing the Convention on the Rights of Persons with Disabilities. *Human Rights Law Review, 8,* 1–34.

Konrad, N., Arboleda-Florez, J., Jager, A.D., Naudts, K., Taborda, J. & Tataru, N. (2007). Consensus paper: Prison psychiatry. *International Journal of Prisoner Health, 3,* 111–113.

Kosak, J. (2005). Mental health treatment and mistreatment in prisons. *William Mitchell Law Review, 32,* 389–418.

Labelle, D. (2008). Bringing human rights home to the world of detention. *Columbia Human Rights Law Review, 40,* 79–133.

Lareau v. Manson, 507 F. Supp. 1177 (D. Conn. 1980), aff'd in part & rev'd in part, 651 F. 2d 96 (2d Cir. 1981).

Liebling, A. (2006). Prisons in transition. *International Journal of Law and Psychiatry, 29,* 422–430.

Lines, R. (2008). The right to health of prisoners in international human rights law. *International Journal of Prisoner Health, 4,* 3–53.

Marschke, L. (2004). Proving deliberate indifference: Next to impossible for mentally ill inmates. *Valparaiso Law Review, 39,* 487–519.

Maurer, M. & Chesney-Lind, M., eds. (2002). *Invisible Punishment: The Collateral Consequences of Mass Imprisonment.* Montreal: McGill-Queen's University Press.

McReynolds, L. & Wasserman, G. (2008). Risk for disciplinary infractions among incarcerated male youths: Influence of psychiatric disorder. *Criminal Justice and Behavior, 35,* 1174–1185.

Megret, F. (2008a). The Disabilities Convention: Human rights of persons with disabilities or disability rights? *Human Rights Quarterly, 30,* 494–516.

Megret, F. (2008b). The Disabilities Convention: Toward a holistic concept of rights. *International Journal of Human Rights, 12,* 261–278.

Melish, T. (2007). The UN Disability Convention: Historic process, strong prospects, and why the U.S. should ratify. *Human Rights Brief, 14,* 37–46.

Neziroğlu, I. (2007). A comparative analysis of mental and psychological suffering as torture, inhuman or degrading treatment or punishment under international human rights treaty law. *Essex Human Rights Review, 4,* 1–16.

Nicholls, T.L., Roesch, R., Olley, M.C., Ogloff, J.R.P. & Hemphill, J.F. (2005). *Jail Screening Assessment Tool (JSAT): Guidelines for Mental Health Screening in Jails.* Burnaby, BC: Mental Health, Law, and Policy Institute, Simon Fraser University.

Nilsen, E. (2007). Decency, dignity, and desert: Restoring ideals of humane punishment to constitutional discourse. *University of California Davis Law Review, 41,* 111–175.

Perlin, M.L. (2007). An internet-based mental disability law program: Implications for social change in nations with developing economies. *Fordham International Law Journal, 30,* 435–454.

Perlin, M.L. (2009). "A change is gonna come": The implications of the United Nations Convention on the Rights of Persons with Disabilities for the domestic practice of constitutional mental disability law. *Northern Illinois University Law Review, 29,* 483–498.

Perlin, M.L. et al. (2006). *International Human Rights and Comparative Mental Disability Law: Documents Supplement.* Durham, NC: Carolina Academic Press.

Perlin, M.L. & Dlugacz, H.A. (2008). *Mental Health Issues in Jails and Prisons: Cases and Materials.* Durham, NC: Carolina Academic Press.

Perlin, M.L. & Dlugacz, H.A. (2009). "It's doom alone that counts": Can international human rights law be an effective source of rights in correctional conditions litigation? *Behavioral Sciences & Law, 27,* 675–694.

Perlin, M.L. & McClain, V. (2009). "Where souls are forgotten": Cultural competencies, forensic evaluations, and international human rights law. *Psychology, Public Policy, and Law, 15,* 257–277.

Peters, J.K. (2006). How children are heard in child protective proceedings, in the United States and around the world in 2005: Survey findings, initial observations, and areas for further study. *Nevada Law Review, 6,* 966–1110.

Pope, K.S. & Gutheil, T.G. (2009). Psychologists abandon the Nuremberg ethic: Concerns for detainee interrogations. *International Journal of Law and Psychiatry, 32,* 161–166.

Rich, W. (2009). The path of mentally ill offenders. *Fordham Urban Law Journal, 36,* 89–119.

Roper v. Simmons, 543 U.S. 551 (2005).

Sen, A. (2006). Human rights and the limits of law. *Cardozo Law Review, 27,* 2913–2927.

State v. Romano, 155 P. 3d 1102 (Hawai'i 2007).

Stein, M.A. & Lord, J. (2008). Jacobus tenBroek, participatory justice, and the UN Convention on the Rights of Persons with Disabilities. *Texas Journal on Civil Liberties & Civil Rights, 13,* 167–185.

Stein, M.A. & Stein, P.J.S. (2007). Beyond disability civil rights. *Hastings Law Journal, 58,* 1203–1240.

Sudbury, J., ed. (2005). *Global Lockdown: Race, Gender and the Prison-Industrial Complex.* New York, NY: Routledge.

Talvi, S.J.A. (2007). *Women behind Bars: The Crisis of Women in the U.S. Prison System.* Emeryville, CA: Seal Press.

Turner, K.P. (2008). Raising the bars: A comparative look at treatment standards for mentally ill prisoners in the United States, United Kingdom, and Australia. *Cardozo Journal of International and Comparative Law, 16,* 409–456.

United Nations Body of Principles for the Protection of all Persons under Any Form of Detention or Imprisonment. (1988). Accessible at http://www.un.org/documents/ga/res/43/a43r173.htm.

Van Zyl Smit, D. (2006). Life imprisonment: Recent issues in national and international law. *International Journal of Law and Psychiatry, 29,* 405–421.

Vasiliades, E. (2005). Solitary confinement and international human rights: Why the U.S. prison system fails global standards. *American University International Law Review, 21,* 71–99.

Vienna Declaration on Crime and Justice (2001). *United Nations Office on Drugs and Crime.* Retrieved October 11, 2010, from http://www.unodc.org/pdf/crime/a_res_55/res5559e.pdf

Ward, T. & Birgden, A. (2007). Human rights and clinical correctional practice. *Aggression and Violent Behavior, 12,* 628–643.

Wasserman, G. et al. (2002). The voice DISC-IV with incarcerated male youth: Prevalence of disorder. *American Academy of Child and Adolescent Psychiatry, 41,* 314–321.

Chapter 7

Adams, D. (2005). The prohibition of widespread rape as a jus cogens. *San Diego International Law Journal, 6,* 357–398.

Allain, A. (2008). *Legal Position of Reservations to the UN Convention on the Rights of Persons with Disabilities.* Belfast, Ireland: Centre on Human Rights for Persons with Disabilities.

Allain, A. (2009). *Treaty Interpretation and the United Nations Convention on the Rights of Persons with Disabilities.* Belfast, Ireland: Centre on Human Rights for Persons with Disabilities.

AM (Somalia) v. Entry Clearance Officer, EWCA Civ 634 (2009).

Andersen-Watts, R. (2008). Recognizing our dangerous gifts: Applying the social model to individuals with mental illness. *Michigan State University Journal of Medicine and Law, 12,* 141–162.

Andrews, P.E. (2006). Some middle-age spread, a few mood swings, and growing exhaustion: The human rights movement at middle age. *Tulsa Law Review, 41,* 693–713.

Banks, A.M. (2009). CEDAW, compliance, and custom: Human rights enforcement in sub-Saharan Africa. *Fordham International Law Journal, 32,* 781–845.

Bernaz, N. (2009). Reforming the UN human rights protection procedures: A legal perspective on the establishment of the universal periodic review mechanism. In *New Institutions for Human Rights Protections* (Boyle, K., ed.). Oxford, UK: Oxford University Press.

Byrnes, A. (2008). The Disability Discrimination Ordinance, the UN Convention on the Rights of Persons with Disabilities, and beyond: Achievements and challenges after ten years of Hong Kong anti-discrimination legislation. Available at: http://law.bepress.com/unswwps/flrps08/art13 (last accessed, June 24, 2010).

Carver, R. (2010). A new answer to an old question: National Human Rights Institutions and the domestication of international law. *Human Rights Law Review, 10,* 1–32.

Cohen, P.S. (1995). Psychiatric commitment in Japan: International concern and domestic reform. *UCLA Pacific Basin Law Journal, 14,* 28–74.

De Burca, G. (2010). The European Union in the negotiation of the UN Disability Convention. *European Law Review, 35,* 174–196.

Declarations and Reservations (2010). *United Nations Enable.* Retrieved September 27, 2010, from http://www.un.org/disabilities/default.asp?id=475

Defeis, E.F. (2004). Universal Declaration of Human Rights: A standard for states. *Seton Hall Legislative Journal, 28,* 259–279.

Dhanda, A. (2007). Legal capacity in the Disability Rights Convention: Stranglehold of the past or lodestar for the future? *Syracuse Journal of International Law and Commerce, 34,* 429–462.

Dillon, S. (2008). What human rights law obscures: Global sex trafficking and the demand for children. *UCLA Women's Law Journal, 17,* 121–186.

Donnelly, M. (2008). From autonomy to dignity: Treatment for mental disorders and the focus for patient rights. *Law in Context, 26,* 37–61.

Farmer, A. & Stinson, K. (2009/2110). Failing the grade: How the use of corporal punishment in U.S. public schools demonstrates the need for U.S. ratification

of the Children's Rights Convention and the Convention on the Rights of Persons with Disabilities. *New York Law School Law Review, 54,* 1035–1069.
Fennell, P. (2008). Human rights, bioethics, and mental disorder. *Medicine and Law, 27,* 95–107.
Flynn, M. (2010). *Olmstead* plans revisited: Lessons learned from the U.N. Convention on the Rights of Persons with Disabilities. *Law and Inequality, 28,* 407–437.
Fritsch, C. (2009). Right to work? A comparative look at China and Japan's labor rights for disabled persons. *Loyola University Chicago International Law Review, 6,* 403–420.
Gable, L. (2007). The proliferation of human rights in global health governance. *Journal of Law, Medicine, and Ethics, 35,* 534–544.
Glor v. Switzerland. (2009). (12444/04), unreported (ECHR, Grand Chamber).
Goldsmith, J.L. & Posner, E. (2005). *The Limits of International Law.* New York: Oxford University Press.
Gottstein, J.B. (2008). Involuntary commitment and forced psychiatric drugging in the trial court: Rights violations as a matter of course. *Alaska Law Review, 25,* 51–105.
Governors of X Endowed Primary School v Special Educational Needs and Disability Tribunal, EWHC 1842 (Admin) (2009).
Gunn, P.C. (2009). Health care refugees. *Loyola University Chicago International Law Review, 6,* 339–364.
Gustavsson, A. & Zakrzewaka-Materys, eds. (1997). *Social Definitions of Disability.* Warsaw, Poland: Wydawniictwo "Zak."
Hendricks, A. (2007). Selected legislation and jurisprudence: The UN Convention on the Rights of Persons with Disabilities. *European Journal of Health Law, 14,* 273–298.
Hendricks, A. & Degener, T. (1994). The evolution of a European perspective on disability legislation. *European Journal of Health Law, 1,* 343–365.
Hernandez, V.T. (2008). Making good on the promise of international law: The Convention on the Rights of Persons with Disabilities and inclusive education in China and India. *Pacific Rim Law and Policy Journal, 17,* 497–527.
Hessel, B.D. (2008). United Nations update. *Human Rights Brief, 15*(3), 52–53.
Heyer, K. (2000). From special needs to equal rights: Japanese disability law. *Asian-Pacific Law and Policy Journal, 1,* 7–21.
http://archive.usun.state.gov/press_releases/20061213_396.html (accessed June 27, 2010).
http://www.un.org/disabilities/default.asp?id=475 (accessed June 27, 2010).
http://www.usun-ny.us/press_releases/20090730_156.html (accessed June 27, 2010).
http://www2.ohchr.org/English/law/parisprinciples.htm (accessed June 27, 2010).
Hunt, P. & Mesquita, J. (2006). Mental disabilities and the human right to the highest attainable standard of health. *Human Rights Quarterly, 28,* 332–356.
In the Matter of Mark C.H.—N.Y.S. 2d—, 2010 WL 1729403 (Sur. 2010).
International Disability Alliance (2008). Position paper on the Convention on the Rights of Persons with Disabilities and other instruments. Accessible at http://psychrights.org/Countries/UN/IDACRPDpaperfinal080425.pdf.

Kiss v. Hungary (2010). European Court of Human Rights. Accessible at http://www.mdac.info/en/european-court-human-rights-upholds-right-vote-per

Kayess, R. & Fogarty, B. (2007). The rights and dignity of persons with disabilities: A United Nations Convention. *Alternative Law Journal, 32,* 22–27, 60.

Kampf, A. (2008). The Disabilities Convention and its consequence for mental health laws in Australia. *Law in Context, 26,* 10–36.

Kanter, A.S. (2009). The United Nations Convention on the Rights of Persons with Disabilities and its implications for the rights of elderly people under international law. *Georgia State University Law Review, 25,* 527–573.

Katz, R.S. (2003). Genocide: The ultimate racial profiling. *Journal of Law and Social Challenges, 5,* 65–92.

Kenney, C. (2009). Disaster in the Amazon: Dodging "boomerang suits" in transnational human rights litigation. *California Law Review, 97,* 857–904.

Koh, H.H. (2007). Restoring America's human rights reputation. *Cornell International Law Journal, 40,* 635–659.

Kumpuvuori, J. & Katsui, (2009). Achieving human security through political advocacy: Linking Ugandan and Finnish DPO advocacy work to Article 14 of the UN CRPD. In *United Nations Convention on the Rights of Persons with Disabilities: Multidisciplinary Perspectives,* 208–225 (Kumpuvuori, J. & Schenin, M., eds.). Turku, Finland: Arkmedia Oy, Vaasa.

Laing, J. (2008). Information technology and biometric databases: Eugenics and other threats to disability rights. *Journal of Legal Technology Risk Management, 3,* 9–34.

Lawrence v. Texas, 539 U.S. 558 (2003).

Lawson, A. (2007). The United Nations Convention on the Rights of Persons with Disabilities: New era or false dawn? *Syracuse Journal of International Law and Commerce, 34,* 563–618.

Lawson, A. (2008). People with psychosocial impairments or conditions, reasonable accommodation and the Convention on the Rights of Persons with Disabilities. *Law in Context, 26,* 62–84.

Liu, S. & Halliday, T. (2009). Recursivity in legal change: Lawyers and reforms of China's criminal procedure law. *Law and Social Inquiry, 34,* 911–948.

Lord, J.E. & Brown, R. (2010). The role of reasonable accommodation in securing substantive equality for persons with disabilities: The UN Convention on the Rights of Persons with Disabilities. Accessible at http://papers.ssrn.com/sol3/papers.cfm?abstract_id=1618903

Lord, J.E. & Stein, M.A. (2009). Social rights and the relational value of the rights to participate in sport, recreation, and play. *Boston University International Law Journal, 27,* 249–281.

Lord, J.E., Suozzi, D. & Taylor, A.L. (2010). Lessons from the experience of the U.N. Convention on the Rights of Persons with Disabilities: Addressing the democratic deficit in global health governance. *Journal of Law, Medicine and Ethics, 38,* 564–579.

Lyon, B. (2010). The unsigned United Nations Migrant Worker Rights Convention: An overlooked opportunity to change the "brown collar" migration paradigm. *New York University Journal of International Law and Politics, 42,* 389–497.

Mahon, C. (2008). Progress at the front: The draft Optional Protocol to the International Covenant on Economic, Social, and Cultural Rights. *Human Rights Law Review, 8,* 617–646.

McBride, A.M., Benítez, C. & Danso, K. (2003). *Civic service worldwide: social development goals and partnerships (CSD Working Paper No. 03–13)*. St. Louis, MO: Washington University, Center for Social Development.
McCallum, R. (2010). *The United Nations Convention on the Rights of Persons with Disabilities: Some Reflections.* Accessible at http://ssrn.com/abstract=1563883
McSherry, B. (2009). International trends in mental health laws: Introduction. *Law in Context, 26,* 1–9.
Megret, F. (2008a). The Disabilities Convention: Human rights of persons with disabilities or disability rights? *Human Rights Quarterly, 30,* 494–516.
Megret, F. (2008b). The Disabilities Convention: Towards a holistic concept of rights. *International Journal of Human Rights, 12,* 261–277.
Melish, T.J. (2007). The UN Disability Convention: Historic process, strong prospects, and why the U.S. should ratify. *Human Rights Brief, 14,* 37–47.
Melish, T.J. (2009). From paradox to subsidiarity: The United States and human rights treaty bodies. *Yale Journal of International Law, 34,* 389–462.
Midgley, J. (1993). Ideological roots of social development strategies. *Social Development Issues, 15,* 1–13.
Midgley, J. (1995). *Social Development: The Developmental Perspective in Social Welfare.* Thousand Oaks, CA: Sage Publications.
Minkowitz, T. (2007). The United Nations Convention on the Rights of Persons with Disabilities and the right to be free from nonconsensual psychiatric interventions. *Syracuse Journal of International Law and Commerce, 34,* 405–427.
Munger, F. (2007). Constitutional reform, legal consciousness, and citizen participation in Thailand. *Cornell International Law Journal, 40,* 455–475.
Munger, F. (2008/2009). Globalization, investing in law, and the careers of lawyers for social causes: Taking on rights in Thailand. *New York Law School Law Review,* 53, 745–802.
Neumayer, E. (2007). Qualified ratification: Explaining reservations to international human rights treaties. *Journal of Legal Studies, 36,* 397–428.
Nicholson v. Knaggs [2009] VSC 64 (unreported) (Vickery, J.).
Parker, C. (2008). UN Convention on the Rights of Persons with Disabilities: A new right to independent living? *European Human Rights Law Review, 4,* 508–523.
Pauwelyn, J. (2005). The Sutherland report: A missed opportunity for genuine debate on trade, globalization and reforming the WTO. *Journal of International Economic Law, 8,* 329–346.
Perlin, M.L. (1998). *Mental Disability Law: Civil and Criminal* (2nd ed., Vol. 1). Newark, NJ: Lexis-Nexis.
Perlin, M.L. (2008a). "Everybody is making love/or else expecting rain": Considering the sexual autonomy rights of persons institutionalized because of mental disability in forensic hospitals and in Asia. *University of Washington Law Review, 83,* 481–508.
Perlin, M.L. (2008b). "I might need a good lawyer, could be your funeral, my trial": A global perspective on the right to counsel in civil commitment cases, and its implications for clinical legal education. *Washington University Journal of Law & Social Policy, 28,* 241–264.
Perlin, M.L. (2009). "A change is gonna come": The implications of the United Nations Convention on the Rights of Persons with Disabilities for the

domestic practice of constitutional mental disability law. *Northern Illinois University Law Review, 29,* 483–498.
Petersen, C.J. (2008). China's ratification of the Convention on the Rights of Persons with Disabilities: The implications for Hong Kong. *Hong Kong Law Journal, 38,* 611–643.
Petersen, C.J. (2010). Inclusive education and conflict resolution: Building a model to implement Article 24 of the Convention on the Rights of Persons with Disabilities in the AsiaPacific. *Hong Kong Law Journal, 40,* 481–512.
Piccard, A.M. (2010). U.S. ratification of CEDAW: From bad to worse? *Law and Inequality, 28,* 119–161.
Principles relating to the Status of National Institutions (The Paris Principles). (1993, December). *Office of the United Nations High Commissioner for Human Rights.* Retrieved September 27, 2010, from http://www2.ohchr.org/English/law/parisprinciples.htm
Quinn, G. (2007). NHRIs and the next steps under the UN Convention on the Human Rights of Persons with Disabilities. Accessible at http://nhri.net/2007/ICC_NHRIs_Disability-G_Quinn_EN.pdf (last accessed June 27, 2010).
Quinn, G. (2009). The United Nations Convention on the Rights of Persons with Disabilities: Toward a new international politics of disability. *Texas Journal on Civil Liberties and Civil Rights, 15,* 33–52.
Quinn, G. & Degener, T. (2002). *Human Rights and Disability: The Current Use and Future Potential Use of United Nations Human Rights Instruments in the Context of Disability.* New York: United Nations.
Ribet, B. (2010). Naming prison rape as disablement: A critical analysis of the Prison Litigation Reform Act, the Americans with Disabilities Act, and the imperatives of survivor-oriented advocacy. *Virginia Journal of Social Policy and the Law, 17,* 281–317.
Rosenthal, E. & Rubenstein, L.S. (1993). International human rights advocacy under the "Principles for the Protection of Persons with Mental Illness. *International Journal of Law and Psychiatry, 16,* 257–300.
Salise, H.J. & Dressing, H. (2005). Involuntary treatment and quality of mental health care: Is there any link? *Current Opinion in Psychiatry, 18,* 576–584.
Salzman, L. (2010). Rethinking guardianship (again): Substituted decision making as a violation of the integration mandate of Title II of the Americans with Disabilities Act. *University of Colorado Law Review, 81,* 157–245.
Sandoval, R.J. (2009). Gender in the Convention on the Rights of Persons with Disabilities. *Alabama Law Review, 60,* 1197–1207.
Schwartz, M. (2007). Deafness in Vietnam: Will the United Nations Convention on the Rights of Persons with Disabilities make a difference? *Syracuse Journal of International Law and Commerce, 34,* 483–515.
Skogly, S.I. (2009). Global responsibility for human rights. *Oxford Journal of Legal Studies, 29,* 827–847.
Stavert, J. (2010). *Glor v. Switzerland*: Article 14 ECHR, disability and non-discrimination. *Edinburgh Law Review, 14,* 141–146.
Stein, M.A. (2007a). A quick overview of the United Nations Convention on the Rights of Persons with Disabilities and its implications for Americans with disabilities. *Mental and Physical Disability Law Reporter, 31,* 679–683.
Stein, M.A. (2007b). Disability human rights. *California Law Review, 95,* 75–121.

Stein, M.A. & Lord, J.E. (2010). Monitoring the Convention on the Rights of Persons with Disabilities: Innovations, opportunities, and future potential. *Human Rights Quarterly, 32,* 2010 WLNR 19717060, accessible at http://ssrn.com/abstract=1533482.

Stein, M.A., Waterstone, M.E. & Wilkins, D.B (2010). Cause lawyering for people with disabilities. *Harvard Law Review, 123,* 1658–1703.

Talbot, R. (2010, July 22). Personal communication.

Talbot, R. (2010, August 26). Personal communication.

The Queen on the Application of Cardiff County Council v Welsh Ministers, (2009). EWHC 3684 (Admin).

The Queen (on the application of Steven Harrison) v The Secretary of State for Health, (2009). EWHC 574 (Admin).

Thio, L-A. (1999). Implementing human rights in ASEAN countries: "Promises to keep and miles to go before I sleep." *Yale Human Rights and Development Journal, 2,* 1–85.

Totah, M. (2003). Fortress Italy: Racial politics and the new immigration amendment in Italy. *Fordham International Law Journal, 26,* 1438–1504.

Townsend v. Calderone, 2010 WL 1999588 (D.N.J. 2010).

Twinomugisha, B.K. (2009). The role of the judiciary in the promotion of democracy in Uganda. *African Human Rights Law Journal, 9,* 1–22.

United Nations. (1986). *Study of the Current Dimension of the Problems of Intolerance and of Discrimination on Grounds of Religion and Belief.* Para. 17. Accessible at http://www2.ohchr.org/english/issues/religion/annual.htm.

United States Mission to the UN. (2006, December). Retrieved September 27, 2010, from http://archive.usun.state.gov/press_releases/20061213_396.html

United States Mission to the UN. (2009, July). Retrieved September 27, 2010, from http://www.usun-ny.us/press_releases/20090730_156.html

Vienna Convention on the Law of Treaties. (1969). 1155 U.N.T.S. 331.

Von Benzon, N.R., Makuch, K. & Makuch, Z. (2008). The right for disabled children to access the natural environment: A law and policy critique. *Willamette Journal of International Law and Dispute Resolution, 16,* 76–102.

Waddington, L. (2007). A new era in human rights protection in the European Community: The implications the United Nations' Convention on the Rights of Persons with Disabilities for the European community. Accessible at http://papers.ssrn.com/sol3/papers.cfm?abstract_id=1026581

Watters, C. & Ingleby, D. (2004). Locations of care: Meeting the mental health and social care needs of refugees in Europe. *International Journal of Law and Psychiatry, 27,* 549–570.

Weller, P. (2009). Human rights and social justice: The Convention on the Rights of Persons with Disabilities and the quiet revolution in international law. *Public Space: The Journal of Law and Social Justice, 4,* 74–91. www.un.org/disabilities/documents/events/csw54_side-event_rangtadasilva.doc

Chapter 8

Fombad, C.M. (2010). Mixed systems in Southern Africa: divergences and convergences. *Tulane European and Civil Law Forum, 25,* 1–21.

Gledhill, K. (2007). Human rights instruments and mental health law: The English experience of the incorporation of the European Convention on Human Rights. *Syracuse Journal of International Law and Commerce, 34,* 359–403.

Himonga, C. (2010). State and individual perspectives of a mixed legal system in Southern African contexts with special reference to personal law. *Tulane European and Civil Law Forum, 25,* 23–36.

Human Rights & Mental Health: Uruguay. (1995). Mental Disability Rights International. Accessible at http://www.mdri.org/mdri-reports-publications.html. (Mental Disability Rights International, 1995).

Human Rights & Mental Health: Mexico. (2000). Mental Disability Rights International. Accesible at http://www.mdri.org/mdri-reports-publications.html. (Mental Disability Rights International, 2000).

Addington v. Texas, 441 U.S. 418 (1979).

Airey v. Ireland, 32 Eur. Ct. H.R. (ser. A) at 15 (1979).

Bach, M. (2007). *Supported Decision Making under Article 12 of the UN Convention on the Rights of Persons with Disabilities: Questions and Challenges.* Accessible at http://www.inclusionireland.ie/documents/Bach-SupportedDecisionMaking-InclusionIrelandNov07.doc.

Banks, R. & Kayess, R. (2007). Disability advocacy: Too much talk and not enough action. In *Justice for People with Disabilities: Legal and Institutional Issues,* 153–168 (Hauritz, M., Sampford, C. & Blencowe, S., eds.). Sydney, Australia: The Foundation Press.

Bartlett, P., Lewis, O. & Thorold, O. (2007). *Mental Disability and the European Convention on Human Rights.* Leiden, The Netherlands: Martinus Nijhoff Publishers.

Bauer, A. (2007). Trends in involuntary psychiatric hospitalization in Israel, 1991–2000. *International Journal of Law and Psychiatry, 30,* 60–70.

Bazelon, D.L. (1973). The defective assistance of counsel. *University of Cincinnati Law Review, 42,* 1–46

Beaupert, F. (2009). Mental health tribunal processes and advocacy arrangements: "Little wins" are "no small feat." *Psychiatry, Psychology, and Law, 16,* 90–107.

Bhaba, F. (2009). Disability equality rights in South Africa: Concepts, interpretation and the transformation imperative. *South Africa Journal of Human Rights, 25,* 218–245.

Bindman, J. et al. (2003). The Human Rights Act and mental health legislation. *British Journal of Psychiatry, 182,* 91–94.

Bisogni, M. (2002). What is the role of the legal representative before the Mental Health Review Tribunal? *Law Society Journal, 40,* 72–74.

Bloch, F.S. (2007). *Access to Justice and the Global Clinical Movement.* NYLS Clinical Research Institute Paper No. 07/08–8 (Oct. 10, 2007). Unpublished manuscript on file with Social Science Research Network). Available at http://papers.ssrn.com/sol3/papers.cfm?abstract_id=1022685.

Carney, T. & Beaupert, F. (2008). Mental health tribunals: Rights drowning in un-"chartered" health waters. *Australian Journal of Human Rights, 13,* 181–208.

Carney, T., Tait, D., Chappell, D. & Beaupert, F. (2007). "Mental health tribunals": "TJ" implications of weighing fairness, freedom, protection and treatment. *Journal of Judicial Administration, 17,* 46–59.

Carney, T. et al. (2008). Advocacy and participation in mental health cases: Realisable rights or pipe dream? *Law in Context, 26,* 125–147.

Chan, G.K.Y. (2007). The right of access to justice: Judicial discourse in Singapore and Malaysia. *Asian Journal of Comparative Law, 2,* 24. Available at http://www.bepress.com/asjcl/vol2/iss1/art2/.

Currie v. Jamaica. (1989). U.N. Human Rights Committee, Communication No. 377/1989, P 13.6, U.N. Doc. CCPR/C/50/D/377/1989 (1994).

Davis, M.F. (2009). In the interests of justice: Human rights and the right to counsel in civil cases. *Touro Law Review, 25,* 147–184.

Dhir, A.A. (2005). Human rights treaty drafting through the lens of mental disability: The proposed International Convention on Protection and Promotion of the Rights and Dignity of Persons with Disabilities. *Stanford Journal of International Law, 41,* 181–216.

Engler, R. (2006). Shaping a context-based civil *Gideon* from the dynamics of social change. *Temple Political & Civil Rights Law Review, 15,* 697–718.

Forster, C.M. & Jivan, V. (2008). Public interest litigation and human rights implementation: The Indian and Australian experience. *Asian Journal of Comparative Law, 3,* 1–36.

GA Resolution. (2006). 61/106, P 12.3, U.N. Doc. A/RES/61/106 (Dec. 13, 2006).

Gable, L. (2007). The proliferation of human rights in global health governance. *Journal of Law Medicine & Ethics, 35,* 534–542.

Geisinger, A. & Stein, M.A. (2007). A theory of expressive international law. *Vanderbilt Law Review, 60,* 75–132.

Honig, J. & Fendell, S. (2000). meeting the needs of female trauma survivors: The effectiveness of the Massachusetts mental health managed care system. *Berkeley Women's Law Journal, 15,* 161–228.

Hortas, L.E. (2004). Asylum protection for the mentally disabled: How the evolution of rights for the mentally ill in the United States created a "social group." *Connecticut Journal of International Law, 20,* 155–183.

Human Rights & Mental Health: Mexico. (2000). Mental Disability Rights International. Retrieved September 30, 2010, from http://www.mdri.org/mdri-reports-publications.html.

Human Rights & Mental Health: Uruguay. (1995). Mental Disability Rights International. Retrieved September 30, 2010, from http://www.mdri.org/mdri-reports-publications.html.

Imai, S. (2002). A counter-pedagogy for social justice: Core skills for community-based lawyering. *Clinical Law Review, 9,* 195–227.

In re Mental Health of K.G.F., 29 P.3d 485 (Mont. 2001).

India Mental Health Act § 91, 1987, No. 14, Acts of Parliament. Available at http://www.disabilityindia.org/mentalact.cfm\

Iya, P. (2005). Enhancing the teaching of human rights in African Universities: What role for law school clinics? *International Journal of Clinical Legal Education, 7,* 20–28.

Johnson, E., Jr. (2000). Equal access to justice: Comparing access to justice in the United States and other industrial democracies. *Fordham International Law Journal,* 24, S83–S110.

Kampf, A. (2008). The Disabilities Convention and its consequence for mental health laws in Australia. *Law in Context, 26,* 10–36.

Kanter, A.S. (2007). The promise and challenge of the United Nations Convention on the Rights of Persons with Disabilities. *Syracuse Journal of International Law and Commerce, 34,* 287–321.

Kaufman, R.E. (2008). Access to the courts as a privilege or immunity of national citizenship. *Connecticut Law Review, 40,* 1477–1530.

Kingdon, D. et al. (2004). Protecting the human rights of people with mental disorder: New recommendations emerging from the Council of Europe. *The British Journal of Psychiatry, 185,* 277–279.

Kumar, C.R. (2008). Corruption, development and good government: Challenges for promoting access to justice in Asia. *Michigan State Journal of International Law, 16,* 475–570.

Lawson, A. (2008). People with psychosocial impairments or conditions, reasonable accommodation and the Convention on the Rights of Persons with Disabilities. *Law in Context, 26,* 62–84.

Lessard v. Schmidt, 349 F. Supp. 1078 (E.D. Wis. 1972).

Lewis, O. (2002). Mental disability law in central and eastern Europe: Paper, practice, promise. *Journal of Mental Health Law, 8,* 293–303.

Lidman, R. (2006). Civil *Gideon* as a human right: Is the U.S. going to join step with the rest of the developed world? *Temple Political and Civil Rights Law Review, 15,* 769–789.

Lottman, M. (1976). Paper victories and hard realities. In *Paper Victories and Hard Realities: the Implementation of the Legal and Constitutional Rights of the Mentally Disabled,* 93 (Bradley, V.J. & Clarke, G.E., eds.). Washington, DC: Health Policy Center, Georgetown University.

Margulies, P. (1992). The cognitive politics of professional conflict: Law reform, mental health treatment technology, and citizen governance. *Harvard Journal of Law & Technology, 5,* 25–63.

McAllister, L.K. (2008). Revisiting a "promising institution": Public law litigation in the civil law world. *Georgia State University Law Review, 24,* 693–734.

McQuoid-Mason, D.J. (2000). The delivery of civil legal aid services in South Africa. *Fordham International law Journal,* 24, S111–S142.

Melish, T. (2007). The UN Disability Convention: Historic process, strong prospects, and why the U.S. should ratify. *Human Rights Brief, 14,* 37–45.

Mental Disability Rights International. (2008). Projects: Neuro-Psychiatric Hospital of Paraguay. *Mental Disability Rights International.* Retrieved September 17, 2008, from http://www.mdri.org/projects/americas/paraguay/index.htm.

Mental Health Act, s. 15 of 2002. (S. Afr.).

Metzger, P. (2007). Doing Katrina time. *Tulane Law Review, 81,* 1175–1218.

Moses, M. (2007, August 13). Analysis of the Uganda Mental Treatment Act from a human rights and public health perspective. *Social Science Research Network.* Retrieved September 19, 2010, from http://papers.ssrn.com/sol3/papers.cfm?abstract_id=1006230.

Paoletti, S. (2006). Deriving support from international law for the right to counsel in the civil cases. *Temple Political and Civil Rights Law Review, 15,* 651–662.

Pearson, M. (2004). Representing the mentally ill: The critical role of advocacy under the Mental Health Act 1986 (Vic). *Alternative Law Journal, 29,* 174–177, 196.

Penal Reform Int'l & Bluhm Legal Clinic, eds. (2007). Access to justice in Africa and beyond: Making the rule of law a reality. South Bend, IN: NITA Press.

Perlin, M.L. (1996). Fatal assumption: A critical evaluation of the role of counsel in mental disability cases. *Law and Human Behavior, 16,* 39–59.

Perlin, M.L. (1997). "Make promises by the hour": Sex, drugs, and the ADA, and psychiatric hospitalization. *DePaul Law Review, 46,* 947–985.
Perlin, M.L. (1998). *Mental Disability Law: Civil and Criminal.* (2nd ed., Vol. 1). Newark, NJ: Lexis Law Publishing.
Perlin, M.L. (2002). "What's good is bad, what's bad is good, you'll find out when you reach the top, you're on the bottom": Are the Americans with Disabilities Act (and *Olmstead v. L.C.*) anything more than "Idiot wind?" *University of Michigan Journal of Law Reform, 35,* 235–261.
Perlin, M.L. et al. (2003a). Therapeutic jurisprudence and outpatient commitment law: Kendra's Law as case study. *Psychology, Public Policy, and Law, 9,* 183–208.
Perlin, M.L. (2003b). "You have discussed lepers and crooks": Sanism in clinical teaching. *Clinical Law Review, 9,* 683–729.
Perlin, M.L. (2007). International human rights law and comparative mental disability law: The universal factors. *Syracuse Journal of International Law & Commerce, 34,* 333–357.
Perlin, M.L. (2008). "I might need a good lawyer, could be your funeral, my trial": Global clinical legal education and the right to counsel in civil commitment cases. *Washington University Journal of Law and Policy, 28,* 241–264.
Perlin, M.L. (2009). "A change is gonna come": The implications of the United Nations Convention on the Rights of Persons with Disabilities for the domestic practice of constitutional mental disability law. *Northern Illinois University Law Review, 29,* 483–498.
Perlin, M.L. et al. (2006a). *International Human Rights and Comparative Mental Disability Law: Cases and Materials.* Durham, NC: Carolina Academic Press.
Perlin, M.L. et al. (2006b). *International Human Rights and Comparative Mental Disability Law: Documents Supplement.* Durham, NC: Carolina Academic Press.
Perlin, M.L. & Sadoff, R.L. (1982). Ethical issues in the representation of individuals in the commitment process. *Law and Contemporary Problems, 45,* 161–192.
Perlin, M.L. & Szeli, E. (2011). Mental health law and human rights: Evolution and contemporary challenges. In *Mental Health and Human Rights* (Dudley, M., ed.). Oxford, UK: Oxford University Press.
Rennie v. Klein, 653 F. 2d 836 (3d Cir. 1981).
Quinn, G. (2007, June). *The UN Convention on the Human Rights of Persons with Disabilities.* Keynote Speech at the European Conference on the Integration of Persons with Disabilities. Berlin.
Rice, S. (2007). A Human Right to Legal Aid (Macquarie Univ. Div. of Law, Working Paper No. 2007–14). *Social Science Research Network.* Retrieved September 19, 2010, from http://papers.ssrn.com/sol3/papers.cfm?abstract_id=1061541
Sesickas, L. (2000). Access to justice in Lithuania. *Fordham International Law Journal, 24,* 159–181.
Smith, R. (2007). Human rights and access to justice. *International Journal of the Legal Profession, 14,* 261–280.
Stein, M.A. (2007). Disability human rights. *California Law Review, 95,* 75–121.
Stein, M.A., Wilkins, D.B. & Waterstone, M.E. (2010). Book review: Cause Lawyering for People with Disabilities. *Harvard Law Review, 123,* 1658–1703.

Stuckey, R.T. (2002). Preparing students to practice law: A global problem in need of global solutions. *South Texas Law Review, 43,* 649–681.
U.N. Econ. & Soc. Council [ECOSOC], Comm. on Econ., Soc., and Cultural Rights, General Comment No. 5, Persons with Disabilities, P 9, U.N. Doc. No. E/1995/22 (Sept. 12, 1994).
Van Ness, S.C. & Perlin, M.L. (1977). Mental health advocacy—The New Jersey experience. In *Mental Health Advocacy: An Emerging Force in Consumers' Rights,* 62–71 (Kopolow, L.E. & Bloom, H., eds.). Washington, DC: U.S. Dep't of Health, Education & Welfare.
Waddington, L. (2007, September 27). A New Era in Human Rights Protection in the European Community: The Implications [of] the United Nations' Convention on the Rights of Persons with Disabilities for the European Community. *Social Sciences Research Network.* Retrieved September 19, 2010, from http://papers.ssrn.com/sol3/papers.cfm?abstract_id=1026581
Williams, V. (2006, November 12). *The Challenge for Australian Jurisdictions to Guarantee Free Qualified Representation Before Mental Health Tribunals and Boards of Review: Learning from the Tasmanian Experience?* Unpublished manuscript, on file with author.
Woo, M. et al. (2007). Migrant access to civil justice in Beijing. *Loyola University Chicago International Law Review, 4,* 101–105.
Wyatt v. Stickney, 325 F. Supp. 781 (M.D. Ala. 1971), aff'd sub. nom. *Wyatt v. Aderholt,* 503 F. 2d 1305 (5th Cir. 1974).
Yew, G.C.K. (2008). Access to justice for the poor: The Singapore judiciary at work. *Pacific Rim Law & Policy Journal, 17,* 595–648.
Zimerman, N. & Tyler, T. (2010). Between access to counsel and access to justice: A psychological perspective. *Fordham Urban Law Journal, 37,* 473–507.

Chapter 9

African Charter on Human and Peoples' Rights, preamble. (1981). African Commission on Human and Peoples' Rights. Retrieved September 30, 2010, from http://www.achpr.org/english/_info/charter_en.html.
Akiyama, A. (2010, March). Disability law in Asia and the Pacific. *Paper presented to conference on The Universal Implementation of the Convention on the Rights of Persons with Disabilities,* National Human Rights Commission of Korea, Seoul, Korea.
Al-Emadi, T.A. & Al-Asdmakh, M.A. (2006). Cultural differences and their impact: Some brief comments. *Chinese Journal of International Law, 5,* 807–810.
Alvarez, J. (2006). International organizations: Then and now. *American Journal of International Law, 100,* 324–347.
Anderson, K. (2000). The Ottawa Convention Banning Landmines, the role of non-governmental organizations and the idea of international civil society. *European Journal of International Law, 11,* 91–120.
Antkowiak, T.M. (2008). Remedial approaches to human rights violations: The Inter-American Court of Human Rights and beyond. *Columbia Journal of Transnational Law, 46,* 351–419.
Arendshorst, J. (2009). The dilemma of non-interference: Myanmar, human rights, and the ASEAN charter. *Northwestern Journal of International Human Rights, 8,* 102–121.

Armstrong, J.D. (1986). Non-governmental organizations. In *Foreign Policy and Human Rights: Issues and Responses*, 243–260 (Vincent, R.J., ed.). Cambridge, UK: Cambridge University Press.

Asian Human Rights Charter. (1998). Accessible at http://tahr.yam.org.tw/ahrc/index.html.

Asplund, K.D. (2009). Resistance to human rights in Indonesia: Asian values and beyond. *Asia-Pacific Journal on Human Rights and the Law, 10*, 27–47.

Banyan (2010, February 6). Asia's never-closer union. *The Economist*, 48.

Barnes, B.E. (2007). *Culture, Conflict, and Mediation in the Asian Pacific.* Lanham, MD: University Press of America.

Bell, D.A. (1996). The East Asian challenge to human rights: reflections on an east west dialogue. *Human Rights Quarterly, 18*, 641–667.

Bell, D.A. (2008). Beyond Liberal Democracy: Political Thinking in an East Asian Context. Princeton, NJ: Princeton University Press.

Blaser, A.W. (1985). Human rights in the third world and development of international nongovernmental organizations. In *Human Rights and Third World Development*, 273–285. (Shepherd, G.W., Jr. & Nanda, V.P., eds.). Westport, CT: Greenwood Press.

Blaser, A.W. (1992). How to advance human rights without really trying: An analysis of nongovernmental tribunals. *Human Rights Quarterly, 14*, 339–370.

Bloise, J.S. (2010). International human rights law in Japan: The cultural factor revisited. Accessible at http://papers.ssrn.com/sol3/papers.cfm?abstract_id=1715348.

Borgen, C.J. (2007). Transnational tribunals and the transmission of norms: The hegemony of process. *George Washington International Law Review, 39*, 685–764.

Brehms, E. (2001). *Human Rights: Universality and Diversity.* The Hague, The Netherlands: Martinus Nijhoff Publishers.

Brown, C. (2001). Human rights. In *The Globalization of World Politics*, 599–616 (Baylis, J. & Smith, S., eds.). Oxford, UK: Oxford University Press.

Brown, C. (2003). The evolution and application of rules concerning independence of the "international judiciary." *Law and Practice of International Courts and Tribunals, 2*, 63–96.

Bruun, O. & Jacobson, M. (2006). Introduction. In *Human Rights and Asian Values: Contesting National Identities and Cultural Representation in Asia.* 1–20. (London, UK: RoutledgeCurzon).

Buchanan, A. & Keohane, R.O. (2006). The legitimacy of global governance institutions. *Ethics and International Affairs, 20*, 405–437.

Burnard, P. et al. (2006). Views of mental illness and mental health care in Thailand: A report of an ethnographic study. *Journal of Psychiatric and Mental Health Nursing, 13*, 742–749.

Burstein, M. (2006). The will to enforce: An examination of the political constraints upon a regional court of human rights. *Berkeley Journal of International Law, 24*, 423–443.

Butegwa, F. (1994). Using the African Charter on Human and Peoples' Rights to secure women's access to land in Africa. In *Human Rights of Women: National and International Perspectives*, 495–514 (Cook, R.J., ed.). Philadelphia: University of Pennsylvania Press.

Byrnes, A., Durbach, A. & Renshaw, C. (2008). Joining the club: The Asia Pacific Forum of National Human Rights Institutions, the Paris Principles, and the advancement of human rights protection in the region. *Australian Journal of Human Rights, 14,* 63–98.

Byung-Sun, O. (1997). Cultural values and human rights: The Korean perspective. In *Human Rights in Asian Cultures, Continuity, and Change: A Regional Report in Support of the UN Decade for Human Rights Education,* 217–249. Osaka, Japan: Hurights Press.

Cabestan, J-P. (2009). Constitutionalism and western legal traditions in human rights in Asian legal systems: With a special focus on Chinese legal systems. In *One Country, Two Systems, Three Legal Orders,* 715–731 (Oliveira, J.C. & Cardinal, P., eds.). Berlin: Springer-Verlag.

Campbell, C. & McDonald, A. (2006). Practice to theory: States of emergency and human rights protection in Asia. In *Human Rights and Asian Values: Contesting National Identities and Cultural Representations in Asia,* 249–279. (Jacobson, M.J. & Bruun, O. eds.). London: RoutledgeCurzon.

Cantoral Benavides Case, Reparations (Art. 63(1) American Convention on Human Rights) Judgment of Dec. 3, 2001, Inter-Am Ct. H.R. (Ser. C) No. 88 (2001), available at http://www1.umn.edu/humanrts/iachr/C/88-ing.html

Cardenas, S. (2007). *Conflict and Compliance: State Responses to International Human Rights Pressure.* Philadelphia: University of Pennsylvania Press.

Carney, T. (2010). A regional Disability Tribunal for Asia and the Pacific: Helping to change the conversation? Accessible at http://ssrn.com/abstract=1688146

Carter, G. (1997). Remembering water: Overcoming historical amnesia in South Africa. *Colorado Journal of International Environmental Law and Policy, 8,* 359–393.

Carver, R. (2010). A new answer to an old question: National Human Rights Institutions and the domestication of international law. *Human Rights Law Review, 10,* 1–32.

Cavallaro, J.L. & Brewer, S.E. (2008). Reevaluating regional human rights litigation in the twenty-first century: The case of the Inter-American court. American Journal of International Law, *102,* 768–827.

Cavallaro, J.L. & Schaffer, E.J. (2004). Less as more: Rethinking supranational litigation of economic and social rights in the Americas. *Hastings Law Journal, 56,* 217–281.

Chanpattana, W. (2010). Asia's mental health crisis in the 21st century. *Journal of ECT, 26,* 2–4.

Chen, A.H.Y. (1999). Towards a legal enlightenment: Discussions in contemporary China on the rule of law. *UCLA Pacific Basin Law Journal, 17,* 125–165.

Cerna, C. (1996). Universality of human rights and cultural diversity: Implementation of human rights in different social-cultural contexts. *Human Rights Quarterly, 16,* 740–752.

Cerna, C. (2004). The Inter-American system for the protection of human rights. *Florida Journal of International Law, 16,* 195–212.

Chaibong, H. (2003). Family versus the individual: The politics of marriage law in Korea. In *Confucianism for the Modern World,* 334–359 (Bell, D. & Chaibong, H., eds.). Cambridge, UK: Cambridge University Press.

Chan, G.K.Y. (2007). The right of access to justice: Judicial discourse in Singapore and Malaysia, *Asian Journal of Comparative Law, 2,* 24. Available at http://www.bepress.com/asjcl/vol2/iss1/art2/

Chan, M.K. (1996). Hong Kong: Colonial legacy, transformation, and challenge. *Annals of the American Academy of Political and Social Science, 547,* 11–23.

Charnovitz, S. (2006a). Recent book on international law—Book review. *American Journal of International Law,* 100, 751–757 (reviews of Non-governmental Organisations in International Law. By Anna-Karin Lindblom. Cambridge, New York: Cambridge University Press, 2005, and NGOs and the United Nations: Institutionalization, Professionalization and Adaptation. By Kerstin Martens. New York: Palgrave Macmillan, 2005.).

Charnovitz, C. (2006b). Nongovernmental organizations and international law. *American Journal of International Law, 100,* 348–372.

Chen, A.H.Y. (2000). The interpretation of the Basic Law—Common law and mainland Chinese perspectives. *Hong Kong Law Journal, 30,* 380–401.

Chen, A.H.Y. (2003). Mediation, litigation and justice: Confucian reflections in a modern liberal society. In *Confucianism for the Modern World,* 257–287 (Bell, D. & Chaibong, H., eds.). Cambridge, UK: Cambridge University Press.

Chen, A.H.Y. (2006). Conclusion: Comparative reflections on human rights in Asia. In *Human Rights in Asia: A Comparative Study of Twelve Asian Jurisdictions, France, and the USA,* 487–516. (Peerenboom, R., Petersen, C.J. & Chen, A.H.Y., eds.). London, UK: Routledge.

Chen, J-h. (2008). Asia values? Why not, but how. In *Human Rights in Asia: A Reassessment of the Asian Values Debate,* 41–61 (Avonius, L. & Kingsbury, D., eds.). New York: Palgrave Macmillan.

Chesterman, S. (2008). Does ASEAN exist? The Association of Southeast Asian Nations as an international legal person. *Singapore Year Book of International Law, 12,* 199–211.

Chiam, S. (2009). Asia's experience in the quest for a regional human rights mechanism. *Victoria University Wellington Law Review, 40,* 127–148.

Clote, P. (2008). Implications of global warming on state sovereignty and Arctic resources under the United Nations Convention on the Law of the Sea: How the Arctic is no longer communis omnium naturali jure. *Richmond Journal of Global Law and Business, 8,* 195–248.

Cobbah, J.A.M. (1987). African values and the human rights debate: An African perspective. *Human Rights Quarterly, 9,* 309–331.

Cohen, A.J. (2006). Debating the globalization of U.S. mediation: Politics, power, and practice in Nepal. *Harvard Negotiation Law Review, 11,* 295–353.

Cohen. D. (2010, March 1). ASEAN's Intergovernmental Commission on Human rights and civil society initiatives in Southeast Asia. *Asia Pacific Bulletin, 51,* unpaginated.

Cohen, P.S. (1995). Psychiatric commitment in Japan: International concern and domestic reform. *UCLA Pacific Basin Law Journal, 14,* 28–74.

Congo v. Ecuador. (1999). Case 11.427, Inter-Am. C.H.R., Report No. 63/99, OEA/Ser. L. /V/II. 102.

Crow, M.E. (2005). From dyad to triad: Reconceptualizing the lawyer-client relationship for litigation in regional human rights commissions. *Michigan Journal of International Law, 26,* 1097–1137.

Dalai Lama (1999). Buddhism, Asian values, and democracy. *Journal of Democracy, 10,* 1–7.

Davis, M.C. (1996). Human rights and the founding of the Hong Kong special administrative region: A framework for analysis. *Columbia Journal of Transnational Law, 34,* 301–334.

Davis, M.C. (1998). Constitutionalism and political culture. *Harvard Human Rights Journal, 11,* 109–147.

Defeis, E.F. (1992). Freedom of speech and international norms: A response to hate speech. *Stanford Journal of International Law, 29,* 57–129.

Delahunty, R.J. & Perez, A.F. (2005). Moral communities or a market state: The Supreme Court's vision of the police power in the age of globalization. *Houston Law Review, 42,* 637–725.

Deng, F.M. (2009). A cultural approach to human rights among the Dinka. In *Human Rights, Southern Voices,* 44–52 (Twining, W., ed.). Cambridge, UK; Cambridge University Press.

Desierto, D.A. (2008). Postcolonial international law discourses on regional developments in South and Southeast Asia. *International Journal of Legal Information,36,* 387–431.

Desierto, D.A. (2009). Universalizing core human rights in the "new" ASEAN: A reassessment of culture and development justifications against the global rejection of impunity. *Göttingen Journal of International Law, 1,* 77–114.

Desierto, D.A. (2010). ASEAN's constitutionalization of international law: Challenges to evolution under the new ASEAN charter. *Columbia Journal of Transnational Law* (in press). Accessible at http://papers.ssrn.com/sol3/papers.cfm?abstract_id=1712831.

Dickinson, L.A. (2003). The promise of hybrid courts. *American Journal of International Law, 97,* 295–310.

Dinokoplia, B. (2009). Strengthening civil society participation and advocacy on human rights protection: The role of national human rights commissions. *Africa Legal Aid Quarterly Journal, 5,* 35–46.

Diokno, J.W. (1980). Asian lawyers, people's rights and human rights. *New Zealand Law Journal, 3,* 43–47.

Diokno, M.S.I. (2006). Once again, the Asian human values debate. In *Human Rights and Asian Values: Contesting National Identities and Cultural Representations in Asia,* 75–91. (Jacobson, M.J. & Bruun, O., eds.). London, UK: RoutledgeCurzon.

Disability at a Glance. (2009). *Disability at a Glance 2009: A Profile of 36 Countries and Areas in Asia and the Pacific.* New York: UN ESCAP.

Donders, Y. (2010). Do cultural diversity and human rights make a good match? *International Social Science Journal,* 15–35.

Donoho, D. (2006). Human rights enforcement in the twenty-first century. *Georgia Journal of International and Comparative Law, 35,* 1–52.

Durbach, A. (2010). Human rights commissions in times of trouble and transition: The case of the national human rights commission of Nepal. Accessible at http://papers.ssrn.com/sol3/papers.cfm?abstract_id=1609452

Durbach, A., Renshaw, C. & Byrnes, A. (2009). "A tongue but no teeth?" The emergence of a regional human rights mechanism in the Asia-Pacific. *Sydney Law Review, 31,* 211–238.

Duxbury, A. (2007). Moving towards or away from institutions? The future of international organizations in Asia and the Pacific. *Singapore Year Book of International Law, 11,* 177–193.

Edwards, G.E. (2010). Assessing the effectiveness of human rights non-governmental organizations (NGOs) from the birth of the United Nations to the 21st century: Ten attributes of highly successful human rights NGOs. *Michigan State Journal of International Law, 18,* 165–228.

Emmerson, D.K. (1995). Singapore and the "Asian values" debate. *Journal of Democracy, 6,* 95–105.

Engle, K. (2000). Culture and human rights: The Asian values debate in context. *New York University Journal of International Law and Politics, 32,* 291–333.

Englehart, N.A. (2000). Rights and culture in the Asian values argument: The rise and fall of Confucian ethics in Singapore. *Human Rights Quarterly, 22,* 548–568.

European Convention on Human Rights. (1950). *Hellenic Resources Network.* Retrieved September 28, 2010, from http://www.hri.org/docs/ECHR50.html

Farran, S. (2009). *Human Rights in the South Pacific: Changes and Challenges.* London: Routledge-Cavendish.

Feng, X. (2002). A review of the development of marriage law in the People's Republic of China. *University of Detroit Mercy Law Review, 79,* 331–398.

Forster, C.M. & Jivan, V. (2008). Public interest litigation and human rights implementation: The Indian and Australian experience. *Asian Journal of Comparative Law, 3,* 1–36.

Freeman, M. (1996). Human rights, democracy, and "Asian values." *The Pacific Review, 9,* 352–366.

Freeman, M. (2006). Universal rights and particular cultures. In *Human Rights and Asian Values: Contesting National Identities and Cultural Representations in Asia,* 43–58. (Jacobson, M.J. & Bruun, O., eds.). London, UK: RoutledgeCurzon.

Friedman, E. (1999). Asia as a fount of universal human rights. In *Debating Human Rights: Critical Essays from the United States and Asia,* 56–79. (Van Ness, P., ed.). London, UK: Routledge.

Friedman, E. (2006). Since there is no east and there is no west, how could either be the best. In *Human Rights and Asian Values: Contesting National Identities and Cultural Representations in Asia,* 21–42. (Jacobson, M.J. & Bruun, O., eds.). London, UK: RoutledgeCurzon.

Fritsch, C. (2009). Right to work? A comparative look at China and Japan's labor rights for disabled persons. *Loyola University Chicago International Law Review, 6,* 403–420.

Gammeltoft, T. & Hernφ, R. (2006). Human rights in Vietnam: Exploring tensions and ambiguities. In *Human Rights and Asian Values: Contesting National Identities and Cultural Representations in Asia,* 159–177. (Jacobson, M.J. & Bruun, O., eds.). London, UK: RoutledgeCurzon.

Gervais, D.J. (2003). Spiritual but not intellectual? The protection of sacred intangible traditional knowledge. *Cardozo Journal of International and Comparative Law, 11,* 467–495.

Gewirtz, D.S. (1994). Toward a quality population: China's eugenic sterilization of the mentally retarded. *New York Law School Journal of International and Comparative Law, 15,* 139–162.

Ghai, Y. (1994). Human rights and governance: The Asia debate. *Australian Year Book of International Law, 15,* 1–34.

Ghai, Y. (2009a). Universalism and relativism: Human rights as a framework for negotiating interethnic claims. In *Human Rights, Southern Voices,* 109–120 (Twining, W., ed.). Cambridge, UK: Cambridge University Press.

Ghai, Y. (2009b). Understanding human rights in Asia. In *Human Rights, Southern Voices,* 120–150 (Twining, W., ed.). Cambridge, UK: Cambridge University Press.

Ginsburg, T. (2010a). Eastphalia as the perfection of Westphalia. *Indiana Journal of Global Legal Studies, 17,* 27–45.

Ginsburg, T. (2010b). Judicial independence in authoritarian regimes: Lessons from Continental Europe. In *Judicial Independence in China: Lessons for Global Rule of Law Promotion,* 234–259. New York: Cambridge University Press.

Godshall, L.E. (2003). Making space for indigenous intellectual property rights under current international environmental law. *Georgetown International Environmental Law Review, 15,* 497–530.

Goldman, R.K. (2009). History and action: The Inter-American human rights system and the role of the inter-American Commission on Human Rights. *Human Rights Quarterly, 31,* 856–887.

Golub, S. (2007). The importance of legal aid in legal reform. In *Access to Justice in Africa and Beyond: Making the Rule of Law a Reality,* xv (Penal Reform Int'l & Bluhm Legal Clinic, eds.). South Bend, IN: NITA Press.

Gotanda, J.Y. (1995). Regional institutions in East Asia and the Pacific: Is the time ripe? *American Society of International Law Proceedings, 89,* 471–483.

Guarnieri, C. (2007). Courts and marginalized groups: Perspectives from Continental Europe. *International Journal of Constitutional Law, 5,* 187–209.

Guo, S. (2009). Implementation of human rights treaties by Chinese courts: Problems and prospects. *Chinese Journal of International Law, 8,* 161–178.

Guzman, A. (2008). International tribunals: A rational choice analysis. *University of Pennsylvania Law Review, 157,* 171–235.

Hafner-Burton, E. & Tsutsui, K. (2005). Human rights in a globalizing world: The paradox of empty promises. *American Journal of Sociology, 110,* 1373–1411.

Hahm, C. & Paik, W. (2003). Legalistic Confucianism and economic development in East Asia. *Journal of East Asian Studies, 3,* 461–491.

Hakimi, M. (2006). The media as participants in the international legal process. *Duke Journal of Comparative and International Law, 16,* 1–33.

Halevy, T. (2008). ADR client strategies in the UK: Leading lawyers on preparing clients, navigating the negotiation process and overcoming obstacles. *Aspatore,* 2008 WL 5662124, *1–*15.

Haley, J.O. (2006). Law and culture in China and Japan: A framework for analysis. *Michigan Journal of International Law, 27,* 895–915.

Halliday, T.C. (2009). Recursivity of global normmaking: A sociolegal agenda. *Annual Review of Law and Social Science, 5,* 16.1–16.27.

Halliday, T.C. & Carruthers, B.G. (2007). The recursivity of law: Global norm making and national lawmaking in the globalization of corporate insolvency regimes. *American Journal of Sociology, 112,* 1135–1202.

Halliday, T.C. & Oshinsky, P. (2006). Globalization of law. *Annual Review of Sociology, 32,* 446–470.

Harding, A. (2007). Buddhism, human rights, and constitutional reform in Thailand. *Asian Journal of Comparative Law, 2,* 1–25.

Harris, S.R. (2000). Asian human rights: Forming a regional covenant. *Asian-Pacific Law & Policy Journal, 1,* 17, 1–22.

Hashimoto, H. (2004). *The Prospects for a Regional Human Rights Mechanism in East Asia.* New York: Routledge.

Hay, K. (2009). A Pacific human rights mechanism: Specific challenges and requirements. *Victoria University of Wellington Law Review, 40,* 195–214.

Helfer, L.R. & Slaughter, A-M. (1997). Toward a theory of effective supranational adjudication. *Yale Law Journal, 107,* 273–391.

Helfer, L.R. & Slaughter, A-M. (2005). Why states create international tribunals: A response to Professors Posner and Yoo. *California Law Review, 93,* 899–955.

Helman, C.G. (2001). *Culture, Health and Illness* (4th ed.). London, UK: Arnold Publ.

Hendriks, A. & Degener, T. (1994). The evolution of a European perspective on disability legislation. *European Journal of Health Law, 1,* 343–365.

Hernandez, V.T. (2008). Making good on the promise of international law: The Convention on the Rights of Persons with Disabilities and inclusive education in China and India. *Pacific Rim Law and Policy Journal, 17,* 497–527.

Heyns, C. & Magnus, K. (2010). Towards minimum standards for regional human rights systems. In *Essays on International Law in Honor of W. Michael Reisman* (Arsanjani, M.H. et al., eds.). In press. Available at http://papers.ssrn.com/sol3/papers.cfm?abstract_id=1572441.

Higgins, R. (1994). *Problems and Process: International Law and How We Use It.* Oxford, UK: Oxford University Press.

Higonnet, E.R. (2006). Restructuring hybrid courts: Local empowerment and national criminal justice reform. *Arizona Journal of International and Comparative Law, 23,* 347–434.

Hoang, N. (2008). Human dignity and fundamental freedoms—Global values of human rights: A response to cultural relativism. Accessible at http://papers.ssrn.com/sol3/papers.cfm?abstract_id=1314288

Hoang, N. (2009). The "Asian values" perspective of human rights: A challenge to universal human rights. Accessible at http://papers.ssrn.com/sol3/papers.cfm?abstract_id=1405436

Honghua, M. (2010). East-Asian order formation and Sino-Japanese relations. *Indiana Journal of Global Law Studies, 17,* 47–82.

Howard, R. (1986). Is there an African concept of human rights? In *Foreign Policy and Human Rights: Issues and Responses,* 11–32 (Vincent, R.J., ed.). Cambridge, UK: Cambridge University Press.

Hsiao, C-Y & Van Riper, M. (2010). Research on caregiving in Chinese families living with mental illness: A critical review. *Journal of Family Nursing, 16,* 68–100.

Hsieh, P.L. (2007). An unrecognized state in foreign and international courts: The case of the Republic of China on Taiwan. *Michigan Journal of International Law, 28,* 765–814.

Hsiung, J.C. (1985). Human rights in an East Asian perspective. In *Human Rights in East Asia: A Cultural Perspective,* 1–30 (Hsiung, J.C., ed.). New York: Paragon House Publishers.

Hsu, C-Y. (1991). Applying Confucian ethics to international relations. *Ethics and International Affairs, 5,* 15–31.

Hui, P.T.C. (2002). Birth control in China: Cultural, gender, socio-economic and legislative perspectives in light of CEDAW standards. *Hong Kong Law Journal, 32,* 187–205.

Human Rights in Asian Cultures, Continuity, and Change: A Regional Report in Support of the UN Decade for Human Rights Education. (1997). Osaka, Japan: Hurights Press.

Hunt, M. (2005). State obligations following from a judgment of the European Court of Human Rights. In *European Court of Human Rights: Remedies and Execution of Judgments,* 25–47 (Christou, T.A. & Raymond, J.P., eds.). London, UK: British Institute of International and Comparative Law.

Hyndman, P. (1992). Appendix 1: Report on a proposed Pacific Charter of Human Rights prepared under the auspices of LAWASIA, May 1989. *Victoria University of Wellington Law Review, 22,* 99–174.

Ikehara, Y. (2010). Disability rights tribunal in Asia and the Pacific. Paper presented to conference on The Universal Implementation of the Convention on the Rights of Persons with Disabilities, National Human Rights Commission of Korea, March, 2010. Seoul, Korea.

Inada, K.K. (1986). A Buddhist response to the nature of human rights. In *Asian Perspectives on Human Rights,* 91–103 (Welch, C.E. & Leary, V.A., eds). Boulder, Colorado: Westview Press.

Information Office of the State Council of the People's Republic of China (2009). Practice and document: National human rights action plan of China (2009–2010). *Chinese Journal of International Law, 8,* 741–777 (Information Office).

International Tribunal for the Law of the Sea. http://www.itlos.org/start2_en.html (last visited April 30, 2010).

Islam, A-U.M. (1997). Public interest litigation: Experiences in South Asia: (Rights in search of remedies). *International Review of Constitutionalism, 7,*129–176.

Iwasaya, Y. (1997). International human rights adjudication in Japan. In *Enforcing International Human Rights in Domestic Courts* 223–293 (Conforti, B. & Francioni, F., eds.). The Hague, Netherlands: Kluwer Law International.

Iyawa, Y. (1997). International human rights adjudication in Japan. In *Enforcing International Human Rights in Domestic Courts,* 223–293 (Conforti, B. & Francioni, F., eds.). The Hague: Kluwer Law International.

Jacobson M. & Bruun, O. (2006). *Human Rights and Asian Values: Contesting National Identities and Cultural Representations in Asia.* London, UK: RoutledgeCurzon.

Jackson, J.H. (1992). Status of treaties in domestic legal systems: A policy analysis. *American Journal of International Law, 86,* 310–340.

Jalal, P.I. (2009). Why do we need a Pacific Human Rights Commission? *Victoria University Wellington Law Review, 40,* 177–194.

Jarmul, H.D. (1995–96). The effect of decisions of regional human rights tribunals on national courts. *New York University Journal of International Law and Politics, 28,* 311–365.

Johnson, L. (1997). Expanding eugenics or improving health care in china: Commentary on the provisions of the standing committee of the Gansu people's congress concerning the prohibition of reproduction by intellectually impaired persons. *Law and Society, 24,* 199–234.

Johnston, K. (2005). Māori women confront discrimination: using international human rights law to challenge discriminatory practices. *Indigenous Law Journal, 4,* 19–67.

Jones, D.M. (2008). Security and democracy: The ASEAN charter and the dilemmas of regionalism in South-east Asia. *International Affairs, 84,* 735–756.

Jones, K. (1988). Buddhism and social action: An exploration. In *The Path of Compassion: Writings on Socially Engaged Buddhism,* 65–81. (Eppsteiner, F., ed.). Berkeley, CA: Parallax Press.

Jones, S. (1996). Regional institutions for protecting human rights in Asia. *Australian Journal of International Affairs, 50,* 269–277.

Jones, S. (1996). Regional institutions for protecting human rights in Asia. *Australian Journal of International Affairs, 50,* 269–277.

Jung, K.D. (1994, November–December). Is culture destiny? The myth of Asia's anti-democratic values. *Foreign Affairs, 73,* 189–194.

Kanter, A.S. (2009). The United Nations Convention on the Rights of Persons with Disabilities and its implications for the rights of elderly people under international law. *Georgia State University Law Review, 25,* 527–573.

Katsumata, H. (2009). ASEAN and human rights: Resisting Western pressure or emulating the West? *The Pacific Review, 22,* 619–637.

Kausikan, B.K.H.P.S. (1995–1996). An East Asian approach to human rights. *Buffalo Journal of International Law, 2,* 263–283.

Kayess, R. & French, P. (2008). Out of darkness into light? Introducing the Convention on the Rights of Persons with Disabilities. *Human Rights Law Review, 8,* 1–34.

Keith, K.J. (2010). International Court of Justice: Reflections on the electoral process. *Chinese Journal of International Law, 9,* 49–80.

Keith, R.C. & Lin, Z. (2001). *Law and Justice in China's New Marketplace.* Hampshire, UK: Palgrave.

Kelsall, M.S. (2010). The new ASEAN Intergovernmental Commission on Human Rights: Toothless tiger or tentative first step? *Asia Pacific Issues, No. 90,* 1–8.

Keown, D. (1998). Are there human rights in Buddhism? In *Buddhism and Human Rights,* 15–42 (Keown, D.V., Prebish, C.S. & Husted, W.R., eds.). Surrey, UK: Curzon.

Keown, D.V., Prebish, C.S. & Husted, W.R., eds. (1998). *Buddhism and Human Rights.* Surrey, UK: Curzon.

Khushalani, Y. (1983). Human rights in Asia and Africa. *Human Rights Law Journal, 4,* 403–442.

Kingdon, D. (2004). Recommendations emerging from the Council of Europe. *British Journal of Psychiatry, 185,* 277–279.

Klein, R. (2001). Cultural relativism, economic development, and international human rights in the Asian context. *Touro International Law Review, 9*, 1–70.

Ko, H. & Koo, J. (2010). Cultural values and the Korean negotiator. *Journal of Korean Law, 9*, 225–244.

Kreder, J.A. (2007). Reconciling individual and group justice with the need for repose in Nazi-looted art disputes. *Brooklyn Law Review, 73*, 155–216.

Kumar, C.R. (2008). Corruption, development and good government: Challenges for promoting access to justice in Asia. *Michigan State Journal of International Law, 16*, 475–570.

Lanfang, F. (2009). Enforcement of arbitral awards between Hong Kong and Mainland China: A successful model? *Chinese Journal of International Law, 8*, 621–636.

Langlois, A.J. (2001). *The Politics of Justice and Human Rights: Southeast Asia and Universalist Theory*. Cambridge, UK: Cambridge University Press.

Law of the People's Republic of China on Maternal and Infant Health Care. (1994). Available at http://www.npc.gov.cn/englishnpc/Law/2007-12/12/content_1383796.htm ("Maternal and Health Care Law").

Lawson, S. (1996). Cultural relativism and democracy: Political myths about "Asia" and the "west."' In *Pathways to Asia: The Politics of Engagement* (Robison, R., ed). Sydney, Australia: Allen and Unwin.

Leary, V.A. (1987). Human rights in the Asian context: Prospects for regional human rights instruments. *Connecticut Journal of International Law, 2*, 319–339.

Leary, V.A. (1990). The Asian region and the international human rights movement. In *Asian Perspectives on Human Rights*, 13–27 (Welch, C.E., Jr. & Leary, V.A., eds.). Boulder, CO: Westview Press.

Ledgerwood, J.L. & Un, K. (2003). Global concepts and local meaning: Human rights and Buddhism in Cambodia. *Journal of Human Rights, 2*, 531–549.

Lee, J. (2009). Legal reform to advance the rights of women in Afghanistan within the framework of Islam. *Santa Clara Law Review, 49*, 531–564.

Lee, M.Y.K. (2008). Universal human dignity: Some reflections in the Asian context. *Asian Journal of Comparative Law, 3*, 1–33.

Lee, S.K. (1993). South Korea: Implementation and application of human rights covenants. *Michigan Journal of International Law, 14*, 705–738.

Levin, M. (2010). Civil procedural justice in Japan. Retrievable at http://papers.ssrn.com/sol3/papers.cfm?abstract_id=1653992

Liebman, B.L. (2009). Assessing China's legal reforms. *Columbia Journal of Asian Law, 23*, 17–33.

Lim, R. (1998). The ASEAN Regional Forum: Building on sand. *Contemporary Southeast Asia, 20*, 115–136.

Linnan, D.K. (1995). Implications for fisheries management of U.S. acceptance of the 1982 Convention on the Law of the Sea. *American Journal of International Law, 89*, 792–834.

Linton, S. (2008). ASEAN states, their reservations to human rights treaties and the proposed ASEAN Commission on Women and Children. *Human Rights Quarterly, 30*, 436–493.

Liu, H-E. (2004). Custody decisions in social and cultural contexts: In-depth and focus group interviews with nineteen judges in Taiwan. *Columbia Journal of Asian Law, 17*, 225–305.

Liu, S. & Halliday, T.C. (2009). Recursivity in legal change: Lawyers and reforms of China's criminal procedure law. *Law & Social Inquiry, 34,* 911–950.

Lo, C-F. (2010). Values to be added to an "Eastphalia order" by the emerging China. *Indiana Journal of Global Studies, 17,* 13–25.

Loh, C. (1995). The Vienna process and the importance of universal standards in Asia. In *Human Rights and Chinese Values: Legal, Philosophical, and Political Perspectives,* 145–167 (Davis, M.C., ed.). Hong Kong: Oxford University Press.

Lynch, C. (2009). Indonesia's use of capital punishment for drug-trafficking crimes: Legal obligations, extralegal factors, and the Bali Nine case. *Columbia Human Rights Law Review, 40,* 523–593.

Mahlman, M. (2010). The Basic Law at 60—Human dignity and the culture of republicanism. *German Law Journal, 11,* 9–31.

Mancuso, S. (2009). Legal transplants and economic development: Civil law vs. common law? In *One Country, Two Systems, Three Legal Orders,* 75–89 (Oliveira, J.C. & Cardinal, P., eds.). Berlin: Springer-Verlag.

Mandiberg, J. (1993). Between a rock and a hard place: The mental health system in Japan. *New Directions for Mental Health Services, 60,* 1–12.

Marfording, A. (1997). Cultural relativism and the construct of culture: An examination of Japan. *Human Rights Quarterly, 19,* 431–448.

Marks, S.P. (2009). The past and future of the separation of human rights into categories. *Maryland International Law Journal, 24,* 209–243.

Marriage Law of the People's Republic of China, Art. 7(b) (2001). Available at http://www.lawinfochina.com/law/display.asp?db=1&id=1793&keyword

Marsh, C. & Payne, D.P. (2007). The globalization of human rights and the socialization of human rights norms. *Brigham Young University Law Review,* 665–687.

Martin, M.D. (2007). The dysfunctional progeny of eugenics: Autonomy gone AWOL. *Cardozo Journal of International and Comparative Law, 15,* 371–421.

Mautner, M. (2008). From "honor" to "dignity": How should a liberal state treat non-liberal cultural groups? *Theoretical Inquiries in Law, 9,* 609–642.

Mauzy, D.K. (1997). The human values and "Asian values" debate in Southeast Asia: Trying to clarify the key issues. *Pacific Review, 19,* 210–236.

Mauzy, D.K. & Milner, R.S. (1995). Human rights in ASEAN states: A Canadian policy perspective. In *New Challenges for ASEAN: Emerging Policy Issues* 115–145 (Acharya, A. & Stubbs, R., eds.). Vancouver, BC: University of British Columbia Press.

McCorquodale, R. (2006). Spreading weeds beyond their garden: Extraterritorial responsibility of states for violations of human rights by corporate nationals. *American Society of International Law Proceedings, 100,* 95–102.

Meijknecht, A. & de Vries, B.S. (2010). Is there a place for minorities' and indigenous peoples' rights within ASEAN? Asian values, ASEAN values, and the protection of Southeast Asian minorities and indigenous peoples. *International Journal of Minority and Group Rights, 17,* 75–110.

Merry, S.E. (2006). Transnational human rights and local activism: Mapping the middle. *American Anthropologist, 108,* 38–51.

Milner, A. (2000). What happened to "Asian values"? In *Towards Recovery in Pacific Asia,* 56–68 (Segal, G. & Goodman, D.S.G., eds.). London, UK: Routledge.

Mohamad, M. (2002). Towards a human rights regime in Southeast Asia: Charting the course of state commitment. *Contemporary Southeast Asia, 24,* 230–251.

Mohamed, A.A. (1999). Individual and NGO participation in human rights litigation before the African Court of Human and Peoples' Rights: Lessons from the European and Inter-American Courts of Human Rights. *Michigan State University-DCL Journal of International Law, 8,* 377–396.

Monshipouri, M. (2001). Promoting universal human rights: Dilemmas of integrating developing countries. *Yale Human Rights and Development Law Journal, 4,* 25–61.

Moyle, K.J. (1997). A cultural exchange: Singapore and the United States can learn from each other in restructuring social security plans. *Pacific Rim Law and Policy Journal, 6,* 449–495.

Mubarak, A.R. (2003), Malaysia's social policies on mental health: A critical theory. *Journal of Health and Social Policy, 17,* 55–72.

Muedini, F.A. (2010). Examining Islam and human rights from the perspective of Sufism. *Muslim World Journal of Human Rights, 7,* 1–23.

Munro, J. (2009). Why states create international human rights mechanisms: The ASEAN Intergovernmental Commission on Human Rights and democratic lock-in theory. *Asia-Pacific Journal on Human Rights and the Law, 10,* 1–26.

Munro, R. (2000). Judicial psychiatry in China and its political abuse. *Columbia Journal of Asian Law, 14,* 1–125.

Munro, R. (2006). *China's Psychiatric Inquisition: Dissent, Psychiatry and the Law in Post-1999 China.* London: Wildy, Simmonds & Hill.

Muntarbhorn, V. (1998). Asia, human rights and the new millennium: Time for a regional human rights charter? *Transnational Law and Contemporary Problems, 8,* 407–418.

Murumba, S.K. (1998). Cross-cultural dimensions of human rights in the twenty-first century. In *Legal Visions of the 21st Century: Essays in Honour of Judge Christopher Weeramantry,* 207–240. (Anghie, A. & Sturgess, G., eds.). The Hague: Kluwer Law International.

Nakamura, T. (2009). Proposal of the Draft Charter of the East Asian community: An overview and the basic principles. In *East Asian Regionalism from a Legal Perspective: Current Features and a Vision for the Future,* 193–214 (Nakamura, T., ed.). London, UK: Routledge.

Ndiaye, (2010). Court and tribunal The advisory function of the International Tribunal for the Law of the Sea. *Chinese Journal of International Law, 9,* 565–587.

Nmehielle, V.O. (2004, # 3). Development of the African human rights system in the last decade. *Human Rights Brief, 11,* 6–11.

Obiora, L.A. (1997). Feminism, globalization, and culture: After Beijing. *Indiana Journal of Global Legal Studies, 4,* 355–406.

Oloka-Onyango, J. (2000). Human rights and sustainable development in contemporary Africa: A new dawn, or retreating horizons? *Buffalo Human Rights Law Review, 6,* 39–76.

Olz, M.A. (1997). Non-governmental organizations in regional human rights systems. *Columbia Human Rights Law Review, 28,* 307–374.

Owada, H. (2009). The rule of law in a globalizing world—An Asian perspective. *Washington University Global Studies Law Review, 8,* 187–205.

Panel Discussion. (2007). The impending Extraordinary Chambers of Cambodia to prosecute the Khmer Rouge. *Santa Clara Journal of International Law, 5,* 326–344.

Pasqualucci, J.M. (2002). Advisory practice of the Inter-American Court of Human Rights: Contributing to the evolution of international human rights law. *Stanford Journal of International Law, 38,* 241–288.

Patten, C. (1998). *East and West: China, Power, and the Future of Asia.* New York: Times Books.

Paul, J. (2000). Cultural resistance to global governance. *Michigan Journal of International Law, 27,* 1–84.

Peerenboom, R. (2003). Beyond universalism and relativism: The evolving debates about "values in Asia." *Indiana International and Comparative Law Review, 14,* 1–85.

Peerenboom, R. (2006). An empirical overview of rights performance in Asia, France, and the USA: The dominance of wealth in the interplay of economics, culture, law, and governance. In *Human Rights in Asia: A Comparative Study of Twelve Asian Jurisdictions, France, and the USA,* 1–64. (Peerenboom, R., Petersen, C.J. & Chen, A.H.Y., eds.). London: Routledge.

Peerenboom, R. (2010). Judicial independence in China: Common myths and unfounded assumptions. In *Judicial Independence in China: Lessons for Global Rule of Law Promotion,* 69–94. New York: Cambridge University Press.

Peerenboom, R. & Chen, W. (2008). *Development of Rule of Law: A Comparison of Taiwan and China.* Available at http://papers.ssrn.com/sol3/papers.cfm?abstract_id=1300862.

Pentelovitch, N.H. (2008). Seeing justice done: The importance of prioritizing outreach efforts at international criminal tribunals. *Georgetown Journal of International Law, 39,* 445–494.

Perera, L.P.N. (1991). *Buddhism and Human Rights: A Buddhist Commentary on the Universal Declaration of Human Rights.* Colombo, Sri Lanka: Karunaratne & Sons.

Perlin, M.L. (2006). "You got no secrets to conceal": Considering the application of the *Tarasoff* doctrine abroad. *University of Cincinnati Law Review, 75,* 611–629.

Perlin, M.L. (2007a). An internet-based mental disability law program: Implications for social change in nations with developing economies. *Fordham International Law Journal, 30,* 435–454.

Perlin, M.L. (2007b). International human rights law and comparative mental disability law: The universal factors. *Syracuse Journal of International Law and Commerce, 34,* 333–357.

Perlin, M.L. (2008a). "Everybody is making love/or else expecting rain": Considering the sexual autonomy rights of persons institutionalized because of mental disability in forensic hospitals and in Asia. *University of Washington Law Review, 83,* 481–508.

Perlin, M.L. (2008b). "I might need a good lawyer, could be your funeral, my trial": A global perspective on the right to counsel in civil commitment cases, and its implications for clinical legal education. *Washington University Journal of Law & Social Policy, 28,* 241–264.

Perlin, M.L. (2009). "A change is gonna come": The implications of the United Nations Convention on the Rights of Persons with Disabilities for the domestic practice of constitutional mental disability law. *Northern Illinois University Law Review, 29,* 483–498.

Perlin, M.L. (2010a). The need for a regional disability rights tribunal in Asia: What can we learn from the Inter-American experience? Paper presented to International Conference on Disability Rights Tribunal in Asia & Pacific, Asia-Pacific Development Center on Disability, October 2010, Bangkok, Thailand.

Perlin, M.L. (2010b). Why a regional tribunal is needed to implement the CRPD. Paper presented to conference on The Universal Implementation of the Convention on the Rights of Persons with Disabilities, National Human Rights Commission of Korea, March 2010. Seoul, Korea. Accessible at http://papers.ssrn.com/sol3/papers.cfm?abstract_id=1744157.

Perlin, M.L. & Ikehara, Y. (2010a). Creation of a disability rights tribunal for Asia and the Pacific: Its impact on China? Paper presented to conference sponsored by the European China Law Studies Association, June 2010. Copenhagen, Denmark. Accessible at http://papers.ssrn.com/sol3/papers.cfm?abstract_id=1744196.

Perlin, M.L. & Ikehara, Y. (2010b). Promoting social change in East Asia: The movement to create a disability rights tribunal and the promise of international online, distance learning. Paper presented at the inaugural conference of the East Asia Law and Society Association, University of Hong Kong, February 2010. Accessible at http://papers.ssrn.com/sol3/papers.cfm?abstract_id=1743741.

Perlin, M., Birgden, A. & Gledhill, K. (2009). "The witness who saw/he left little doubt": A comparative consideration of expert testimony in mental disability law cases in common and civil law systems. *Journal of Investigative Psychology and Offender Profiling, 6,* 59–88.

Persaud, S.N. (2009). Eternal law: The underpinnings of dharma and karma in the justice system. *Richmond Journal of Law and the Public Interest, 13,* 49–90.

Petersen, C.J. (2000). The failure of the Hong Kong Court of Appeal to recognize and remedy disability discrimination. *Hong Kong Law Journal, 30,* 6–21.

Petersen, C.J. (2002). The right to equality in the public sector: An assessment of post-colonial Hong Kong. *Hong Kong Law Journal, 32,* 103–134.

Petersen, C.J. (2005). A progressive law with weak enforcement? An empirical study of Hong Kong's disability law. *Disability Studies Quarterly, 25,* 1–21.

Petersen, C.J. (2006). From British colony to special administrative region of China: Embracing human rights in Hong Kong. In *Human Rights in Asia: A Comparative Legal Study of Twelve Asian Jurisdictions, France and the USA,* 224–264 (Peerenboom, R., Petersen, C.J. & Chen, A.H.Y., eds.). London: Routledge.

Petersen, C.J. (2007). Trafficking of mainland Chinese women into Hong Kong's sex industry: Problems of identification and response. *Asia-Pacific Journal on Human Rights and the Law, 2,* 35–84.

Petersen, C.J. (2008). China's ratification of the Convention on the Rights of Persons with Disabilities: The implications for Hong Kong. *Hong Kong Law Journal, 38,* 611–643.

Petersen, C.J. (2010a). Inclusive education and conflict resolution: Building a model to implement Article 24 of the Convention on the Rights of Persons with Disabilities in the Asia Pacific. *Hong Kong Law Journal, 40,* 481–512.

Petersen, C.J. (2010b). Population policy and eugenic theory: Implications of China's ratification of the United Nations Convention on the Rights of Persons with Disabilities. *China: An International Journal, 8,* 85–109.

Petersmann, E-U. (2006). Justice as conflict resolution: Proliferation, fragmentation, and decentralization of dispute settlement in international trade. *University of Pennsylvania Journal of International Economic Law, 27,* 273–366.

Phan, H,D. (2009). A blueprint for a Southeast Asian Court of Human Rights. *Asian-Pacific Law and Policy Journal, 10,* 384–433.

Pollis, A. (1996). Cultural relativism revisited: Through a state prism. *Human Rights Quarterly, 18,* 316–344.

Posner, E.A. (2008). Human welfare, not human rights. *Columbia Law Review, 108,* 1758–1800.

Preis, A-B.S. (1995). Human rights as cultural practice: An anthropological critique. *Human Rights Quarterly, 18,* 286–315.

Purohit and Moore v The Gambia. (2003). Comm. No. 241/2001, 2003 ahrlr 96 (achpr 2003). 1 IHRR 257 (Afr. Comm'n on Human and Peoples' Rights).

R. v. Sec'y of State for Transp., ex parte Factortame Ltd. (No. 2), (1991). 1 AC 603 (H.L.).

Ramsay, G. (2010) Mainland Chinese family caregiver narratives in mental illness: Disruption and continuity. *Asian Studies Review, 34,* 83–103.

Rao, A. (1995). The politics of gender and culture in international human rights discourse. In *Women's Rights Human Rights: International Feminist Perspectives,* 167–188 (Peters, J. & Wolper, A., eds.). New York: Routledge.

Raub, L. (2009). Positioning hybrid tribunals in international criminal justice. *International Law and Politics, 41,* 1013–1053.

Renshaw, C., Byrnes, A. & Durbach, A. (2009). Implementing human rights in the Pacific through National Human Rights Institutions: The experience of Fiji. *Victoria University of Wellington Law Review, 40,* 251–277.

Renteln, A.D. (1985). The unanswered challenge of relativism and the consequences for human rights. *Human Rights Quarterly, 7,* 514–540.

Renteln, A.D. (1990). *International Human Rights: Universalism versus Relativism.* Newbury Park, CA: Sage Publications.

Robison, R. (1996). The politics of "Asian values." *Pacific Review, 9,* 309–327.

Romano, C.P.R. (2009). Can you hear me now? The case for extending the international judicial network. *Chicago Journal of International Law, 10,* 233–273.

Rose, C. (2010). An emerging norm: The duty of states to provide reparations for human rights violations by non-state actors. *Hastings International and Comparative Law Review, 33,* 307–343.

Rosenne, S. (1995). Establishing the International Tribunal for the Law of the Sea. *American Journal of International Law, 89,* 806–814.

Sarfaty, G.A. (2007). International norm diffusion in the Pimicikamak Cree nation: A model of legal mediation. *Harvard International Law Journal, 48,* 441–482.

Saul, B., Mowbray, J. & Bagoomians, I. (2010). Resistance to regional human rights cooperation in the Asia-Pacific: Demythologising regional exceptionalism by learning from the Americas, Europe, and Africa. To be published in *Human Rights In The Asia-Pacific Region: Towards Institution Building,.* (Nasu, H. &. Saul, B, eds). Accessible at http://papers.ssrn.com/sol3/papers.cfm?abstract_id=1699551.

Schmid, J.C. (2006). Advisory opinions on human rights: Moving beyond a pyrrhic victory. *Duke Journal of Comparative and International Law, 16*, 415–455.

Schoener, W. (1997). Non-governmental organizations and global activism: Legal and informal approaches. *Indiana Journal of Global Legal Studies, 4*, 537–569.

Se, T. & Karatasu, R. (2004). A conception of human rights based on Japanese culture: Promoting cross-cultural debates. *Journal of Human Rights, 3*, 269–289.

Selected Human Rights Documents. (2000). *Asia-Pacific Journal on Human Rights and the Law, 1*, 126–143.

Sen, A. (1997). *Human Rights and Asian Values.* New York: Carnegie Council on Ethics and International Affairs.

Sen, A. (1999). Democracy as a universal value. *Journal of Democracy, 10*, 3–17.

Sengupta, I. (2010). Disunity in diversity: Struggling for an Asian Human Rights Charter. Accessible at http://papers.ssrn.com/sol3/papers.cfm?abstract_id=1650484

Seymour, D. (2003). The extension of the European Convention On Human Rights To Central And Eastern Europe: Prospects and risks. *Connecticut Journal of International Law, 8*, 243–261.

Shany, Y. (2010). Assessing the effectiveness of international courts: Can the unquantifiable be quantified? *International Law Forum of the Hebrew University of Jerusalem.* Accessible at http://www.effective-intl-adjudication.org/admin/Reports/6522776dd407e9c3875da218ebc70d5bUnquantifiable.pdf

Shelton, D. (2009). Form, function, and the powers of international courts. *Chicago Journal of International Law, 9*, 537–571.

Shelton, D. (2010). *Regional Protection of Human Rights.* New York: Oxford University Press.

Shinfuku, N. (1998). Mental health services in Asia: International perspective and challenge for the coming years. *Psychiatry and Clinical Neurosciences, 52*, 269–274.

Shivji, I. (1989). *The Concept of Human Rights in Africa.* Dakar, Senegal: CODESRIA.

Simon, K. (2010). International non-governmental organizations and non-profit organizations. *International Lawyer, 44*, 399–414.

Sloane, R.D. (2001). Outrelativizing relativism: A liberal defense of the universality of international human rights. *Vanderbilt Journal of Transnational Law, 34*, 527–595.

Sosnov, M. (2008). The adjudication of genocide: Gacaca and the road to reconciliation in Rwanda. *Denver Journal of International Law and Policy, 36*, 125–153.

Sossin, L. (2009). God at work: Religion in the workplace and the limits of pluralism in Canada. *Comparative Labor Law and Policy Journal, 30*, 485–505.

Spaak, T. (2007). Moral relativism and human rights. *Buffalo Human Rights Law Review, 13*, 73–85.

Splittgerber, S. (1996). The need for greater regional protection for the human rights of women: The cases of rape in Bosnia and Guatemala. *Wisconsin International Law Journal, 15*, 185–227.

Stacy, H.M. (2009). *Human Rights for the 21st Century: Sovereignty, Civil Society, Culture.* Stanford, CA: Stanford University Press.

Standaert, P.E. (1999). The friendly settlement of human rights abuses in the Americas. *Duke Journal of Comparative and International Law, 9,* 519–542.

Steiner, H.J., Alston, P. & Goodman, R. (2008). *International Human Rights in Context: Law, Politics, Morals* (3d ed.). Oxford, UK: Oxford University Press.

Stokke, H. (2006). Modernization without westernization? Asian values and human rights discourse in the east and west. In *Human Rights and Asian Values: Contesting National Identities and Cultural Representations in Asia,* 134–158. (Jacobson, M.J. & Bruun, O., eds.). London, UK: RoutledgeCurzon.

Subedi, S.P. (1999). Are the principles of human rights "western" ideas? An analysis of the claim of the "Asian" concept of human rights from the perspective of Hinduism. *California Western International Law Journal, 30,* 45–68.

Svensson, M. (2002). *Debating Human Rights in China: A Conceptual and Political History.* Oxford, UK: Rowman & Littlefield Publishers, Inc.

Svensson, M. (2006). The Chinese debate on Asian values and human rights: Some reflections on relativism, nationalism, and Orientalism. In *Human Rights and Asian Values: Contesting National Identities and Cultural Representations in Asia,* 199–226. (Jacobson, M.J. & Bruun, O., eds.). London: RoutledgeCurzon.

Tasman, A., Sartorius, N. & Saraceno, B. (2009). Addressing mental health resource deficiencies in Pacific Rim countries. *Asia-Pacific Psychiatry, 1,* 3–8.

Tay, S.S.C. (1996). Human rights, culture and the Singapore example. *McGill Law Journal, 41,* 743.

Templeman, L. (1991). Treaty-making and the British parliament. *Chicago-Kent Law Review, 67,* 459–484.

Tesón, F.R. (1984–1985). International human rights and cultural relativism. *Virginia Journal of International Law, 25,* 869–898.

Tiba, F.K. (2006). What caused the multiplicity of international courts and tribunals? *Gonzaga Journal of International Law, 10,* 202–226.

The ASEAN Charter (2008), *available at* http:// www.aseansec.org/publications/ ASEANCharter.pdf

Thio, L-A. (1997). The impact of internationalisation on domestic governance: Gender egalitarianism & the transformative potential of CEDAW. *Singapore Journal of International and Comparative Law, 1,* 278–350.

Thio, L-A. (1999). Implementing human rights in ASEAN countries: "Promises to keep and miles to go before I sleep." *Yale Human Rights and Development Journal, 2,* 1–85.

Thomuschat, C. (2008). International courts and tribunals. In *Max Planck Encyclopedia of Public International Law* (Wolfrum, R., ed.). Accessible at http://www.mpepil.com/

Thorp, J. (2001/2002). Welcome ex-dictators, torturers and tyrants: Comparative approaches to handling ex-dictators and past human rights abuses. *Gonzaga Law Review, 37,* 167–199.

Thurman, R.A.F. (1988). Nagarjuna's guidelines for Buddhist social activism. In *The Path of Compassion: Writings on Socially Engaged Buddhism,* 120–144. (Eppsteiner, F., ed.). Berkeley, CA: Parallax Press.

Toki, V. & Baird, N. (2009). An indigenous Pacific human rights mechanism: Some building blocks. *Victoria University of Wellington Law Review, 40,* 215–236.

Torok, J.H. (2005). Asian American jurisprudence: On curriculum. *Michigan State Law Review*, 635–711.
Toufayan, M. (2010). Identity, effectiveness, and newness in transjudicialism's coming of age. *Michigan Journal of International Law, 31*, 307–383.
Traer, R. (1995). Buddhist affirmations of human rights. *Journal of Buddhist Ethics, 2*, 1–12.
Trindade, A.A.C. (2000). Current state and perspectives of the Inter-American system of human rights protection at the dawn of the new century. *Tulane Journal of International and Comparative Law 8*, 5–37.
Tsang, H.W.H. et al. (2007). A cross-cultural study of employers' concerns about hiring people with psychotic disorder: Implications for recovery. *Social Psychiatry and Psychiatric Epidemiology, 42*, 723–733.
Trivedi, J.K., Narang, P. & Dhyani, M. (2007). Mental health legislation in South Asia with special reference to India: Shortcomings and solutions. *Mental Health Review Journal, 12*, 22–29.
Tuen, J.T-H. (1999). Effects of the economic crisis on the placement of people with disabilities in Singapore. *Asia and Pacific Journal on Disability, 2*. Accessible at http://www.dinf.ne.jp/doc/english/asia/resource/z00ap/004/z00ap00409.html.
Tvatova, R. (2010). Central Asian states and international law: Between post-Soviet culture and Eurasian civilization. *Chinese Journal of International Law, 9*, 205–220.
Twinomugisha, B.K. (2009). The role of the judiciary in the promotion of democracy in Uganda. *African Human Rights Law Journal, 9*, 1–22.
Tyagi, Y.K. (1981). Third world response to human rights. *Indian Journal of International Law, 21*, 119–140.
Udombana, N.J. (2004). Between promise and performance: Revisiting states' obligations under the African Human Rights Charter. *Stanford Journal of International Law, 40*, 105–142.
United Nations Economic and Social Commission for Asia and the Pacific. http://www.unescap.org/about/index.asp (last visited May 7, 2010).
VanGrasstek, C. & Sauvé, P. (2006). The consistency of WTO rules: Can the single undertaking be squared with variable geometry? *Journal of International Economic Law, 9*, 837–844.
Van Schaack, B. (2001). In defense of civil redress: The domestic enforcement of human rights norms in the context of the proposed Hague Judgments Convention. *Harvard International Law Journal, 42*, 141–200.
Varayudej, S. (2006). Right to democracy in international law: Its implications for Asia. *Annual Survey of International and Comparative Law, 12*, 1–17.
Velásquez Rodriguez v. Honduras, Inter-Am. Ct. H.R. (ser. C), No. 4, 28 ILM 294 (1989).
Viljoen, F. & Louw, L. (2007). State compliance with the recommendations of the African Commission on Human and Peoples' Rights, 1994–2004. *American Journal of International Law, 101*, 1–34.
Vo, V.A. (2006). Human rights and Asian values in Vietnam. In *Human Rights and Asian Values: Contesting National Identities and Cultural Representations in Asia*, 92–110 (Jacobson, M.J. & Bruun, O., eds.). London: RoutledgeCurzon.
Wan, M. (2007). Human rights lawmaking in China: Domestic policies, international law, and international politics. *Human Rights Quarterly, 29*, 727–753.

Wang, Y.S. (2009). The triumph of Confucianism: How a subjugated legal system is failing a generation of Chinese women and girls. *Cardozo Journal of Law and Gender, 15,* 691–720.

Weinstein, N. (2010). Establishing the Disability Rights Tribunal for Asia and the Pacific. Unpublished paper; on file with author.

Weisburd, M.A. (2002). "Vertical" conflict between international and national tribunals. *American Society of International Law Proceedings, 96,* 42–53.

Weissbrodt, D. (1977). The role of international nongovernmental organizations in the implementation of human rights. *Texas International Law Journal, 12,* 293–320.

Weldehaimanot, S. (2009). Unlocking the African Court of Justice and Human Rights. *Journal of African and International Law, 2,* 167–187.

Weston, B.H., Lukes, R.A. & Hnatt, K.M. (1987). Regional human rights regimes: A comparison and appraisal. *Vanderbilt Journal of Transnational Law, 20,* 585–637.

Wexler, D.B. (2008). Two decades of therapeutic jurisprudence. *Touro Law Review, 24,* 17–28.

Wexler, D.B. & Winick, B.J., eds. (1996). *Law in a Therapeutic Key: Recent Developments in Therapeutic Jurisprudence.* Durham, NC: Carolina Academic Press.

Whiting, A. (2003). Situating Suhakam: Human rights debates and Malaysia's National Human Rights Commission. *Stanford Journal of International Law, 39,* 59–98.

Wilde, R. (1998). NGO proposals for an Asia-Pacific human rights system. *Yale Human Rights and Development Journal, 1,* 137–142.

Williams, C. (2006). International human rights and Confucianism. *Asia-Pacific Journal on Human Rights and the Law, 1,* 38–66.

Wilson, R.J. & Perlin, J. (2003). The Inter-American Human Rights System: Activities from late 2000 through October 2002. *American University International Law Review, 18,* 651–752.

Winick, B.J. (2005). *Civil Commitment: A Therapeutic Jurisprudence Model.* Durham, NC: Carolina Academic Press.

Wong, B.K.Y. (2000). Traditional Chinese philosophy and dispute resolution. *Hong Kong Law Journal, 30,* 304–319.

Wood, S.G. & Scharrfs, B.G. (2002). Applicability of human rights standards to private corporations: An American perspective. *American Journal of Comparative Law, 50,* 531–566.

Wuiling, C. (2006). Assessing criminal justice and human rights models in the fight against sex trafficking: A case study of the ASEAN region. *Essex Human Rights Review, 3,* 46–63.

Yamaga-Karns, K. (1995). Pressing Japan: Illegal foreign workers under international human rights law and the role of cultural relativism. *Texas International Law Journal, 30,* 559–581.

Yamane, H. (1982). Human rights for the peoples of Asia. *Human Rights Teaching, 3,* 18–22.

Yee, S. (2004). The role of law in the formation of regional perspectives of human rights and regional systems for the protection of human rights: The European and Asian models as illustrations. *Singapore Year Book of International Law, 8,* 157–164.

Yu'e, M. (2009). Disability discrimination in employment. In *Taking employment discrimination seriously: Chinese and European perspectives* 85–112 (Leiden, The Netherlands: Martinus Nijhoff Publishers).

Yun, K. (2007). How Japan's recent efforts to reduce sex trafficking can be improved through international human rights enforcement mechanisms: Fulfilling Japan's global legal obligations. *Buffalo Human Rights Law Review, 13,* 205–253.

Zechetner, E. (1997). In the name of culture: Cultural relativism and the abuse of the individual. *Journal of Anthropological Research, 53,* 319–347.

Chapter 10

Allan, A. & Allan, M.M. (2000). The South African Truth and Reconciliation Commission as a therapeutic tool. *Behavioral Sciences and the Law, 18,* 459–477.

Aponte Toro, R.P. (1999). Sanity in international relations: An experience on therapeutic jurisprudence. *University of Miami Inter-American Law Review, 30,* 659–684.

Baker, G. (2008). Rediscovering therapeutic jurisprudence in overlooked areas of the law—How exposing its presence in the environmental justice movement can legitimize the paradigm and make the case for its inclusion into all aspects of legal education and the practice of law. *Florida Coastal Law Review, 9,* 215–236.

Barton, T.D. (1999). Therapeutic jurisprudence, preventive law, and creative problem solving. *Psychology, Public Policy, and Law, 5,* 921–943.

Birgden, A. (2002). Therapeutic jurisprudence and "good lives": A rehabilitation framework for corrections. *Australian Psychologist, 37,* 180–186.

Birgden, A. (2004). Therapeutic jurisprudence and responsivity: Finding the will and the way in offender rehabilitation. *Psychology, Crime, and Law, 10,* 283–295.

Carasik, L. (2006). Justice in the balance: An evaluation of one clinic's ability to harmonize teaching practical skills, ethics and professionalism with a social justice mission. *Southern California Review of Law & Social Justice, 16,* 23–91.

Cooper, J.M. (1999). State of the nation: Therapeutic jurisprudence and the evolution of the right of self-determination in international law. *Behavioral Sciences & the Law, 17,* 607–643.

Day, A. & Casey, S. (2009). Values in forensic and correctional psychology. *Aggression and Violent Behavior, 14,* 231–238.

Dickie, I. (2008). Ethical dilemmas, forensic psychology, and therapeutic jurisprudence. *Thomas Jefferson Law Review, 30,* 455–461.

Diesfeld, K. & Freckelton, I. (2006). Mental health law and therapeutic jurisprudence. In *Disputes and Dilemmas in Health Law,* 91–114 (Freckelton, I. & Peterson, K., eds.). Sydney, Australia: The Federation Press.

Diesfeld, K. & McKenna, B. (2006). The therapeutic intent of the New Zealand Mental Health Review Tribunal. *Psychiatry, Psychology and Law, 13,* 100–109.

Diesfeld, K. & McKenna, B. (2007). The unintended impact of the therapeutic intentions of the New Zealand Mental Health Review Tribunal? Therapeutic jurisprudence perspectives. Journal of Law and Medicine, *14,* 566–576.

Dlugacz, H.A. (2008/2009). Outpatient commitment: Some thoughts on promoting a meaningful dialogue. *New York Law School Law Review, 53,* 79–96.

Fischer, J. (2006). A comparative look at the right to refuse treatment for involuntarily hospitalized persons with a mental illness. *Hastings International and Comparative Law Review, 29,* 153–185.

Freckelton, I. (2003). Mental-health review tribunal decision-making: A therapeutic jurisprudence lens. *Psychiatry, Psychology, and Law, 10,* 44–62.

Freckelton, I. (2008). Therapeutic jurisprudence misunderstood and misrepresented: The price and risks of influence. *Thomas Jefferson Law Review, 30,* 575–591.

Freeman, M.B. (2010). Florida collaborative family law: The good, the bad, and the (hopefully) getting better. *Florida Coastal Law Review, 11,* 237–256.

Frueh, J. (2008). The *Anders* brief in appeals from civil commitment. *Yale Law Journal, 118,* 272–318.

Hinshaw, C.D. (2005). Taking a gamble: Applying therapeutic jurisprudence to compulsive gambling and establishing gambling treatment courts. *Gaming Law Review, 9,* 333–342.

Hurwitz, D.R. (2003). Lawyering for justice and the inevitability of international human rights clinics. *Yale Journal of International Law, 28,* 505–549.

In re Mental Health of K.G.F., 29 P. 3d 485 (Mont. 2001).

Kahn, M. (2002). Jurisprudential countertransference. *Touro Law Review, 18,* 459–477.

Keywood, K. (2005). Detaining mentally disordered patients lacking capacity: The arbitrariness of informal detention and the common law doctrine of necessity. *Medical Law Review, 13,* 108–115.

Kinderman, P. & Tai, S. (2008) Psychological models of mental disorder, human rights, and compulsory mental health care in the community. *International Journal of Law and Psychiatry, 31,* 479–486.

King, M.S. (2008). Restorative justice, therapeutic jurisprudence and the rise of emotionally intelligent justice. *Melbourne University Law Review, 32,* 1096–1126.

King, M.S. & Guthrie, R. (2008). Therapeutic jurisprudence, human rights, and the Northern Territory emergency response. *Precedent, 89,* 39–41.

Kirchengast, T. (2007). Victim influence: Therapeutic jurisprudence and sentencing law in the New South Wales Court of Criminal Appeal. *Flinders Journal of Law Reform, 10,* 143–159.

Kruse, K. (2008). The human dignity of clients, *Cornell Law Review, 93,* 1343–1364.

Lawson, A. (2008). People with psychosocial impairments or conditions, reasonable accommodation and the Convention on the Rights of Persons with Disabilities. *Law in Context, 26,* 62–84.

Lind, E.A. & Tyler, T.R. (1988). *The Social Psychology of Procedural Justice.* New York: Plenum Press.

Luban, D. (2007), Lawyers as upholders of human dignity (when they aren't busy assaulting it). In *Legal Ethics and Human Dignity* 65–96. (Luban, D., ed.). Cambridge, UK: Cambridge University Press.

McCrudden, C. (2000). A common law of human rights? Transnational judicial conversations on constitutional rights. *Oxford Journal of Legal Studies, 20,* 499–532.

McSherry, B. (2009). Mental health laws for those "compliant" with treatment. *Journal of Law and Medicine, 17,* 9–15.
Munir, M.A. (2007). Therapeutic jurisprudence in Pakistan: Juvenile delinquency and the role of the defense lawyer. In *Transforming Legal Processes in Court and Beyond,* 85–106. (Reinhardt, G. & Cannon, A., eds.). Melbourne, Australia: Australasian Institute of Judicial Administration Incorporated.
Munro, R. (2000). Judicial psychiatry in China and its political abuses. *Columbia Journal of Asian Law, 14,* 1–128.
New York State Ass'n for Retarded Children, Inc. v. Rockefeller, 357 F. Supp. 752 (E.D.N.Y. 1973).
Nicholson, C.M.A. (2008). The impact of child labor legislation on child-headed households in South Africa. *Thomas Jefferson Law Review, 30,* 407–427.
Olmstead v. L.C., 527 U.S. 581 (1999).
Olowu, D. (2007). Therapeutic jurisprudence: An inquiry into its significance for international criminal justice. *Revista Juridica Universidad de Puerto Rico, 76,* 129–150.
Olowu, D. (2010). Therapeutic jurisprudence: Transforming legal education and humanising criminal justice in Africa. *De Jure, 1,* 95–116.
Ostas, D.T. (2010). Civil disobedience in a business context: Examining the social obligation to obey inane laws. *American Business Law Journal, 47,* 291–312.
Perlin, M.L. (1994). Therapeutic jurisprudence: Understanding the sanist and pretextual bases of mental disability law. *New England Journal on Criminal and Civil Confinement, 20,* 369–382.
Perlin, M.L. (1996). "The executioner's face is always well-hidden": The role of counsel and the courts in determining who dies. *New York Law School Law Review, 41,* 201–236.
Perlin, M.L. (1999)."Half-wracked prejudice leaped forth": Sanism, pretextuality, and why and how mental disability law developed as it did. *Journal of Contemporary Legal Issues, 10,* 3–36.
Perlin, M.L. (2000a). A law of healing. *University of Cincinnati Law Review, 68,* 407–433.
Perlin, M.L. (2000b). "Their promises of paradise": Will *Olmstead v. L.C.* resuscitate the constitutional "least restrictive alternative" principle in mental disability law? *Houston Law Review, 37,* 999–1054.
Perlin, M.L. (2002). Chimes of freedom: International human rights and institutional mental disability law. *New York Law School Journal of International and Comparative Law, 21,* 423–433.
Perlin, M.L. (2002–2003). "Things have changed": Looking at non-institutional mental disability law through the sanism filter. *New York Law School Law Review, 46,* 535–546.
Perlin, M.L. (2003a). "She breaks just like a little girl": Neonaticide, the insanity defense, and the irrelevance of ordinary common sense. *William & Mary Journal of Women and Law, 10,* 1–34.
Perlin, M.L. (2003b). "You have discussed lepers and crooks": Sanism in clinical teaching. *Clinical Law Review, 9,* 683–729.
Perlin, M.L. (2005). "And my best friend, my doctor, won't even say what it is I've got": The role and significance of counsel in right to refuse treatment cases. *San Diego Law Review, 42,* 735–755.

Perlin, M.L. (2008). "Everybody is making love/or else expecting rain": Considering the sexual autonomy rights of persons institutionalized because of mental disability in forensic hospitals and in Asia. *University of Washington Law Review, 83,* 481–508.

Perlin, M.L. (2009). A therapeutic jurisprudence inquiry into the roles of dignity and humiliation in the law. *Human Dignity and Humiliation Studies.* Retrieved September 24, 2010, from http://www.humiliationstudies.org/whoweare/annualmeeting14.php.

Perlin, M.L. (2010). "They keep it all hid": The ghettoization of mental disability law and its implications for legal education. *Saint Louis University Law Journal, 54,* 857–876.

Perlin, M.L. (2011a). "Abandoned love": The impact of *Wyatt v. Stickney* on the intersection between international human rights and domestic mental disability law. *Law and Psychology* (in press).

Perlin, M.L. (2011b). Considering pathological altruism in the law from therapeutic jurisprudence and neuroscience perspectives. In *Pathological Altruism* (Oakley, B. et al., eds.). New York: Oxford University Press. In press.

Perlin, M.L. & Dorfman, D.A. (1996). Is it more than "dodging lions and wastin' time"? Adequacy of counsel, questions of competence, and the judicial process in individual right to refuse treatment cases. *Psychology, Public Policy, and Law, 2,* 114–136.

Perlin, M.L., Gould, K.K. & Dorfman, D.A. (1995). Therapeutic jurisprudence and the civil rights of institutionalized mentally disabled persons: Hopeless oxymoron or path to redemption? *Psychology, Public Policy, and Law, 1,* 80–119.

Perlmutter, B. (2005). George's story: Voice and transformation through the teaching and practice of therapeutic jurisprudence in a law school child advocacy clinic. *Saint Thomas Law Review, 17,* 561–621.

Petersen, C.J. (2010). Inclusive education and conflict resolution: Building a model to implement Article 24 of the Convention on the Rights of Persons with Disabilities in the Asia Pacific. *Hong Kong Law Journal, 40,* 481–512.

Petrila, J. (1993). Paternalism and the unfulfilled promise of "Essays in Therapeutic Jurisprudence." *New York Law School Journal of Human Rights, 10,* 877–905.

Pope, K.S. & Gutheil, T.G. (2009). Psychologists abandon the Nuremberg ethic: Concerns for detainee interrogations. *International Journal of Law and Psychiatry, 32,* 161–166.

Prior, P.M. (2003). Removing children from the care of adults with diagnosed mental illnesses—A clash of human rights? *European Journal of Social Work, 6,* 179–190.

R. v. Bournewood Community and Mental Health N.H.S. Trust ex parte *L (Secretary of State for Health and others intervening)* A.C. 458, H.L. (1999).

Ramirez, J., Jr. & Ronner, A.D. (2004). Voiceless Billy Budd: Melville's tribute to the Sixth Amendment, *California Western Law Review, 41,* 103–145.

Rigby, D. (2006). Tasmanian mental health representation project—A practical experience in therapeutic jurisprudence. Paper presented to the 3d International Conference on Therapeutic Jurisprudence, Perth, Australia. Accessible at http://www.aija.org.au/TherapJurisp06/Papers/Rigby.pdf.

Ronner, A. (2002). Songs of validation, voice, and voluntary participation: Therapeutic jurisprudence, Miranda and juveniles. *University of Cincinnati Law Review, 71,* 89–120.
Ronner, A. (2008). The learned-helpless lawyer: Clinical legal education and therapeutic jurisprudence as antidotes to Bartleby syndrome. *Touro Law Review, 24,* 601–664.
Ronner, A. (2010). *Law, Literature and Therapeutic Jurisprudence.* Durham, NC: Carolina Academic Press.
Rotman, E. (2008). Therapeutic jurisprudence and terrorism. *Thomas Jefferson Law Review, 30,* 525–545.
Salisbury, C.S., (2005). From violence and victimization to voice and validation: Incorporating therapeutic jurisprudence in a children's law clinic. *Saint Thomas Law Review, 17,* 623–676.
Slobogin, C. (1999a). The admissibility of behavioral science information in criminal trials from primitivism to Daubert to voice. *Psychology, Public Policy, and Law, 5,* 100–119.
Slobogin, C. (1999b). Therapeutic jurisprudence: Five dilemmas to ponder. *Psychology, Public Policy, and Law, 1,* 193–219.
Spaulding, W. et al. (2000). Applications of therapeutic jurisprudence in rehabilitation for people with severe and disabling mental illness. *Thomas M. Cooley Law Review, 17,* 135–170.
Steinberger, C.B. (2003). Persistence and change in the life of the law: Can therapeutic jurisprudence make a difference? *Law and Psychology Review, 27,* 55–72.
Stolle, D.P., Wexler, D.B. & Winick, B.J. (2000). *Practicing Therapeutic Jurisprudence: Law as a Helping Profession.* Durham, NC: Carolina Academic Press.
Tait, D. (2003). The ritual environment of the Mental Health Tribunal Hearing: Inquiries and reflections. *Psychiatry, Psychology and Law, 10,* 91–96.
Talley, K.O. (2008/2009). Independent protection and advocacy: The role of counsel in institutional settings. *New York Law School Law Review, 53,* 55–78.
Twinomugisha, B.K. (2009). The role of the judiciary in the promotion of democracy in Uganda. *African Human Rights Law Journal, 9,* 1–22.
Tyler, T.R. & Huo Y.J. (2002). *Trust in the Law.* New York: Russell Sage Foundation.
Volpp, L. (2000). Righting wrongs. *UCLA Law Review,* 47, 1815–1837.
Waldman, E. (2008). Therapeutic jurisprudence: Growing up and looking forward. *Thomas Jefferson Law Review, 30,* 345–349.
Ward, T. & Birgden, A. (2007). Human rights and clinical correctional practice. *Aggression and Violent Behavior, 12,* 628–643.
Ward, T. & Birgden, A. (2009). Accountability and dignity: Ethical issues in correctional and forensic practice. *Aggression and Violent Behavior, 14,* 227–231.
Ward, T. & Salmon, K. (2009). The ethics of punishment: Correctional practice implications. *Aggression and Violent Behavior 14,* 239–247.
Wexler, D.B. (1977). Criminal commitment contingency structures. In *Perspectives in Law and Psychology—The Criminal Justice System,* 121–138 (Vol. 1) (Sales, B.D., ed.). New York: Plenum Press.

Wexler, D.B., ed. (1990). *Therapeutic Jurisprudence: The Law as a Therapeutic Agent.* Durham, NC: Carolina Academic Press.
Wexler, D.B. (1993). Therapeutic jurisprudence and changing concepts of legal scholarship. *Behavioral Sciences & Law, 11,* 17–29.
Wexler, D.B. (2000). Practicing therapeutic jurisprudence: Psycholegal soft spots and strategies. In *Practicing Therapeutic Jurisprudence: Law as a Helping Profession,* 45–68 (Stolle, D.P. Wexler, D.B. & Winick, B.J., eds.). Durham, NC: Carolina Academic Press.
Wexler, D.B. (2008). Two decades of therapeutic jurisprudence, *Touro Law Review, 24,* 17–28.
Wexler, D.B. (2009). Post on therapeutic jurisprudence. LISTSERV (May 5, 2009). Accessible at http://lists.topica.com/lists/tjsp/read?sort=d&start=1728
Wexler, D.B. (2010). From theory to practice and back again in therapeutic jurisprudence: Now comes the hard part. *Social Science Research Network.* Retrieved September 30, 2010, from http://papers.ssrn.com/sol3/papers.cfm?abstract_id=1580129
Wexler, D.B., ed. (2008). *Rehabilitating Lawyers: Principles of Therapeutic Jurisprudence for Criminal Law Practice.* Durham, NC: Carolina Academic Press.
Wexler, D.B. & Winick, B.J., eds. (1996). *Law in a Therapeutic Key: Recent Developments in Therapeutic Jurisprudence.(*Durham, NC: Carolina Academic Press.
WHO Policy Brief (2008). Developing effective mental health laws in Africa. Available at http://www.who.int/mental_health/policy/development/MHPB7.pdf. (Policy Brief)
Winick, B.J. (1997). Coercion and mental health treatment. *Denver University Law Review, 74,* 1145–1168.
Winick, B.J. (1999). Therapeutic jurisprudence and the civil commitment hearing. *Journal of Contemporary Legal Issues, 10,* 37–56.
Winick, B.J. (2002). Therapeutic jurisprudence and the treatment of people with mental illness in eastern Europe: Construing international human rights law. *New York Law School Journal of International & Comparative Law, 21,* 537–572.
Winick, B. (2003a). A therapeutic jurisprudence model for civil commitment. In *Involuntary Detention and Therapeutic Jurisprudence: International Perspectives on Civil Commitment,* 23–54 (Diesfeld, K. & Freckelton, I., eds.). Hampshire, UK: Ashgate Press.
Winick, B.J. (2003b). Therapeutic jurisprudence and problem solving courts. *Fordham Urban Law Journal, 30,* 1055–1084.
Winick, B.J. (2005). *Civil Commitment: A Therapeutic Jurisprudence Model.* Durham, NC: Carolina Academic Press.
Winick, B.J. (2009). Foreword: Therapeutic jurisprudence perspectives on dealing with victims of crime. *Nova Law Review, 33,* 535–541.
Winick, B.J. (2010). Personal communication (e-mail, June 30, 2010).
Winick, B.J. & Lerner-Wren, G. (2002). Do juveniles facing civil commitment have a right to counsel? A therapeutic jurisprudence brief. *University of Cincinnati Law Review, 71,* 115–118.
Winick, B.J. & Wexler, D.B. (2002). Drug treatment court: Therapeutic jurisprudence applied. *Touro Law Review, 18,* 479–485.
Wyatt v. Stickney, 344 F. Supp 373 (M.D. Ala. 1972).

Chapter 11

Bartlett, P., Lewis, O. & Thorold, O. (2007). *Mental Disability and the European Convention on Human Rights*. Leiden, The Netherlands: Martinus Nijhoff Publishers.

Butler, G. (2009). The essence of human rights: A religious critique. *University of Richmond Law Review, 43*, 1255–1317.

Dhir, A.A. (2008). Relationships of force: Exploring the legal and social issues surrounding mental disability. *Windsor Review of Legal and Social Issues, 25*, 103–112.

Gostin, L.O. (2008). "Old" and "new" institutions for persons with mental illness: Treatment, punishment or preventive confinement. *Public Health, 122*, 906–913.

In re Mental Health of K.G.F., 29 P.3d 485 (Mont. 2001).

Kinley, D. (2007). Human rights fundamentalisms. *Sydney Law Review, 29*, 545–575.

In the Matter of Mark C.H. (2010).—N.Y.S. 2d—, 2010 WL 1729403 (Sur. 2010).

Lippmann, L. & Goldberg, I.I. (1973). *The Right to Education: Anatomy of the Pennsylvania Case and Its Implication for Exceptional Children*. New York: Columbia University Teachers College Press.

McCrudden, C. (2008). Human dignity and judicial interpretation of human rights. *European Journal of International Law, 19*, 655–723.

Perlin, M.L. (1991). Competency, deinstitutionalization, and homelessness: A story of marginalization. *Houston Law Review, 28*, 63–142.

Perlin, M.L. (1994). *The Jurisprudence of the Insanity Defense*. Durham, NC: Carolina Academic Press.

Perlin, M.L. (2000). *The Hidden Prejudice: Mental Disability on Trial*. Washington, DC: American Psychological Association Press.

Perlin, M.L. (2002). "Chimes of Freedom": International human rights and institutional mental disability law. *New York Law School Journal of International and Comparative Law, 21*, 423–433.

Perlin, M.L. (2003). "You have discussed lepers and crooks": Sanism in clinical teaching. *Clinical Law Review, 9*, 683–729.

Perlin, M.L. (2005). "And my best friend, my doctor/won't even say what it is I've got: The role and significance of counsel in right to refuse treatment cases. *San Diego Law Review, 42*, 735–755.

Perlin, M.L. (2009). Beyond Article 12: Implications of the Convention on the Rights of Persons with Disabilities for the advocacy movement in the US and abroad (with special attention to Asia). Paper presented to National Association of Rights, Protection and Advocacy Conference, September 2009. Phoenix, Arizona.

Perlin, M.L. & Dlugacz, H.A. (2009). "It's doom alone that counts": Can international human rights law be an effective source of rights in correctional conditions litigation? *Behavioral Sciences and the Law, 27*, 675–694.

Perlin, M.L. & Ikehara, Y. (2010). Promoting social change in East Asia: The movement to create a disability rights tribunal and the promise of international online, distance learning. Paper presented at the inaugural conference of the East Asia Law and Society Association, University of

Hong Kong, February, 2010. Accessible at http://papers.ssrn.com/sol3/papers.cfm?abstract_id=1743741.

Prior, P.M. (2007) Mentally disordered offenders and the European Court of Human Rights, *International Journal of Law and Psychiatry, 30,* 546–557.

Ronner, A. (2002). Songs of validation, voice, and voluntary participation: Therapeutic jurisprudence, Miranda and juveniles. *University of Cincinnati Law Review, 71,* 89–120.

Ronner, A. (2008). The learned-helpless lawyer: Clinical legal education and therapeutic jurisprudence as antidotes to Bartleby syndrome. *Touro Law Review, 24,* 601–664.

Rosenthal, E. & Rubenstein, L.S. (1993). International human rights advocacy under the "Principles for the Protection of Persons with Mental Illness." *International Journal of Law and Psychiatry, 16,* 257–300.

Stacy, H.M. (2009). *Human Rights for the 21st Century: Sovereignty, Civil Society, Culture.* Stanford, CA: Stanford University Press.

Twinomugisha, B.K. (2009). The role of the judiciary in the promotion of democracy in Uganda. *African Human Rights Law Journal, 9,* 1–22.

Index